The *Ātman-Brahman* in Ancient Buddhism

The *Ātman-Brahman* in Ancient Buddhism

by
Kamaleswar Bhattacharya

Canon Publications

Canon Publications
Cotopaxi, Colorado 81223, U.S.A.
ISBN 978-0-88181-006-6
ISBN 0-88181-006-1

published April 2015
corrected reprint with new introduction, August 2015

This book was originally published in French: *L'Ātman-Brahman dans le Bouddhisme ancien,* Publications de l'École française d'Extrême-Orient, vol. 90; Paris, 1973.

Contents

anattani attamānaṃ passa lokaṃ sadevakaṃ |
niviṭṭhaṃ nāmarūpasmiṃ idaṃ saccan ti maññati || *Sn.* 756

Publisher's Foreword

After realizing the importance of this 1973 French book by Kamaleswar Bhattacharya, I first contacted him about an English translation of it in 2001. At that time he already had a typescript English translation of it, made by someone other than himself, whose name we never learned. From this typescript, some parts faint to the point of illegibility due to a worn typewriter ribbon, and with many corrections and changes added in hard to decipher handwriting (presumably Bhattacharya's), Nancy input an electronic copy. A printout of this was mailed to Bhattacharya for his corrections and revisions. Over the course of several years, due to his many other commitments, revised printouts went back and forth between France and the U.S.A. several times. He left the main text almost entirely unchanged from the French. To the notes he added an occasional reference here and there. In the end, he had the book as he wanted it, and had even taken much time and trouble to update all the "see" references to conform to the new pagination of the English book. All that remained were the four indexes. Then by chance, several months after the fact, we learned that he had passed away on March 16, 2014. He certainly wanted this book to be published. So we felt it our responsibility to publish it, even without the indexes. At last, 42 years after its publication in French, Bhattacharya's important research on this subject is made available in English.

Kamaleswar Bhattacharya was born in 1928 in northeast India. After mastering Sanskrit in a way that is only possible in India, he came to Paris in 1955 on a French Government Scholarship. He there received his doctorate in 1962, for work on the Sanskrit inscriptions of Cambodia. With the support of Louis Renou, he became Attaché de Recherche at the Centre National de la Recherche Scientifique in 1960. He retired from there as Directeur de Recherche in 1996.

Bhattacharya's thesis in this book is, in our time, epoch-making, although twelve hundred years ago it would not have been necessary. While no one doubts that the Buddha denied the *ātman*, the self, the question is: Which *ātman*? Buddhism, as understood in the modern era, has taken this to be the universal *ātman* taught in the Hindu Upaniṣads, equivalent to *brahman*. What we find in the Buddha's words as recorded in the Buddhist scriptures, however, is only a denial of any permanent self in the ever-changing aggregates that form a person. In decades of teaching, the Buddha had many opportunities to clearly deny the universal *ātman* if that was his intention. He did not do so. Bhattacharya's research is the most important study of this fundamentally important question to have appeared. Other studies of this question exist, coming to the same conclusion, but in general they have not been taken seriously. Bhattacharya's research, because of the high level of his scholarship, has to be taken seriously. One may disagree with it, but it cannot be dismissed or ignored.

David and Nancy Reigle
Canon Publications

New Introduction

The most serious objection to Kamaleswar Bhattacharya's thesis that the Buddha did not deny the universal *ātman* may be put in the form of this question: Why, then, did Buddhists down through the ages think he did? Reply: Actually, they did not think this, as far as we can tell from their writings that refute the *ātman* and teach the *anātman* or no-self doctrine. The idea of the *ātman* as the impersonal universal *ātman* did not become dominant in India until some time after the eighth century C.E. Before then, throughout the Buddhist period, the dominant idea of the *ātman* in India was that of a permanent personal *ātman*. Judging from their writings, the Indian Buddhist teachers from Nāgārjuna to Āryadeva to Asaṅga to Vasubandhu to Bhavya to Candrakīrti to Dharmakīrti to Śāntarakṣita thought that the Buddha's *anātman* teaching was directed against a permanent personal *ātman*.

The Question of Which Self

Due to an unforeseen twist of history, we find ourselves today thinking that Buddhism with its *anātman* doctrine denied an *ātman* that it apparently did not deny. When we think of the *ātman*, we usually think of a universal self that is impersonal and all-pervasive, the one self of all. This is the idea of the *ātman* that has become dominant in India during the last thousand years, under the influence of the Advaita Vedānta school of Hinduism. The *ātman* is there identified with *brahman*, the absolute reality, and is described as non-dual (*advaita*). So it is beyond subject-object duality, and hence beyond the reach of thought or speech, and it is beyond the pairs of opposites such as existence and non-existence, or eternal and non-eternal. Naturally, then, this is the *ātman* we think of when we hear of the Buddhist teaching of *anātman*, no-self. However, this is not the idea of the *ātman* that prevailed in India throughout the Buddhist period; that is, up till about a thousand years ago.

The *ātman* idea that was dominant in India during the Buddhist period was that of a permanent personal self. There was supposed to be something in an individual that explained the continuity of the sense of personal identity from youth to old age, and even from waking to sleeping to waking, and that persisted from life to life. This was the personal *ātman*. This personal *ātman* was usually held to be a *kartṛ*, a "doer" or "agent," and/or a *bhoktṛ*, an "enjoyer" or "experiencer." That is, according to different schools, it had at least some ability to act, and/or had some ability to experience the results of action. At the same time, it was regarded as being permanent. It is this permanent personal self that the Indian Buddhist teachers argued against in their refutations of the *ātman*. Their arguments were not directed against an impersonal universal *ātman*.

The Buddha had taught *anātman*, no-self, and this became one of the three defining characteristics of the Buddhist teachings, along with suffering, and impermanence. The Indian Buddhist teachers wrote that our clinging to the idea of a personal self is what binds us to the cycle of life and death, what causes us suffering. The idea of a permanent personal self is what they understood the *anātman* teaching to refer to, as far as we can judge from their critiques of the *ātman* idea. When Vasubandhu wrote that you cannot achieve enlightenment if you believe in a self, it is not the impersonal universal *ātman* that he was talking about. He was critiquing the idea of an individual personal self, an idea that was held by numerous other Buddhists of the time, as well as by Hindus of the time. The one self of all that we now think of when we think of the *ātman* is an idea that had not yet come to dominate the Indian scene.

Indian Buddhist Teachers against Some Self

The most influential Buddhist refutation of the *ātman* is probably that written in about the fourth century C.E. by Vasubandhu. Vasubandhu systematized the early Buddhist teachings in his *Abhidharma-kośa* in eight chapters, to which he added a supplementary ninth chapter on the "person" (*pudgala*). This refutation of the *ātman* devotes most of its space to refuting the person posited by the Buddhist Pudgalavādins (Vātsīputrīyas or Sāṃmatīyas). This person or self was held to be indeterminate (*avaktavya*), in that it is neither the five aggregates (*skandha*) nor is it other than them. Later in this chapter some space is given to refuting the non-Buddhist (*tīrthika*) ideas of the *ātman*, identified by the sub-commentator Yaśomitra as those of Sāṃkhya, Vaiyākaraṇa (the grammarians), and Vaiśeṣika. One of these is the idea of a permanent *kartṛ*, "doer" or "agent," and *bhoktṛ*, "enjoyer" or "experiencer" (p. 476, P. Pradhan Sanskrit edition). There is no mention of the Advaita Vedānta idea of an impersonal universal *ātman.*

Preceding Vasubandhu by perhaps a couple of centuries, we have the brief examination of the *ātman* (and *dharma*-s) by Nāgārjuna in chapter 18 of his *Mūla-madhyamaka-kārikā,* consisting of twelve verses. In this book, Nāgārjuna was primarily addressing the earlier schools of Buddhism in his attempt to establish the teachings of what later became known as Mahāyāna Buddhism. As may be seen by his use of the terms *ātmīya,* "pertaining or belonging to me," *mama,* "of me, mine," and *ahaṃkāra,* "sense of I," in verses 2-4 of this chapter, Nāgārjuna is here examining the idea of a personal self. This is confirmed by the four major Indian commentaries on Nāgārjuna's text: the *Akutobhayā* incorrectly attributed to Nāgārjuna, and those by Buddhapālita, Bhavya or Bhā[va]viveka, and Candrakīrti. Although they bring in non-Buddhist ideas of the *ātman,* e.g., a *kartṛ,* doer and a *bhoktṛ,* enjoyer, these commentaries make no mention of the Advaita Vedānta idea of the one universal *ātman.*

Nāgārjuna's disciple Āryadeva gave us a refutation of the *ātman* that is specifically directed at non-Buddhist (*tīrthika*) ideas of the *ātman*. This is chapter 10 of his *Catuḥśataka*, consisting of twenty-five verses, and there is a commentary by Candrakīrti on this book. Āryadeva critiques the Hindu Vaiśeṣika, Sāṃkhya, and Nyāya ideas of the self, all ideas of a permanent personal self. Again, there is no mention of the Advaita Vedānta idea of an impersonal universal *ātman*.

Contemporary with Vasubandhu we have a refutation of the *ātman* in the *Yogācāra-bhūmi*, written by Asaṅga (so Tibetan tradition) or by Maitreya (so Chinese tradition). It is the segment on *ātma-vāda*, the doctrine of the self, which is the fourth of sixteen segments on the doctrines of others, *para-vāda*, found in the third section (including *bhūmi*-s 3-5) of the *Yogācāra-bhūmi* (pp. 129-137, V. Bhattacharya Sanskrit edition). It begins by defining its subject as *ātman* (self) or *sattva* (living being) or *jīva* (individual soul) or *poṣa* (man) or *pudgala* (person). Obviously, it is speaking of the doctrine of a personal self, not a universal self.

The most important Buddhist refutation of the *ātman* for historical purposes is that by Bhavya in his *Madhyamaka-hṛdaya*, because it is the earliest text so far known that describes and critiques the Vedānta system by name. This text examines and critiques the various philosophical systems prevalent in India at that time, circa mid-sixth century C.E., so the Vedānta that he critiques preceded the Advaita Vedānta of Śaṅkarācārya. Unexpectedly, much of Bhavya's refutation of the *ātman* in the Vedānta chapter, chapter 8 consisting of 104 verses, is of an *ātman* that is a *kartṛ*, doer and a *bhoktṛ*, enjoyer. These are what Bhavya's primary refutation of the *ātman* was directed against that he had already made earlier in this book, where he refuted the Sāṃkhya and Vaiśeṣika ideas of the *ātman* (chapter 3 on reality, verses 94-98, and chapters 6 and 7 on the Sāṃkhya and Vaiśeṣika philosophical systems). Apparently the *ātman* of the Vedānta known to Bhavya, although universal (i.e., *eka*, "one"), was yet a *kartṛ*, doer as in Vaiśeṣika, and a *bhoktṛ*, enjoyer as in Sāṃkhya and Vaiśeṣika.

Bhavya's refutation of the *ātman* idea of the Vedānta known to him hinges on the contradiction between it being posited as unitary (*eka*), illustrated by the simile of the space within a pot, and yet being a *kartṛ*, doer and a *bhoktṛ*, enjoyer. He wrote that without the false ideas of the *ātman* as a *kartṛ* and a *bhoktṛ*, the remaining Vedānta ideas of the *ātman* (some of which were appropriated from the Buddhists, such as that reality can only be beyond thought and speech, verses 85-86) are no different than the correct Buddhist ideas of *svabhāva*, an "inherent nature." Thus, both the *ātman* and *svabhāva* are unborn (*ajāta*), one (*eka*), all-pervasive (*sarvaga*), permanent (*nitya*), imperishable (*acyuta*), supreme (*para*), and beyond thought and speech (verses 89-94, Chr. Lindtner Sanskrit edition). He then addresses the Vedāntins (verse 95), saying that if you, sirs, also intended such an *ātman*, there is no fault (*nirdoṣa*) and it is logically appropriate (*upapattika*). So (verses 97-98) abandon your false ideas of an *ātman*, a *kartṛ* and a *bhoktṛ*, and come over to the Buddhist teachings.

Where Nāgārjuna critiques the idea that the *ātman* is either the aggregates (*skandha*) or is other than the aggregates (*Mūla-madhyamaka-kārikā* 18.1), some in our time have thought that by the latter alternative Nāgārjuna denied the Advaita Vedānta idea of the *ātman*, an impersonal universal *ātman*. None of the four major Indian commentaries thereon explain it in such a way. Bhavya explains an *ātman* other than the aggregates as the Vaiśeṣika idea of the *ātman* as a permanent *kartṛ*, doer, and the Sāṃkhya idea of the *ātman* as a *bhoktṛ*, enjoyer. He did not mention the Vedānta idea of the *ātman*, which at that time apparently included these two ideas. Only later would we see the emergence of Advaita Vedānta in which these two ideas were rejected and only the ones accepted by Bhavya remained.

Another Madhyamaka commentator, Candrakīrti, gave us a refutation of the *ātman* in his *Madhyamakāvatāra*, chapter 6, verses 120-165, with his own commentary thereon. He begins (verse 120) by saying that all afflictions and faults arise from *sat-kāya-dṛṣṭi*, the incorrect view of taking the perishable assemblage, i.e., the body, etc., to be an enduring self, so the *ātman* should be refuted. He then (verse 121) defines the *ātman* of the non-Buddhists, using the Hindu Sāṃkhya definition: it is a permanent self that is a *bhoktṛ*, enjoyer but not a *kartṛ*, doer. He says that other non-Buddhist ideas of the *ātman* are only small variations of this. Thus in his commentary on this verse he brings in the Vaiśeṣika definition of the *ātman* in full, in brief a *kartṛ* and a *bhoktṛ*, and at the very end he adds one sentence on the Veda-vāda, i.e., Vedānta, idea of the self: the one self is differentiated in various bodies like the space in a pot. The clear implication is that in the Vedānta known to Candrakīrti, like in that known to Bhavya before him, the *ātman*, although one, was regarded as a *kartṛ*, doer and a *bhoktṛ*, enjoyer. That is, although ultimately universal, it is still a personal *ātman*, not an impersonal *ātman*.

Dharmakīrti, famous for his treatises on reasoning, has given critiques of the *ātman* in various parts of these, especially in his *Pramāṇa-vārttika* and his commentary on its Svārthānumāna section. Most of these have been conveniently gathered together in a 2013 book by Vincent Eltschinger and Isabelle Ratié, *Self, No-Self, and Salvation: Dharmakīrti's Critique of the Notions of Self and Person*. Like the other Indian Buddhist teachers, Dharmakīrti refutes the person (*pudgala*) posited by the Buddhist Pudgalavādins, and the Hindu Nyāya and Vaiśeṣika and Sāṃkhya ideas of the *ātman*, a permanent personal self. He does not refer to the Advaita Vedānta idea of the impersonal universal *ātman*.

The most extensive Buddhist refutation specifically of the *ātman* is that by Śāntarakṣita in his *Tattva-saṃgraha* and the commentary thereon by his disciple Kamalaśīla, who are dated in the eight century C.E. Śāntarakṣita devoted verses 171-221 to a critique of the Nyāya and Vaiśeṣika idea of the *ātman*, verses 222-284 to the Mīmāṃsā idea of the *ātman*, verses 285-310 to the Sāṃkhya idea, verses 311-327 to the Digambara Jaina idea, and only verses 328-335 to the Advaita [Vedānta] idea of the *ātman*. The Advaita idea here described is that the *ātman* is *jñāna*, "knowledge, cognition," or *vijñāna*, "consciousness," which is one (*eka*) and permanent (*nitya*), and the world is a transformation of consciousness (*vijñāna-pariṇāma*). Of course, this is not the *ātman* idea of the Advaita Vedānta of Śaṅkarācārya. For Śaṅkara and his famous doctrine of *māyā*, "illusion," the world is not a transformation of consciousness. It is a superimposition of a false appearance on the one unchanging *brahman*, and the *ātman* is *brahman*.

Śāntarakṣita and Kamalaśīla gave us the last major refutation of the *ātman* written by Indian Buddhist teachers, and they obviously wrote before the promulgation by Śaṅkarācārya of the Advaita Vedānta idea of the impersonal universal *ātman*.

Śaṅkarācārya, who is usually dated in the eighth century C.E., formulated the Advaita Vedānta teachings on the basis of selected passages of the Upaniṣads. These taught that the *ātman* is *brahman*, the absolute reality, non-dual (*advaita*), one without a second, and Śaṅkara attempted to show that this is the purport of all the Upaniṣads. This *ātman* is necessarily universal and impersonal; it cannot be individual or personal. It follows from this that the *ātman* cannot be a *kartṛ*, a "doer" or "agent," or a *bhoktṛ*, an "enjoyer" or "experiencer." Indeed, Śaṅkarācārya, like the Indian Buddhist teachers, made the refutation of this idea of the personal self a central theme of his writings. At the beginning of his introduction to his most definitive work, the *Brahma-sūtra-bhāṣya*, he describes the problem of the (personal) self, "a natural human behaviour based on self-identification in the form of 'I am this' or 'This is mine'." At the conclusion of his introduction, after describing how "one superimposes external characteristics on the Self," he writes (as translated by Swami Gambhirananda):

> Thus occurs this superimposition that has neither beginning nor end but flows on eternally, that appears as the manifested universe and its apprehension, that conjures up agentship [*kartṛ-tva*] and enjoyership [*bhoktṛ-tva*], and that is perceived by all persons. In order to eradicate this source of evil and in order to acquire the knowledge of the unity of the Self, is begun a discussion (after the study) of all the Upaniṣads.

In view of all the above, we can see why Kamaleswar Bhattacharya wrote near the end of his chapter 1 (p. 34): "Before stating that Buddhism has denied the *ātman*, modern authors should, therefore, have been precise as to which *ātman* is meant." The question, "which atman?" pertains to the first part of his thesis, enunciated on the first page of his Preface: "the Buddha does not deny the Upaniṣadic *ātman*," i.e., the universal *ātman* that Advaita Vedānta takes as the purport of all the Upaniṣads. That the Buddha did not deny the universal *ātman*, is, I think, demonstrable. The Indian Buddhist teachers uniformly describe the *ātman* that they understood the Buddha to have denied as an enduring personal *ātman*, rather than an impersonal universal *ātman*.

The Resulting Question

The second part of Kamaleswar Bhattacharya's thesis, "on the contrary, he indirectly affirms it, *in denying that which is falsely believed to be the ātman*," is another question. If the Buddha's denial of a permanent personal self was intended to indirectly affirm an impersonal universal *ātman*, we would expect to find at least some affirmations of a universal *ātman* in the Buddhist scriptures. We do find these, in a small number of Buddhist scriptures, especially in the *tathāgata-garbha* sūtras. The *tathāgata-garbha* sūtras teach the *tathāgata-garbha*, a buddha nature that is found in everyone. They openly equate this with the *ātman*, which they distinguish from the personal *ātman* by describing it as the perfection of *ātman* (*ātma-pāramitā*). One of these *tathāgata-garbha* sūtras is the Mahāyāna *Mahāparinirvāṇa-sūtra*, purporting to give the Buddha's final teachings before he achieved *parinirvāṇa*, i.e., died. If the *tathāgata-garbha* teaching was in fact the Buddha's final view on this question, then his denial of a permanent personal self in his other scriptures would indeed indirectly affirm an impersonal universal *ātman*.

An often-quoted passage from the *Laṅkāvatāra-sūtra* distinguishes the *tathāgata-garbha* from the *ātman* taught by the non-Buddhists, and says that the teaching of the *tathāgata-garbha* was used by the Buddhas to help those who are afraid of the no-self (*nairātyma*) teaching. Kamaleswar Bhattacharya quotes this passage in full (pp. 193-196). He notes that the *ātman* it speaks of is there described as a *kartṛ*, doer. As was made clear by the refutations of the *ātman* written by the Indian Buddhist teachers, this is a personal *ātman*. This passage, then, distinguishes the *tathāgata-garbha* from the permanent personal *ātman* taught by the non-Buddhists, not from the impersonal universal *ātman* that the Advaita Vedānta non-Buddhists would later promulgate. As for the suggestion that the *tathāgata-garbha* teaching is only provisional, used to help those who are afraid of the no-self teaching, both the *tathāgata-garbha* and the no-self teachings are referred to as skillful means in this passage. Different truths can be used as skillful means. In the whole rest of the *Laṅkāvatāra-sūtra* the *tathāgata-garbha* teaching is presented as ultimate truth.

The Buddhist teaching of no-self, *anātman* or *nairātyma*, certainly denies a permanent personal self, thus denying that which is falsely believed to be the *ātman*. That this indirectly affirms some reality, whatever it may be, is also stated by Nāgārjuna and elaborated by his four major Indian commentators. Nāgārjuna in his *Mūla-madhyamaka-kārikā* 18.6 writes that both *ātman* and *anātman*, and also neither *ātman* nor *anātman*, were taught by the buddhas. Candrakīrti in his commentary thereon explains that just as the view of *ātman* is not reality (*tattva*), so also its opposite, the view of *anātman* is not reality. Both are only views, which the best trainees leave behind. Nāgārjuna in the next verse begins his definition of reality, saying that the true nature (*dharmatā*) is beyond the range of thought and speech. The same is said in the *Mahāparinirvāṇa-sūtra*, but is more specific at the end, bringing in the *tathāgata-garbha* (Mark Blum translation, p. 160): "Whether one speaks of self, nonself, the denial of self, or the denial of nonself, one only renounces attachments [to those views], he does not renounce *this* view of self. This view of self I call 'buddha-nature'."

Kamaleswar Bhattacharya in this book has gathered together considerable evidence that indirectly affirms an impersonal universal *ātman*, primarily from the Pāli Buddhist canon. He did not draw this evidence from the *tathāgata-garbha* sūtras with their perfection of *ātman* (except by way of one long opening quote from the *Ratna-gotra-vibhāga*). In the end, the question of whether the Buddha indirectly affirmed the Upaniṣadic *ātman* is a matter for each person to decide by examining the evidence and choosing which teachings make the most sense to them. Kamaleswar Bhattacharya's book gives us a choice that most people in our time did not think existed in Buddhism.

Summing Up

In this book, Kamaleswar Bhattacharya has provided us with a sustained argument for a position that only a small number of Buddhist scholars today are sympathetic with: "the Buddha does not deny the Upaniṣadic *ātman*." While it, unlike others, has been taken seriously by Buddhist scholars (those who could read the French original), it has not convinced the majority of them. For this reason I have added this new introduction laying out the refutations of the *ātman* by the Indian Buddhist teachers, showing that a permanent personal *ātman* is what they thought the Buddha denied. We see everywhere in Buddhist writings published today, even by the best Buddhist scholars, the assumption that the Buddha denied the impersonal universal *ātman*. They have simply not taken account of the fact that the dominance of this idea in India did not occur until after the Buddhist period. It is my hope that the publication of this book in English translation will make it much more widely accessible. Perhaps now, after the author's death, it will receive the attention it deserves.

David Reigle

Preface

This book came into being by chance. I had intended, in fulfillment of a long-standing promise,[1] to write a book on Buddhism in ancient Cambodia. An encounter with a stanza on an inscription led me, however, to make a thorough study of the problem of the *ātman* in Buddhism.

Does this problem actually exist? Does not Buddhism deny the *ātman*? These are questions that may well be asked.

I have but one answer which I have tried to formulate in various ways in this book, on the basis, invariably, of a study of the Pāli canon and of the Nikāyas in particular, that is: the Buddha does not deny the Upaniṣadic *ātman*; on the contrary, he indirectly affirms it, *in denying that which is falsely believed to be the ātman.*

The one request I would make of such eminent scholars as have devoted their lives to the study of Buddhism is that they adopt a genuinely Buddhist attitude and read this book before saying, "That is impossible."

I must explain the particular structure of this book. Most of its chapters were presented between 1963-67, as annual reports of the Centre National de la Recherche Scientifique. In the course of time these reports had undergone modification as regards their contents but I have, perhaps mistakenly, kept their original form. Most of the appendices derive from what were initially only notes. Sometimes (for example, with reference to the *nāmarūpa*, Appendix IV), I do no more than give outlines of research which may have been done in detail.

To explain Upaniṣadic and Buddhist philosophy, I have had recourse, from time to time, to parallels with western philosophy. The apparent similarities doubtless require deeper study; but I have no other aim here than that of rendering this exposition as comprehensible as possible. Besides, a number of the comparisons found here are those I tested with students at Brown University, Providence, Rhode Island, U.S.A. I should say here that the development of this work owes much to that teaching experience. My congenial and attentive students frequently opened new horizons to me with their comments.

I owe something to each one of the authors mentioned in this book and am especially indebted to those who have studied this problem before me, particularly, Hermann Oldenberg, Ananda Coomaraswamy and Sarvepalli Radhakrishnan.[2] The works of T.R.V. Murti and of K. Venkata Ramanam have aided me greatly in my comprehension of the Madhyamaka.

As far as possible I have refrained from bestowing a polemic character upon this book. I have concerned myself with saying what I have to say rather than with judging others and have mentioned no author for purposes of criticism except on points where this has seemed essential.

Had the conditions under which I have had to work been better, the result would certainly have been closer to the one dreamed of but there have been difficulties over consulting indispensable books. . . .

I am indebted to that excellent Sanskritist, Jeffrey L. Masson, who not only put his own library in Providence at my disposal but also obtained a great many essential Pāli and Sanskrit texts from Harvard for me. I regret not having had access to a number of sources of secondary importance.

Alexander B. Griswold took the trouble to read the manuscript and his opinion was a crucial influence on the decision to publish this work. I offer him my heartfelt thanks.

Mention cannot be omitted of the fruitful interviews I had in Paris with Walpola Rāhula Thera, Tripiṭakavāgīśvarācārya. Despite a divergence of opinion, he was kind enough to clarify a number of points for me.

I remember, with regrets, three departed mentors: Louis Renou, Paul Mus and George Cœdès. All three followed my efforts with great benevolence, right from the inception of my research into the Sanskrit epigraphy of Cambodia. Where this present work is concerned it is to Louis Renou that most is owed. This great Indologist had no patience with "adventurous" spirits and it must be said that he received some of my first reports rather coldly. Yet it is a pleasure to remember how, after he had read the second chapter on *Brahman* (ch. II), he declared himself "convinced."

Once again, I should like to thank J. Filliozat, Director of the Ecole française d'Extrême-Orient and, also, the Centre National de la Recherche Scientifique for all their help, without which this book would not exist.

Notes to Preface

1. *Les Religions brāhmaniques dans l'ancien Cambodge, d'après l'epigraphie et l'iconographie* (=*Publications de l'Ecole française d'Extrême-Orient*, XLIX, 1961), p. 5.

2. The question of the relationships between Buddhism and the Upaniṣads is of perennial interest to researchers. Cf. P. Horsch, "Buddhismus und Upaniṣaden," in *Pratidānam: Indian, Iranian and Indo-European Studies Presented to F.B.J. Kuiper on his Sixtieth Birthday* (The Hague-Paris, Mouton, 1968), pp. 462-477.

Chapter One

Ātman Anātman

A Sanskrit inscription from Cambodia, inscription B from Bàt Cũṃ (reign of Rājendravarman: 944-968 A.D.), begins with the following stanza:[1]

Buddho bodhiṃ vidadhyād vo yena nairātmyadarśanam |
viruddhasyāpi sādhūktaṃ sādhanaṃ paramātmanaḥ ||

The concept of *paramātman* is in contradiction (*viruddha*) with the doctrine of *nairātmya*; nevertheless, the Buddha taught that same doctrine as a means (*sādhana*) of attaining to *paramātman*!

G. Cœdès, when he edited and translated this inscription in 1908, saw in it a contamination of Buddhism by Hinduism in Cambodia. Today we are able to dismiss this hypothesis, thanks to the *Mahāyāna-Sūtrālaṃkāra*, edited and translated by S. Lévi in 1907 and 1911. Stanza 23 of Chapter IX in fact says:

śūnyatāyāṃ viśuddhāyāṃ nairātmyātmāgralābhataḥ[2] |
buddhāḥ suddhātmalābhitvād gatā ātmamahātmatām ||

The commentator, in accordance with the text,[3] writes:

tatra cānāsrave dhātau buddhānāṃ paramātmā nirdiśyate.—kiṃ kāraṇam?—agranairātmyātmakatvāt. agraṃ nairātmyaṃ viśuddhā tathatā, sā ca buddhānām ātmā, svabhāvārthena. tasyāṃ viśuddhāyām agraṃ nairātmyam ātmānaṃ buddhā labhante śuddham. ataḥ śuddhātmalābhitvād buddhā ātmamāhātmyaṃ prāptā ity anenābhisaṃdhinā buddhānām anāsrave dhātau paramātmā vyavasthāpyate.

According to the translation by S. Lévi, slightly modified:

In utterly pure Emptiness,[4] the Buddhas have attained to the summit of the *ātman*, which consists in Impersonality.[5] Since they have found, thus, the pure *ātman*, they have reached the heights of *ātman*.

And, in this Plan Without-Outflowing, is indicated the *paramātman* of the Buddhas—How so?—Because their *ātman* consists in the essential Impersonality. The essential Impersonality is the absolutely pure Thus-ness,[6] and it is the *ātman* in the sense of the own-nature[7] of the Buddhas. When it is absolutely pure, the Buddhas attain to the essential Impersonality which is the pure *ātman*. Attaining to the pure *ātman*, the Buddhas attain to the greatness of the *ātman*. And it is with that intention that the *paramātman* of the Buddhas is classified in the Plan Without-Outflowing.

The commentary to the *Ratnagotravibhāga* clarifies this thought further:

tatra yā rūpādike vastuny anitye nityam iti saṃjñā, duḥkhe sukham iti, anātmany ātmeti, aśubhe śubham iti saṃjñā, ayam ucyate caturvidho viparyāsaḥ. etad-viparyayeṇa caturvidha evāviparyāso veditavyaḥ.—katamaś caturvidhaḥ?—yā tasminn eva rūpādike vastuny anityasaṃjñā, duḥkhasaṃjñā, anātmasaṃjñā, aśubha-saṃjñā, ayam ucyate caturvidhaviparyāsaviparyayaḥ.—sa khalv eṣa nityādilakṣaṇaṃ Tathāgatadharmakāyam adhikṛtyeha viparyāso 'bhipreto yasya pratipakṣeṇa catur-ākārā Tathāgatadharmakāyaguṇapāramitā vyavasthāpitā, tadyathā nityapāramitā, sukhapāramitā, ātmapāramitā, śubhapāramiteti. eṣa ca grantho vistareṇa yathāsūtram anugantavyaḥ: viparyastā, Bhagavan, sattvā upātteṣu pañcasūpādānaskandheṣu. te bhavanty anitye nitya-saṃjñinaḥ, duḥkhe sukhasaṃjñinaḥ, anātmany ātma-saṃjñinaḥ, aśubhe śubhasaṃjñinaḥ. sarvaśrāvakapratyeka-buddhā api, Bhagavan, śūnyatājñānenādṛṣṭapūrve sarva-jñajñānaviṣaye Tathāgatadharmakāye viparyastāḥ. ye,

Bhagavan, sattvāḥ syur Bhagavataḥ putrā aurasā nityasaṃjñina ātmasaṃjñinaḥ, sukhasaṃjñinaḥ, śubhasaṃjñinas te, Bhagavan, sattvāḥ syur aviparyastāḥ; syus te, Bhagavan, samyagdarśinaḥ.—tat kasmād dhetoḥ?—Tathāgatadharmakāya eva, Bhagavan, nityapāramitā, sukhapāramitā, ātmapāramitā, śubhapāramitā. ye, Bhagavan, sattvās Tathāgatadharmakāyam evaṃ paśyanti te samyak paśyanti; ye samyak paśyanti te Bhagavataḥ putrā aurasā iti vistaraḥ.

. . . pañcasūpādānaskandheṣv ātmadarśinām anyatīrthyānām asadātmagrahābhirativiparyayeṇa prajñāpāramitābhāvanāyāḥ paramātmapāramitādhigamaḥ phalaṃ draṣṭavyam. sarve hy anyatīrthyā rūpādikam atatsvabhāvaṃ vastv ātmety upagatāḥ. tac caiṣāṃ vastu yathāgraham ātmalakṣaṇena visaṃvāditatvāt[8] *sarvakālam anātmā. Tathāgataḥ punar yathābhūtajñānena sarvadharmanairātmyaparapāramiprāptaḥ.*[9] *tac cāsya nairātmyam anātmalakṣaṇena*[10] *yathādarśanam avisaṃvāditatvāt*[8] *sarvakālam ātmābhipretaḥ, nairātmyam evātmeti*[8] *kṛtvā. yathoktaṃ sthito 'sthānayogeneti.*

The idea of the permanent (*nitya*) in what is impermanent (*anitya*), of happiness (*sukha*) in what is sorrowful (*duḥkha*), of the *ātman* in what is non-*ātman* (*anātman*), of the pure (*śubha*) in what is impure (*aśubha*), that is to say, in such things as the corporeal form (*rūpa*), etc., that is what is called: the fourfold misapprehension (*viparyāsa*).[11] By the inversion of this, it is to be understood that the non-misapprehension (*aviparyāsa*) is also fourfold. What is this fourfold non-misapprehension?—The concept of the impermanent, of sorrow, of the *anātman* and of the impure, in these same things, that is: the corporeal form etc.,—this is what is called: the fourfold inversion of misapprehension (*viparyāsa-viparyaya*). —In relation, however, to the *dharmakāya*[12] of the Tathāgata, whose characteristic is being permanent (*nitya*), etc., this non-misapprehension itself is regarded as a misapprehension, in opposition to which is set the Perfection[13] of quality of the *dharmakāya* of the Tathāgata, Perfection which takes on four forms: being permanent (*nitya*), being happy (*sukha*), being *ātman* and being pure (*śubha*). This text must be understood in detail, according to the (*Śrīmālādevīsiṃhanāda-*) *Sūtra*: 'Lord, beings are misled as regards the five groups of elements of existence they have assumed (*upātteṣu pañcasūpādānaskandheṣu*);[14] they have the idea of the permanent in what is impermanent, of happiness in what is sorrowful, of the *ātman* in what is non-*ātman*, of purity in the impure. All the Śrāvakas and Pratyekabuddhas, on the other hand, Lord, are mistaken with regard to the *dharmakāya* of the Tathāgata, which is the object of knowledge of the Omniscient; they are without vision of it, lacking any intuition of Emptiness (*śūnyatājñānenādṛṣṭapūrve sarvajñajñānaviṣaye Tathāgatadharmakāye viparyastāḥ*). Beings, Lord, who are the true sons (*putrā aurasāḥ*) of the Lord, possessed of ideas of the Permanent, of the *ātman*, of Happiness and of Purity: these beings, Lord, are not misled; they see truly, Lord.— . . . Why so?—It is the *dharmakāya* of the Tathāgata, Lord, which constitutes the Perfections: being permanent, being happy, being *ātman* and being pure. Beings, Lord, who see the *dharmakāya* of the Tathāgata thus, see truly, and those who see truly are the true sons of the Lord.'

Adepts of other doctrines (*anyatīrthyāḥ*)[15] see the *ātman* in the five groups of elements of existence. They are thus attached to the grasping of an *ātman* which does not exist (*asadātmagrahābhirati*).[16] Inversely to this attachment, the *Prajñāpāramitā* is practiced, and the fruit of that practice is the attainment of Perfection: the *paramātman* (*paramātmapāramitādhigama*). All adepts of other doctrines, in fact, consider as *ātman* something that has not its own nature (*atatsvabhāva*), that is: corporeal form, etc. That thing is always non-*ātman* (*sarvakālam anātmā*) for, under whatsoever aspect it is grasped, it is at variance with the characteristics of the *ātman* (*yathāgraham ātmalakṣaṇena visaṃvāditatvāt*).[17] The Tathāgata, on the other hand, by virtue of his absolute knowledge (*yathābhūtajñānena*), has gained perfect intuition of the

> Impersonality of all separate elements.[18] This Impersonality accords, from every point of view (*yathādarśanam*), with the characteristics of the *ātman.*[19] It is thus always regarded as *ātman*, because it is Impersonality which is *ātman* (*nairātmyam evātmeti kṛtvā*). Similarly, it is said: 'he holds by not holding' (*sthito 'sthānayogena*).[20]

The idea of *paramātman* is thus not contradictory to the doctrine of *nairātmya*; the two terms rather designate the same thing from two different points of view. Regarding the passage from the *Mahāyāna-Sūtrālaṃkāra*, R. Grousset has rightly said:

> Perhaps it may be permissible to note that such a conception recalls, curiously enough, material from some of the Upaniṣads; the *ātman* consisting essentially in *nairātmya*, or, if preferred, the person being resolved in its very depths in impersonality, we there approach the impersonal *ātman* of the *Bṛhadāraṇyaka*. And this return to the most ancient Brahminical past presages the future . . . if we envisage the *ātman* of some Upaniṣads and of Śaṅkara, so impersonal, so neutral, so unqualified and so similar to emptiness, we shall be struck by how negligible is the distance which separates it from the *ātman nirātman* of Asaṅga.[21]

Let us recall that, in the *Tattirīya-Upaniṣad*, the *brahman-ātman* is already called *anātmya.*[22] The *Maitri*, for its part, employs the terms *nirātman* and *nirātmaka.*[23] There is one point, however, on which we are at variance with the author we have just quoted: where he sees, first, a severance (ancient Buddhism) and then a 'return' (Mahāyāna), we have come to recognize a continuity.

What is the Upaniṣadic *ātman*?—The *ātman* is not the individual ego but rather 'the super-reality of the *jīva*, the individual ego.'[24] The *ātman* is neither the body nor the totality of the psycho-physical elements which make up the empirical individual.[25] The 'body'[26] is no more than a 'support' (*adhiṣṭhāna*) of the incorporeal (*aśarīra*) *ātman*[27]—of the *ātman* 'without *ātman*' (*anātmya, nirātman, nirātmaka*).[28] "Just as the beast is yoked to the cart, so the *prāṇa* (that is, the *ātman*)[29] is yoked to this body."[30] The *ātman* is the 'inner ruler' (*antaryāmin*) which resides in the Universe but is distinct from and unknown to the Universe. All our activities derive from it; there is no other seer than it, no other hearer, no other thinker and no other knower. Even so, it remains invisible itself, inaudible, unthinkable, unknowable.[31] The *ātman* is the "inner light" (*antarjyotis*) of man.[32]

The corporeal (*saśarīra*) *ātman* is mortal; it experiences pleasure and pain. But the incorporeal (*aśarīra*) *ātman*, the authentic *ātman*, is immortal; it is exempt from all pleasure and from all suffering.[33]

In no wise does the Buddha deny this absolute reality, this "super-reality of the individual ego." He merely condemns the opinion, current at his time, which identifies the *ātman* with that individual ego. He condemns the "children" (*bāla*)[34] who aspire to become permanent, not by immersing themselves in the Permanent, beyond the empirical categories of space, time and causality,[35] but by virtue of a temporal acquisition, *post mortem*, of that ideal state, in a higher world.[36]

The Buddha is neither a "pessimist" nor a "nihilist";[37] in no wise does he advocate the destruction (*uccheda, vināsa, vibhava*) of the existing individual (*sato sattassa*).[38] He shows, on the contrary, the way which leads from the ephemeral to the Eternal, from the mortal to the Immortal, from the sorrow of the finite to the Bliss of the Infinite.[39]

Nirvāṇa/nibbāna, or the extinction of the ego, is not a "nothingness" but, on the contrary, the plenitude of Being, beyond the limitations of the empirical world.[40]

The Buddha did not say, "There is no *ātman*." He simply said, in speaking of the *skandha/khandhas*, ephemeral and painful, which constitute the psycho-physical being of a man: *n'etaṃ mama, n'eso 'ham asmi, na m'eso attā*, "This is not mine, I am not this, this is not my *ātman*."[41]

It is because we do not see things as they really are (*yathābhūtaṃ*), because we look at the outside and not at the inside,[42] that we consider as our *ātman* that which it is not, and that we see, in the annihilation of what is passing, our own annihilation. The Buddha, no more than the sages of the Upaniṣads, does not seek the end of sorrow in annihilation.

If, however, it is not our body,[43] it is, at least, our individual consciousness which we consider to be our essence. What am I without my consciousness? I am reduced to nothingness; I no longer know who I am nor whether there is an external world.[44]

Such is the opinion, in general, of men and of gods, indicated as much by Pāli texts as by the Upaniṣads.[45] And their answer is identical: it is neither the body nor the totality of psycho-physical components which constitutes our essence. Our essence is the *ātman* which is beyond all these elements. It is neither a thing nor a state, but an inexpressible experience, in which all distinction between subject and object vanishes, where the individual I melts into universal Being. The question "what am I?" is no longer asked. As a man plunged in deep sleep, or in the embrace of a beloved woman,[46] so the man who experiences the *ātman* no longer possesses any individual consciousness. All opposition between the interior and the exterior disappears in Unity. The *ātman* sees the *ātman*, the *ātman* hears the *ātman*, the *ātman* knows the *ātman*, for there is nothing but *ātman*, subject knowing and object known.[47]

Sorrow lies in Desire, which belongs to our finitude,[48] itself due to Ignorance (*avidyā/avijjā*):[49] this consists in seeing something permanent in what is impermanent, the *ātman* in the non-*ātman* (that is, in the psycho-physical elements which compose our empirical individuality). If the Buddha—like the sages of the Upaniṣads—proved the destruction of something, it was but sorrow and its cause.[50] He, like them, lets us have a glimpse of that supreme experience which is beyond birth and death, "from which there is no return." But it is for us to realize it in ourselves by our own efforts.[51]

To know the *ātman-brahman* is, in effect, to become it.[52] It is not enough to conceive of it objectively. As long as we do nothing but conceive of it, we are far from knowing it: the *ātman*, the Self, remains an object to us, and, therefore, a non-Self. We imagine the *ātman* as this or that element of our empirical individuality and, when that no longer satisfies us, being impermanent and sorrowful, we end, either in nihilism or in a kind of eternalism,[53] which consists in seeing the *ātman* in a happy and eternal life to which we accede after death.[54] We aspire to that life and we perform good deeds but we forget that, in doing all this, we are maintaining within ourselves a focus of desire.[55]

The *ātman*, the Absolute, is beyond the relation implied by all thought. It is said that "it is established in its own greatness"; but that very expression is not adequate, for, simple as it is, it nevertheless implies a relation: the Absolute is no longer the Absolute, but a distinction made within it.[56] It is possible to speak of it in negative terms only: *neti neti* . . . "it is not so, not so. . . ."[57] All the "theories of the *ātman*" (*ātmavāda/attavāda*), which attempt to express it in terms of habitual thought, are therefore ultimately false and are thus best avoided.

Buddhism and the Upaniṣads agree in saying that absolute Truth cannot be attained through theoretical knowledge. Blind attachment to a doctrine such as that of the *ātman*, as blind attachment to moral and ritual practices (*śīlavrata/sīlabbata*),[58] serves only to make us "swollen headed"; it does not reveal the Truth to us. That is why the Buddha condemns the *attavādupādāna*, along with the three other *upādānas*;[59] this should not be seen as a negation of the *ātman*.[60]

The Buddha does not deny the *ātman*, he merely condemns attachment to theories (*vāda*) concerning the *ātman*. The Upaniṣads, too, say:

> *nāyam ātmā pravacanena labhyo*
> *na medhayā na bahunā śrutena* |
> *yam evaiṣa vṛṇute tena labhyas*
> *tasyaiṣa ātmā vivṛṇute tanūṃ svām* ||

> This *ātman* cannot be attained to through teachings, nor through the intellect, nor through great knowledge. Only the one it elects may attain to it; it is to him that the *ātman* reveals its true nature.[61]

All truths as can be formulated are, in fact, but approximations of Truth, which is inexpressible; none of them can be identified with Truth itself. They aid us in reaching it, they guide our progress towards it; but they must be transcended if it is to be reached.[62] In reasoned knowledge, the subject sees his object from the outside. He is focussed upon his object, which object is right in front of him; he does not coincide with his object.[63] This knowledge is, thus, imperfect. According to the *point of view* of the subject, he grasps only *partial expressions* of his object and not the object itself at all.[64] Genuine and complete knowledge is direct experience, where the subject and the object are one. This is also why this knowledge is incommunicable. Expressed in language it ceases to be itself; we can speak only of a divided thing. "That which is expressible is held in the subject-object split. Even if the process of clarification is continued to infinity by consciousness, it never attains to the plenitude of the origin."[65] Therefore it is said, "It is for you to make the effort; the Tathāgatas merely enunciate (that which escapes enunciation)."[66] The teaching of the Buddha is compared to a boat necessary for crossing a river but not to be carried on the shoulders, once the river has been crossed (*nittharaṇatthāya no gahaṇatthāya*).[67]

Is there then any access to the Absolute other than through recourse to the empirical? The answer given by our texts is definite; it is by way of the empirical that we attain to the Absolute.[68] "The investigator proceeds from the obvious and outer to the deeper and the inward."[69] Starting from inert matter (*anna*), we raise ourselves to increasingly spiritual realities (which are, as well, increasingly "actual" manifestations of the *ātman*): life (*prāṇa* = vital breath[70]), will (*manas*), consciousness (*vijñāna*); then we surpass consciousness itself to attain at last, beyond any intermediary, the vision of the Plenitude. That vision is called *ānanda* "Bliss," or *abhaya* "fearlessness," since it transcends all the antinomies (*dvandva*) of the empirical world.[71] It is reached only by the "negative way." As we progress, we superimpose on the Absolute less and less limiting determinations. We pass through each stage by denying the "superimposition." We say, "It is not so, not so . . ." (*neti neti*),[72] so as to penetrate further. Do we then achieve a nothingness? No. For negation here is, in reality, a *negation of negation.* We may explain the philosophy of the Upaniṣads in the words Karl Jaspers applies to that of Plotinus: if the Absolute "is not that which it is not, this is in no wise because it is less than what it is not, but because it is greater." And, "since it is more than what it is not, far from excluding that, it includes it in itself."[73] Negation thus leads, not to the void of nothingness but to Plenitude. Absolute being, which opens to us on completion of our evolution, comprises life, will and consciousness, although it goes beyond them.

Thus, it is not outside of ourselves that we grasp the Real: through all eternity the Real is present in us, but we do not see it, blinded as we are by our false conceptions. Our Deliverance is nothing but the wiping away of the erroneous constructions of our mind (*kalpana-kṣaya*): we do not become, at the moment of our Deliverance, something new which has not previously existed but simply *discover* our true nature, veiled until then by "ignorance."[74] Our psycho-physical existence is not an obstacle to Deliverance; we have only to sublimate it. "Behind all our growth is the perfection of ourselves which animates it; we are constantly becoming until we possess our being. The changing consciousness goes on until it is able to transcend change.[75] The Beyond is the absolute fulfilment of our self-existence. It is *ānanda,* the truth behind matter, life, mind, intelligence, that controls them all by exceeding them."[76]—We have no need to put an end to our phenomenal existence,[77] it matters only that we lead our human life in a spirit of perfect *detachment,*[78] gaze fixed upon the supreme goal of our existence which is Being itself. The objects of desire (*kāma*) cannot themselves contaminate us, if they are pursued in that spirit. Evil comes from attachment and not from life; Deliverance has to be attained through this very life. That is the profound truth, which Ariṭṭha, the *gaddhabādhipubba*,[79] had not understood.[80]

The Pāli texts are never weary of reiterating that ties arise from the fact that one sees *ātman* in what is non-*ātman*, that is to say in the *upādānaskandhas*.[81] The Buddha therefore exhorts us to understand these things as they actually are—ephemeral and insubstantial[82]—to "take refuge in the *ātman*" and to aspire to the immutable state which is Nirvāṇa.[83]

These statements should be compared to the well-known account in the *Mahāvagga*:[84]

> After preaching the Doctrine in Benares, the Buddha made his way towards Uruvelā. Leaving the road, he went into a forest and sat down under a tree. At that moment, thirty friends, all young princes, were amusing themselves with their wives in a corner of the wood. One of them was not married so he had brought along a courtesan and, whilst they were disporting themselves, she ran off with their belongings. The young men pursued her and, arriving at the spot where the Buddha was, they asked him if he had seen a woman pass. When they had told their story, the Buddha, in his turn, asked them: "Which would be better for you, to seek for a woman or to seek for the *ātman*?"—*katamaṃ nu kho tumhākaṃ varaṃ, yaṃ vā tumhe itthiṃ gaveseyyātha yaṃ vā attānaṃ gaveseyyātha?*[85]—They replied saying it would be better to seek for the *ātman* and were converted.

Let us remember the celebrated words of Yājñavalkya to Maitreyī, in the *Bṛhadāraṇyaka-Upaniṣad*:

> Verily, not for the love of the husband is the husband dear, but for love of the *ātman* is a husband dear.
>
> Verily, not for the love of a wife is a wife dear, but for love of the *ātman* a wife is dear.

Verily, not for love of the sons are sons dear, but for love of the *ātman* sons are dear.

Verily, it is not for love of wealth that wealth is dear, but for love of the *ātman* wealth is dear.

Verily, not for love of all is all dear, but for love of the *ātman* all is dear.

Verily, it is the *ātman* that should be seen, that should be heard of, that should be pondered, and that should be firmly meditated upon.

O Maitreyī, it is only by seeing, hearing of, reflecting upon, and understanding the *ātman*, that one knows all that is.[86]

Communion with the *ātman*—if it may be so expressed—is a form of existence "in which all desire is fulfilled, where there is desire only for the *ātman*, where there is no more desire, nor affliction."[87]

The *ātman* is the "Reality of the real" (*satyasya satyam*).[88] All positive realities shown to us by experience in the sensible world are but the shadow of the *ātman*. In grasping this we grasp all the rest; for example, it is in laying hold of a musical instrument that one lays hold of the sound it emits,[89] in laying hold of the clay, that we lay hold of all the objects derived from it.[90] The *ātman* is the ultimate Reality upon which the empirical world is founded; its "modifications" (*vikāra*), that is, the individual things and beings, are "mere names which rest upon speech" (*vācārambhaṇaṃ vikāro nāmadheyam*).[91]

❖

We have already spoken of the practical consequences of this doctrine. Let us now look at them more closely.

This doctrine naturally implies detachment from all that is finite. But it would be wrong to represent this detachment as isolation from the world: the Absolute, according to our doctrine, is not to be sought beyond the world, but in the world itself: it is its most profound spiritual reality.[92] "Enjoy with detachment" (*tyaktena bhuñjīthāḥ*), says the *Īśā-*

Upaniṣad.[93] We must love husband, wife, children, riches, etc., not to mention our own person, not for themselves—for they have no existence in themselves—but for the One, or the All, of which they are but aspects. There is no question of renouncing the world and all its charms; rather, instead of restricting our individual life to itself, we must integrate it into the totality of existence.

One who has realized the *ātman* is not outside the world, but he looks upon the world with new eyes: he is as a "creator of the world" (*viśvakṛt*).[94] Nothing has changed with regard to the contours of forms; but the world takes on new significance for him. He sees the *ātman* everywhere in the world and, as a result, identifies with the world.[95] Even traditional rituals change in value: according to the *Bṛhadāraṇyaka-Upaniṣad,* 1, 4, 16, the "five great sacrifices" are but sacrifices to the *ātman.*[96]

Such a man is beyond covetousness, hates and everything which divides the beings of this world.[97] Concepts of "I" and of the "other" are illusory to him.[98] He finds himself in all beings and all beings in himself. Thus he experiences the joys and sorrows of all beings and, without ever acting for himself *as an individual,* he spontaneously works for the good of All. The egoistic love of "I" and "mine," which ordinarily characterizes men, gives place to universal Love.[99] Here is the metaphysical foundation of the Buddhist (and Hindu[100]) cardinal virtues of Friendship (*maitrī*) and of Compassion (*karuṇā*), from which flow all other virtues.

We must acknowledge that it is only in Mahāyānic texts that this conception is clearly expressed. According to them, *maitrī* and *karuṇā* (or *kṛpā*) are founded on the "intuition of the identity of beings" (*sattveṣu samatājñānam*).[101] All beings are identical, since they are not beings in themselves, but have their entire reality in the indivisible universal principle. Buddhists call this principle *śūnyatā, tathatā, bhūtakoṭi, dharma-dhātu, dharma-kāya* . . . and also *ātman,* in the Upaniṣadic sense.[102] Thus we read in the *Mahāyāna-Sūtrālaṃkāra:*[103]

saṃskāramātraṃ jagad etya buddhyā
nirātmakaṃ duḥkhavirūḍhimātram |
vihāya yānarthamayātmadṛṣṭiḥ
mahātmadṛṣṭiṃ śrayate mahārtham ||
vinātmadṛṣṭyā ya ihātmadṛṣṭir
vināpi duḥkhena suduḥkhitaś ca |
sarvārthakartā na ca kārakāṅkṣī
yathātmanaḥ svātmahitāni kṛtvā ||
yo muktacittaḥ parayā vimuktyā
baddhaś ca gāḍhāyatabandhanena |
duḥkhasya paryantam apaśyamānaḥ
prayujyate caiva karoti caiva ||
svaṃ duḥkham udvoḍhum ihāsamartho
lokaḥ kutaḥ piṇḍitam anyaduḥkham |
janmaikam ālokayate tv acinto
viparyayāt tasya tu bodhisattvaḥ ||
yat prema yā vatsalatā prayogaḥ
sattveṣv akhedaś ca jinātmajānām |
āścaryam etat paramaṃ bhaveṣu
na caiva sattvātmasamānabhāvāt ||

Coming to understand that the world is Nothing but constructs, without personality, Nothing-but-which tends towards sorrow, then, rejecting the View of I which is without meaning, he resorts to the View of the great I which has a great Meaning.

He, (the Bodhisattva) who, without the View of I, possesses here the View of I, he, who free from sorrow is sore afflicted, he who works for all without expectation of any reward, as though he were doing good, on his own behalf, for his own person!

He, who, with thought delivered by supreme liberation, is also bound by a close and far-reaching bond,[104] he, who without seeing the limit of his pain,[105] occupies himself and works!

The world, here, is not capable of bearing its own pain; how much less the mass of pain of others! In its thoughtlessness, it has eyes only for its own birth. The Bodhisattva is just the opposite.

> The tenderness of the sons of the Victors towards creatures, their love, their occupation, their tirelessness, is the supreme marvel of the worlds! Or rather, No! since other and self are identical to them.

We give here, in modified form, the translation by S. Lévi. *Mahātmadṛṣṭi* (st. 37), is rendered by "the great View of I." This should, however, be "the View of the Great I" (= of the universal I, *mahātman*). This is contrasted, in our stanza, with the "View of I" (limited, individual). Such, too, is the opposition indicated in st. 38: "He, who without the view of the (limited) I, possesses here the View of the (universal) I." It is, in truth, the illusion of the individual I which divides beings, whereas the intuition of the universal I, of the authentic I, unites them. Unequivocally, Jayavarman VII, the great Buddhist king of Cambodia, has his son who is also his panegyrist, say:

anekadhānekajagatsu bhinno
'py ātmaikatā tu sphuṭam asya satyā |
sukhāni duḥkhāni yad ātmabhājām
ātmany adhāt suhṛdaye yadīye ||

> Though the *ātman* is divided in various ways in various beings, he has realized its unity in a manifest fashion, in that he has taken into his compassionate *ātman* the joys and sorrows of those who participate in the *ātman*.[106]

However, this conception does not seem to be foreign to the Pāli Canon. The *Aṅguttara-Nikāya* makes a distinction between two types of individuals: a limited type, who moves in the finite and, it follows, in sorrow (*appātumo* [= Sanskrit *alpātmā*], *appa-dukkha-vihārī*), and a universal and incommensurable type (*mahattā* [= Sanskrit *mahātmā*], *appamāṇa-vihārī*). The acts of the latter, whether good or bad, do not affect him, for all that he does, he does without egoistic desire: a pinch of salt put into a glass of water makes all the water undrinkable, but it is quite otherwise if this same pinch of salt is thrown into the Ganges.[107] He works spontaneously for the good of the world; liberated as he is from his contingent finitude, he helps others to liberate themselves,—not by "altruism," for there is nothing in the world which is "other" to him, but because he has taken cognizance of his true being, which is universal Being.[108] In fact, his deliverance is not complete for him as long as the entire world is not delivered, since he and the world are identical.[109]

It is the Mahāyāna which has, incontestably, formulated the ultimate conclusions of this doctrine. As we know, at the centre of the Mahāyāna, is to be found the ideal of the Bodhisattva, that "great being" (*mahāsattva*), that "great *Ātman*" (*mahātman*), who renounces Nirvāṇa because he has not yet preached the *dharma* to all beings of all worlds.[110] It would seen, however, that the Arahant has too often been presented as a monster of egoism, caring only for his own salvation! This is how one of the authors who has concentrated on the problem, expresses it:

> The Buddhist sage, the Arhat—not to mention a Buddha—is far above the world: he neither despises nor loves it, but feels only compassion; and this feeling is not one of 'sympathy' in the Christian sense, nor of 'being one with the sinful world'; rather it is experienced from 'outside,' as by a spectator who has himself escaped from the misery and looks out upon a struggling mankind from the consciousness of his own invulnerability to suffering.[111]

An eminent representative of Buddhism has, however, written:

> He [the Arahant] is free from all egoistic desires, from hate, ignorance, vanity, pride and from all impediments; he is pure and gentle, full of universal love, of compassion, kindness, sympathy, understanding and tolerance. He serves others in the purest possible manner, for he takes no more thought for himself, seeks for no gain, accumulates nothing, not even spiritual possessions. . . .[112]

Yet the point of view which would seem most exact is that of Har Dayal:

> Such an *arhat* also went forth as a preacher and taught the doctrine of the Buddha to the people. The Master had exhorted his disciples to wander and preach the truth for the welfare and liberation of the multitude, as he loved his fellow-creatures and had pity on them.[113]
>
> Such was the ideal of the *arhat*, as it was understood during the three centuries after Gautama Buddha's death. But it seems that the Buddhist monks began to neglect certain important aspects of it in the second century B.C., and emphasised a few duties to the exclusion of others. They became too self-centred and contemplative, and did not evince the old zeal for missionary activity among the people. They seem to have cared only for their own liberation from sin and sorrow. They were indifferent to the duty of teaching and helping all human beings. The *bodhisattva* doctrine was promulgated by some Buddhist leaders as a protest against this lack of true spiritual fervour and altruism[114] among the monks of that period. The coldness and aloofness of the *arhats* led to a movement in favour of the old gospel of 'saving all creatures.' The *bodhisattva* ideal can be understood only against this background of a saintly and serene, but inactive and indolent monastic Order.[115]

❖

Neither the Upaniṣads nor Buddhism deny the empirical reality of the individual.[116] They only deny it ontological substantiality. The psycho-physical being exists, empirically. But that existence is not the supreme goal of man, who must become universal Being. That universal Being is in us, is ourselves; we do not however know it, due to the fact that our consciousness is not yet sufficiently opened out. "Individual consciousness is born of limitation and, as Plotinus puts it (VI, 5, 12), of non-being. 'It is through non-being that you have become someone.' But that individual consciousness will disappear as we become conscious of what we really are, and we will find ourselves to be identical with universal being. Relieved of all individuality, 'you no longer say of yourself: this is what I am; you relinquish all limits so as to become universal being. And yet you were it from the start; but, as you were something else besides, that surplus diminished you; for that surplus did not come from being, since nothing can be added to being, but from non-being.'"[117]

In order to rediscover our true being, we must free ourselves of our contingent individuality. That 'purification,' however, operates only progressively, from existence to existence. We have to tread a long road, before arriving at it.[118] Buddhism recommends "the middle way" (*madhyamā pratipad/majjhimā paṭipadā*), which avoids the two extreme positions (*anta*): "is" (*asti/atthi*), "is not" (*nāsti/n' atthi*),—that of "eternalism" (*śāśvatavāda/sassatavāda*) and that of "nihilism" (*ucchedavāda*).[119] The things of the world endure neither forever nor for a short time. The psycho-physical vehicle, a kind of chariot,[120] continues to roll, so to speak, from one existence to the next,—neither identical nor different,—until the individual rediscovers his true being. The concept of *karman* plays a major role in that doctrine. It is our acts which govern our becoming, as long as we are in the world of becoming. "With the present *nāmarūpa*[121] one performs a good or a bad act; and as a result of this act another *nāmarūpa* is born." "A *nāmarūpa* dies, and another is born; but the latter proceeds from the former." "The chain of phenomena continues: one appears just as another disappears; there is, as it were, neither precedent nor successor among them. Consequently, neither the same nor another attains to the ultimate aggregation of the (individual) consciousness."[122]

The Upaniṣads, too, exalted the role of *karman*, as the determining factor in the successive rebirths of man. Let us recall the celebrated passage in the *Bṛhadāraṇyaka-Upaniṣad* (III, 2, 13), which would seem to be saying:[123] when, at death, all the psychic and corporeal elements of the individual are dissolved in the corresponding parts of the macrocosm: the voice in fire, the breath in the wind, the eye in the sun, the mind in the moon, the ear in the regions of the sky, the body in the earth, the *ātman* in space,[124] the body hairs in the plants, the hair in the trees, the blood and sperm in the waters, *karman* alone subsists in order to determine future existence. "And, speaking, it was of action (*karman*) that they (Yājñavalkya and Ārtabhāga) spoke, and, praising, it was action (*karman*) that they praised: one becomes good through good action, bad through bad action."[125] Elsewhere, however, (IV, 3, 35 - 4, 6), the *Bṛhadāraṇyaka* seems to recognize a kind of "subtle body"—the *sūkṣma*° or *liṅgaśarīra* of Sāṃkhya and of classical Vedānta—which transmigrates from one existence to another.[126] It is true that some canonical Buddhist texts also appear to speak of transmigration.[127] All the same, Buddhism in general refuses to admit such a conception. As Warren has emphasized, rebirth, in Buddhism, is not transmigration ("Rebirth is not transmigration").[128]—Yet, if the being who is reborn is not the same as the one who dies, neither is it another, for it is the product of its *karman.* The various individual existences are but links in an uninterrupted chain; they belong to a "series" (*saṃtati, saṃtāna*).[129]

Some fine passages in the *Bṛhadāraṇyaka* tell of the migration of phenomenal man through existences:

> As a heavily laden cart goes creaking on its way, just so does this (corporeal) *ātman* (*śārīra ātmā*), mounted by the spiritual *ātman* (*prājñenātmanā*), go along groaning, when man breathes his last.[130]

> As a caterpillar at the end of a blade of grass, draws itself in for a new advance, so this (corporeal) *ātman,* shaking off this inanimate body, draws itself in for a new advance.[131]

> As an artist, taking the material of a figure, fashions it in a new, more beautiful form, so this (corporeal) *ātman,* when it has shaken off this inanimate body,[132] makes for itself a new, a more beautiful form, of *pitṛ* or of *gandharva,* of *deva* or of Prajāpati or of Brahmā or of other beings.[133]

It is not the spiritual *ātman* (*prājña ātmā*), the authentic *ātman*, which transmigrates from one body to another: it is in itself everywhere. Throughout all the happenings of our phenomenal existence, however, it is within us as our "inner light." It is what makes us act (*kārayitṛ*) without itself acting (*akartṛ*).[134] And, by virtue of our acts, we give ourselves increasingly beautiful forms of existence,—forms in which, we may say, its presence becomes more and more "actual."[135] But do we ever arrive at the goal?

> 'The man of desire goes, by virtue of his *karman*,
> To the goal to which his mind is attached.
> When he has worn out the effects of his *karman*,[136]
> Whatever that may have been,
> From the world where it had taken him he returns
> Here below to accomplish new acts.'

> So much for one who desires. As for one who does not desire, who is without desire, who is liberated from desire, who has attained the object of his desire, who desires nothing but the *ātman*, his breaths do not escape him;[137] being nothing but *brahman*, he enters into *brahman*.
>
> This is what the following stanza says:
>
> 'When they are all rejected,
> The desires he carried in his heart,
> Then the mortal becomes immortal;
> And here below he attains the *brahman*.'
>
> As the dead skin of a snake rests abandoned on an anthill, so rests the body. As for the incorporeal, immortal breath,[138] it is pure *brahman*, pure light.[139]

It is then, in the last analysis, desire (*kāma*) which determines our phenomenal becoming. "This *puruṣa* is but desire: in fact, as is its desire, so is its will; as its will, so its acts; and it reaps according to its acts."[140] As Śaṅkara makes clear, commenting on this passage, acts, good or bad, bear fruits only when they are accompanied by egoistical desires; they are sterile if their agent is without desire. It is thus desire which is the "root of *saṃsāra*" (*saṃsārasya mūlam*).[141] We find the same idea in the *Aṅguttara-Nikāya*.[142] Now, desire exists only because we are shut up in the I of limited consciousness. How could he who has identified himself with universal Being have egoistic desires? We experience the sorrows of existence because we move in the finite (*appātumo, appa-dukkha-vihārī*).[143] One who has transcended his individual consciousness to become universal Consciousness,[144] who has become the Great Ātman (*mahattā*), is delivered from *saṃsāra*: acts, good or bad, no longer have any hold on him because he is liberated from desire; and, thus he is no longer subject to becoming.[145]

As long, however, as the individual consciousness (*vijñāna /viññāṇa*) is "established" (*patiṭṭhita*), man is involved in *saṃsāra*: one *nāmarūpa* is succeeded by another.[146] The *vijñāna /viññāṇa* is, therefore, as some texts say, the "seed" (*bīja*) of becoming.[147]

By the "establishment" of *viññāṇa*, should be understood attachment to our empirical individuality, made up of the *rūpa*, of the *vedanā*, of the *saññā*, of the *saṃkhārā*s (and of *viññāṇa*?) [= *nāmarūpa*[148]]. In fact, as long as we are attached to our individuality, made up of the *khandha*s, the *viññāṇa* finds a "point of support" (*ārammaṇa*), a "foundation" (*patiṭṭhā*). And phenomenal man identifies, in some manner, with that individual consciousness, for, without it, the *nāmarūpa* has no *raison d'être*.[149] When he is detached from his individuality, he is delivered (*vimutta*).[150]—The *nāmarūpa* and the *viññāṇa* condition each other, it is said. They are like two bundles of reeds which stand, one leaning on the other. When one of these bundles falls the other falls as well: in the same way, when the *nāmarūpa* ceases to function (that is to say when we cease to be attached to it), the *viññāṇa*, no longer having a point of support, also ceases, and, when the *viññāṇa* has ceased to function, the current *nāmarūpa* loses its *raison d'être* and no other *nāmarūpa* is produced: the phenomenal series is irrevocably broken.[151]

It is not, nevertheless, the same *viññāṇa* which goes from one existence to the next: the monk Sāti, who professes this opinion, is guilty of heresy.[152] "After death, according to acts, there appears in the mother's womb the knowledge aggregate [or consciousness: *vijñāna*] (six groups of knowledge) inseparable from four other aggregates. The knowledge in question is the fruit of retribution (*vipākaphala*) and, as such, undefined from the moral point of view (*avyākṛta*). It is the explanation of the new existence for, 'if, after the descent into the maternal womb, the knowledge goes, the embryo will not be born.'"[153] The *pratisandhivijñāna* "does not pass from the preceding existence into the present one, but comes into existence by virtue of conditions realized in the previous existence: acts, volitions, propensities, objects, etc. The echo thrown back by the mountain is not the cry of a passerby, but it would not be produced if no cry were given. In this process, there is neither identity nor difference: the thought at rebirth is not confused with the thought at death, but is its tributary. In the same way, butter is not milk, but without milk there can be no butter."[154]

Phenomenal man is, therefore, an uninterrupted flux of individual consciousness (*vijñānasrotas °pravāha °saṃtati*).[155] Our last phenomenal existence is also "the last aggregate of *viññāṇa*" (*pacchimaviññāṇasaṃgaha*).[156] We may recall the famous episodes concerning Godhika and Vakkali: Māra seeks the *viññāṇa* of these two saints who have committed suicide,[157] but does not find it, because it is nowhere "established."[158] We may also recall the passage from the *Majjhima-Nikāya*, already cited, where the Buddha declares that the gods themselves, starting with Indra, Brahmā and Prajāpati, do not succeed in finding the *viññāṇa* of the Tathāgata.[159] These texts make us think, on the other hand, of the famous words of Yājñavalkya: *na pretya saṃjñāsti* "there is no consciousness after Deliverance": words which troubled Maitreyī, for whom the disappearance of the individual consciousness signified the annihilation of the conscious subject.[160] The *samaṇas* and *brāhmaṇas* of the Buddha's time also accused him of being nihilistic, because he professed this same doctrine.[161] But, says Yājñavalkya, "this *ātman*, in truth, is imperishable; it is, by its nature, indestructible."[162] The Buddha himself also protests against the nihilistic interpretation of his doctrine: he does not advocate, says he, the "destruction of the existing individual" (*sato sattassa ucchedaṃ vināsaṃ vibhavaṃ*).[163]

In fact, the disappearance of individual consciousness could only be interpreted as the annihilation of the conscious subject if this implied the disappearance of all consciousness. But this is not at all the case. "It is in knowing that he does not know; knowledge does not escape from the knower he is, for it is indestructible; *only, there is no second, no object other and separated, that he is capable of apprehending.*"[164] "Where there is the appearance of duality (*dvaitam iva*), one feels the other, one sees the other, one hears the other, one hails the other, one thinks about the other, one knows the other; but when all has become his own self (*ātmaiva*), what will he feel, and with what? Whom will he see, and with what? Whom will he hear, and with what? Whom will he hail, and with what? Whom will he think, and with what? Whom will he know, and with what?"[165]

In what then does this knowledge consist? It may perhaps be said that the subject knows himself. Yet Yājñavalkya dismisses this hypothesis: "That by which he knows everything, by what could he know it? By what, my dear, could one know the knower?"[166] The subject cannot be the object of his own act.[167] We have to do here rather with a "certitude" than with "knowledge."[168]

If Deliverance were nothing but a new form of individual existence in a higher world, we might think that the flux of phenomenal *vijñāna* continues to flow beyond deliverance. Yet, time and again, the Upaniṣads and Buddhism have emphasized the insufficiency of this conception.[169] Deliverance does not consist in a prolongation of the individuality under any form whatsoever—for all existence is transitory and, therefore, sorrowful—but in going beyond it by identifying with universal Being. How, then, can one speak of the specific consciousness of the Delivered? Specific consciousness has no "point of support" (*ārammaṇa*), no "foundation" (*patiṭṭhā*) other than in individuality.[170] Now, the Delivered is one who has transcended his individuality.[171] He *has*, therefore, *no* particular consciousness: he *is* Consciousness. Beyond all inner and outer distinctions, he is only a "homogeneous mass of consciousness" (*anantaro 'bāhyaḥ kṛtsnaḥ prajñāna-ghana eva*).[172]

The Buddhist texts we have been studying do not, it is true, have recourse to so many words. Nevertheless, the interpretation we have given is perfectly in accord with a canonic text. The *Kevaddha* (*Kevaṭṭa*)-*Sutta* speaks, indeed, of a universal and absolute *viññāṇa*, transcending the phenomenal *viññāṇa* of each individual:

> *viññāṇaṃ anidassanaṃ anantaṃ sabbatopabhaṃ* |
> *ettha āpo ca paṭhavī tejo vāyo na gādhati* ||
> *ettha dīghañ ca rassañ ca aṇuṃ thūlaṃ subhāsubhaṃ* |
> *ettha nāmañ ca rūpañ ca asesaṃ uparujjhati* |
> *viññāṇassa nirodhena etth' etaṃ uparujjhati* ||

> *Viññāṇa*, undemonstrable, infinite, radiating from all sides. Neither earth, water, fire nor wind finds a footing there. There do the long and short, fine and coarse, good and evil, name and form (= individuality) cease to be, leaving no trace behind. There do all these cease to be, following upon the cessation of *viññāṇa*.[173]

As Buddhaghosa explains, the first of these *viññāṇa*s is a "name of Nirvāṇa" (*nibbānassa nāmaṃ*), while the second is the phenomenal *viññāṇa* (*carimaka-viññāṇam pi abhisaṃkhāra-viññāṇam pi*).[174]

❖

The Buddha sometimes speaks of the individual as an entity which is more than a "series of phenomena." It is the *puggala*,[175] he says, which, by reason of its "thirst" (*taṇhā*), assumes, in the course of existences, "burdens," that is: the *upādānakkhandhas*, and then is delivered, in putting down the last burden.[176] But there is no need to conclude, along with the Pudgalavādin,[177] that the Buddha is affirming here the ontological substantiality of the individual. Neither is there the need to think, along with subtle scholastics, that the "burden" (*bhāra*) is the totality of the old *skandhas* which engender new ones, and the "carrier of the burden" (*bhārahāra* = *pudgala/puggala*), the new *skandhas* which are engendered.[178] We may be content to suppose that the Buddha is simply conforming to the world's usage. Does he not say: "I am not in disagreement with the world, it is the world which is in disagreement with me?"[179]

The belief in the existence of an eternal I is folly; but the belief in the non-existence of an I is even greater folly. "Who believes in the soul falls into the extreme view of eternity (*śāśvatānta*); who believes that the soul does not exist falls into the extreme view of annihilation (*ucchedānta*). Light error, heavy error."[180]—Whosoever thinks that the individual is no more than an insubstantial compound of *skandha/khandha*, without at the same time being aware of the universal principle which is the foundation of all individual phenomena, is detached from all moral responsibility regarding himself and his kind; he "lets fall" his good deeds, whose fruits he does not aspire to reap, for the individual, being insubstantial in his innermost depths, must perish. The goal of all existence appears to him to be absolute annihilation. The Buddha thus did not deny the I for those whose spiritual vision did not go beyond it. "Ānanda, the heterodox monk Vatsagotra came to ask me this question: 'Is there or is there not a soul?' I did not reply to him. In fact, to answer that there is a soul, would have been to contradict the truth of things, for there is no *dharma* that is a soul nor that has any relationship with one; and if I had replied that there is no soul, I would have increased Vatsagotra's folly, for he would have thought: 'I had a soul and that soul now does not exist.'"[181] "Taking into account the damage done by heresy[182] and, on the other hand, of the downfall of good deeds, the Buddhas teach the Law in the same way that the tigress carries its offspring."[183]

Absolute Truth is not taught. It must be experienced by oneself; one must become it. The Upaniṣads and the Buddha only *indicate* it, it is for us to realize it in ourselves.[184] We cannot, however, do this unless we are already spiritually prepared. Those who are still tied to phenomena must purify themselves progressively. They should not be told that the individual is nothing but an insubstantial composite of *upādānaskandhas*: on the contrary, they should be told that the individual is an actual agent who, by virtue of his desire, assumes the "burden" (*bhāra*) and then puts it down when he is freed from desire. This, it is said, is why the Buddhas have proclaimed two truths: an absolute truth (*paramārtha/paramattha*) and a conventional truth (*saṃmuti*),[185] or, as the Mahāyānic texts explain, they have adapted their teachings to the needs of various categories of men, in the same way as a doctor prescribes different remedies according to the maladies of his patients:[186]

> There are people in this world, whose eye of understanding is completely covered with that thick film that is the erroneous thesis and incorrect view of the non-existence of the I. They do not see the mass of things, although it does not exceed the domain of the purely mundane vision. Although they are based in conventional truth, they conform only to the sole reality of that which is named: earth, water, fire and wind, and say that the mind is but the product of the maturation of the great elements which constitute the first embryonic stage, etc.,—as one may notice that alcoholic drinks, which are but the product of the maturation of various substances such as roots, boiled rice, water, the ferment, etc., have the power of producing intoxication, weakness, etc.[187] They deny past and future (*pūrvāntāparānta°*) and they deny the other world and the I, saying: 'This world does not exist, the other world does not exist, there is no maturation of the

fruits of good and evil deeds, there is no spontaneously appearing being,[188] etc. In denying all that, they turn away from the projecting of various excellent and desirable fruits, such as the heavens and supreme Bliss; they are continually engaged in producing bad actions and are on their way to falling into precipices such as hell, etc. It is to put a stop to the erroneous views of these people that the blessed Buddhas—who conform to the dispositions of beings[189] amongst which there are eighty-four thousand different states of mind, who endeavour to fulfil the vows they have taken to save all beings, who are provided with the tools of wisdom, of compassion and of the means of salvation, who are without equal, who are the only friends of the world,[190] who want to heal all the serious illnesses which the passions are, who are the great kings of medicine, and who desire to show their favour to the people to be converted, from the lower, middle and higher classes—have sometimes spoken of the I. Their goal is the stopping of the bad deeds, etc., of people to be converted from the lower class who accomplish bad deeds. But this only pertains to the mundane level . . .

There are those who are like birds tied by the strong and very lengthy strings of the love of I and mine, which gives rise to the belief in the actual existence of I, and who, even though they have gone very far and accomplish only good deeds, being turned away from the path of evil deeds (*kuśalakarmakāriṇo 'kuśalakarmapathavyāvṛttāḥ*), cannot go beyond birth in the three spheres of existence and go to the city of Nirvāṇa,[191] which is salvation and where there is neither old age nor death. To these people to be converted from the middle class, the blessed Buddhas, who are desirous of showing their favour to the people to be converted, have taught the non-I, in order to weaken their attachment to the false view of personality and to bring into being the desire for Nirvāṇa.

There are those who have obtained the maturation of the seed, that is to say, of adhesion to the deep law, thanks to earlier distinguished practice. To these people to be converted from the higher class, for whom Nirvāṇa is close, who are free of the love of I and who are capable of penetrating the true meaning, ultimate and profound, of the sacred words of the Chief of silent ones, the Buddhas, after having perceived their excellent aspiration, have taught that there is neither I nor non-I.

Just as the view of the I is not true, so that which stands against it, the view of the non-I, is not true either.[192] Thus it is taught: 'There is neither I nor non-I.'

The Pudgalavādins made themselves guilty of heresy, not insofar as they affirmed the reality of the individual—for orthodox Buddhism has never denied this—but because they affirmed its *substantial* reality. Whilst orthodox Buddhists consider it as a simple "designation" (*prajñaptisant*) of a "phenomenal series," the Pudgalavādin sustained it as "substance" (*dravyasant*).[193] Their doctrine is known mainly through the critiques of their adversaries; we learn from these that they conceived of the individual (*pudgala*) as an entity of which it can be said neither that it is identical to the *skandhas*, nor that it is distinct from them.[194] The relationship which exists between them would be similar to that between fire and fuel: a thesis which all orthodox Buddhist schools dispute.

In some ways the doctrine of these "pseudo-Buddhists" (*saugatammanya*)[195] brings to mind the *naiyāyika-vaiśeṣika* doctrine relative to the *ātman*,[196] and orthodox Buddhists, when they criticize it, do use the term *ātman* as a synonym of *pudgala*.[197] Unfortunately, however, modern authors do not always manage to distinguish between the *ātman-pudgala* and the *ātman-brahman* of the Upaniṣads. Whence the theory of the "negation of the *ātman*." They like, for instance, to evoke in support of this thesis the venerable image of the chariot,[198] made famous by a passage in the *Milinda-pañhā*;[199] but what is forgotten is that this image is meant solely to indicate the purely phenomenal character of the empirical individual: just as "chariot" is only a conventional name (*sammuti, vohāra* . . .) given to an aggregate of various elements, all subject to destruction, so *satta, pudgala*, etc., are only conventional names given to a composite of *upādānakkhandhas*, all ephemeral. That which our texts deny is the so-called ontological substantiality of the individual and not at all the *ātman*, the universal, indivisible principle, which animates all psycho-physical vehicles, but which everywhere remains in itself and, thus, does not mix with them.[200] It is, as the *Maitri-Upaniṣad* says, because of that which comes to him from outside that man is *rathita*; when he is relieved, he discovers his true being, the *ātman.*[201] The *ātman* is not the chariot (*ratha*), but the "master of the chariot" (*rathin*),[202] its "inciter" (*pracodayitṛ*).[203] Even though it moves in all bodies (*pratiśarīreṣu carati*), it "rests in its own greatness" (*sve mahimni tiṣṭhati*),[204] above phenomena (*uparistha*),[205] not subject to their contact "like a drop of water on a lotus petal" (*bindur iva puṣkare*).[206] It is eternally pure (*śuddha*), peaceful (*śānta*), without individuality (*nirātman*)[207] . . . , "empty" (*śūnya*).[208] It is what makes us act (*kārayitṛ*), but it does not act itself (*akartṛ*). Being "in itself" (*svastha*), it is "as a spectator" (*prekṣakavat*) of our acts, good and bad, which do not affect it at all (*sitāsitaiḥ karmaphalair anabhibhūtaḥ*).[209]

Do the Buddhist texts know this spiritual principle? It is tempting to think of *Jātaka* VI, pp. 252-253, where it is said that the body is the chariot, whose driver is the *ātman* (*kāyo te rathasaññāto . . . attā va sārathi*). If one looks more closely at the text, however, one notices that the word *attan* is in this case nothing but a synonym for *manas.*[210] We may recall that, according to the *Kaṭha-Upaniṣad* (III, 3 and 9), it is the *buddhi* or the *vijñāna* which is the "driver" (*sārathi*) of the chariot.[211] There are, however, in the Pāli Canon, passages which call the "driver," sometimes the Buddha, sometimes the Dhamma.[212] The Tathāgata, in fact, as we have seen above,[213] is not other than the *ātman.* He may thus be considered as the driver of all psycho-physical vehicles. But he is also identical to Dhamma. It is not, he says, in his "stinking body" (*pūtikāya*) that the Buddha should be seen. "One who sees Dhamma sees me, and one who sees me sees the Dhamma."[214] And, when he exhorts his disciples to take refuge in the *ātman* and in the Dhamma, he certainly seems to be indicating that these two last are one.[215]

It is, in fact, by that which is good in ourselves that we triumph over that which is bad, by the *kalyāṇātman* that we triumph over the *pāpātman*.[216] Our phenomenal existence is not the enemy of our true being. The same chariot, according to our dispositions, drives to *saṃsāra* and to *mokṣa*.[217] The conflict exists only if we are attached to the chariot without being aware of the "master of the chariot," who we really are. If, on the contrary, we go through our phenomenal existence in order to sublimate it, *mokṣa* becomes the crowning of *saṃsāra*, or, as the *Gītā* says, our (phenomenal) *ātman* becomes "the friend" of our (true) *ātman*:

uddhared ātmanātmānaṃ nātmānam avasādayet |
ātmaiva hy ātmano bandhur ātmaiva ripur ātmanaḥ ||

May one be saved by himself,[218] may one not let himself perish. The (phenomenal) *ātman* is the friend of the (true) *ātman*, and it is also its enemy.

bandhur ātmātmanas tasya yenātmaivātmanā jitaḥ |
anātmanas tu śatrutve vartetātmaiva śatruvat ||

For the man who has overcome the phenomenal *ātman* with the (true) *ātman*, the (phenomenal) *ātman* is the friend of the true *ātman*. But for one who has not realized his (true) *ātman*,[219] it is his (phenomenal) *ātman* which behaves as an enemy.[220]

jitātmanaḥ praśāntasya paramātmā samāhitaḥ |
śītoṣṇasukhaduḥkheṣu tathā mānāpamānayoḥ ||

The supreme *ātman* (*paramātman*) of one who has overcome the (phenomenal) *ātman* and who is perfectly peaceful, is collected within itself, in heat as in cold, in pleasure as in sorrow, in honour as in dishonour.[221]

These stanzas will help us to understand what the *Dhammapada* is telling us:

> *attā hi attano nātho ko hi nātho paro siyā* |
> *attanā hi sudantena nāthaṃ labhati dullabhaṃ* ||

> The *ātman* is the refuge[222] of the self. What other refuge can there be? When the (phenomenal) *ātman* is properly subdued, a refuge, difficult to find, is obtained.[223]

> *attanā coday' attānaṃ paṭimāse 'ttam attanā* |
> *so attagutto satimā sukhaṃ bhikkhu vihāhisi* ||
> *attā hi attano nātho attā hi attano gati* |
> *tasmā saññamay' attānaṃ assaṃ bhadraṃ va vāṇijo* ||

> Goad yourself by the *ātman*; examine yourself by the *ātman*. Protected by the *ātman* and attentive, you will live, O Bhikṣu, in happiness.
>
> The *ātman* is the refuge of the self; the *ātman* is the destination of the self. Therefore, control your (phenomenal) *ātman* as the merchant does a good horse.[224]

The Pudgalavādins, it is true, evoked these stanzas (or analogues) in support of their thesis.[225] They did not, however, take into account a fundamental difference: whereas their *pudgala* is a moral agent, the true spiritual *ātman* of the Buddhist texts, as that of the Upaniṣads and of the *Gītā*, "is beyond good and evil."[226] Not being an agent itself, it is as a "witness" (*sākṣin*) of our acts, good and bad.[227]

❖

It thus seems established that where, in Buddhist literature, a "negation of the *ātman*" might be seen, it is, in fact, a condemnation, either of (1) the common opinion, according to which the *ātman* would be the psycho-physical being (*sakkāyadiṭṭhi* = Sanskrit *satkāyadṛṣṭi*),[228] or (2) of the theory of the Pudgalavādins, or, lastly (3), of the attachment to all theory relating to the *ātman*—Absolute.[229] Nowhere is there question of the negation of the true spiritual *ātman* of the Upaniṣads.

The traditional interpretation, which reduces the words of the Master: *n' etaṃ mama, n' eso 'ham asmi, na m' eso attā*, "This is not mine, I am not this, this is not my *ātman*,"[230] to a negation intended to dispel the *satkāyadṛṣṭi*,[231] is but a partial explanation. The Naiyāyika Uddyotakara saw the essential truth: "One," he said, "who does not accept the *ātman* cannot make sense of these words of the Tathāgata: 'Bhadanta, I am not the *rūpa*, etc., nor are you, Bhikṣu, the *rūpa*, etc.' This negation is a specific negation (*viśeṣapratiṣedha*), not a universal negation (*sāmānyapratiṣedha*). One who does not accept the *ātman* must employ a universal negation: 'I am not,' 'You are not.' A specific negation always implies a corresponding affirmation: when, for example, I say, 'I do not see with my left eye,' it is understood that I do see with my right eye. . . ."[232]

After all that we have written up to now, there can be no question of confusing Buddhism with Nyāya. Moreover, a passage from the *Mahānidāna-Sutta*[233] seems formally to exclude such a parallel. The *ātman*, says our text, is not sensation (*vedanā*), since the latter is subject to the vicissitudes proper to all empirical things; an invariable I is not to be found there. Could the *ātman*, the ego, therefore be other than sensation? Perhaps: but when I feel nothing, can I still say "I am" (*asmi*)?[234] A third hypothesis is possible, and one that is reminiscent of the theory of Nyāya-Vaiśeṣika: the *ātman* is not sensation; it is not however deprived of sensation. It feels, for its attribute is sensation (*vedanā-dhamma*). But this hypothesis is worth no more than the previous one: when all sensation has disappeared, can I still say "I am"? In these circumstances, there is no *ātman* in the sense of an individual, in whatever manner this might be imagined.

Uddyotakara is certainly mistaken when he sees in these words of the Buddha an affirmation of the *ātman* as conceived by the Naiyāyikas, that is: as the individual ego, distinct from the aggregates.[235] This fundamental error should not, however, cause us to forget the force of the logic which he employs to prove that the Buddha did not deny all *ātman*.

We have seen that, according to the Mahāyānist texts cited above,[236] the *nairātmya* is not the negation of the "supreme *ātman*" (*paramātman*), the "Great Ātman" (*mahātman*), the *ātman* "without a second" (*advaya*). We find this idea again in the *Nairātmyaparipṛcchā*, attributed to Aśvaghoṣa.[237] "Is there a *paramātman* in the body or not" (*kim asti śarīre paramātmā, kim vā nāsti*)? "Neither one nor the other can be said" (*dvayam atra nocyate*). The *paramātman*, the Absolute, is beyond all objective grasping (*upalambha*).[238] It is "empty as space" (*śūnyam ākāśam iva*). Here again is a passage which is very enlightening; it is due to Vasubandhu, author of the *Viṃśatikā*:

> *yo bālair dharmāṇāṃ svabhāvo grāhyagrāhakādiḥ parikalpitas tena kalpitenātmanā teṣāṃ nairātmyam, na tv anabhilāpyenātmanā yo buddhānāṃ viṣayaḥ.*

> The own-nature of phenomena, consisting in graspable and grasper,[239] as childish minds imagine it, that is the imaginary Self of phenomena; and it is through this imaginary Self that phenomena are without-self; but not by the ineffable Self which is the domain of the Buddhas.[240]

It is in fact only this imaginary *ātman* (*kalpita ātmā*)—the so-called ontological substantiality of individual phenomena —that the Buddha denies, not the true, spiritual *ātman*, the universal base. "There is, monks, a non-born, non-produced, non-created, non-formed. If there were not, monks, a non-born, non-produced, non-created, non-formed, there would be no issue for the born, the produced, the created, the formed."[241] Those who claim that the Buddha has negated the *ātman*—if we are to believe the Pāli texts, they must have been quite numerous, at the epoch of the Buddha, and amongst his disciples themselves—see the *ātman* precisely in that which is non-*ātman*, that is to say, in the psycho-physical elements of their phenomenal existence. They accuse the Buddha of preaching a nihilistic doctrine, because he advocates *nirvāṇa*, the extinction of the individual ego.[242] But, replies the Buddha, if the psycho-physical elements of our existence are neither ourselves nor anything belonging to us, how can it be said that their annihilation is our own annihilation? On the contrary, it is by transcending our phenomenal existence that we discover our true being. We may recall the parable of Jetavana:

> Monks, if someone came into this copse of Jeta where we are, and took for burning, the grass, wood, branches, leaves, could you say that he took you and burned you?—No, Lord, for all that is not us, none of that belongs to us.—In the same way, monks, reject what is not of yourselves. . . .[243]

❖

Before stating that Buddhism has denied the *ātman*, modern authors should, therefore, have been precise as to which *ātman* is meant. If this thesis continues to be maintained, it must also be said that the Upaniṣads have denied the *ātman*. These, when they state that *ātman-brahman* is the sole Reality, are in fact denying that psycho-physical being which men, too often, consider as the *ātman*.[244] As we have seen above, the very terms *anātmya, nirātman* and *nirātmaka* are used there to designate the *ātman-brahman*, the transcendent Impersonality.[245] The *Mahāyāna-Sūtrālaṃkāra* and the commentary to the *Ratnagotravibhāga* do naught else but continue this tradition when they treat *nairātmya* as a synonym of *mahātman/paramātman*.[246] Classical Vedānta, on the other hand, uses the term *anātman* in exactly the same sense as does Buddhism, that is, to designate the psycho-physical phenomenon.[247]

Unfortunately, some Vedantists themselves, when dealing with Buddhism, are the first to misunderstand the Upaniṣadic *ātman*. Such, for example, is the case with Professor Murti:

> . . . the *ātman* is the root-cause of all attachment, desire, aversion, and pain. When we take anything as self (substantial and permanent), we become attached to it and dislike other things that are opposed to it. *Sakkāyadiṭṭhi* (Substance-view) is *avidyā* (ignorance) *par excellence*, and from it proceed all passions. Denial of *Satkāya* (*ātman* or Substance) is the very pivot of the Buddhist metaphysics and doctrine of salvation. (The Upaniṣadic verse: *ātmānaṃ ced vijānīyād*, etc.,[248] can, with a slight change, be made to express the Buddhist formula:
>
> *ātmānaṃ ced vijānīyān nāsty ayam iti pūruṣaḥ;*
> *kim icchan kasya kāmāya tv anusaṃjvared ātmānam*).[249]

Let us note that there is attachment and aversion only at the level of self and other. When this level is transcended, when everything has become my *ātman*, who can be attached, and to what, who can hate, and what?[250]

The Upaniṣadic formulae, *tat tvam asi* "you are that" and *ahaṃ brahmāsmi* "I am *brahman*," have often been wrongly interpreted. It has been understood that the individual subject (*tvam, aham*), as such, was the absolute Being (*tat* = *brahman*). And, so goes the argument, Buddhism, having refused true reality to the individual subject, could not recognize an Absolute in the way that the Upaniṣads do.[251]—Yet, there is nothing in the Upaniṣads which substantiates such an interpretation. The individual is identical to the Absolute only in its "subtle essence" (*aṇiman*), and not in itself. It is thus that the *ātman* of each one (identical to *brahman*) is the *ātman* of all things: *sa ya eṣo 'ṇimā, aitadātmyam idaṃ sarvam, tat satyam, sa ātmā, tat tvam asi.*[252]—In the same way as these positive formulae deny any true reality to the empirical individual, by affirming that absolute Being is the sole Reality,[253] so, it seems to us, the negative formulae of the Buddha: *n' etaṃ mama, n' eso 'ham asmi, na m' eso attā*, are saying, inversely, that the Absolute is the sole Reality, by refusing any true reality to the empirical individual: *tat tvam asi* = *nāsi tvam etat; n' eso 'ham asmi* = *so 'ham asmi* (= *ahaṃ brahmāsmi*).

Doubtless it will be said that this is an error. Buddhism, which condemns the "idea: 'I am'" (*asmimāna*), cannot accept the statement: "I am *brahman*."—The fact is, however, that the *asmimāna* has its origin in attachment, vague though it may be, to our empirical individuality.[254] Now, I am only able to say: "I am *brahman*," when I have transcended my empirical individuality. I am not able to become the *ātman-brahman*, universal Consciousness, and remain an "I" at the same time. "The idea of 'I'"—writes Śaṅkara—"has its origin in the objective *ātman* (the non-*ātman*); it has for its domain what merely rests upon speech. It thus regains no validity when that *ātman* which is its origin has, itself, been denied."[255] To anticipate what will be the subject of the next chapter, let us point out that, according to a Pāli text itself, an Arahant who has "become the brahman" (*brahmabhūta*),[256] is one whose *asmimāna* has been "completely uprooted."[257]

Professor Murti asks:[258] "If the *ātman* had been a cardinal doctrine with Buddhism, why was it so securely hidden under a bushel that even the immediate followers of the Master had no inkling of it? The Upaniṣads, on the other hand, blazen forth the reality of the *ātman* in every page, in every line almost."

In truth, it is of the *ātman* that the Buddha speaks when he tells us what it is not (*anattā*). As Śaṅkara would say, it is with reference to something real that the unreal may be negated: it is, for example, with reference to the real rope that the illusion of the snake may be denied.[259] And Professor Murti himself writes elsewhere in his work (pp. 234-235):

> Negation itself is significant because there is an underlying reality—the subjacent ground. If there were no transcendent ground, how could any view be condemned as false? A view is false, because it *falsifies the real*, makes the thing appear other than what it is in itself. Falsity implies the real *that* is falsified. (Author's italics.)

If the Buddha insists upon this negative aspect of the *ātman*, it is to disperse the pernicious opinion, too widespread in the world, according to which the *ātman* would be the psycho-physical being, in other words, the *sakkāya-diṭṭhi*, the error *par excellence*. "The *samaṇas* and the *brāhmaṇas*," says one of our texts, "who envisage the *ātman* in various ways, envisage either the aggregate of *upādānakkhandhas*, or one amongst them."[260] Let us not forget that Buddhism is, first and foremost, a doctrine of salvation: "As the ocean has but one taste, the taste of salt, so monks, this doctrine and this discipline have but one taste, the taste of Deliverance."[261] Now, the *sakkāya-diṭṭhi* is the origin of all our bondage. It is only because we have identified with our psycho-physical individuality that we have the illusory ideas of "I" and of "mine" (*ahaṃkāra, mamaṃkāra*).[262] And, as long as the *sakkāya-diṭṭhi* is not dispersed by true knowledge of Reality, no deliverance is possible. How can one who is attached to his sorrowful existence, saying: "This is mine, I am this, this is my *ātman*," understand his own sorrow and divest himself of it?[263] The Buddha thus demonstrates the falsity of this view, by analyzing the psycho-physical elements of our phenomenal existence: what is impermanent and sorrowful can be neither the *ātman* nor anything pertaining to the *ātman* (*attaniya*). As Karl Jaspers puts it so well, "that which is not the Self is thought of here in terms of the measure of the true Self."[264]

It would be absurd to think that the Buddha, who condemns all attachment to "theories" (*dṛṣṭi/diṭṭhi*), who says that he has gone beyond the domain of *diṭṭhi*,[265] makes a "theory" of the *anattā* itself. The idea of the *anattā* is meant only to do away with the false opinion about the *ātman* and to prepare us thus for the direct intuition of the spiritual *ātman: nittharaṇatthāya no gahaṇatthāya.*[266] Such, in fact, is the conclusion that the Māhāyanist schools will draw, and with good reason.[267]

It may however be asked: why did the Buddha not speak more about the *ātman*? We will reply: it is because the Upaniṣads had already spoken enough about it. The Buddha has no wish to be a philosopher, but a saviour,[268] or, if preferred, "Buddha exhorts us to be philosophical enough to recognise the limits of philosophy."[269] He holds more strictly to the "negative way,"[270] than do the Upaniṣads themselves.

❖

There certainly are positive expressions, relative to the *ātman,* in the Pāli Canon: the Buddha exhorts us to "take refuge in the *ātman,*" to "aspire to the Great Ātman."[271] But these positive expressions—often moreover wrongly interpreted[272]—are almost drowned in the mass of negative expressions. The formulae which sum up the whole doctrine, relative to the *ātman,* of the Buddha are: *n' etaṃ mama, n' eso 'ham asmi, na m' eso attā.* They take the place of the positive formulae of the Upaniṣads: *tat tvam asi, ahaṃ brahmāsmi.* It is this predilection for negative expression which would seem to have been responsible for the pernicious theory of the "negation of the *ātman.*" It is certainly permissible to speak here, using the words of Barth, of a "metaphysical shipwreck."[273] Here is a revealing passage from the *Abhidharmakośa*:[274]

> ***Ābhidharmika.***—"How would you explain the Sūtra which says: 'To recognize an I in what is not I, this is a misunderstanding of idea, of thought, of view'?"[275]
>
> ***Pudgalavādin.***—"This Sūtra says that it is a misunderstanding to recognize an I in what is not an I; it does not say that it is a misunderstanding to recognise an I in what is an I."
>
> ***Ābhidharmika.***—"What should be understood by 'what is not an I'? Will you say that this has to do with the *skandha*s, *āyatana*s and *dhātu*s? It is contrary to your theory that the Pudgala is neither identical to the colour-figure, etc., nor different from the colour-figure, etc. Moreover, the Sūtra says: 'O Bhikṣus, know that all Brahmins and religious people who consider the I, consider but the five elements-of-attachment.'[276] Thus, it is not in an I, because of an I, that an I is recognized, but only in the *dharma*s which are not an I and which are falsely imagined to be an I."

The Pudgalavādin is certainly wrong, but the Ābhidharmika is equally wrong. It is the Mahāyānist schools which put things right:

> To take that which is not the *ātman*,—the corporeal form, etc.—for the *ātman*, is an error, and, to consider that which is non-*ātman* as non-*ātman* is a non-error. But, in relation to the *dharmakāya* of the Tathāgata, which is the *ātman*, this non-error is itself an error.[277]

Men, in general, see the *ātman* in that which is not *ātman*, that is to say in the psycho-physical elements of phenomenal existence: they are attached thus to taking hold of an *ātman* which does not exist (*asadātmagrahābhirati*). It is therefore good for them to understand that the psycho-physical being is not the *ātman*. But one should not be attached to this idea as if it were a dogma. It is but a stage in spiritual progress. It must itself be surpassed in the experience of that which *is* the *ātman*, universal Being, the unchangeable ground of all changing individual phenomena.

However, the Śrāvakas and the Pratyekabuddhas, says the Sūtra which our text cites, envisage only phenomena; they have but a sterile idea of *anātman* and they have no intuition of transcendent Impersonality (*nairātmya*), which is the *dharmakāya* of the Tathāgata and the true spiritual *ātman*.[278]

Notes to Chapter One

1. G. Cœdès, "Les inscriptions de Bàt Cŭṃ," *JA.* 1908 (2), pp. 230 and 241, st. I (cf. pp. 241-242, n. 4).

2. S. Lévi's reading is here modified after G. M. Nagao, *Index to the Mahāyāna-Sūtrālaṃkāra*, I (Tokyo, 1958), p. xiii. See also "For a New Edition of the *Mahāyānasūtrālaṃkāra*," *Journal of the Nepal Research Centre*, XII (2001), p. 6 (read *viśuddhā* for *viśuddhāya*).

3. This does not always seem to be the case. Cf. *infra*, p. 55; p. 102, n. 194. Cf. also, below, the interpretation of *nairātmyātmāgra-lābhataḥ*. We do not touch here upon the much discussed question of the identification of the author or authors of this text and of its commentary. We would only say that they do not seem to us to have been composed by one and the same person.

4. *Śūnyatā*: cf. *infra*, pp. 131-132.

5. This is how we understand the expression *nairātmyātmāgra-lābhataḥ*. The commentator gives a different interpretation.

6. In the translation of the *Mahāyāna-Sūtrālaṃkāra*, S. Lévi uses the term *Quiddité*. But, in his translation of the *Triṃśikā*, he substitutes the word *Ainsité*, thusness, "modelled exactly upon the original (*tathā* = ainsi + °*tā* = suf. té) and which gives the meaning more precisely" (*Matériaux pour l'étude du Système Vijñaptimātra* [Paris, 1932], p. 118, n. 3). Vasubandhu defines *tathatā*: *sarvakālaṃ tathā-bhāvāt.* (*Triṃśikā*, 25; cf. Candrakīrti, *MKV.*, p. 265 [*infra*, p. 132]: *tathābhāvo 'vikāritvaṃ sadaiva sthāyitā.*)

7. On the equivalence *svabhāva* (or *svarūpa*) = *ātman*, cf. *infra*, p. 114, n. 249.

8. On this reading, see L. Schmithausen, "Philologische Bemerkungen zum Ratnagotravibhāga," *WZKS.* XV (1971), p. 143.

9. On the reading, cf. below, n. 18.

10. Cf. below, n. 19.

11. Cf. *infra*, p. 74, n. 81.

12. On the subject of *dharmakāya*, see *infra*, pp. 29-30, and ch. II.

13. On the term *pāramitā*, see Lamotte, *Traité*, II, p. 1058, n. 2; Edgerton, *Dictionary*, s.v.

14. Cf. *infra*, p. 172, n. 160.

15. On *tīrthika/tīrthya*, cf. "Supplément aux Recherches sur le Vocabulaire des inscriptions sanskrites du Cambodge," I, *BEFEO.* LIII, 1 (1966), pp. 274-275.

16. Cf. below, n. 60; pp. 33-34, 37.

17. The *ātman* is permanent (*nitya*), happy (*sukha*), pure (*śubha*), whereas the *rūpa* and other *skandha* are impermanent (*anitya*), sorrowful (*duḥkha*), impure (*aśubha*).

18. *sarvadharmanairātmyaparapāramiprāptaḥ* (edition, p. xvi: "Corrections"), or *sarvadharmanairātmyaparapāram abhiprāptaḥ* (p. 31)?

19. Instead of *anātmalakṣaṇena* we read: *ātmalakṣaṇena.* On the one hand, the view of the *anyatīrthyāḥ* is contradictory to the char-acteristics of the *ātman* (*ātmalakṣaṇena visaṃvāditatvāt*); on the other hand, the view of the Tathāgatas accords with them (*avisaṃvāditatvāt*).

20. *ASP.*, p. 4 (1. 25), etc.—Cf. *MKV.*, p. 265 (*infra*, p. 164, n. 95): *adarśanayogena viṣayatvam upayāti; ibid.*, p. 373: *anadhigamanayogena svayam adhigacchanti* (cf. May, n. 10.3: p. 73 and n. 103). Cf. also the *cittam acittam* of *Prajñāpāramitās*: Lamotte, *Vimalakīrti*, pp. 56 ff. (cf. *Laṅk.* III, 30; *Triṃśikā*, 29; *infra*, n. 173).

Ratnagotravibhāga, pp. 30-31. See also Jikido Takasaki, *A Study on the Ratnagotravibhāga (Uttaratantra), Being a Treatise on the Tathāgatagarbha Theory of Mahāyāna Buddhism* (= *Serie Orientale Roma*, XXXIII, 1966), pp. 207 ff. The author justly remarks: "Here *'ātman'* should be understood in the sense of the *'dharmakāya'* or *'dharmadhātu'* as the universal essence or truth itself, which represents, in its turn, the Non-substantiality (*nairātmya*) of separate elements and individuals" (p. 207, n. 66).—We will speak later of other Mahāyānic texts (*infra*, p. 78, n. 90; pp. 13-15, 33, 111; p. 119, n. 278; cf. pp. 193 ff.).

21. R. Grousset, *Les philosophies indiennes*, II (Paris, 1931), p. 28.

22. *TU.* II, 7.

23. *MaiU.* II, 4; VI, 20. 21. 28.—Cf. *infra*, p. 34 and n. 245.

24. Radhakrishnan, *Up.*, p. 74.

25. *ChU.* VIII, 7-12; *TU.* II and III.—Cf. below, pp. 9-10.

26. The word *śarīra*, in its widest sense, designates not only the "gross body," but the "subtle body" too. In other words, it designates the psycho-physical complex. See *infra*, n. 245 (p. 113).

27. *ChU.* VIII, 12, 1. Cf. *Kaṭha Up.* II, 22.

28. Above.

29. The Upaniṣads often use the word *prāṇa* as a synonym for *ātman-brahman* (cf. *Bṛhadāraṇyaka, infra*, n. 88; p. 20 and n. 138, with Śaṅkara). This is certainly a harking-back to the primitive meaning of the word *ātman* "vital breath" (assimilated, on the cosmic level to the Wind, *Vāta/Vāyu*).[a] *Prāṇa-brahman-ātman* is not however the

vital breath, but its base (*prāṇasya prāṇaḥ*, *BĀU.* IV, 4, 18 [cf. *Kena-Up.* I, 2]; cf. II, 1, 20; 5, 15; Śaṅkara on *Muṇḍ.Up.* III, 1, 4: *prāṇa* = *prāṇasya prāṇaḥ*). It is itself *aprāṇa* (*BĀU.* III, 8, 8 [*infra*, p. 166, n. 114]; cf. *Muṇḍ.Up.* II, 1, 2). How is comparison of this *prāṇa* "without *prāṇa*" and the *ātman* "without *ātman*" (below), foundation of all *ātmans* (*asminn ātmani . . . sarva eta ātmānaḥ samarpitāḥ*, *BĀU.* II, 5, 15), to be avoided? Note too that the *Chāndogya-Upaniṣad* (VI, 3, 2-3; 11, 1-3; cf. *Amṛtabindu-Up.* 13 [in *Thirty-Two Upaniṣads* = *Ānandāśrama Sanskrit Series*, 29, Poona, 1895]) uses the term *jīva* to designate the *ātman*; a term later reserved for the psycho-physical phenomenon. Cf. *MaiU.* VI, 19: *aprāṇād iha yasmāt saṃbhūtaḥ prāṇasaṃjñako jīvas tasmāt prāṇo vai turyākhye dhārayet prāṇam.—aprāṇāt prāṇādi-viśeṣarahitāc cidātmana eveha dehe yasmāt prāṇasaṃjñako jivaḥ saṃbhūtaḥ, prāṇadhāriṇopādhinā prāṇasaṃjñaṃ prāpya jīvo jāta iti yāvat, tasmāt prāṇo vai svabhāvato 'prāṇo 'pi prāṇa iti prasiddhaḥ sa turyākhye 'vasthātrayātīte 'prāṇe prāṇam ātmānaṃ dhārayet, prāṇātmabhāvanāṃ hitvāprāṇacidātmabhāvanāṃ kuryād ity arthaḥ*, Rāmatīrtha. (On *tur[ī]ya*, see *infra*, p. 67.)—On all this, cf. *infra*, pp. 190-191.

---

a. This, at least, is the opinion of the majority of authors. Cf. Oldenberg, *LUAB.*[2], p. 45: "The primary meaning of 'Ātman' is without doubt 'Atem' (breath), and the Sanskrit word is certainly etymologically related to the German equivalent."—*Contra*, Deussen, *AGPh.* I, 1, p. 285 (cf. article in *ERE.* II, p. 195; *contra*, Keith, *RPhVU.* II, p. 451); L. Renou, "On the word Ātman," *Vāk*, 2, p. 151.—The passage of the meaning of "vital breath" to that of "individual" is easy to imagine: the essence of the individual—his soul—was supposed to reside in the vital breath ("recalls Akkadian *napištu* 'vital breath, life, individual,'" A. Minard, *Trois énigmes sur les Cent Chemins*, II [= *Publications de l'Institut de Civilisation indienne*, fascicle 3, Paris, 1956], p. 335, § 910 a).

30. *sa yathā prayogya ācaraṇe yuktaḥ, evam evāyam asmiñ charīre prāṇo yuktaḥ*, *ChU.* VIII, 12, 3.—Cf. *BĀU.* IV, 3, 35: *tadyathānaḥ susamāhitam utsarjad yāyād evam evāyaṃ śārīra ātmā prājñen-ātmanānvārūḍha utsarjan yāti.—Kaṭha-Up.* III, 3: *ātmānaṃ rathinaṃ viddhi śarīraṃ ratham eva tu.—Chāgaleya-Up.* 7 (edition-translation by L. Renou, Paris, 1959; cf. Belvalkar-Ranade, pp. 257-258).—*MaiU.* II, 3-4: *śakaṭam ivācetanam idaṃ śarīraṃ, kasyaiṣa khalv īdṛśo mahimātīndriyabhūtasya yenaitadvidham etac cetanavat pratiṣṭhāpitam,*

pracodayitā vāsya . . . yo ha khalu vāvoparisthaḥ śrūyate guṇeṣv ivordhva-retasaḥ sa vā eṣa śuddhaḥ pūtaḥ śūnyaḥ śānto 'prāṇo nirātmānanto 'kṣayyaḥ sthiraḥ śāśvato 'jaḥ svatantraḥ sve mahimni tiṣṭhati; anenedaṃ śarīraṃ cetanavat pratiṣṭhāpitam, pracodayitā vaiṣo 'py asya.—Ibid., II, 6; VI, 4.

Cf. *infra*, pp. 28 ff.—"The contrast with the Platonic metaphor in the *Phaidros* is as obvious as the parallel," Keith, *RPhVU.* II, p. 555, n. 6.

31. *BĀU.* III, 7. Cf. *ibid.*, III, 8, 11; 4, 2.—The *ātman* is at once the farthest away and the closest: *dūrāt sudūre tad ihāntike ca, Muṇḍ.Up.* III, 1, 7. Cf. *Īśā-Up.* 4-5; *Kaṭha-Up.* II, 21-22.—*BhG.* XIII, 15-16:

bahir antaś ca bhūtānām acaraṃ caram eva ca ।
sūkṣmatvāt tad avijñeyaṃ dūrasthaṃ cāntike ca tat ॥
avibhaktaṃ ca bhūteṣu vibhaktam iva ca sthitam ।

Aṣṭāvakra-Gītā, I, 19-20:

yathaivādarśamadhyasthe rūpe 'ntaḥ paritas tu saḥ ।
tathaivāsmin śarīre 'ntaḥ paritaḥ parameśvaraḥ ॥
ekaṃ sarvagataṃ vyoma bahir antar yathā ghaṭe ।
nityaṃ nirantaraṃ brahma sarvabhūtagaṇe tathā ॥

Viṣṇudharmottara, I, 67, 20 (ed. Veṅkaṭeśvara Press, Bombay): *bhūtāntarastho 'pi na bhūtasaṃstha āścaryam etan mama devadeva.*—See also *infra*, p. 59, n. e.

E. Bréhier (*La philosophie de Plotin* [Paris, 1928], pp. 164-165), says: ". . . Plotinus' own doctrine is that Platonic transcendence, well understood, fundamentally implies immanence, in other terms, that there cannot be true continuity in the domain of spiritual realities, if there is not absorption of the inferior reality into the superior reality. It is not the immanence, as the Stoics conceived of it, that is to say, the circulation or dispersion of the first principle through the things, but quite the contrary, what may be called immanence in the transcendent, an absorption of things into their principle.[a] . . . Immanence, thus understood, seems to Plotinus to be, not the opposite, but on the contrary, the condition of true transcendence."

These remarks are also true for the Upaniṣads. Cf. especially, the analysis of the *Taittirīya-Upaniṣad* (II and III): "The higher includes the lower and goes beyond it," Radhakrishnan, *Up.*, p. 557. It may be said, even so, by reversing the terms, that the transcendence of *brahman-ātman*, in the Upaniṣads, as of the One, for Plotinus, is the condition of its true immanence. How could one and the same being be everywhere in its entirety, if everywhere it were not in itself (*svastha*,

MaiU. II, 7 [cf. below, p. 29]; *uparistha* "situated above [phenomena]," *ibid.*, II, 4 [cf. above, n. 30; below, p. 29 and n. 205]), in other words, if it were lost in the things by being mixed with them? "It would cease to be the universal being . . . ; it would be, by accident, the being of another thing," Plotinus, *Enneads,* VI, 4, 3 [trans. Bréhier, coll. Budé], cf. also Meister Eckhart: "That which is one in many things must necessarily be above the things" (*Traités et Sermons,* translated from the German by F. A. and J. M. with an introduction by M. de Gandillac, Paris 1942, p. 160 [Sermon No. 9]).

We may therefore say, with Radhakrishnan (*Indian Philosophy*², I, p. 184): "Brahman is in the world, though not as the world," or (*ibid.*, p. 203): "The Upaniṣads declare that the universe is in God. But they never hold that the universe is God." Cf. Śaṅkara: "Though the cause (that is to say, the *brahman*) and effect (i.e. the world) are not distinct, one from the other, it is the effect which has the cause for essence, and not the cause which has the effect for essence" (*ananyatve 'pi kārya-kāraṇayoḥ kāryasya kāraṇātmatvam, na tu kāraṇasya kāryātmatvam, Brahmasūtra-bhāṣya,* II, 1, 9, p. 446); "It is the outspread universe which has for its own nature the *brahman,* it is not the *brahman* which has the outspread universe for its own nature" (*brahmasvabhāvo hi prapañco na prapañcasvabhāvaṃ brahma, ibid.*, III, 2, 21, p. 712). It is the *nāman* and the *rūpa* which have the *brahman* for essence, it is not the *brahman* which has the *nāman* and the *rūpa* for essence (. . . *nāmarūpe . . . brahmaṇaivātmavatī, na brahma tadātmakam, Taittirīyopaniṣad-bhāṣya,* II, 6, *infra,* p. 232, n. 14).—*BhG.* VII, 12; IX, 4-5, with notes by Radhakrishnan (*The Bhagavadgītā*² [London, 1949, etc.], pp. 217, 239-240).—Belvalkar-Ranade, p. 384.

---

a. The author makes cross reference here to Arnou, *Le Désir de Dieu,* p. 162, sq.

32. *BĀU.* VI, 3.—The *brahman-ātman* is called "the light of lights" (*jyotiṣāṃ jyotis*), *BĀU.* IV, 4, 16; *Muṇḍ.Up.*, II, 2, 9; *BhG* XIII, 17. Cf. *Kaṭha-Up.* V, 15 (= *Muṇḍ.Up.* II, 2, 10 = *Śvet.Up.* VI, 14); cf. *BhG* XV, 6; *Ud.* I, 10, p. 9 [*Netti,* p. 150].—*antaḥ śarīre jyotirmayo hi śubhraḥ* [*ātmā*], *Muṇḍ.Up.* III, 1, 5. See also *ChU.* VIII, 3, 4; 12, 3 (cf. *MaiU.* II, 2).—*Infra,* n. 83.

33. *ChU.* VIII, 12, 1. Cf. *Kaṭha-Up.* II, 22.

34. The "ignorant" are called *bāla* "children" because their consciousness is not fully opened out. Cf. *infra,* p. 209 and n. 13, with reference to *avidyā/avijjā.*

35. *deśa-kāla-nimitta,* as the Vedānta was later to say (cf. Deussen, *AGPh.* I, 2, 137).

36. *attani vā, bhikkhave, sati, attaniyaṃ me ti assa?—evaṃ, bhante.—attaniye vā, bhikkhave, sati, attā me ti assa?—evaṃ bhante.—attani ca, bhikkhave, attaniye ca saccato thetato anupalabbhamāne, yaṃ p' idaṃ diṭṭhiṭṭhānaṃ: so loko so attā, so pecca bhavissāmi nicco dhuvo sassato avipariṇāmadhammo, sassatisamaṃ tath' eva ṭhassāmīti, nan' āyaṃ, bhikkhave kevalo paripūro bāladhammo? M.* I, p. 138.—Cf. *infra,* nn. 53, 54, 243.

The *ātman* is not an object to be "grasped": *anupalabbhamāna* (cf. *anupalabbhiyamāna,* below, n. 38; cf. also *ananuvejja, infra,* n. 38, and pp. 187 ff.), but transcendent to the empirical I, it is our true essence, that we must discover in our own depths. *nānātmalābhavad aprāptaprāptilakṣaṇa ātmalābhaḥ, labdhṛlabdhavyayor bhedābhāvāt,* Śaṅkara, *Bṛhadāraṇyakopaniṣad-bhāṣya,* I, 4, 7 (p. 144).

Oldenberg, who translates the expression *anupalabbhamāna* by "nicht zu erfassen" (i.e. not comprehensible) (*Buddha* [ed. 1961], p. 255; cf. *LUAB.*², p. 258; on this see also below, n. 243), clarifies: "Thus it appears that a categorical statement regarding the problem of a Self which is incomprehensible and belongs to an order of things beyond, is to be avoided." (*LUAB.*², p. 309, n. 194 [cf. *infra,* n. 119].) However, the same author wonders whether this passage does not constitute a polemic against the Upaniṣads (*LUAB.*², p. 258, n. 1). This idea is affirmed by other more recent authors: thus, H. von Glasenapp, *Vedānta und Buddhismus* (= *Abhandlungen der Akademie der Wissenschaften und der Literatur in Mainz: Geistes- und Sozialwissenschaftlichen Klasse,* 1950, NR. 11), p. 4 (1014); W. Rāhula, *L'enseignement du Bouddha* (Paris, 1961), p. 86 and n. 17. But it is incorrect, as we shall see further on (nn. 53, 54). H. von Glasenapp quotes *BĀU.* IV, 4, 13. The meaning of this passage is however quite otherwise (cf. *infra,* p. 13). The doctrine criticized in the passage of the *Majjhima-Nikāya* rather reminds us of the famous doctrine of Śāṇḍilya where the influence of ancient ritualist-theist representations is encountered (cf. Deussen, *AGPh.* I, 2, p. 308; Keith, *RPhVU.* II, p. 582; Belvalkar-Ranade, p. 386). This doctrine, found in the *Chāndogya-Upaniṣad,* already appears in Book X of the *Śatapatha-Brāhmaṇa: sa prāṇasyātmā, eṣa ma ātmā, etam ita ātmānaṃ pretyābhisaṃbhaviṣyāmi* (*ŚB.* X, 6, 3, 2).—*eṣa ma ātmāntar hṛdaye, etad brahma, etam itaḥ pretyābhisaṃbhavitāsmi* (*ChU.* III, 14, 4). [Here, the word *pretya* is to be taken in the literal sense and not in the figurative sense as elsewhere; below, n. 160.] The internal contradiction of this doctrine is: "Who does not feel the inner contradiction of these words, and that, if the Ātman really is my soul, there is no need to go out in search of it!" Deussen, *AGPh.* I, 2, p. 309; cf. p. 321.—See also Śaṅkara, *Chāndogyopaniṣadbhāṣya,* III, 14, 4. Cf. *Some Thoughts,* pp. 9 ff.

37. These terms are justifiable only at the level of empirical consciousness. The Absolute, to which no category of empirical knowledge applies, appears, indeed, to be simply a "non-being" (*asant*). Cf. Śaṅkara, *Brahmasūtra-bhāṣya,* II, 1, 17; Duessen, *AGPh.* I, 2, pp. 117-118. The Upaniṣads and Buddhism are, on the other hand, certainly pessimistic doctrines, insofar as they affirm the world to be full of sorrow. But, instead of being "endless complaints against the vanity of life" (Oldenberg-Foucher, *Buddha*[4], p. 248), they deny the true reality of perceptible existence, and raise themselves to a height where there is neither sorrow nor pleasure, where all the conflicts between opposites are resolved into an absolute harmony (*paramaṃ sāmyam, Muṇḍ.Up.* III, 1, 3). Deliverance, thus understood, is neither an annihilation nor a passage from earthly sorrow to celestial happiness, but freedom from all the limitations of the empirical world,—a passage from the limitations of the finite to the plenitude of the Infinite. Cf. *infra,* nn. 54, 71; pp. 12 ff. See also Hiriyanna, *The Quest after Perfection* (Mysore, 1952), pp. 56-57, 111.

It is Barth who has stated the truth, "Thus these doctrines appear to us, originally, to breathe speculative daring rather than lassitude and suffering. It is nonetheless true . . . that, in the long run, in spite of their incontestable grandeur, they had a depressing effect on the Hindu mind" (*Œuvres,* I, p. 84). Cf. also *infra,* pp. 235-236.

38. *evaṃ vimuttacittaṃ kho, bhikkave, bhikkhuṃ sa-Indā devā sa-Brahmakā sa-Pajāpatikā anvesaṃ nādhigacchanti: idaṃ nissitaṃ Tathāgatassa viññāṇan ti.—taṃ kissa hetu?—diṭṭhe vāhaṃ, bhikkhave, dhamme Tathāgataṃ ananuvejjo ti vadāmi. evaṃvādiṃ kho maṃ, bhikkhave, evamakkhāyiṃ eke samaṇabrāhmaṇā asatā tucchā musā abhūtena abbhācikkhanti: Venayiko samaṇo Gotamo, sato sattassa ucchedaṃ vināsaṃ vibhavaṃ paññāpetīti. yathā vāhaṃ, bhikkhave, na, yathā cāhaṃ na vadāmī, tathā maṃ te bhonto samaṇabrāhmaṇā asatā tucchā musā abhūtena abbhācikkhanti: Venayiko . . . paññāpetīti. pubbe cāhaṃ, bhikkhave, etarahi ca dukkhañ c' eva paññāpemi dukkhassa ca nirodhaṃ, M.* I, p. 140. (Cf. *infra,* n. 45; pp. 8, 22-23.)

Cf. *S.* XXII, 85: The *ātman-Tathāgata* (this identification is clearly indicated in the text) is neither one of the *upādānakkhandhas* nor their totality, but something more profound, which is not destroyed with the cessation of the phenomenal existence of the individual.[a] It is the Being itself, which cannot be "grasped" by thought (*anupalabbhiyamāna*: cf. *anupalabbhamāna*, above, n. 36, and *ananuvejja*, in the passage just quoted; see *infra*, n. 243, and pp. 187 ff.).—See also *S.* XXII, 86; XLIV, 2.

Ud. VIII, 3, pp. 80-81 (= *It.*, p. 37 = *Netti*, p. 62; cf. *infra*, pp. 33, 135-136):

atthi, bikkhave, ajātaṃ abhūtaṃ akataṃ asaṃkhataṃ. no ce taṃ, bikkhave, abhavissa ajātaṃ abhūtaṃ akataṃ asaṃkhataṃ, na yidha jātassa bhūtassa katassa saṃkhatassa nissaraṇaṃ paññāyetha. yasmā ca kho, bikkhave, atthi ajātaṃ abhūtaṃ akataṃ asaṃkhataṃ, tasmā jātassa bhūtassa katassa saṃkhatassa nissaraṇaṃ paññāyati.

Dhp. 97: *assaddho akataññū ca sandhicchedo ca yo naro* | *hatāvakāso vantāso sa ve uttamaporiso* || (cf. *infra*, p. 182 and n. 35).—*Ibid.*, 383: *saṃkhārānaṃ khayaṃ ñatvā akataññū 'si brāhmaṇa* ||

akata, etc. = Nirvāṇa/Nibbāna. Cf. *ChU.* VIII, 13: *akṛtaṃ kṛtātmā brahmalokam abhisaṃbhavāmi.* (The expression *brahmaloka* does not mean "the world of Brahmā" here [or "the world of *brahman*"!], *brahmaṇo lokaḥ*, but "the world which is *brahman*," *brahmaiva lokaḥ*: cf. Deussen, *AGPh.* I, 2, p. 131; see also Śaṅkara, *Brahmasūtrabhāṣya*, I, 3, 15. In the same way, *brahmapuram* = *brahmaiva puram*, Śaṅkara on *ChU.* VIII, 1, 5; *nirvāṇapuram* = *nirvāṇam eva puram*, below, n. 191. On *ChU.* VIII, 13, see also Appendix II.)

ajātaṃ, ajaraṃ, amataṃ, asokaṃ (nibbānaṃ), *M.* I, pp. 163, 167, 173.—*ajaraṃ, amaraṃ, asokaṃ, abhayaṃ (nibbānaṃ)*, *Therīgāthā*, 512.

Cf. *BĀU.* IV, 4, 25: *sa vā eṣa mahān aja ātmājaro 'maro 'mṛto 'bhayo brahma.*— *ChU.* VIII, 1, 5, 7, 1: *ātmā . . . vijaro vimṛtyur viśokaḥ . . .*; VIII, 3, 4, (= *MaiU.* II, 2): *eṣa ātmeti hovāca, etad amṛtam abhayam, etad brahmeti.* (On *abhaya*, cf. *infra*, n. 71).—*Kaṭha-Up.* II, 18 (cf. *BhG.* II, 20): *na jāyate mriyate vā vipaścin nāyaṃ kutaścin na babhūva kaścit.*—*Vivekacūḍāmaṇi*, 134: *na jāyate no mriyate na vardhate na kṣīyate no vikaroti nityaḥ.* See also *Ratnagotravibhāga*, I, 80.

Note that the "unborn, unproduced, uncreated, unformed" (*ajāta, abhūta, akata, asaṃkhata*), in a word, the Unconditioned, is not another world, situated beyond the "born, produced, created, formed" (*jāta, bhūta, kata, saṃkhata*). It is in us, is our very selves: it is our essential nature. It must, then, be discovered in the depths of our being, by transcending our phenomenal existence. It is not "by a local movement" (*gamanena*) that the "end of the world" (*lokassa anto* = *dukkhassa anto* "end of suffering"), is attained to, "where one is not born, does not grow old, does not die, where there is neither death nor rebirth" (*yattha na jāyati na jīyati na mīyati na cavati na uppajjati*). "But, I tell you, it is in this body, endowed with consciousness, which is no more than a fathom in height, that are found the origin of the world, the cessation of the world, and the way which leads to the cessation of the world" (*api ca khvāhaṃ, āvuso, imasmiñ ñeva vyāmamatte kaḷevare saññimhi samanake lokañ ca paññāpemi lokasamudayañ ca lokanirodhañ ca lokanirodhagāminiñ ca paṭipadaṃ*). And he who thus knows, in himself, the "end of the world," aspires neither to this world nor to the other (*nāsiṃsati lokam imaṃ parañ ca*). *S.* I, pp. 61-62 = *A.* II, pp. 47-49 (an oft-quoted passage, most recently by P. Mus, "Où finit Puruṣa?" in *Mélanges Louis Renou*, p. 562).—This is a formulation of the "Four Noble Truths" (*Cattāri Ariyasaccāni*), which is unusual. The "world" (*loka*) here means the empirical world, which is the place of our becoming (this is the reason why it is identified as sorrow, *dukkha*). But this world has its "origin" (*samudaya*) in ourselves,—in our imperfect consciousness, which confuses appearance and Being, and which is therefore called "ignorance" (*avidyā/avijjā*: cf. *infra*, p. 209 and n. 13). It must therefore also have its "end" (*anta*) or "cessation" (*nirodha*) in ourselves, in the full unfolding of our consciousness. And the "way which leads to the cessation of the world" (*lokanirodhagāminī paṭipadā* = *dukkha-nirodhagāminī paṭipadā* of the "Four Noble Truths") is the "noble eightfold path" (*ariyo aṭṭhaṅgiko maggo*) or *brahmacariya* (*lokantagū vusitabrahmacariyo*, *S.* I, p. 62, *gāthā*; cf. *infra*, p. 122 and n. 9; p. 128). We do not consider it a betrayal of the thought of the Buddha, to have him saying: Man is a finite being; however, his finitude, unlike that of inferior beings, is *open*: he contains in himself, not only Infinity, which is his true nature (as it is for all other beings) but also, by virtue of his consciousness, the capacity to discover that nature: through consciousness, he is capable of going beyond consciousness to become Consciousness (cf. *infra*, n. 149).—See also *infra*, n. 60; p. 157, n. 60; pp. 137 ff.; Appendix VI. "It was a great opportunity for exegesis, but B[uddhaghosa] makes no use of it," Mrs. Rhys Davids, *The Book of the Kindred Sayings*, I (= *Pāli Text Society Translation Series*, No. 7, London, 1917), p. 86, n. 3. (Cf. *infra*, pp. 187 ff.)

a. Cf. *BĀU.* IV, 5, 14, with Deussen, *Up.*, p. 485, n., and *AGPh.* I, 2, p. 314 (on *mātrāsaṃsarga* [Mādhyaṃdina], cf. Śaṅkara, *Brahmasūtra-bhāṣya,* I, 4, 22, p. 418: *mātrābhis tv asya bhūtendriyalakṣaṇābhir avidyākṛtābhir* asaṃsargo *vidyayā bhavati*; see also *Chāndogyopaniṣadbhāṣya,* VI, 3, 2; Kumārila, *Ślokavārttika, Ātmavāda,* 147, with Pārthasārathimiśra [ed. Svāmī Dvārikādāsa Śāstrī, Varanasi, Tara Publications, 1978]); *ChU.* VIII, 1, 5 (*na vadhenāsya hanyate*); *ibid.*, VI, 11, 3 (*jīvāpetaṃ vāva kiledaṃ mriyate, na jīvo mriyate*); *Kaṭha-Up.* II, 18 [*BhG.* II, 20] (*ajo nityaḥ śāśvato 'yaṃ purāṇo na hanyate hanyamāne śarīre*); *BhG.* VIII, 20 (*sarveṣu bhūteṣu naśyatsu na vinaśyati*); *ibid.*, XIII, 27 (*samaṃ sarveṣu bhūteṣu tiṣṭhantaṃ parameśvaram* | *vinaśyatsv avinaśyantaṃ yaḥ paśyati sa paśyati* ||); *Vivekacūḍāmaṇi,* 134 (*vilīyamāne 'pi vapuṣy amuṣmin na līyate kumbha ivāmbaraḥ svayam*); cf. also *ibid.*, 560 ff.; *Amṛtabindu-Up.* 13-14 (edition quoted); *Māṇḍ-Kār.* III, 3-4; *Madhyamaka-hṛdaya,* VIII, 9-10 (V. V. Gokhale, "The Vedānta Philosophy described by Bhavya in his *Madhyamakahṛdaya,*" *IIJ.* II [1958], no. 3, pp. 174-175).—*upādhipralaya evāyaṃ nātmavilayaḥ,* Śaṅkara, *Brahmasūtra-bhāṣya,* II, 3, 17 (p. 603). Compare with Jaspers: "That which is destroyed by death is appearance, not Being itself." (*Philosophie,* II [Berlin 1932], p. 222.) See also below, nn. 83, 86.

39. Cf. *infra,* n. 71.

40. Cf. the texts that have just been cited, n. 38. See also ch. II.

41. This doctrine, which is often the subject of lengthy developments (we will meet with it in the second sermon of Benares, under the name of *Anattalakkhaṇa-Sutta: Mahāvagga,* I, 6, 38 ff. [*Vin.* I, pp. 13-14]; *S.* XXII, 59 [vol. III, pp. 66-68]), is found summarized in these terms:

yad aniccaṃ taṃ dukkhaṃ; yaṃ dukkhaṃ tad anattā; yad anattā taṃ n' etaṃ mama, n' eso 'ham asmi, na m' eso attā ti evam etaṃ yathābhūtaṃ sammappaññāya daṭṭhabbaṃ, S. III, pp. 22-23, 44-45, 82-83, 84; IV, pp. 1-3.—Cf. *infra,* pp. 31 ff., 35-39, 207 ff.

42. Cf. *Kaṭha-Up.* IV, 1-2.

43. The Asura Virocana of the *Chāndogya-Upaniṣad* (VIII, 8) is, as Keith has so admirably said (*RPhVU.* II, p. 517), "the prototype of all men who merely see in the body the hope of immortality, and, therefore, deck it out on death with gay raiment."

44. Thought of Indra, in *ChU.* VIII, 11. *nāha khalv ayam evaṃ saṃpraty ātmānaṃ jānāti, ayam aham asmīti, no evemāni bhūtāni, vināśam evāpīto bhavati.*—Cf. the thought of Maitreyī, in *BĀU.* II, 4, 13, and

IV, 5, 14; Gauḍapāda, *Māṇḍ.Kār.* III, 39, with Śaṅkara's commentary (*infra*, p. 68).

45. Compare, with the Upaniṣadic passages quoted in the previous note, the passage of the *Majjhima-Nikāya* (I, p. 140), quoted above, n. 38. See also pp. 22-23.—According to the terms of the *Brahmajāla-Sutta* (*D.* I, 2, 13; vol. I, p. 21), these would be the *ekacca-sassatikā ekacca-asassatikā*: all that which is corporeal is perishable, but the consciousness (*citta, manas, viññāṇa*; cf. *infra*, n. 211) does not perish. *yaṃ kho idaṃ vuccati cakkhun ti pi sotan ti pi ghānan ti pi jivhā ti pi kāyo ti pi, ayaṃ attā anicco addhuvo asassato vipariṇāma-dhammo: yañ ca kho idaṃ vuccati cittan ti vā mano ti vā viññāṇan ti vā, ayaṃ attā nicco dhuvo sassato avipariṇāmadhammo, sassatisamaṃ tath' eva ṭhassatīti.*

46. *priyayā striyā saṃpariṣvaktaḥ*, *BĀU.* IV, 3, 21. We have here (cf. Plotinus, *Enneads*, VI, 7, 34) a mention of that conception of love where the lover and the beloved are one. See *infra*, pp. 11-12 and n. 86.—With regard to deep sleep (*suṣupti-* or *suṣuptam*), cf. *infra*, pp. 67-68.

47. *BĀU*, II, 4, 12-14 (cf. IV, 5, 13-15); IV, 3, 19-33; *ChU.* VI, 8-10; VII, 24, 1; VIII, 11.—Cf. *infra*, pp. 23-24.

48. Cf. *infra*, p. 21.

49. On the meaning of *avidyā/avijjā*, see *infra*, p. 209 and n. 13.

50. Cf. *M.*, I, p. 140, quoted above, n. 38.

51. Cf. *infra*, p. 9.

52. *ātmany evātmānaṃ paśyati* (*BĀU.* IV, 4, 23).—*abhayaṃ hi vai brahma bhavati ya evaṃ veda* (*ibid.*, IV, 4, 25).—*sa yo ha vai tat paramaṃ brahma veda brahmaiva bhavati* (*Muṇḍ.Up.* III, 2, 9).—*saṃviśaty ātmanātmānam* (*Māṇḍ.Up.* 12); etc. See also *infra*, n. 245 end (*Mai.U.* VI, 20).—Cf. Kālidāsa, *Kumārasaṃbhava*, III, 50 (ed. Parvaṇīkara-Paraba, Bombay, Nirṇaya-Sāgara Press, 1886): *ātmānam ātmany avalokayantam* (*svātirekeṇa paramātmano 'bhāvād iti bhāvaḥ*, Mallinātha).

Is the *Suttanipāta* engaging in a polemic against the Upaniṣads, when it says, in verse 477: *attanā attānaṃ nānupassati*? It is not, for the *ātman* it speaks of is only the individual, so-called *ātman.* Cf. *Paramatthajotikā* (II, 2, p. 410): *attanā attānaṃ nānupassatīti ñāṇa-sampayuttena cittena vipassanto attano khandhesu aññaṃ attānaṃ nāma na passati, khandhamattam eva passati.*—The expression means, simply, that the Buddha has transcended his empirical individuality. (Cf. also *Papañcasūdanī*, I, pp. 70-71, on *M.* I, p. 8 [cit. *Paramattha-jotikā, loc. cit.*].)

53. *S.* III, p. 98 identifies, in fact, the doctrine criticized in the passage of the *Majjhima-Nikāya* quoted above (n. 36: *so loko so attā, so pecca bhavissāmi nicco dhuvo sassato avipariṇāmadhammo, sassatisamaṃ tath' eva ṭhassāmi*) with "eternalism" (*sassatadiṭṭhi* = Sanskrit *śāśvata-dṛṣṭi* = *śāśvatavāda*). [Cf. also *Bauddhavidyāsudhākaraḥ: Studies in Honour of Heinz Bechert on the Occasion of His 65th Birthday* (Swisttal-Odendorf, 1997: *Indica et Tibetica,* 30), pp. 26-27.] This formulation of eternalism is different from that found in, for instance, the *Brahmajāla-Sutta* (*D.* I, pp. 13 ff.). Cf. also *infra,* p. 18 and n. 119.—These two formulations have, however, a point in common: they both consider eternity as time prolonged, either in this world (*Brahmajāla-Sutta*), or in another world (text under consideration here). Such an eternity is illusory, from the Upaniṣadic and Buddhist point of view (cf. below, n. 54). Some modern authors have, it is true, identified the *śāśvatavāda/sassatavāda* with the Upaniṣadic doctrine; but this is an error. If the expression "eternal" itself is to be condemned, then it must be thought that Buddhism condemns itself. Is not Nirvāṇa, which is not subject to temporal becoming, "eternal"? *appabhavattā ajarāmaraṇaṃ; pabhavajarāmaraṇānaṃ abhāvato niccaṃ,* Buddhaghosa, *Visuddhimagga,* XVI, 71 [ed. Warren-Kosambi, *HOS.* 41).—Cf. *PTS. Dictionary,* s.v. *nibbāna,* p. 364; Vidhuśekhara Bhaṭṭācārya, *Gauḍapādīyam Āgamaśāstram* (University of Calcutta, 1950), *Avataraṇikā,* pp. 92-93.

54. Happiness does not belong to any world, for all existence, having its origin in time, must also have an end (*yaṃ kiñci samudaya-dhammaṃ sabban taṃ nirodha-dhammaṃ,* and analogous formulae, *passim*); now that which is impermanent is sorrowful (*yad aniccaṃ taṃ dukkhaṃ*). Aspiration to happiness in the beyond is therefore likened to the love of a man for an imaginary woman, or again, to the building of a stairway to climb up into an imaginary palace (*D.* I., pp. 192 ff.).—Cf. *Vivekacūḍāmaṇi,* 21: *dehādibrahmaparyante anitye bhogavastuni.* (Apropos Brahmā[s], cf. *infra,* p. 99; p. 146, n. g.)

BĀU. I, 4, 15: *atha yo ha vā asmāl lokāt svaṃ lokam adṛṣṭvā praiti, sa enam avidito na bhunakti . . . yad iha vā apy anevaṃvin mahat puṇyaṃ karma karoti, tad dhāsyāntataḥ kṣīyata eva. ātmānam eva lokam upāsīta; sa ya ātmānam eva lokam upāste, na hāsya karma kṣīyate, asmād dhy eva ātmano yad yat kāmayate tat tat sṛjate.—Ibid.,* III, 8, 10: *yo vā etad akṣaraṃ, Gārgi, aviditvāsmiṃl loke juhoti yajate tapas tapyate bahūni varṣasahasrāṇi, antavad evāsya tad bhavati; yo vā etad akṣaraṃ, Gārgi, aviditvāsmāl lokāt praiti, sa kṛpaṇaḥ: atha ya etad akṣaraṃ, Gārgi, viditvāsmāl lokāt praiti, sa brāhmaṇaḥ.* (On the word *brāhmaṇa*, see *infra*, p. 127 and n. 43).—*Ibid.*, IV, 4, 6-7: *tad eva saktaḥ saha karmaṇaiti liṅgaṃ mano yatra niṣaktam asya | prāpyāntaṃ karmaṇas tasya yat kiṃ ceha karoty ayam | tasmāl lokāt punar aity asmai lokāya karmaṇe || iti nu kāmayamānaḥ. athākāmayamānaḥ: yo 'kāmo niṣkāma āptakāma ātmakāmaḥ, na tasya prāṇā utkrāmanti* (cf. III, 2, 11), *brahmaiva san brahmāpyeti. tad eṣa śloko bhavati* (= *Kaṭha-Up.* VI, 14; cf. also *Muṇḍ.Up.* III, 2, 2):

yadā sarve pramucyante kāmā ye 'sya hṛdi śritāḥ |
atha martyo 'mṛto bhavaty atra brahma samaśnuta || iti—

ChU. VIII, 1, 6 (cf. VII, 25, 2): *tadyatheha karmajito lokaḥ kṣīyate, evam evāmutra puṇyajito lokaḥ kṣīyate. tad ya ihātmānam ananuvidya vrajanty etāṃś ca satyān kāmān, teṣāṃ sarveṣu lokeṣv akāmacāro bhavati.*—*Ibid.*, II, 23, 1-2: *trayo dharmaskandhāḥ . . . sarva ete puṇyalokā bhavanti, brahmasaṃstho 'mṛtatvam eti.*—Cf. *Muṇḍ.Up.* I, 2; *infra*, pp. 20, 180.

It seems clear to us, in the light of these passages, that the one from *Majjhima-Nikāya*, which we have quoted above, n. 36, is not, as has often been thought, a polemic against the Upaniṣads, but that, on the contrary, it states their major doctrine, that is: the *ātman* is not something from which we are separated and which we must attain to in another world, instead it is our true being, that we must discover in the depths of ourselves.

"Deliverance is different from existence in *svarga* or paradise. The latter is a part of the manifested world. The soul may live there for ages and yet return to earth, an heir to its deeds. Deliverance, on the other hand, is a state of permanent union with the Highest Self. Life in paradise is a prolongation of self-centred life, while life eternal is liberation from it. While the former is time extended, the latter is time transcended," Radhakrishnan, *Up.*, pp. 117-118. Cf. also Deussen, *AGPh.* I, 2, pp. 314-315 ("Schopenhauer's definition of immortality as an indestructability without duration,"); Hiriyanna, *Popular Essays in Indian Philosophy* (Mysore, 1952), p. 80.—Compare with Jaspers: "Then Being is not beyond death in time, but rather, in the actual depths of existence as Eternity" (*Philosophie,* III [Berlin, 1932], p. 93).—"If, by eternity, we understand not endless duration in time, but timelessness, then he who lives in the present lives eternally," Wittgenstein, *Tractus logico-philosophicus,* 6.4311 (*The German text of Ludwig Wittgenstein's* Logisch-philosophische Abhandlung, with a new Translation by D. F. Pears and B. F. McGuinness, and with the Introduction by Bertrand Russell, London, 1961). See also *infra*, n. 160; p. 144.

55. We "reinforce the I," to use J. Krishnamurti's expression.

56. *sa, bhagavaḥ, kasmin pratiṣṭhita iti; sve mahimni, yadi vā na mahimnīti, ChU.* VII, 24, 1. Śaṅkara clarifies: the affirmative sentence "it is established in its own greatness" expresses only an empirical truth; from the point of view of the absolute Truth (*paramārtha*), we do not even say that it is established in its own greatness, for it is nowhere established (*apratiṣṭhitaḥ kvacid api*). *sve mahimnīti sva ātmīye mahimni māhātmye vibhūtau pratiṣṭhito bhūmā, yadi pratiṣṭhām icchasi kvacit; yadi vā paramārtham eva pṛcchasi, na mahimny api pratiṣṭhita iti brūmaḥ. apratiṣṭhito 'nāśrito bhūmā kvacid apīty arthaḥ.* (*Chāndogyo-paniṣad-bhāṣya,* VII, 24, 1.)

57. *BĀU.* II, 3, 6; III, 9, 26; IV, 2, 4; 4, 22; 5, 15. Cf. *Ārṣeya-Upaniṣad* (edition-translation by Belvalkar, in *Proceedings and Transactions of the Third Oriental Conference,* Madras, 1925, pp. 31 and ff.; analyzed in Belvalkar-Ranade, pp. 297-300; a better edition is that of V. P. Limaye and R. R. Vadekar, in *Eighteen Principal Upaniṣads,* I, Poona, *Vaidika-saṃśodhana-maṇḍala,* 1958).—Gauḍapāda, *Māṇḍ.Kār.* III, 26; Śaṅkara, *Brahmasūtra-bhāṣya,* III, 2, 22; *Upadeśasāhasrī, padya,* 11; Deussen, *AGPh.* I, 2, pp. 134 ff. Cf. below, p. 10, where negation as *method* will be spoken of.

58. Moral and ritual practices are means and not ends in themselves. They are of value only insofar as they purify our mind, thus preparing for us the way to knowledge, that is, to the realization of our unity with the Absolute, which is the true Good, "beyond good and evil." Morality is, therefore, compared (as is theoretical knowledge: *infra,* p. 9) to a boat, necessary for crossing a river, but which should not be carried on the shoulders when the river is crossed: *kullūpamaṃ vo, bhikkhave, dhammaṃ desitam ājānantehi dhammā pi vo pahātabbā, pag eva adhammā, M.* I, p. 135 (p. 180 in the Nālandā edition). Cf. Śaṅkara, *Vākyabhāṣya* on *Kena-Up.*, Introduction, p. 4: *upāyabhūtāni hi karmāṇi saṃskāradvāreṇa jñānasya . . . na hi nadyāḥ pārago nāvaṃ na muñcati yatheṣṭadeśagamanaṃ prati svātantrye sati* (cf. *Upadeśasāhasrī, padya,* XIV, 13). [Analogous idea in Saint Augustine and Meister Eckhart: see Coomaraswamy, *Hinduism and Buddhism* (New York, n.d.), p. 81, n. 249; *The Living Thoughts of Gotama the Buddha* (London, 1948), p. 31].—*Sn.* 520, 547 (cf. *ChU.* IV, 14, 3; *BhG.* V, 10), 715, 790, 839, 900; *Dhp.* 39, 267, 412 (= *Sn.* 636).—*Kauṣ.Up.* I, 4: *tadyathā rathena dhāvayan rathacakre paryavekṣeta, evam ahorātre paryavekṣate, evaṃ sukṛta-duṣkṛte, sarvāṇi ca dvandvāni; sa eṣa visukṛto viduṣkṛto brahmavidvān brahmaivābhipraiti.*—*BĀU.* IV, 3, 22:

ananvāgataṃ puṇyena, ananvāgataṃ pāpena.—*Ibid.*, IV, 4, 22-23: *na sādhunā karmaṇā bhūyān, no evāsādhunā kanīyān.* See also *Kauṣ.Up.* III, 1 and 8. *ChU.* VIII, 4, 1: *na sukṛtaṃ na duṣkṛtam.*—*TU.* II, 9 (passage cited below, n. 71).—*Kaṭha-Up.* II, 14: *anyatra dharmād anyatrādharmāt.*—*Muṇḍ.Up.* III, 1, 3: *vidvān puṇya-pāpe vidhūya nirañjanaḥ paramaṃ sāmyam upaiti.*—*MaiU.* VI, 18: *vidvān puṇya-pāpe vihāya pare 'vyaye sarvam ekīkaroti.*—*Kaivalya-Up.* 23 (*infra*, n. 173); *Subāla-Up.* XV (Radhakrishnan, *Up.*, p. 890); *BhG.* II, 50; *Aṣṭāvakra-Gītā*, IV, 3-4; *Vivekacūḍāmaṇi*, 503-505, 545-546.—*Śivadharmottara*, folio 50b (manuscript in the Sylvain Lévi collection, Institut de Civilisation indienne de l'Université de Paris): *dharmarajjvā vrajed ūrdhvaṃ pāparajjvā vrajaty adhaḥ* | *dvayaṃ jñānāsinā cchit[t]vā videhaḥ śāntim arcchati* || This idea is to be found again in the 18th c., coming from Rām-prasād: cf. M. Lupsa, *Chants à Kālī de Rāmprasād* (= *Publications de l'Institut français d'Indologie*, 30, Pondicherry, 1967), pp. 102 and 103 no. 83.

See also Radhakrishnan, *Indian Philosophy*², I, pp. 227 ff.; *Eastern Religions and Western Thought*² (Oxford University Press, 1940), pp. 102 ff.; *Up.*, pp. 121-121, with notes; Keith, *RPhVU.* II, pp. 582, 586, ll. 22-29; Hiriyanna, *The Quest after Perfection*, Essay VIII; *Outlines of Indian Philosophy* (London, 1932, etc.), pp. 381-382; Kokileswar Sastri, *An Introduction to Advaita Philosophy*, (University of Calcutta, 1924), ch. IV; M. K. Venkatarama Iyer, *Advaita Vedānta according to Śaṅkara* (London 1964), pp. 60-61. Cf. *infra*, pp. 15-16 and n. 107; p. 29; n. 216; p. 31 and n. 227; p. 184, n. 31; Appendix I.

59. Cf. *infra*, p. 173, n. 161.

60. Contrary to what is written by, for example, E. J. Thomas, *The History of Buddhist Thought*² (London, 1951 [reprint: 1953]), p. 98, and W. Rāhula, *op. cit.*, p. 86.

The word *diṭṭhi* (= Sanskrit *dṛṣṭi*), in *diṭṭhupādāna*, does not necessarily mean "false opinion" (*micchā-diṭṭhi* = Sanskrit *mithyā-dṛṣṭi*), the meaning seen in it by scholasticism (*Dhammasaṅgaṇi*, 1215; *Vibhaṅga*, p. 375; Buddhaghosa, *Sumaṅgalavilāsinī*, III, p. 1024; *Visuddhimagga*, XVII, 243 [edited quoted]): it can simply mean "theory" (literally, the word means "point of view"), and thus be the opposite of intuitive and immediate knowledge, *paññā* (= Sanskrit *prajñā*). Cf. *M.*, Sutta 72; *Sn.* 796 ff., 837 ff., 878 ff., 1078 ff.; *Laṅk.* I, 1; p. 9, l. 5 from bottom.—Cf. the word *darśana*, "system," "isolated fixation" (Betty Heimann, "Opposites: Contrasts or Complements in early Greek and Indian Philosophy?" in *Brahma-vidyā, The Adyar*

Library Bulletin, Jubilee Volume, XXV, parts 1-4 [1961], p. 225). See also, on this subject, Venkata Ramanan, p. 342b, n. 92.

It is the attachment to the facts of discursive knowledge that the Buddha condemns. The Tathāgata, who has seen things as they really are (*yathābhūtaṃ*), has gone beyond the realm of *diṭṭhi*: *diṭṭhigatan ti kho, Vaccha, apanītam etaṃ Tathāgatassa, M.* I, p. 486. Those who remain attached there see only aspects of the Truth, and nothing of the Truth itself (*ekaṅgadassino*): cf. below, n. 64. The *dhamma/nibbāna* (cf. ch. II), it is further stated, is beyond reason (*atakkāvacara*): *M.* I, pp. 167, 487; *It.*, p. 37; etc. Reason (*tarka*) has only empirical truth (*saṃvṛti-satya*) for its domain, not absolute Truth (*paramārtha*); it is the refuge of "children" (cf. *supra*, n. 34) [*bālāśraya*], of those who have not seen the true Truth (*adṛṣṭa-satya*): *MSA*, I, 12 and commentary.

On the question which occupies us here, the following verse of the *Mahāyāna-Sūtrālaṃkāra* is of particular interest:

> *na cātmadṛṣṭiḥ svayam ātmalakṣaṇā*
> *na cāpi duḥsaṃsthitatā vilakṣaṇā* |
> *dvayān na cānyad bhrama eṣa tūditas*
> *tataś ca mokṣo bhramamātrasaṃkṣayaḥ* || (*MSA*. VI, 2).

"The view of the *ātman* does not have itself for Indication the *ātman*; nor does Malformation (*duḥsaṃsthitatā* = *pañcopādāna-skandhāḥ*, according to the commentary) differ in Indication.[a] It is however incorrect to consider that there is nothing except these two;[b] Deliverance is therefore nothing other than the destruction of error."

It is thus that we propose to translate this stanza, rejecting the interpretation given in the commentary (cf. *supra*, n. 3), followed by S. Lévi:

. . . *nāpy ato dvayād* (that is to say, of the *ātmadṛṣṭi* and of the *duḥsaṃsthitatā*) *anyad ātmalakṣaṇam upapadyate. tasmān nāsty ātmā. bhrama eṣa tūtpanno yeyam ātmadṛṣṭiḥ. tasmād eva cātmābhāvān mokṣo 'pi bhramamātrasaṃkṣayo veditavyaḥ, na tu kaścin muktaḥ.* (Commentary.)

". . . Et il n'y a rien en dehors des deux; ce (= l'*ātman*) n'est donc qu'un préjugé, et la délivrance est la destruction de Rien-qu'un-préjugé." (S. Lévi; cf. also E. Frauwallner, *Die Philosophie des Buddhismus* [Berlin, 1956], p. 313.)

In the transcendent sense, it is true, there is neither individual (this is the sense in which the commentator takes the word *ātman*), nor bond, nor deliverance. Our stanza however does not contain simply a negation; it contains, as well, if we understand it properly, an affirmation, that of the true spiritual *ātman*, transcending the empirical I and ungraspable by discursive thought.—If there is no deliverance (*mokṣa*), in the usual sense of the term, it is because our true being, the *ātman*, is eternally free. It is by error that we consider the *ātman*, sometimes as an entity from which we are separated in space and time, sometimes as identical to our apparent reality, to the psycho-physical being: deliverance, then, appears to us, either as the conquest of something exterior to us,[c] or as pure annihilation.[d] But our authentic nature, unaltered by the conditions of our phenomenal existence,[e] is always present in the depths of our own being: we simply have to re-cognize it, re-discover it, by parting the veils of false conceptions which separate us from it.[f] There is, in the transcendent sense, no distinction between *saṃsāra* and *nirvāṇa*: *MK.* XXV, 19-20 (cf. XVI, 4-10); *MSA.* VI, 5 and commentary; *Laṅk.*, p. 76, ll. 7 ff.; *Mahāyānaviṃśikā*, 15 (G. Tucci, *Minor Buddhist Texts*, I [= *Serie Orientale Roma*, IX, 1956], p. 203); Lamotte, *Somme*, II, 2, p. 265; *Vimalakīrti*, pp. 315-316 (*Vimalakīrtinirdeśa*, VIII, 29, p. 88); cf. D. T. Suzuki, *Outlines of Mahāyāna Buddhism* (London, 1907), pp. 352-357; Th. Stcherbatsky, *The Conception of Buddhist Nirvāṇa* (Leningrad, 1927), p. 48; Murti, pp. 162-163, 232-233, 273-274; Venkata Ramanan, pp. 52, 66, 97, 113, 122, 258-259, 324, 329; S. N. Dasgupta, *Indian Idealism* (Cambridge University Press, 1933 [reprint: 1962]), pp. 98-99. See also Oldenberg, *Buddha* (ed. 1961), p. 203, passage in italics (= Oldenberg-Foucher[4], p. 241, n. 1).—*Supra*, n. 38 (last paragraph); *infra*, p. 157, n. 60; pp. 137 ff.; Appendix VI.

na nirvāsi nirvāṇena nirvāṇaṃ tvayi saṃsthitam |
buddhaboddhavyarahitaṃ sadasatpakṣavarjitam || *Laṅk.* II, 7.

"You do not vanish into Nirvāṇa; Nirvāṇa is in you.[g] There is in it neither subject knowing nor object known, neither is there the thesis of being, nor that of non-being."[h]

Cf. Deussen, *AGPh.* I, 2, pp. 310 ff.; Oldenberg, *LUAB.*[2], pp. 117-118.—Śaṅkara, *Muṇḍakopaniṣad-bhāṣya*, III, 2, 6: *avidyādisaṃsārabandhāpanayanam eva mokṣam icchanti brahmavido na tu kāryabhūtam.*—*Ibid.*, III, 2, 9: *avidyāpratibandhamātro hi mokṣo nānyaḥ pratibandhaḥ, nityatvād ātmabhūtatvāc ca.*—*Brahmasūtra-bhāṣya*, IV, 4, 2 (p. 1006): *phalatvaprasiddhir api mokṣasya bandhanivṛttimātrāpekṣā, nāpūrvopajananāpekṣā.*—*Bṛhadāraṇyakopaniṣad-bhāṣya*, IV, 4, 6 (pp. 663-664):

na hi vastuto muktāmuktatvaviśeṣo 'sti, ātmano nityaikarūpatvāt; kiṃ tu tadviṣayāvidyāpohyate śāstropadeśajanitavijñānena.—Commentary on *Māṇḍ.Kār.* III, 5: *bandhamokṣādayo vyāvahārikā na virudhyante.* See also *Vivekacūḍāmaṇi*, 46-47, 50 ff., 194 ff., 478, 510, 531 ff., 569-574 (st. 574 = *Amṛtabindu-Up.* 10 [edition cited] = *Māṇḍ.Kār.* II, 32); *Aṣṭāvakra-Gītā*, I, 11; II, 18, 20; XV, 18.—"The condition of *mokṣa* . . . differs from *saṃsāra* merely in a change of outlook, and there is no factual change whatsoever . . . *Mokṣa* means the revelation of the intrinsic nature of *ātman*; and, as it is self-manifesting, it requires no direct aid whatsoever for revealing itself. It shines by its own light, when once the obstruction to its full manifestation is removed," Hiriyanna, *The Quest after Perfection*, pp. 86-87; cf. p. 74. (On the Sāṃkhya point of view, cf. R. Garbe, *Die Sāṃkhya-Philosophie*[2] [Leipzig, 1917], p. 389.)

mokṣasya na hi vāso 'sti na grāmāntaram eva vā |
ajñānahṛdayagranthināśo mokṣa iti smṛtaḥ ||

Śivagītā, cited by Radhakrishnan, *Up.*, p. 118, n. 6. Cf. Śaṅkara on *Kaṭha-Up.* III, 12; *Vivekacūḍāmaṇi*, 557-558; *Brahma-Purāṇa*, cited by Śaṅkara (?), *Śvetāśvataropaniṣad-bhāṣya*, p. 34 (on *Śvet.Up.* I, 11); Abhinavagupta, *Paramārthasāra*, v. 60 (edition-translation by L. Silburn [= *Publications de l'Institut de Civilisation indienne*, fascicule 5, Paris, 1957]; cf. S. S. Suryanarayana Sastri, "Paramārthasāra," *NIA.* I, 1 [April 1938], p. 40).—See also *infra*, p. 95.

We may compare with Plotinus: "Our fatherland is the place from which we come, and our father is there. What then is this voyage and this flight? It is not with our feet that it is accomplished, for our feet always carry us from one land to another; neither is it necessary to prepare harness nor any boat, but it is necessary to stop looking and, closing the eyes, to exchange that way of seeing for another, and awaken that faculty that everyone possesses, but which few turn to use" (*Enneads*, I, 6, 8).—"If you are capable of attaining, or rather, if you are in the universal being, you will not seek any further; if you renounce doing so, you will incline elsewhere, you will fall and you will no longer see its presence because you are looking elsewhere. But if you search no more, how are you going to experience its presence? It is because you are near to it and because you have not come to a stop at a particular being; you do not even say any more of yourself: this is what I am; you abandon all limits to become universal being. Nevertheless, you were it before; but as you were from the outset something else as well, this surplus reduced you; for the surplus did not come from being, since nothing is added to being, but from non-being. Through this non-being, you have become someone, and you are not universal being unless you abandon this non-being. You thus increase yourself by abandoning everything else and, by virtue of this abandonment, the universal being is present. As long as you are with everything else, it does not manifest. It does not have to come to be present; it is you who have gone; to go, is not to leave it to go somewhere else; for it is there; but, though remaining close to it, you are turned away from it" (*ibid.*, VI, 5, 12; trans. Bréhier).

Scholastics explain *attavāda* by *sakkāyadiṭṭhi* (= Sanskrit *satkāya-dṛṣṭi*): *Dhammasaṅgaṇi*, 1217; *Vibhaṅga*, p. 375; Buddhaghosa, *Papañca-sūdanī*, II, p. 112; *Visuddhimagga*, XVII, 243 (cf. *Sāratthappakāsinī*, II, p. 15). Cf. Sthiramati, *Triṃśikā-bhāṣya*, p. 23, l. 12: *upādānaskandheṣv ātmeti darśanam ātmadṛṣṭiḥ satkāyadṛṣṭir ity arthaḥ.* See also *Abhidharma-kośabhāṣya*, V, 9, p. 283 (*AK.* V, p. 22).

This interpretation manifestly rests upon the fact that the conception of *ātman* usually criticized by the Pāli texts is that which identifies the *ātman* with the *upādānaskandhas*: cf. *S.* XXII, 47 (vol. III, p. 46): *ye hi keci, bhikkhave, samaṇā vā brāhmaṇā vā anekavihitaṃ attānaṃ samanupassamānā samanupassanti, sabbe te pañcupādāna-kkhandhe samanupassanti, etesaṃ vā aññataraṃ. M.*, Sutta 35, attributes this conception to the Nigaṇṭhaputta Saccaka; but some disciples of the Buddha are themselves guilty of heresy in adopting it: thus Yamaka, *S.* XXII, 85.

But rather than limit ourselves to a single *vāda*, would it not be preferable to say, in accordance with the totality of Buddhist literature, that the expressions *attavāda, attadiṭṭhi* include all *vāda*s whatsoever? The *ātman* is not the idea of it as conceived by us: *nātmadṛṣṭiḥ svayam ātmalakṣaṇā.*—See also Rāhula, *op. cit.*, p. 86.

In short, whatever may be the meaning of *attavāda* ("theory of the *ātman*," or "view of the *ātman* [in that which is not the *ātman*, that is to say, the *upādānaskandhas*]"), there is nothing which would allow us to say that the Buddha denied the *ātman*.

---

a. S. Lévi's translation.

b. *dvayān na cānyad bhrama eṣa tūditaḥ.*—*taditas*, in the text, is nothing but a misreading (or misprint?) for *tūditas*, as S. Lévi noted in his personal copy of the work (which may be consulted at the Institut de Civilisation indienne de l'Université de Paris). One should not therefore take into account the correction proposed by E. Leumann: *tad-gatas* (St. Schayer, "Die Erlösungslehren der Yogācāra's nach dem Sūtrālaṃkāra des Asaṅga," *Zeitschrift für Indologie und Iranistik*, II [1923], p. 117, n. 2).

c. Cf. *supra*, p. 6 and n. 36.

d. The heresy of Yamaka, *S.* XXII, 85: *tathāhaṃ Bhagavatā dhammaṃ desitaṃ ājānāmi, yathā khīṇāsavo bhikkhu kāyassa bhedā ucchijjati vinassati, na hoti paraṃ maraṇā ti.*—Cf. *supra*, n. 38.

e. Cf. *MaiU.* III, 2: *amṛto 'syātmā bindur iva puṣkare.*—*Kaṭha-Up.* V, 11:

sūryo yathā sarvalokasya cakṣur
na lipyate cākṣuṣair bāhyadoṣaiḥ |
ekas tathā sarvabhūtāntarātmā
na lipyate lokaduḥkhena bāhyaḥ ||

BhG. XIII, 31-32:

anāditvān nirguṇatvāt paramātmāyam avyayaḥ |
śarīrastho 'pi kaunteya na karoti na lipyate ||
yathā sarvagataṃ saukṣmyād ākāśaṃ nopalipyate |
sarvatrāvasthito dehe tathātmā nopalipyate ||

See also *Māṇḍ.Kār.* III, 5; *Madhyamakahṛdaya*, VIII, 12 (Gokhale, *loc. cit.*, p. 175); *Ratnagotravibhāga*, I, 52.—*Supra*, n. 31; p. 29.

f. The *ātman-brahman* is compared to a treasure buried in the depths of our being. Even though established in us from all eternity, we do not see it, distracted as we are by the world of appearances: *tadyathāpi hiraṇyanidhiṃ nihitam akṣetrajñā upary upari saṃcaranto na vindeyuḥ, evam evemāḥ sarvāḥ prajā ahar ahar gacchantya etaṃ brahmalokaṃ na vindanti, anṛtena hi pratyūḍhāḥ*, *ChU.* VIII, 3, 2. (For *anṛta*, cf. *infra*, n. 91. On *brahmaloka*, see *supra*, p. 47.—*ahar ahar gacchantyaḥ*: it refers to the state of profound sleep, cf. *ChU.* VI, 9, 2, and *infra*, p. 69, n. c).—Cf. *MaiU.* VI, 28; *Vivekacūḍāmaṇi*, 65, 302.—*Ātmabodha*, 44:

ātmā tu satataṃ prāpto 'py aprāptavad avidyayā |
tannāśe prāptavad bhāti svakaṇṭhābharaṇaṃ yathā ||

The image of a treasure is found again in Mahāyānic texts, apropos the *ātman-Tathāgatagarbha.* Cf. Lamotte, *Vimalakīrti*, p. 56 (Mahāyānic *Mahāparinirvāṇa-Sūtra*). See also *infra*, pp. 193 and 194.

g. The translation of Suzuki (*The Laṅkāvatāra Sūtra* [London, 1932], p. 23; cf. also La Vallée Poussin, *Siddhi*, II, p. 668): "Thou dost not vanish in Nirvāṇa, nor is Nirvāṇa abiding in thee" (*na nirvāsi nirvāṇe na nirvāṇaṃ tvayi saṃsthitam*), does not seem to be exact.

h. *sadasatpakṣavarjitam*: cf. *ṚV.* X, 129, 1-2; *ŚB.* X, 5, 3, 1.—*Śvet. Up.* IV, 18: *yadātamas tan na divā na rātrir na san na cāsac chiva eva kevalaḥ.*—*BhG.* XIII, 12: *jñeyaṃ yat tat pravakṣyāmi yaj jñātvāmṛtam aśnute | anādimat paraṃ brahma na sat tan nāsad ucyate ||*—*Subāla-Up.* XIII (Radhakrishnan, *Up.*, p. 888); *Kaivalya-Up.* 24 (*infra*, p. 98, n. 173).—BEFEO. III, p. 22, st. I ("stèle des hôpitaux" of Jayavarman VII, Buddhist king of Cambodia, at Sai Fong [1186 A.D.]): *bhāvābhāva-dvayātīto 'dvayātmā yo* [*Buddho*] *nirātmakaḥ.*—Murti, pp. 228 ff.—*Infra*, p. 188.

61. *Kaṭha-Up.* II, 23; *Muṇḍ.Up.* III, 2, 3. Cf. *TU.* II, 4 and 9: *yato vāco nivartante aprāpya manasā saha* ("Whence words return along with the mind, without having attained it").—*Kena.Up.* I, 3-9; II, 1-3; *Kaṭha-Up.* II, 7, 9; VI, 12-13; *Muṇḍ.Up.* III, 1, 8; *BhG.* II, 29.—*MKV.*, p. 57: *paramārtho hy āryāṇāṃ tūṣṇīṃbhāvaḥ* (cf. J. W. De Jong, "Textcritical Notes on the Prasannapadā," *IIJ.* 20 [1978], p. 33).—*Ibid.*, p. 264 (word of Buddha): *anakṣarasya dharmasya śrutiḥ kā | śrūyate deśyate cāpi samāropād anakṣaraḥ ||*—*Laṅk.*, p. 16: *na maunais tathāgatair bhāṣitam, maunā hi tathāgatāḥ . . .* —*Ibid.*, II, 119: *tattvaṃ hy akṣaravarjitaṃ.*—*Ibid.*, III, 7: *yasyāṃ ca rātryāṃ dhigamo yasyāṃ ca parinirvṛtaḥ | etasminn antare nāsti mayā kiṃcit prakāśitam ||*—*Ibid.*, *Sagāthaka*, v. 220: *paramārthas tv anakṣaraḥ.*—*MK.* XXV, 24 (cf. *infra*, p. 70, n. e; n. 243): *sarvopalambhopaśamaḥ prapañcopaśamaḥ śivaḥ | na kvacit kasyacit kaścid dharmo Buddhena deśitaḥ ||*—*Niraupamya-stava*, 7: *nodāhṛtaṃ tvayā kiṃcid ekam apy akṣaraṃ vibho.*—*Paramārtha-stava*, 1: *vākpathātītagocaram.* [G. Tucci, "Two Hymns of the Catuḥ-stava of Nāgārjuna," *JRAS.* 1932, pp. 309-325.]

See, especially, V. Bhattacharya, *The Basic Conception of Buddhism* (University of Calcutta, 1934), pp. 19 ff., and *Gauḍapādīyam Āgamaśāstram*, pp. 198 ff.—Cf. Radhakrishnan, *Gautama the Buddha*[2] (Bombay, Hind Kitabs, 1946), p. 62, n. 3; Murti, pp. 231, 232, 244; Venkata Ramanan, pp. 273-274; *Vimalakīrtinirdeśa*, VIII, 33 (Lamotte, *Vimalakīrti*, pp. 317-318) [cf. Suzuki, *Outlines . . .*, p. 107].

"The final answer to the question of the nature of the Ātman is that recorded for us in a legend by Śaṅkara: Vāṣkali asked Bāhva as to the nature of the Brahman: the latter remained silent, and on being pressed for an answer replied, 'I teach you, indeed, but you understand not: silence is Ātman,'" Keith, *RPhVU.* II, p. 522 (cf. Śaṅkara, *Brahmasūtra-bhāṣya*, III, 2, 17; Deussen *AGPh.* I, 2, p. 143; *upaśānto 'yam ātmā* = "this *ātman* is appeased": cf. Nāgārjuna, *MK.* XXV, 24 [above]; XVIII, 9).—"Not the muteness of nescience, but the silence of that knowledge beyond knowledge, of the supreme fullness of insight and inner sensibility," Oldenberg, *LUAB.*[2], p. 116.—To be compared with Jaspers: "The ultimate of thought, as of communication, is silence" (*Vernunft und Existenz* [= *Aula-Voordrachten der Rijksuniversiteit te Groningen*, No. 1, 1935], p. 74).

Appropriate remarks from Stcherbatsky, *op. cit.*, pp. 21-22, against La Vallée Poussin and Keith, who make an "agnostic" out of the Buddha. See also Radhakrishnan, *Indian Philosophy*[2], I, Appendix, §§ VI-VII; *Gautama the Buddha*[2], pp. 43 ff.; Murti, ch. II.

In the verse of the *Kaṭha-* and of the *Muṇḍaka-Upaniṣad* which we have quoted, the notion of grace makes its first appearance in India ("Only, one who is elected may attain it . . ."): Barth, *Œuvres*, I, p. 76, n. 1; Deussen, *AGPh.* I, 2, p. 72; R. G. Bhandarkar, *Vaiṣṇavism, Śaivism and Minor Religious Systems* (= *Grundriss der indo-arischen Philologie und Altertumskunde*, III. Band, 6. Heft, Strassburg, 1913), p. 29; etc.—But, for us, that matters little. "When, however, we lapse back from this state into ordinary consciousness, we represent the self as another with its transcendent majesty. We quake and shiver, bleed and moan with a longing gaze at it. We dare not even lift up our eyes. We are filled with a desire to escape from the world of discord and struggle. In this mood we represent the supreme as the sovereign personality encompassing this whole world, working through the cosmos and ourselves for the realization of the universal kingdom. If the personal concept is more prominent, the individual seeks his development in a humble, trustful submission to God. We may adopt the mode of *bhakti* or devotion, or the method of *jñāna* or contemplation by which the self, set free from all that is not self, regains its pure dignity. *The attainment of spiritual status when refracted in the logical universe appears as a revelation of grace,*" Radhakrishnan, *Eastern Religion and Western Thought*[2], pp. 28-29 (our italics).—See also "Le 'védisme' de certains textes hindouistes," *JA.* 1967, p. 210 and n. 59.

62. Cf. *BĀU*, IV, 4, 10 (= *Īśā-Up.* 9):

andhaṃ tamaḥ praviśanti ye 'vidyām upāsate |
tato bhūya iva tamo ya u vidyāyāṃ ratāḥ ||

Cf. also *BĀU.* III, 5 (repeated in *Subāla-Up.* XIII: Radhakrishnan, *Up.*, p. 888), with Saṅkara, *Brahmasūtra-bhāṣya*, III, 4, 50 (differently, *Bṛhadāraṇyakopaniṣad-bhāṣya*), and Deussen, *Up.*, p. 435; Radhakrishnan, *Up.*, p. 222.—*BĀU.* IV, 4, 21; the story of the *bāliśa* in the *Chāgaleya-Upaniṣad* (cf. L. Renou, *Chāgaleya-Upaniṣad* [Paris, 1959], p. 8, n. 14).

Sn. 800 (cf. 911): *attaṃ pahāya anupādiyāno ñāṇe pi so nissayaṃ no karoti.*

MK. XIII, 8:

śūnyatā sarvadṛṣṭīnāṃ proktā niḥsaraṇaṃ jinaiḥ |
yeṣāṃ tu śūnyatādṛṣṭis tān asādhyān babhāṣire ||

Ratnakūṭa (= *Kāśyapaparivarta*), cited *MKV.*, p. 248-249 (ed. A. von Staël-Holstein [Shanghai, 1926], §§ 64-65, pp. 95, 97). Cf. Stcherbatsky, *op. cit.*, pp. 49-50; Murti, pp. 160 ff.; Venkata Ramanan, pp. 130-133, 136, 168, 172.

Samādhirāja-Sūtra, XXXII, 3 (ed. P. L. Vaidya, Darbhanga, 1961 [= *Buddhist Sanskrit Texts*, No. 2]):

bahavo 'cintiyā dharmā ye śabdena prakāśitāḥ |
yas tatra niviśec chabde saṃdhābhāṣyaṃ na jānati ||

A formulated truth is comparable to a finger with which one indicates something. One who looks only at the end of the finger does not see the object indicated; similarly, one who is attached only to the word cannot perceive the Truth: *Laṅk.*, p. 196 (cf. VI, 3); Lamotte, *Traité*, I, p. 538 (cf. Venkata Ramanan, p. 130).

See also *Amṛtanāda-Up.* 1 (in *Thirty-two Upaniṣads* = *Ānandāśrama Sanskrit Series*, 29, Poona, 1895); *Amṛtabindu-Up.* 18 *(ibid.)*; *Viveka-cūḍāmaṇi*, 56 ff., 356, 476-477; *Aṣṭāvakra-Gītā*, XVI, 1.

To meditate, it is necessary to know; but, without the help of meditation, true knowledge is not obtained:

n' atthi jhānaṃ apaññassa paññā n' atthi ajjhāyato |
yamhi jhānañ ca paññā ca sa ve nibbānasantike ||

Dhp. 372.—Cf. *Śivadharmottara*, fol. 49 b (manuscript cited above, p. 54, n. 58):

nāsti jñānaṃ vinā dhyānaṃ nāsti jñānam ayoginaḥ |
jñānaṃ dhyānaṃ ca yasyāsti tīrṇas tena bhavārṇavaḥ ||

Jñāna is abstract theoretical knowledge, which can be acquired through the reading of books and from masters; *vijñāna* is the *anubhava* or "integral experience": F. Edgerton, *"Jñāna and vijñāna,"* in *Festschrift M. Winternitz* (Leipzig, 1933), pp. 217-220; cf. Hiriyanna, *The Quest after Perfection*, pp. 60, 108-109; *Popular Essays in Indian Philosophy*, pp. 14 ff.; O. Lacombe, *"Jñānaṃ savijñānam,"* in *Mélanges Louis Renou*, pp. 439 ff. (In the Buddhist texts in Sanskrit, it is *vijñāna* which designates "empirical discursive knowledge," and *jñāna*, "metaphysical intuitive knowledge": May, n. 252; wrongly, Edgerton, *Dictionary*, s.v. *vijñāna*.)

paravediyaṃ diṭṭhim upātivatto, Sn. 474. Cf. *M.* II, pp. 234-235 (cited by Jayatilleke, p. 276); V. Trenckner, etc., *A Critical Pāli Dictionary* (Copenhagen, 1924—), s.v. *a-para-(p)paccaya* (cf. *a-para-pratyaya, MK.* XVIII, 9, with the commentary by Candrakīrti).—See also *infra*, pp. 181-182.

An opposition between *jñāna* and *darśana* is also spoken of. Thus, Venkata Ramanan, p. 355 a-b, n. 10: "After reading or reciting the scriptures following other people, to weigh or consider (the meaning of what is read or recited), this is *jñāna*; (thereupon) to realize the truth in one's self is *darśana*; the one is not necessarily free from doubt, whereas the other is the direct personal knowledge, clear understanding free from doubt."—The word *darśana* is employed here in the sense opposite to that noted above, n. 60 (on the various meanings of the word, see May, n. 10). Note that the word *dṛṣṭi/diṭṭhi* is also sometimes employed in this sense: *dhammañ ca ñāsi paramāya diṭṭhiyā, Sn.* 471; *anuttarā ca te nātha dṛṣṭis tattvadarśinī, Niraupamya-stava,* 2 (reference, above, n. 61).—On *dassana*, in the *Nikāyas*, see Jayatilleke, Index, s.v. *ñāṇa*.—Cf. *infra*, n. 86 end; p. 185, n. 34.

63. *sthāpayann agrataḥ kiṃcit tanmātre nāvatiṣṭhate,* Vasubandhu, *Triṃśikā,* 27.—Cf. Jaspers, *Introduction à la Philosophie* (= *Einführung in die Philosophie*; translation by J. Hersch, ed. 10/18, Paris, 1965), pp. 28-29.

64. *ekaṅgadassino, Ud.* VI, 4, p. 69. Our text illustrates this idea by means of a well-known parable: an elephant is presented to those blind from birth who imagine it, one as a pot, another as a fan, another as a plough, another as a broom and so on, according to whether they touch the head, an ear, the trunk or the tail of the animal; but they don't know what an elephant is. Each one, however, keeps to his idea, and a fistfight ensues from the conflict of opinions (origin of philosophical quarrels).—Cf. *Sn.* 878 ff.; Lamotte, *Traité,* I, pp. 39 ff.; Venkata Ramanan, pp. 128-130; and the definitions, "incomplete" (*akṛtsna*), "one-footed" (*ekapād*), of *brahman-ātman* which the *Bṛhadāraṇyaka-Upaniṣad* criticizes (I, 4, 7; II, 1 [cf. *Kauṣ.Up.* IV]; III, 9, 10-17. 26; IV, 1-2). The *Chāndogya* (V, 11-18; cf. *ŚB.* X, 6, 1) offers an exact parallel with the account of the *Udāna,* when it criticizes the views of six learned brahmins, with regard to the *ātman vaiśvānara* (Agni *vaiśvānara* in the *ŚB.*). These brahmins, incapable of embracing with thought Reality in its fullness, take the parts for the whole; and Śaṅkara, commenting on this text, recalls

precisely that parable of the elephant and the people blind from birth (*hasti-darśana iva jātyandhāḥ, Chāndogyopaniṣad-bhāṣya,* V, 18, 1).—See also *Ārṣeya-Upaniṣad* (cited above, n. 57).—*Infra*, n. 71 end.

Is the whole obtained by adding together the parts?—No, it is not, for, to speak truly, "They are not *component parts,* but *partial expressions,* which is an entirely different thing" (Bergson, *Introduction à la Métaphysique,* in *La Pensée et le Mouvant,* 63rd edition, Paris, Presses universitaires de France, 1966, p. 192).—See also Belvalkar-Ranade, p. 384.

65. Jaspers, *Introduction à la Philosophie,* p. 34 (edition cited).

66. *tumhehi kiccam ātappaṃ, akkhātāro tathāgatā, Dhp.* 276.—To be compared with Plotinus, *Enneads,* VI, 9, 4: ". . . our words and our writings tend towards it; they bring us out of language so as to awaken us to contemplation; in some way they show the path to one who wants to contemplate. For, one goes as far as teaching him the route and the road; as for contemplation, it is the work of the one who himself wants to contemplate" (Trans. Bréhier). Cf. also Jaspers: "I have nothing to proclaim. It is up to the hearer, not merely to follow the statements of the speaker, but to examine them within his own being and at best to take them as an occasion of ascertaining something for himself" (*Der philosophische Glaube* [Zürich, 1948], p. 127).

See also Oldenberg, *Buddha* (ed. 1961), p. 302 [= Oldenberg-Foucher[4], p. 365]; Coomaraswamy, *The Living Thoughts of Gotama the Buddha,* p. 22; Rāhula, *op. cit.*, ch. I; Lamotte, *Histoire,* p. 50; Radhakrishnan, *Gautama the Buddha*[2], pp. 11 ff., 64-65.—*Infra,* pp. 133, 181-182.

67. *M.* I, pp. 134-135, 260-261. Cf. *Sn.* 21; Lamotte, *Traité,* I, p. 64 and n. 1. See also above, n. 58; and "Suppléments aux Recherches sur le Vocabulaire des inscriptions sanskrites du Cambodge," I, *BEFEO.* LIII, 1 (1966), pp. 274-275.

"But one who studies, solely to arrive at a personal point of view, considers books and studies as steps of a ladder, which must carry him to the heights of knowledge. Once a level has been passed, it no longer preoccupies him. Those, on the other hand, who study solely to fill up their memory, do not use the steps of the ladder to raise themselves higher, but they collect them carefully and impose upon themselves the task of carrying them, delighted with the feeling that the weight of their burden is increasing; this is why they always stay on the ground. They carry what should have carried themselves," Schopenhauer, *Le Monde comme Volonté et comme Représentation*

(French translation by A. Burdeau, new edition, revised and corrected by R. Roos, Paris, 1966), p. 758.—"In the light of his early reading of Schopenhauer, it is not uninteresting to compare this figure with the image of the ladder which once climbed must be thrown away, used by Wittgenstein at the end of the *Tractatus* to show how the propositions of his book should be read and understood," P. Gardiner, *Schopenhauer* ("Penguin Books," 1963), p. 226, n. Cf. also Jayatilleke, p. 357, n. 3.

68. *vyavahāram anāśritya paramārtho na deśyate*, *MK.* XXIV, 10.—*upāyabhūtaṃ vyavahārasatyam, upeyabhūtaṃ paramārthasatyam*, *Madhyamakāvatāra*, VI, 80, cited *BCAP.* p. 179.—

tathya-saṃvṛti-sopānam antareṇa vipaścitaḥ |
tattva-prāsāda-śikharārohaṇaṃ na hi yujyate ||

verse cited *AAĀ.*, p. 346.—Cf. Murti, pp. 232, 253 (cf. pp. 154 ff.); Venkata Ramanan, pp. 40-41, 84 ff., 260-261; and our translation of the *Vigrahavyāvartanī*, in *Journal of Indian Philosophy*, I, 3 (November 1971: Th. Stcherbatsky Centennial Issue), pp. 236-237, v. XXVIII.

In the text cited above, n. 38 (last paragraph), the Buddha says: Only, one who knows the world can attain to the "end of the world," *lokavidū . . . lokantagū* (*S.* I, p. 62, *gāthā*).

69. Radhakrishnan, *Up.*, p. 554. Cf. Augustine, *Confessions*, VII, 23, cited *ibid.*, p. 557 (cf. *Indian Philosophy*[2], II, p. 480, n. 4).

70. Cf. *supra*, n. 29.

71. *TU.* II and III.—The idea expressed by this text is already found, in less developed form, in *ChU.* VIII, 7-12 (cf. Keith, *RPhVU.* II, pp. 517-518; Dasgupta, *op. cit.*, pp. 13-14; Radhakrishnan, *Up.*, p. 510). See also *Ait.Ār.* II, 3, 2, and the long, and rather disorganized, development contained in *ChU.* VII (cf. Belvalkar-Ranade, pp. 230 ff.).—*Infra*, n. 135.

Beatitude *(ānanda)*, in the *Taittirīya-Upaniṣad*, is manifestly opposed to fear *(bhaya)*, which has its origins in the sense of the dualities of the empirical world.[a] Thus *TU.* II, 9 (cf. *BĀU.* IV, 4, 22):

yato vāco nivartante aprāpya manasā saha |
ānandaṃ brahmaṇo vidvān na bibheti kutaścana ||

etaṃ ha vāva na tapati: kim ahaṃ sādhu nākaravam, kim ahaṃ pāpam akaravam iti. sa ya evaṃ vidvān ete ātmānaṃ spṛṇute, ubhe hy evaiṣa ete ātmānaṃ spṛṇute ya evaṃ veda.

Cf. *ibid.*, II, 7: *yadā hy evaiṣa etasminn adṛśye 'nātmye 'nirukte 'nilayane 'bhayaṃ pratiṣṭhāṃ vindate, atha so 'bhayaṃ gato bhavati. yadā hy etasminn udaram antaraṃ*[b] *kurute, atha tasya bhayaṃ bhavati. tat tv eva bhayaṃ viduṣo 'manvānasya.* [Let us note the expression *viduṣo 'manvānasya,* "of the scholar who does not understand," or (which comes to the same thing) *viduṣo manvānasya,* "of one who thinks himself wise" (because he makes of *brahman* an object of knowledge, and who thus does not understand). Cf. *TU.* I, 4, 1: *brahmaṇaḥ kośo 'si medhayāpihitaḥ.*]

BĀU. I, 4, 2: *yan mad anyan nāsti, kasmān nu bibhemi . . . dvitīyād vai bhayaṃ bhavati.* When everything has become my *ātman,* when otherness is transcended, of whom or what could I be afraid? Cf. *MaiU.* VI, 30: *pareṣv ātmavad vigatabhayaḥ.* (*sarvātmabrahmarūpatvāt pareṣu jīvāntareṣv ātmavad ātmanīva vigatabhayo nirātaṅkaḥ, na cāsya dvitīyadarśananimittaṃ bhayaṃ bhavatīty arthaḥ. ātmā hy eṣāṃ sa bhavatīti śrutyantarāt* [*BĀU.* I, 4, 10], Rāmatīrtha.)

Brahman-ātman = *abhaya:* cf. *BĀU.* IV, 2, 4; 3, 21; 4, 25; *ChU.* VIII, 3, 4 (= *MaiU.* II, 2); *Kaṭha-Up.* III, 2; *Praśna-Up.* V, 7. See also above, n. 38, and cf. *BhG.* XV, 5:

> *nirmānamohā jitasaṅgadoṣā*
> *adhyātmanityā vinivṛttakāmāḥ* |
> *dvandvair vimuktāḥ sukhaduḥkhasaṃjñair*
> *gacchanty amūḍhāḥ padam avyayaṃ tat* ||

(Cf. *ibid.*, II, 45: *nirdvandvo nityasattvastho niryogakṣema ātmavān.*)

Mbh. XII, 9924:

> *ubhe satyānṛte tyaktvā śokānandau priyāpriye* |
> *bhayābhaye ca saṃtyajya saṃpraśānto nirāmayaḥ* ||

Cf. Hiriyanna, *Popular Essays in Indian Philosophy,* pp. 80-81: ". . . the joy . . . is of a superior transcendental kind, such as is meant by the old saying: *sukhaṃ duḥkhasukhātyayaḥ.* Rather it is not joy at all, in the common acceptation of the term, but peace or repose that ever is the same."

The same idea, *Ud.* I, 10, p. 9 (= *Netti,* p. 150): *atha rūpā arūpā ca sukhadukkhā pamuccati.* Cf. *Kevaddha (Kevaṭṭa)-Sutta,* below, p. 24; *S.* XXXVI, 3, 6, 3 (vol. IV, p. 205); and *Sn.* 228:

> *ye suppayuttā manasā daḷhena*
> *nikkāmino Gotamasāsanamhi* |
> *te pattipattā amataṃ vigayha*
> *laddhā mudhā nibbutiṃ bhuñjamānā* ||

—*nibbānaṃ paramaṃ sukhaṃ, M.* I, p. 508; *Dhp.* 204. See also *infra,* pp. 121-122, 239 (*A.* IV, p. 14); *Ud.* VIII, 10 (*infra,* p. 166, n. 116).—*nibbānaṃ abhayaṃ, Therīgāthā,* cited above, n. 38. Cf. Radhakrishnan, *Indian Philosophy*², I, p. 448: *Nirvāṇa* = "completeness of being, eternal beatitude exalted high above the joys and sorrows of the world." See also Rāhula, *op. cit.*, p. 69.

In the ancient Upaniṣads, *ānanda* is not the object of an experience, but that experience itself, in which disappears, as in deep sleep (cf. *BĀU.* II, 1, 19; IV, 3, 19-33), all distinction between subject and object; man torn from the I of limited consciousness, identifies with the universal Being. Cf. Śaṅkara on *BĀU.* III, 9, 28, 7; Deussen, *AGPh.* I, 2, pp. 90, 129-134.

It is however characteristic of the ulterior spiritualization that the state of deep dreamless sleep (*suṣupti-* or *suṣuptam*), as well as the beatitude (*ānanda*) inherent in it, is no longer considered the supreme goal (*paramā gatiḥ, BĀU.* IV, 3, 32) of man but simply a transitory state, where the absence of duality is only apparent, because it contains the seed (*bīja*) of objective consciousness: sleep over, man returns to the dreaming and waking states. To the three states known to the ancient Upaniṣads,[c]—that of waking, that of dreaming and that of sleeping,—is thus added a "fourth" (*caturtha, tur[ī]ya*), which is not a "state," because it is "invisible" (*adṛṣṭa*), "impalpable" (*avyavahārya*),[d] "ungraspable" (*agrāhya*), "without distinctive mark" (*alakṣaṇa*), "imponderable" (*acintya*), "unnamable" (*avyapadeśya*). The play of phenomena ends there (*prapañcopaśama*).[e] Man, illumined by the light of the *ātman*, becomes that light itself.[f] The "fourth"—the *ātman*—has for its essence simply certitude regarding itself (*ekātmapratyayasāra*).[g] *Māṇḍ.Up.*; *MaiU.* VI, 19 (*supra*, n. 29); VII, 11. Cf. Gauḍapāda, *Māṇḍ.Kār.* I, 11-16; III, 33 ff., with commentary by Śaṅkara.—Śaṅkara, *Brahmasūtra-bhāṣya*, II, 1, 9 (p. 447):

suṣuptisamādhyādāv api satyāṃ svābhāvikyām avibhāgaprāptau mithyājñānasyānapoditatvāt pūrvavat punaḥ prabodhe vibhāgo bhavati.—*Ibid.*, II, 3, 31 (p. 612): *suṣuptād utthānam avidyātmakabījasadbhāvakāritam.*—*Ibid.*, III, 2, 9 (p. 705): *sa evāyam upādhiḥ svāpaprabodhayor bījāṅkuranyāyena.* Cf. Śaṅkara, *Upadeśasāhasrī, padya,* XVI, 18: *jāgratsvapnau tayor bījaṃ suṣuptākhyaṃ tamomayam.*—*Ibid.*, XVII, 26: *suṣuptākhyaṃ tamo 'jñānaṃ bījaṃ svapnaprabodhayoḥ.*—*Vivekacūḍāmaṇi*, 121: *bījātmanāvasthitir eva buddheḥ.* Cf. Deussen, *AGPh.* I, 2, pp. 278 ff. (interpretation wrong; as in Oltramare, *L'histoire des idées théosophiques dans l'Inde,* I [= *Annales du Musée Guimet, Bibliothèque d'études,* t. XXIII, Paris, 1906], p. 124). Important notes by Radhakrishnan on the *Māṇḍūkya-Upaniṣad* (Radhakrishnan, *Up.*, pp. 695 ff.). See also Belvalkar-Ranade, pp. 322 ff.

Note the comparison between *suṣupti* and *samādhi.* Gauḍapāda criticizes the *yogins*, who seek only to escape momentarily from the sorrowful world, by way of *samādhi.* Lacking intuition of the Truth, they take the empirical I for an authentic I, and, accordingly, they experience the greatest terror in the face of the only valid *yoga,* as taught by Vedānta, that is "*yoga* without contact" (*asparśayoga*), or the experience of the *ātman,* in which disappears individual consciousness (which, from the empirical point of view, appears to be nothing but annihilation). This fear is all the more ridiculous since it is precisely in the experience of the *ātman* that all the torments of the empirical world are quietened (cf. above):

asparśayogo vai nāma durdarśaḥ sarvayogibhiḥ |
yogino bibhyati hy asmād abhaye bhayadarśinaḥ ||

Māṇḍ.Kār. III, 39 (cf. IV, 2).—Cf. Śaṅkara: *asparśayogo nāmāyaṃ sarvasaṃbandhākhyasparśavarjitatvād asparśayogo nāma vai smaryate, prasiddha upaniṣatsu. duḥkhena dṛśyata iti durdarśaḥ. sarvayogibhiḥ: vedāntavihitavijñānarahitaiḥ sarvayogibhiḥ. ātmasatyānubodhāyāsalabhya evety arthaḥ. yogino bibhyati hy asmāt sarvabhayavarjitād api, ātmanāśarūpam imaṃ yogaṃ manyamānā bhayaṃ kurvanti. abhaye 'smin bhayadarśinaḥ: bhayanimittātmanāśadarśanaśīlā avivekina ity arthaḥ.* See also *supra*, p. 7, and cf. *Aṣṭāvakra-Gītā,* cited below, p. 80.—*abhaye bhayadarśinaḥ*: cf. what Nāgārjuna writes on the subject of ignorant people, when they hear Nirvāṇa spoken of:

sarvaduḥkhakṣayaṃ dharmaṃ śrutvaivam aparīkṣakaḥ |
saṃtrasyaty aparijñānād abhayasthānakātaraḥ ||

(*Ratnāvalī*, I, 39 [ed. M. Hahn, Bonn, 1982 (*Indica et Tibetica,* 1); cf. v. 77]).—Cf. *infra*, p. 195 and n. 50.

Gauḍapāda, it is true, recommends the yogic method, but simply as a subordinate method for arriving at the goal (III, 40 ff.; cf. Śaṅkara on III, 48: *sarvo 'py ayaṃ manonigrahādir mṛllohādivat sṛṣṭir upāsanā coktā paramārthasvarūpapratipattyupāyatvena, na paramārthasatyeti*).—Cf. *BhG.*, ch. VI. See also *JA.* 1972, pp. 96-97.

The three ways of representing the *ātman* (as *oḷārika,* as *manomaya,* and as *saññāmaya*), which the *Poṭṭhapāda-Sutta* of *Dīgha-Nikāya* criticizes (I, pp. 186-187; cf. pp. 195 ff.), recall, there can be no doubt about it, the *annamaya-*, the *manomaya-*, and the *vijñānamaya-ātman* of the *Taittirīya-Upaniṣad.* Cf. Hajime Nakamura, "Upaniṣadic tradition and the early school of Vedānta as noticed in Buddhist Scripture," *HJAS.* 18 (1955), p. 79; Jayatilleke, pp. 317 ff. (on the equivalence *saṃjñā/saññā = vijñāna/viññāṇa*, cf. below, n. 160). See also, apropos the seven theories of the *ātman* which the *Brahmajāla-Sutta* criticizes (*D.* I, pp. 34-36), Rhys Davids, *Dialogues of the Buddha,* I (= *Sacred Books of the Buddhists,* edited by F. Max Müller, vol. II, London, 1899 [reprint: 1956]), p. 48, n. 3.—Contrary, however, to what these authors think, there is no question, in the Pāli texts, of polemics against the *Taittirīya-Upaniṣad*: whereas the Pāli texts condemn fixed "points of view" (*diṭṭhi*), relative to the *ātman,* the *Taittirīya-Upaniṣad* speaks of "envelopes" (*kośa*)[h] of the ineffable Reality, and of a progressive search, which proceeds from the most superficial to the most profound: the *ānandamaya-ātman,* ultimate term of this progression, is not an object of knowledge as opposed to a knowing subject, but the Reality itself in its plenitude, before which speech ceases along with thought (*yato vāco nivartante aprāpya manasā saha*). Basically, therefore, the Pāli texts say exactly the same thing as the Upaniṣads: the Truth, one and absolute, is not the field of discursive knowledge (which tends inevitably to divide it up into particular concepts, limited and contradictory: cf. *supra,* n. 64), but it is the object of the sage's most intimate experience. —Cf. F. O. Schrader, "On the problem of Nirvāṇa," *JPTS.* 1904-1905, p. 168: ". . . the sixty-two *diṭṭhigatāni* [of the *Brahmajāla-Sutta*] are not condemned in every respect by the Buddha, but only as far as their imperfectness and exclusiveness are concerned." See also *Some Thoughts,* p. 18, n. 51.

---

a. In fact, the *ānanda/abhaya* transcends even the empirical opposition between *bhaya* and *abhaya* (cf. below, *Mbh.* XII, 9924). The words *ānanda, abhaya* do nothing but *indicate* an inexpressible experience.

b. Cf. *Bhāgavata-Purāṇa,* III, 29, 26:

ātmanaś ca parasyāpi yaḥ karoty antarodaram |
tasya bhinnadṛśo mṛtyur vidadhe bhayam ulbaṇam ||

Śaṅkara: *ud aram* = *alpam api.* Cf. also *Vivekacūḍāmaṇi,* 330:

yadā kadā vāpi vipaścid eṣa
brahmaṇy anante 'py aṇumātrabhedam |
paśyaty athāmuṣya bhayaṃ tadaiva
yad vīkṣitaṃ bhinnatayā pramādāt ||

c. The *Chāndogya-Upaniṣad,* however, seems already to recognize, implicitly, a fourth, when it says, for example, that creatures do not know the *ātman-brahman,* though they daily attain to it in the state of deep sleep (VIII, 3, 2, *supra,* p. 59, n. f), and that they only know it when they are illumined by its light (VIII, 3, 4; 12, 3). Cf. Śaṅkara, *Chāndogyopaniṣad-bhāṣya*, VI, 9, 2-3; VIII, 3, 2-4; VIII, 11-12; *Brahmasūtra-bhāṣya*, I, 3, 19; II, 1, 9; II, 3, 31; III, 2, 9; IV, 4, 2. See also Belvalkar-Ranade, pp. 241, 323, 364 (last line), 373.

d. "unbetastbar" (intangible) [Deussen].

e. *prapañcopaśamaṃ śāntaṃ śivam advaitam*, *Māṇḍ.Up.* 7. Cf. Nāgārjuna, *MK.* XXV, 24: *sarvopalambhopaśamaḥ prapañcopaśamaḥ śivaḥ.* (*draṣṭavyopaśama*, *ibid.*, V, 8; cf. *infra*, p. 164, n. 95.) See also Radhagovinda Basak, *Lectures on Buddha and Buddhism* (Calcutta, 1961), p. 114. We may recall that the Buddhist Tantras adopt the theory of four "states" (La Vallée Poussin, *Siddhi*, II, p. 803).

f. *paraṃ jyotir upasaṃpadya svena rūpeṇābhiniṣpadyate*, *ChU.* VIII, 3, 4; 12, 3 (cf. *MaiU.* II, 2). Cf. *infra*, n. 83; p. 95.—On what follows in *ChU.* VIII, 12, 3 (*sa tatra paryeti jakṣat krīḍan ramamāṇaḥ strībhir vā yānair vā jñātibhir vā nopajanaṃ smarann idaṃ śarīram*), cf. Deussen, *Up.*, p. 195: "The following sensuous description is undoubtedly a later addition." In fact, the description rather fits the dream state than that of Deliverance: cf. *BĀU.* IV, 3, 10-13. Zaehner (*Hinduism* [New York, Oxford University Press, 1955], p. 75) is wrong about the meaning of the passage of the *Chāndogya-Upaniṣad*. Elsewhere, he cites *svena svena rūpeṇa*, although, in the text, we find only: *svena rūpeṇa*! It is true that in the Adyar Library Edition, *Daśopanishads with the Commentary of Śrī Upanishad-Brahma-Yogin*, vol. II (1936), we read *svena svena rūpeṇa*, but this must be a printer's error: in *ChU.* VIII, 3, 4 of the same edition, we find only *svena rūpeṇa*, and that reading is confirmed by the commentaries on the two passages.

g. "Certitude," not "knowledge": cf. *infra*, p. 23.

h. If we may be permitted to digress here: usually five *kośa*s are seen in the *Taittirīya-Upaniṣad*. This, however, is a mistake. In actual fact there is only question, in this text, of four *kośa*s (the *annamaya-*, the *prāṇamaya-*, the *manomaya-* and the *vijñānamaya-ātman* are in fact *kośa*s, even though not expressly designated by this name; but the *ānandamaya-ātman* is not a *kośa*). It is only in later texts that the theory of the *pañca kośāḥ* is met with, the *ānandamaya* being considered as the deepest "sheath" in which Reality is enclosed. The *annamayakośa* is the "gross body" (*sthūlaśarīra*) of man, the *prāṇamaya-*, the *manomaya-* and the *vijñānamaya-kośa* together constitute his "subtle body" (*liṅgaśarīra*), whilst the *ānandamayakośa* constitutes his "causal body" (*kāraṇaśarīra*). See *Paiṅgala-Up.* II, 4 (ed. A.

Mahādeva Śāstrī, in the *Sāmānya Vedānta Upanishads*, Madras, Adyar Library, 1921); *Sarvasaropaniṣad* (= *Sarvopaniṣatsāra*), 5 (in *The Sāmānya Vedānta Upaniṣads*; 2 in *Thirty-two Upaniṣads* [= *Ānandāśrama Sanskrit Series*, 29], Poona, 1895).—Contrary to what Deussen writes, *AGPh.* I, 2, p. 255, the word *kośa*, in *MaiU.* VI, 27 *(hṛdy ākāśamayaṃ kośam ānandaṃ paramālayam)*, does not mean "sheath." Rāmatīrtha glosses it by *bhāṇḍāgāra: kośo bhāṇḍāgāras tadvat sarvavastvāśrayatvāt.* Let us note, too, that *MaiU.* VI, 28 speaks of only four *kośas*: *caturjālaṃ brahmakośaṃ praṇudet* "Let the sheath of *brahman* with its four networks be moved away" (cf. J. Filliozat, *Les relations extérieures de l'Inde*, I [= *Publications de l'Institut français d'Indologie*, 2, Pondicherry, 1956], p. 42). Rāmatīrtha pointlessly introduces here the concept of *ānandamaya-kośa: catvāri jālāny upary upari veṣṭanāni yasmiṃs tac caturjālaṃ brahmakośaṃ brahmaṇaḥ kośavadācchādakam annamayaprāṇamayamanomayavijñānamayākhyaiś caturbhiḥ kośaiḥ pariveṣṭitam ānandamayakośaṃ praṇudet prerayed bhindyād iti yāvat.* The expression *caturjālaṃ brahmakośaṃ* [*prapadye*] occurs also in *Taittirīya-Āraṇyaka*, II, 19 (*annamayaprāṇamayamanomayavijñānamayaiś caturbhir jālaiḥ āvaraṇaiḥ āvṛtaṃ mukhyaṃ brahmasthānam*, Bhaṭṭabhāskara: *The Taittirīya Āraṇyaka* with the commentary of Bhaṭṭa Bhāskara Miśra, ed. A Mahadeva Sastri and K. Rangacharya, reprint, Delhi, Motilal Banarsidass, 1985, I, p. 252).

This development is a corollary to what we have indicated above: the degradation of the state of *suṣupti* to a passing state, and the introduction of a "fourth" which is beyond all relationship and which thus is neither an effect nor a cause (*Māṇḍ.Kār.* I, 11). The purely theoretical nature of this development is understood, however, when it is seen that the terms *ānanda* and *sukha* continue to be employed to designate the Absolute. Śaṅkara, in his commentary on the *Brahmasūtras*, after having given the impression of considering, in accordance with Bādarāyaṇa, *ānandamaya* as the supreme Reality (from his commentary on *Sūtra* I, 1, 12 to the beginning of his commentary on *Sūtra* I, 1, 19), suddenly adopts the theory of *pañca kośāḥ* and places the Absolute above *ānandamaya* (*Brahmasūtra-bhāṣya*, I, 1, 12-19; cf. III, 3, 11-13.—Cf. Deussen, *Das System des Vedānta* [Leipzig, 1883], pp. 149-151; G. Thibaut, *The Vedānta-Sūtras with the commentary of Śaṅkarācārya*, I [= *Sacred Books of the East*, edited by F. Max Müller, Vol. XXXIV, Oxford, 1890], p. xxxiii and n. 1; p. 71, n. 1; L. Renou, *Śaṅkara: Prolégomènes au* Vedānta [Paris, 1951], p. 65, n. 2. The theory according to which the passage would be an interpolation has been definitively demolished by Y. Kanakura, "Über die Interpolation des Śāṅkarabhāṣya zum Brahmasūtra," *Festgabe Jacobi* [= *Beiträge zur Literaturwissenschaft und Geistesgeschichte Indiens*, herausgegeben von W. Kirfel, Bonn, 1926], pp. 383-385. See also Daniel H. H. Ingalls, "The Study of Śaṅkarācārya," *Annals of the Bhandarkar Oriental Research Institute*, XXXIII [1952], p. 10). This is also the opinion that he expresses in his commentary on the *Tattirīya-Upaniṣad*. The difficulty is surmounted by means of a distinction between *ānanda* and *ānandamaya: ānandamaya ānandaprāyo nānanda eva, anātyantikatvāt*, Śaṅkara on *Māṇḍ.Up.* 5. *Ānandajñāna: na hi suṣupte nirupādhikānandatvaṃ prājñasyābhyupagantuṃ śakyam, tasya kāraṇopahitatvāt; anyathā muktatvāt punarutthānāyogāt. tasmād ānandaprācuryam evāsya svīkartuṃ yuktam ity arthaḥ*. In other words, when the expression *ānandamaya* is used, it is not the Absolute, the unconditioned *ānanda*, which is to be understood (*nirupādhikānanda*), but only an inferior reality "rich in *ānanda*" (*ānandaprāya*). This distinction may already have existed in the mind of the author of the *Māṇḍūkya-Upaniṣad*; but it is only by means of an artifice that Śaṅkara introduces it into the *Taittirīya*. The parallelism between *TU.* II, 5 and III, 6 proves that the *ānandamaya-ātman* of the first passage = the *ānanda* of the second; but, according to Śaṅkara, it is *TU.* III, 6 which speaks of *brahman*, whereas, in *TU.* II, 5, the question is merely that of a "modification" (*vikāra*) of the *brahman-ānanda*!

72. *Supra*, p. 8.—In the later Vedānta, this method is called *adhyāropāpavādanyāya*, "method of superimposition and of negation."

73. *Les grands philosophes* (= *Die grossen Philosophen*, I, translated under the direction of J. Hersch, Paris, 1963), p. 655.

74. Cf. *infra*, n. 160.

75. On the role of the consciousness, cf. *supra*, n. 38 (last paragraph); *infra*, n. 149.

76. Radhakrishnan, *Up.*, p. 558.

77. To Buddhism, the "thirst for non-existence" (*vibhava-taṇhā*) is as bad as the "thirst for existence" (*bhava-taṇhā*). Cf. Rāhula, *op. cit.*, p. 52. How could it be otherwise? As is well expressed in the *Aṣṭāvakra-Gītā* (XVI, 6 ff.), attachment *(rāga)* and aversion *(dveṣa)* are but two faces of the same thing. Aversion is only attachment disguised. Only the man very much attached to the world can want to leave it, in order to avoid its miseries (*hātum icchati saṃsāraṃ rāgī duḥkhajihāsayā*, v. 9). Schopenhauer has said the same: "Far from

being a negation of Will, suicide is a mark of intense affirmation of the Will . . . He who kills himself would like to live; he is unhappy only with his lot." (*Le Monde comme Volonté et comme Représentation*, p. 499 [edition cited]).

According to a certain conception—a later one, as we shall show further on—suicide is permitted only to those who have already transcended their phenomenal existence and who, thus, aspire neither to life nor to death: *S.* I, pp. 120 ff. (story of Godhika); III, pp. 119 ff. (story of Vakkali); *M.* III, pp. 263 ff.; *S.* IV, pp. 55 ff. (story of Channa); *Mbh.* XIII, 1749. Cf. La Vallée Poussin, "Quelques observations sur le suicide dans le Bouddhisme ancien," *Bulletin de la Classe des Lettres et des Sciences morales et politiques*, Académie royale de Belgique, séance du 1er décembre 1919, Bruxelles, 1919, pp. 685-693; Lamotte, *Traité*, II, pp. 740-742 in note; J. Filliozat, "La mort volontaire par le feu et la tradition bouddhique indienne," *JA.* 1963, pp. 21-51; Lamotte, "Le Suicide religieux dans le bouddhisme ancien," *Bulletin de la Classe des Lettres et des Sciences morals et politiques*, Académie royale de Belgique, 5e série, t. LI, Bruxelles, 1965, pp. 156 ff.; D. Seyfort Ruegg, *Buddha-nature, Mind and the Problem of Gradualism in a Comparative Perspective, On the Transmission and Reception of Buddhism in India and Tibet*, London, School of Oriental and African Studies, University of London, 1989 (*Jordan Lectures in Comparative Religion* XIII), pp. 147 ff.—*Infra*, p. 175, n. 174; Appendix V.

78. Cf. *infra*, nn. 92 and 93.

79. "Who had been a vulture trainer in a former life" (*PTS. Dictionary*).

80. *so vata, bhikkhave aññatr' eva kāmehi aññatra kāmasaññāya aññatra kāmavitakkehi kāme paṭisevissatīti n' etaṃ ṭhānaṃ vijjati, M.* I, p. 133.

The idea often reappears in Buddhist and Vedāntic texts. Cf. *A.* IV, 36, 3 (vol. II, p. 38 = *S.* XXII, 94, 26-27, vol. III, p. 140); *ibid.*, IV, 36, 4 (vol. II, p. 39); *ibid.*, vol. III, p. 347 (= *Theragāthā*, 700-701); *Sn.* 213, 625 (= *Dhp.* 401), 812, 845; *Kāśyapaparivarta*, § 38, p. 67 (ed. A. von Staël-Holstein); *Saundarananda*, XIII, 4-6 (ed. E. H. Johnston, *Punjab University Oriental Publications*, Oxford University Press, 1928); *Ratnagotravibhāga*, I, 71-72; *Daśabhūmika-Sūtra*, *gāthā*, V, 29 (ed. P. L. Vaidya, Darbhanga, 1967 [= *Buddhist Sanskrit Texts*, No. 7]); *Ratnolkādhāraṇī*, cited in *Śikṣāsamuccaya*, p. 176, v. 3 (ed. P. L. Vaidya, Darbhanga, 1961 [= *Buddhist Sanskrit Texts*, No. 11]); *Vimalakīrti-*

nirdeśa, I, 10, p. 8 (14) [Lamotte, *Vimalakīrti*, p. 111 (17)].—*Viveka-cūḍāmaṇi*, 536, 541, 552; *Aṣṭāvakra-Gītā*, IX, 8.

The world of multiple colors is, to be sure, an object of desire; but it is not itself the desire; the desire is in us: *n' ete kāmā yāni citrāni loke, saṃkapparāgo purissasa kāmo.* The world remains what it is: it is the sage who retains his desire: *tiṭṭhanti citrāni tath' eva loke, ath' ettha dhīrā vinayanti chandaṃ.*—*S.* I, p. 22; *A.* III, p. 411; cf. *Kathāvatthu*, VIII, 4; Buddhaghosa, *Sāratthappakāsinī*, I, p. 63; *Paramatthajotikā*, II, 2, pp. 539-540; *Abhidharmakośabhāṣya*, III, 3 [*AK.* III, pp. 7-8]; *Udānavarga*, II, 7 (ed. F. Bernhard, Göttingen, 1965 [= *Abhandlungen der Akademie der Wissenschaften in Göttingen: Philologisch-historische Klasse*, Dritte Folge, Nr. 54; *Sanskrittexte aus den Turfanfunden* X]). See also *infra*, p. 172, n. 160. Kālidāsa has summarized this idea in a sentence of the *Kumārasaṃbhava* (I, 59 [60 in the critical edition of the Sāhitya Akademi, New Delhi, 1962]): *vikārahetau sati vikriyante yeṣāṃ na cetāṃsi ta eva dhīrāḥ* "Only those whose minds are not troubled when a source of trouble exists are sages."

In the Tantras, through the exaggerations, the same tendency is discernible. Cf. La Vallée Poussin, "A propos du Cittaviśuddhi-prakaraṇa d'Āryadeva," in *Bulletin of the School of Oriental Studies*, VI (1930-32), pp. 411 ff.

81. One of the four "misapprehensions" (*viparyāsa/vipallāsa*), *A.* II, p. 52 (= *Paṭisaṃbhidāmagga*, II, p. 80). Cf. *Abhidharmakośabhāṣya*, V, 8, p. 283 (*AK.* V, p. 21); Commentary to the *Ratnagotravibhāga*, quoted and translated above, pp. 2-5.—As this last text eloquently establishes, the authentic counterpart of the misapprehension of the *ātman* in the non-*ātman*, that is to say, in the *upādānaskandhas*, is the view of the *ātman* in the true *ātman*, which is the *dharmakāya* of the Tathāgata. See also *infra*, p. 39 (and n. 278).

82. Cf. *MaiU.* IV, 2.—*Ātmabodha*, 31:
āvidyakaṃ śarīrādi dṛśyaṃ budbudavat kṣaram |
etadvilakṣaṇaṃ vidyād ahaṃ brahmeti nirmalam ||

83. *evaṃ khandhe avekkheyya bhikkhu āraddhavīriyo* |
divā vā yadi vā rattiṃ sampajāno paṭissato ||
jaheyya sabbasaṃyogaṃ kareyya saraṇ' attano |
careyyādittasīso va patthayaṃ accutaṃ padaṃ ||

S. XXII, 95 (vol. III, p. 143; ed. Nālandā, vol. II, p. 360). Cf. *ibid.*, 43 (vol. III, pp. 42-43); XLVII, 9 (vol. V, p. 154); 13 (vol. V, p. 163); 14 (vol. V, p. 164); *D.* II, pp. 100, 120; III, pp. 58, 77; *Dhp.* 46, 170, 236 and 238 (*so karohi dīpam attano*); *Sn.* 501 (*ye attadīpā vicaranti loke, akiñcanā sabbadhi vippamuttā*). See also *Sn.* 756-758.

On the subject of the expression *attadīpa*, cf. *BĀU.* IV, 3, 6; *ChU.* VIII, 3, 4; 12, 3 (cf. *MaiU.* II, 2).—*Śvet.Up.* II, 15:

> *yadātmatattvena tu brahmatattvaṃ*
> *dīpopameneha yuktaḥ prapaśyet* |
> *ajaṃ dhruvaṃ sarvatattvair viśuddhaṃ*
> *jñātvā devaṃ mucyate sarvapāśaiḥ* ||

MaiU. VI, 20: *yadātmanātmānam aṇor aṇīyāṃsaṃ dyotamānaṃ manaḥkṣayāt paśyati . . . Ibid.*, VI, 30: *anantā raśmayas tasya dīpavad yaḥ sthito hṛdi.*

Cf. *supra*, p. 6 and n. 32; Mrs. Rhys Davids, *The Birth of Indian Psychology and its Development in Buddhism* (= *Buddhist Psychology*[3], London, 1936), pp. 209-210; Coomaraswamy, *Hinduism and Buddhism*, p. 77, n. 187. See also *Les Religions brahmaniques dans l'ancien Cambodge, d'après l'épigraphie et l'iconographie* (= *Publications de l'École française de'Extrême-Orient*, XLIX, Paris, 1961), pp. 57-58.

According to the traditional interpretation (cf. besides the commentaries, N. P. Chakravarti, *L'Udānavarga sanskrit*, I [Paris 1930], pp. 192-193; E. Waldschmidt, *Das Mahāparinirvāṇa-Sūtra*, II [=*Abhandlungen der Deutschen Akademie der Wissenschaften zu Berlin: Klasse für Sprachen, Literatur und Kunst*, 1950, Nr. 2, 1951], p. 200), the word *dīpa*, in the Pāli texts which we have quoted, means "island" (Sanskrit *dvīpa*, and not *dīpa* "light"). Cf. however *S.* I, p. 169 (*infra*, pp. 179-180): *attā sudanto purisassa joti.* See also J. Brough, *The Gāndhārī Dharmapada* (London, 1962), pp. 209-211.—Be that as it may, the general meaning of these texts is clear: it is just what we have indicated. Compared with the parallel texts (cf. especially, *S.* XXII, 43. 95; XLVII, 13. 14; see also Waldschmidt, *op. cit.* pp. 198-200), the passage of the *Mahāparinibbāna-Sutta* (*D.* II, p. 100) can only have one meaning (contrary to what Rāhula writes, *op. cit.*, p. 89; cf. also Murti, p. 23, n. 1): All the conditioned realities of the world are perishable. The Tathāgata himself—an octogenarian—must die. He is no more than an "old chariot" (*jarasakaṭa*: cf. the familiar image of the chariot, below, p. 28). The conditions of our temporal existence cannot be done away with. We can, however, *transcend* them. Even more: the supreme goal of our existence is to transcend them, for, in time, we are more than time. What the Buddha is saying to Ānanda (who is distressed by the thought of losing him) is this: That which I am, you are. Separated in our temporal existence, we are one in the Transcendence. Make, therefore, this timeless *ātman* manifest in you, as I have done myself (*kataṃ me saraṇam attano, D.* II, p. 120); I will thus be to you eternally present. "Dwell, Ānanda, making of the *ātman* your light, of the *ātman*, and of the *ātman* alone, your refuge; making of *dhamma* your light, of *dhamma*, and of *dhamma* alone your refuge." (We shall return further on to the equivalence *attan* = *dhamma*, which this passage clearly indicates, pp. 29-30 and n. 215.)—Cf. *supra*, n. 38 (and a); *infra*, n. 86.

84. I, 14 (*Vin.* I, p. 23).—Analogous account from Buddhaghosa, *Visuddhimagga*, XII, 82 (cf. the following note).

85. Rhys Davids-Oldenberg, *Vinaya Texts*, I (= *Sacred Books of the East*, edited by F. Max Müller, vol. XIII, Oxford, 1881), p. 117: "Which would be better for you; that you should go in search of a woman or that you should go in search of yourselves?" Cf. also E. J. Thomas, *op. cit.*, p. 101; Rāhula, *op. cit.*, p. 90.—Bhikkhu Ñāṇamoli, *The Path of Purification* (Colombo, 1956), p. 430: "But which is better for you, to seek the king or to seek [your] self?" (*kiṃ pana te rājānaṃ gavesituṃ varaṃ udāhu attānaṃ? Visuddhimagga*, XII, 82 [edition cited]).—But it is difficult to understand what is meant, in these passages, by "your-self (°selves)," if not the *ātman*, our true Reality, transcending our empirical reality. The ambiguity of these passages comes, no doubt, from the fact that the word *ātman* is employed also as a reflexive pronoun. Metaphysics, however, is in accordance with the grammar: when it is said "seek the *ātman*," what is really being said is "seek oneself." (Cf. *infra*, n. 218.)

Precise translations by I. B. Horner, *The Book of the Discipline*, IV (= *Sacred Books of the Buddhists*, XIV, London, 1951), p. 32, and by Pe Maung Tin, *The Path of Purity*, II (= *Pāli Text Society Translation Series*, No. 17, London, 1929), p. 456 (cf. n. 1). See also Mrs. Rhys Davids, "A Hallmark of Man and of Religion," *NIA*. I, 1 (April 1938), p. 79.—*attānaṃ gaveseyyātha*: cf. *ChU.* VIII, 7, 1: *ātmā anveṣṭavyaḥ*.

86. *na vā are patyuḥ kāmāya patiḥ priyo bhavati, ātmanas tu kāmāya patiḥ priyo bhavati. na vā are jāyāyai kāmāya jāyā priyā bhavati, ātmanas tu kāmāya jāyā priyā bhavati. na vā are putrāṇāṃ kāmāya putrāḥ priyā bhavanti, ātmanas tu kāmāya putrāḥ priyā bhavanti. na vā are vittasya kāmāya vittaṃ bhavati, ātmanas tu kāmāya vittaṃ priyaṃ bhavati . . . ātmanas tu kāmāya sarvaṃ priyaṃ bhavati. ātmā vā are draṣṭavyaḥ śrotavyo mantavyo nididhyāsitavyaḥ. Maitreyī, ātmano vā are darśanena śravaṇena matyā vijñānenedaṃ sarvaṃ viditam, BĀU.* II, 4, 5 (cf. IV, 5, 6). [Trans. Senart, modified; cf. A. Minard, *Trois énigmes* . . . , II, p. 169, § 412a.]—Cf. *ibid.*, I, 4, 8; III, 5; IV, 4, 22.

Against the interpretation according to which what would be in question here would be "a profession of brutal egoism," see A. Foucher in Senart, *Bṛhadāraṇyaka-Upaniṣad* (Paris, 1934), p. xv; C. Formichi, "On the real meaning of the dialogue between Yājñavalkya and Maitreyī," in *Indian Studies in Honor of Charles Rockwell Lanman* (Cambridge, Mass., Harvard University Press, 1929), pp. 75-77; Hiriyanna, *The Quest after Perfection*, pp. 89-91.

BĀU. I, 4, 8 makes an important point: The *ātman* is dearer than son, riches and all the things of the exterior world. All particular objects of our love are perishable, but one who loves the *ātman* (the One or the All) is never separated from the object of his love (*sa ya ātmānam eva priyam upāste, na hāsya priyaṃ pramāyukaṃ bhavati*).—Cf. *supra*, p. 74, n. 83 end. See also *ChU.* VIII, 3, 1-2; *Vivekacūḍāmaṇi*, 105-106.

Note that love for the One does not exclude love for a particular being. On the contrary, it is the perfect love of lovers, where one identifies with the other, which illustrates, for Yājñavalkya, the experience of the One (*supra*, p. 7 and n. 46).

ātmā . . . draṣṭavyaḥ śrotavyo mantavyo nididhyāsitavyaḥ: according to the later interpretation, this concerns the four stages of spiritual knowledge, that is: *śravaṇa, manana, nididhyāsana* and *darśana.* Thus, Śaṅkara: *śrotavyaḥ pūrvam ācāryata āgamataś ca. paścān mantavyas tarkataḥ. tato nididhyāsitavyo niścayena dhyātavyaḥ. evaṃ hy asau dṛṣṭo bhavati śravaṇamanananididhyāsanasādhanair nirvartitaiḥ. yadaikatvam etāny upagatāni tadā samyagdarśanaṃ brahmaikatvaviṣayaṃ prasīdati, nānyathā śravaṇamātreṇa.* (*Bṛhadāraṇyakopaniṣad-bhāṣya*, II, 4, 5; cf. IV, 5, 6.) See also P. Hacker, *Untersuchungen über Texte des frühen Advaitavāda*: 1. *Die Schüler Śaṅkaras* (= *Abhandlungen der Akademie der Wissenschaften und der Literatur in Mainz: Geistes- und Sozialwissenschaftlichen Klasse*, 1950, NR. 26), pp. 152-153 (2058-2059). Cf. *infra*, p. 185, n. 34.—"*Diṭṭhaṃ, Sutaṃ, Mutaṃ, Viññātaṃ*," *Buddhist Studies in Honour of Walpola Rahula* (London, 1980), pp. 10-15; *Some Thoughts*, pp. 13-15.

87. *tad vā asyaitad āptakāmam ātmakāmam akāmaṃ rūpaṃ śokāntaram, BĀU.* IV, 3, 21. Cf. *ibid.*, IV, 4, 6.—*Ibid.*, IV, 4, 12:

ātmānaṃ ced vijānīyād ayam asmīti pūruṣaḥ |
kim icchan kasya kāmāya śarīram anusaṃjvaret ||

See also *ChU.* VII, 25, 2; VIII, 1, 5-6; 7, 1; 12, 6; *BhG.* III, 17.—We shall return to this question further on (pp. 13, 35).

88. *BĀU.* II, 1, 20 (= II, 3, 6). Cf. *MaiU.* VI, 32 (which combines

BĀU. II, 1, 20 and II, 4, 10).—By the "real" (*satya*), we should understand the empirical reality. Cf. *BĀU.* I, 6, 3: *tad etad amṛtaṃ satyena cchannam; prāṇo* (= *ātmā: supra*, n. 29) *vā amṛtam, nāmarūpe satyam; tābhyām ayaṃ prāṇaś channaḥ* (cf. *infra*, pp. 228-229).—*TU.* II, 6: *satyam abhavat; yad idaṃ kiṃ ca tat satyam ity ācakṣate* (the punctuation adopted here—contrary to Śaṅkara and the modern interpreters—is supported by Bhaṭṭabhāskara's commentary upon the *Taittirīya-Āraṇyaka*, Part II, pp. 47-48, edition cited). See also Deussen, *AGPh.* I, 2, pp. 69, 119, 209.—Cf. *infra*, p. 131.

89. *BĀU.* II, 4, 7-9 (cf. IV, 5, 8-10).

90. *ChU.* VI, 1, 4.—The *ātman* is the ground of all true knowledge, for, in it all subject-object duality is transcended. Let us recall that the *Suvikrāntavikrāmi-paripṛcchā-Prajñāpāramitā-Sūtra* also posits the *ātman* "without a second" (*advaya*) as the supreme principle of knowledge: *yo hy advayam ātmānaṃ prajānāti sa Buddhaṃ Dharmaṃ ca prajānāti.—tat kasya hetoḥ?—ātmabhāvaṃ sa bhāvayati sarvadharmāṇāṃ yenādvayaparijñayā sarvadharmāḥ parijñātāḥ; ātmasvabhāvaniyatā hi sarvadharmāḥ. yo hy advayadharmaṃ prājānīte sa buddhadharmān prajānīte; advayadharmaparijñayā buddhadharmaparijñā, ātmaparijñayā sarvatraidhātukaparijñā. ātmaparijñeti, Suvikrāntavikrāmin, pāram etat sarvadharmāṇām.* (*Suvikrāntavikrāmi-paripṛcchā-Prajñāpāramitā-Sūtra*, edited with an Introductory Essay by Ryusho Hikata, Kyushu University, Fukuoka, Japan, 1958, p. 20; cf. *Mahāyāna-Sūtra-Saṃgraha*, edited by P. L. Vaidya, part I [= *Buddhist Sanskrit Texts*, No. 17, Darbhanga, 1961], p. 11.)

Compare with Meister Eckhart: "When one know creatures as they are in themselves—what I shall call evening knowledge—one sees creation only in distinct images. But when one knows creatures in God—what I shall call morning knowledge—one sees a creature without the least distinction, without any of the images which represent it and without resemblance to anything whatever, in the Unity which is God himself." ("De l'homme noble," in *Traités et Sermons*, p. 110 [translation cited].)

Of course, what is morning for the sages is evening for others and vice versa:

> *yā niśā sarvabhūtānāṃ tasyāṃ jāgarti saṃyamī* |
> *yasyāṃ jāgrati bhūtāni sā niśā paśyato muneḥ* ||

BhG. II, 69. (Verse cited by Ānandavardhana as an example of *dhvani*: *Dhvanyāloka*, p. 125, ed. Durgāprasād-Parab, Bombay, Nirṇayasāgara Press, 1891 [= Kāvyamālā 25].)

As clarified by Śaṅkara, the night (*niśā*) of sages (or the day for others) is the night of "ignorance," characterized by the subject-object split (*grāhyagrāhakabhedalakṣaṇāyām avidyāniśāyām* [*Bhagavad-gītā-bhāṣya*, II, 69; cf. *infra*, n. 167]). Cf. also *Laṅk.*, *Sagāthaka*, v. 178:

> *bālānāṃ na tathā khyāti yathā khyāti manīṣiṇām* |
> *manīṣiṇāṃ tathā khyāti sarvadharmā alakṣaṇāḥ* ||

(On *bāla*, cf. *supra*, n. 34, and on *alakṣaṇa*, *infra*, p. 164, n. 94.)

91. *ChU.* VI, 1, 4-6. Cf. *ibid.*, VI, 4, 1 ff. (it may be thought that the primordial "three forms" [*trīṇi rūpāṇi*], which this last passage is concerned with, represent limited aspects of the One: cf. *infra*, p. 162, n. 82).

Such, it seems to us, is the true sense of the words *vācārambhaṇam*, etc.: *vācārambhaṇaṃ vāgārambhaṇaṃ vāgālambanam ity etat . . . vāgālambanamātraṃ nāmaiva kevalam, na vikāro nāma vastv asti*, Śaṅkara, *Chāndogyopaniṣad-bhāṣya*, VI, 1, 4 (differently, *Brahmasūtra-bhāṣya*, II, 1, 14). See also *infra*, p. 36; p. 162, n. 82; p. 229.—Recent discussions on *vācārambhaṇa*: J. A. B. van Buitenen, in *Indian Linguistics*, XVI (= *Suniti Kumar Chatterji Jubilee Volume*, 1955), pp. 157 ff.; *IIJ.* II (1958), no. 4, pp. 295 ff.; F. B. J. Kuiper, in *IIJ.* I (1957), no. 2, pp. 155 ff.; *ibid.*, II, no. 4, pp. 306 ff.

The world is true insofar as it has for essence the Being in itself, of which it is the "modification" (*vikāra*), or, as Śaṅkara puts it, "reflection" (*ābhāsa, pratibimba, chāyā*); but it is false, if we take it for a thing in itself, separating it from its foundation: *sarvaṃ ca nāmarūpādi sadātmanaiva satyaṃ vikārajātam, svatas tv anṛtam eva . . . sadātmanā sarvavyavahārāṇāṃ sarvavikārāṇāṃ ca satyatvam, sato 'nyatve cānṛtatvam*, Śaṅkara, *Chāndogyopaniṣad-bhāṣya*, VI, 3, 2.—Neither the Upaniṣads nor Śaṅkara say that the world is illusion: they simply say that things and individual beings are the appearances of *brahman-ātman*, universal foundation, and, consequently, they do not possess true reality, independent of the Being which appears. There is no "modification" which is a "thing in itself!" *na vikāro nāma vastv asti*, Śaṅkara, *Chāndogyopaniṣad-bhāṣya*, VI, 1, 4, below. Cf. *Brahma-sūtra-bhāṣya*, II, 1, 14 (p. 454): *na tu vastuvṛttena vikāro nāma kaścid asti . . . brahmavyatirekeṇa kāryajātasyābhāvaḥ.* See also Radhakrishnan, *Eastern Religions and Western Thought*[2], p. 31; *The Hindu View of Life*, p. 48 (American edition; Macmillan, New York, n.d.).

92. Cf. the poem by Tagore, *Mukti* (*Sañcayitā*[2], p. 375):

. . . .

. . . . pradīper mato
samasta saṃsāra mor lakkha barttikāy
jvālāye tulibe ālo tomāri śikhāy
tomāra mandira mājhe | |
. . . .

"I recognize no God except the God that is to be found in the hearts of the dumb millions. They do not recognize His presence; I do," Gandhi, *In Search of the Supreme*, compiled and edited by V. B. Kher, Ahmedabad, Navajivan Publishing House, vol. I, 1961, p. 29.

That which constitutes our "bond," is made by our being shut up in the I of a limited consciousness. This obstacle is only in ourselves. Consequently, liberty (*svārājya*) is not obtained through isolation from the rest of existence (which would, on the contrary, prolong the bond and aggravate it). As the *Aṣṭāvakra-Gītā* (I, 15) expresses it, once again so well, the very fact of devoting oneself to *samādhi* is, for the man who does so, his bond (*ayam eva hi te bandhaḥ samādhim anutiṣṭhasi*). [Cf. *supra*, p. 68.]

Our unity with the All has to be regained, beyond the sensible appearances which divide us, and thus we must deliver ourselves from our isolation: ". . . to overcome the barrier of separation from the rest of existence and to realize *advaitam*, the Supreme Unity which is *anantam*, infinitude . . . to go beyond the world of appearances, in which facts as facts are alien to us, like the mere sounds of foreign music . . . an emancipation in the inner truth of all things, where the endless Many reveal the One," Tagore, *The Religion of Man* ("Unwin Books," London, 1961), pp. 115-116. Cf. the celebrated poem, *Nirjharer svapnabhaṅga* (*Sañcayitā*[3], pp. 5-6), commented upon by the poet himself: ". . . the sudden expansion of my consciousness in the superpersonal world of man" (*The Religion of Man*, p. 58).

Cf. Radhakrishnan, *Indian Philosophy*[2], I, pp. 207 ff.; *Up.* pp. 106, 123, 126-127; *Bhagavadgītā*[2], pp. 184, 292-293; *Eastern Religions and Western Thought*[2], pp. 45-46, 52-54, 93, 97 ff., 108-109; Hiriyanna, *The Quest after Perfection,* Essays I, II, IV, and p. 110; *Popular Essays in Indian Philosophy*, pp. 10-11, 21, 22-23, 82, 86-87, 114; Dhirendra Mohan Datta, *The Philosophy of Mahatma Gandhi* (Madison, The University of Wisconsin Press, 1953), pp. 44, 65 ff.; Kshiti Mohan Sen, *Hinduism* ("Penguin Books," 1961), pp. 24 ff.—Compare with Teilhard de Chardin: "God awaits us at the end of Evolution; surmounting the world, does not mean scorning it or rejecting it, but crossing it and sublimating it" (*L'avenir de l'homme* [= *Œuvres*, 5, Paris,

Éditions du Seuil, 1959], pp. 104-105). "Instead of leaving behind, it (detachment) carries on; instead of cutting, it raises up: no longer rupture, but crossing, no longer evasion, but emergence" (*ibid.*, p. 125).—"There, truly liberated from the world, he is at last entirely open to the world," Jaspers, *Introduction à la Philosophie*, p. 67 (edition cited). See also *infra*, n. 110.

93. 1.—Cf. Radhakrishnan, *Eastern Religions and Western Thought*[2], p. 131; *Up.*, p. 567. We are aware that this verse is sometimes translated differently; but Śaṅkara seems to be right in glossing *tyaktena* by *tyāgena*. What is it that has to be renounced? Only what is contingent,—the "modifications" called "name," "form" and "action" (cf. *infra*, p. 229),—by virtue of awareness of the absolute Reality, which is our true Being. And it is not a question of "renouncing," literally, for the text speaks of "enjoying" (*bhuj-*); whereas the son, the servant, etc., when they are renounced or dead, no longer serve us. The word *tyāga* means, to Śaṅkara, "detachment" rather than "renunciation" . . . *sarvam eva nāmarūpakarmākhyaṃ vikārajātaṃ paramārthasatyātmabhāvanayā tyaktaṃ syāt . . . na hi tyakto mṛtaḥ putro vā bhṛtyo vā ātmasaṃbandhitāyā abhāvād ātmānaṃ pālayati. atas tyāgenety ayam evārthaḥ.*

94. *BĀU.* IV, 4, 13.—Josiah Royce has well brought out this transfiguration (*The World and the Individual, First Series: The Four Historical Conceptions of Being* [Dover edition, New York, 1959], p. 160).

95. *BĀU.* IV, 4, 13. Cf. *ibid.*, 22.—Śaṅkara.

96. Cf. Deussen, *AGPh.* I, 2, p. 59.—We will speak again of the *ātmayajña* (pp. 179 ff.).

97. There is no longer any object, other and separated, which he can covet, since all belongs to him or, rather, is himself: *ātmana evedaṃ sarvam ātmaiva ca sarvam*, Śaṅkara on *Īśā-Up.* I.

98. Cf. *Ud.* VI, 6, p. 70.

99. *Īśā-Up.* 6-7.

sarvabhūtastham ātmānaṃ sarvabhūtāni cātmani ।
īkṣate yogayuktātmā sarvatra samadarśanaḥ ॥
yo māṃ paśyati sarvatra sarvaṃ ca mayi paśyati ।
tasyāhaṃ na praṇaśyāmi sa ca me na praṇaśyati ॥
sarvabhūtasthitaṃ yo māṃ paśyaty ekatvam āsthitaḥ ।
sarvathā vartamāno 'pi sa yogī mayi vartate ॥
ātmaupamyena sarvatra samaṃ paśyati yo 'rjuna ।
sukhaṃ vā yadi vā duḥkhaṃ sa yogī paramo mataḥ ॥

BhG. VI, 29-32.

vidyāvinayasaṃpanne brāhmaṇe gavi hastini ।
śuni caiva śvapāke ca paṇḍitāḥ samadarśinaḥ ॥
labhante brahmanirvāṇam ṛṣayaḥ kṣīṇakalmaṣāḥ ।
chinnadvaidhā yatātmānaḥ sarvabhūtahite ratāḥ ॥

Ibid., V, 18 and 25. Cf. XII, 4. (On *brahmanirvāṇa*, cf. ch. II.)

samaṃ paśyan hi sarvatra samavasthitam īśvaram ।
na hinasty ātmanātmānaṃ tato yāti parāṃ gatim ॥

Ibid., XIII, 28 (cf. note of F. Edgerton, *The Bhagavadgītā* ["Harper Torchbooks," New York, 1964]).

adveṣṭā sarvabhūtānāṃ maitraḥ karuṇa eva ca ।
nirmamo nirahaṃkāraḥ samaduḥkhasukhaḥ kṣamī ॥

Ibid., XII, 13 (cf. XI, 55).

brahmabhūtaḥ prasannātmā na śocati na kāṅkṣati ।
samaḥ sarveṣu bhūteṣu madbhaktiṃ labhate parām ॥

Ibid., XVIII, 54. (On *brahmabhūta*, cf. ch. II.)

Cf. *Kaivalya-Up.* 10 (in *The Śaiva Upaniṣads with the Commentary of Śrī Upaniṣad-Brahma-Yogin*, edited by Pandit A. Mahādeva Śāstrī, Madras, Adyar Library, 1950); *Mbh.* XII, 8751 ff., 9923; XIII, 5569 ff.; etc.; Manu, XII, 91 (*infra*, p. 181 and n. 29), 118, 125; *Bhāgavata-Purāṇa*, III, 29, 17 (*maitryā caivātmatulyeṣu*); *Madhyamakahṛdaya*, VIII, 8 (Gokhale, *loc. cit.*, p. 173).—Mrs. Rhys Davids, *The Birth of Indian Psychology* . . . , pp. 46-47.—Tagore, *The Religion of Man*, ch. VI and VII; *Mukti* (*loc. cit.*): *prema mor bhakti-rūpe rahibe phaliyā*.—Gandhi: "And I worship the God that is Truth or Truth which is God through the service of these millions" (*In search of the Supreme*, I, p. 29). Datta (*op. cit.*) writes: "*Ahiṃsā* carried, for Gandhi, also the positive spirit of treating all beings as one's very self (*ātmavat sarvabhūteṣu*) repeatedly taught in the *Gītā* and other Indian scriptures . . . without *ahiṃsā* Truth cannot be realized. Truth for him was God that pervaded all beings, and preserved and unified them through love. God can be realized by loving God, and to love God is to love the beings in whom He is incarnate. So he says, 'When you want to find Truth as God the only inevitable means is Love, i.e. non-violence'" (pp. 93-94). "Behind all these vows and virtues of Gandhi lay his simple spiritual perception of every being as the manifestation of the Self or God that is present in all. Love for all beings flowed from this perception and all virtues from this love" (p. 104).

See also Schopenhauer, *Le Monde comme Volonté et comme Représentation*, p. 471 (edition cited); *Le Fondement de la Morale* (translation by M.-R. Bastian, Paris, 1937), ch. XXII; Deussen, *On the Philosophy of the Vedānta in its Relations to Occidental Metaphysics*: an address delivered before the Bombay Branch of the Royal Asiatic Society, Saturday the 25th February, 1893 (Bombay, 1893), p. 14.—Cf. Appendix I.

100. Cf. the preceding note.—*maitro brāhmaṇa ucyate*, says Manu, II, 87; XI, 35 (cf. *infra*, p. 154, n. 43).

101. *MSA*. IX, 70-71.—Cf. the passages of the *Bhagavadgītā*, cited above, n. 99.—Manu, XII, 125:

evaṃ yaḥ sarvabhūteṣu paśyaty ātmānam ātmanā |
sa sarvasamatām etya brahmābhyeti paraṃ padam ||

Ibid., VI, 44: *samatā caiva sarvasminn etan muktasya lakṣaṇam.*

102. *Supra*, pp. 1 ff.

103. XIV, 37-41.

104. *gāḍhāyatabandhanena.* (S. Lévi: "the tightened bond of Places." Does he confuse *āyata* with *āyatana*?)—Cf. the following note, and Appendix V, p. 235.

105. *duḥkhasya paryantam apaśyamānaḥ.* (S. Lévi: "without regard to the end of suffering.") If the suffering of the Bodhisattva were individual, it would have a "limit" (*paryanta*). But, for him, the sorrow of others is his own sorrow, *sattvātmasamānabhāvāt* (st. 41). He therefore sees no limit to his suffering.

106. G. Cœdès, "La stèle de Ta-Prohm" [1186 A.D.], *BEFEO*. VI, pp. 53 and 73, st. XXV (slightly modified translation). P. Mus, "Le sourire d'Angkor," *Artibus Asiae*, XXIV, 3/4 (1961) [= *Felicitation Volume presented to Professor George Cœdès on the occasion of his Seventy-fifth Birthday*], p. 381, cites that stanza. Compare G. Cœdès, *Inscriptions du Cambodge*, I (Hanoi, 1937), p. 257, st. XVII (translated in our *Religions brahmaniques* . . . , p. 76, n. 2). Lastly, on the question, see *BCA*. VI, 126 and Commentary; St. Schayer, *Vorarbeiten zur Geschichte der mahāyānistischen Erlösungslehren* (= *Untersuchungen zur Geschichte des Buddhismus*, V, München-Neubiberg, 1921), p. 35; Murti, p. 283.

107. *A*. III, 99 (vol. I, pp. 249 ff.). Cf. *ibid.*, 33 (vol. I, pp. 134 ff.). —*Īśā-Up.* 2; *BhG*. IV, 18 ff.—*sarvabhūtātmabhūtātmā kurvann api na lipyate* . . . *padmapattram ivāmbhasā*, *BhG*. V, 7 and 10 (cf. *ChU*. IV, 14, 3; see also *infra*, p. 29).—

yasya nāhaṃkṛto bhāvo buddhir yasya na lipyate |
hatvāpi sa imāṃl lokān na hanti na nibadhyate || *Ibid.*, XVIII, 17.

Cf. *supra*, n. 58, and Appendix 1; *infra*, p. 21.

108. *śāntā mahānto nivasanti santo*
vasantaval lokahitaṃ carantaḥ |
tīrṇāḥ svayaṃ bhīmabhavārṇavaṃ janān
ahetunānyān api tārayantaḥ ||
ayaṃ svabhāvaḥ svata eva yat para-
śramāpanodapravaṇaṃ mahātmanām |
sudhāṃśur eṣa svayam arkakarkaśa-
prabhābhitaptām avati kṣitiṃ kila ||
Vivekacūḍāmaṇi, 37-38 (cf. *infra*, p. 216).

Sn. 571: *tuvaṃ anusaye chetvā tiṇṇo tāres' imaṃ pajaṃ.*

"My life is one indivisible whole, and all my activities run into one another, and they all have their rise in my insatiable love of mankind," Gandhi, quoted by Datta, *op. cit.*, p. 76. Tagore was fully aware of the "technical" meaning of the word *Mahātmā* ("the Man who has made himself one with the Being of the universe," Romain Rolland, *Mahatma Gandhi*), when he applied this epithet to Gandhi. Addressing the inmates of the Satyāgraha Ashram in Sabarmati, on the 4th of December 1922, in the absence of Gandhi who was in prison, the poet said:

"I am sure, you all feel that the spirit of Mahatmaji is working among you. What is the true meaning of the great word Mahātmā? It implies the emancipated soul that realizes itself in all souls. It means the life that is no longer confined within itself, but finds its larger soul of *Ātman*, of Spirit. Then, in such realization, it becomes Mahātmā. For it includes all spirits in itself . . . He [the Mahātmā] is the Infinite Soul, whose activities are for the Whole." (*Truth called them differently: Tagore-Gandhi Controversy*, compiled and edited by R. K. Prabhu and Ravindra Kelekar, Ahmedabad, Navajivan Publishing House, 1961, pp. 10-11.)

See also Coomaraswamy, "Mahātmā," in *Mahātmā Gandhi: Essays and reflections on his life and work, presented to him on his Seventieth Birthday*, October 2nd, 1939, edited by S. Radhakrishnan (London, Allen and Unwin², 1949), pp. 63-67.—Radhakrishnan, *Up.*, pp. 129-130.

109. Cf. *MSA*. XIV, 39, above, p. 14. See also *infra*, p. 235.

110. In fact, it concerns Nirvāṇa only in the narrow sense of *anupadhiśeṣa* (or *nirupadhiśeṣa)-nirvāṇa*, corresponding to the *videhamukti* of Vedānta (*infra*, p. 144). The Bodhisattva, who has realized his identity with the Whole, has already attained Nirvāṇa, if by the word is understood the extinction of the sense of ego. "He is born (*jāyate*) as delivered (*mukta*), he comes into existence

(*utpadyate*) as delivered. Born as delivered, coming into existence as delivered, he has the force (*bala*) and the power (*anubhāva*) to preach the law which delivers the shackled beings (*baddhasattva*) from their bond (*bandhana*)," Lamotte, *Vimalakīrti*, p. 232 (cf. *Vimalakīrtinirdeśa*, IV, 15, p. 51). Technically, the Nirvāṇa of the Bodhisattva is called *apratiṣṭhitanirvāṇa*: cf. *ibid.*, pp. 143-144, nn.

As the *Aṣṭasāhasrikā Prajñāpāramitā* says, to evade the world of becoming is to impose on oneself a limitation (*baddhasīmāno hi te saṃsārasrotasaḥ*), it is not true liberty. The Bodhisattva is truly free, because he ceaselessly assumes existences, without being constrained to do so.—*ASP.*, p. 17 (cf. *AAĀ.*, p. 330).

Let us recall that Hindu literature also speaks of ancient sages having, in some way, delayed their complete Deliverance (*videha-mukti*), by freely taking on individual existences in order to save the world.—Śaṅkara, *Brahmasūtra-bhāṣya*, III, 3, 32. Cf. Radhakrishnan, *Up.*, p. 127: "Possessing the immortality of non-birth, the redeemed self still assumes, by free volition, an individual form in the manifested world. Birth is a becoming of the Supreme in the cosmic being. This becoming is not inconsistent with Being. It becomes a means and not an obstacle to the enjoyment of life eternal. To be released from the chain of birth and death is not to flee from the world of becoming. Bondage does not consist in the assumption of birth or individuality, but in the persistence of the ignorant sense of the separate, selfish ego. It is not the embodiment that creates the bondage, but the frame of mind. To the free spirit life has no terrors. He wishes to conquer life for God. He uses the world as the mould and condition for the manifestation of his spiritual freedom. He may assume birth for the purpose of helping the world.[a] There will be individualisation without an ego-sense. The play of the individual consciousness can take many forms, assume many aspects and poises. All through, however, he lives in the truth of the cosmic play with no delusion, released from ego, in full control of the manifested being."—"May I be born and reborn again and suffer a thousand miseries if I am able to worship *the only God* in whom I believe, *the sum total of all souls*, and above all my God, the wicked, my God the afflicted, my God the poor of all races," Vivekānanda, quoted by Datta, *op. cit.*, p. 68.

---

a. *lokānugraha evaiko hetus te janmakarmaṇoḥ*, Kālidāsa, *Raghuvaṃśa*, X, 31.

111. Schayer, *Vorarbeiten* . . . , pp. 20-21.

112. Rāhula, *op. cit.*, pp. 68-69.

113. *caratha, bhikkhave, cārikaṃ bahujanahitāya bahujanasukhāya lokānukampāya atthāya hitāya sukhāya devamanussānaṃ, Vin.* I, p. 21. Cf. *D.* II, pp. 45 ff., 119-120, 224-225; III, 127-128; *S.* I, p. 105; *A.* I, p. 22; *It.* 84; *Sn.* 693.—*ASP.*, p. 125.

114. Cf. *supra*, p. 16.

115. Har Dayal, *The Bodhisattva Doctrine in Buddhist Sanskrit Literature* (London, 1932), pp. 2-3.—Cf. *infra*, pp. 235-236.

116. Cf. Radhakrishnan, *Up.*, pp. 93-94: "There does not seem to be any suggestion that the individual egos are unreal. They all exist only through the Self and have no reality apart from it. The insistence on the unity of the Supreme Self as the constituent reality of the world and of the individual souls does not negate the empirical reality of the latter."

117. Bréhier, *La philosophie de Plotin*, p. 111. Cf. *supra*, pp. 57-58. —*MaiU.* IV, 4, below, p. 29 and n. 201.

118. The belief in a multiplicity of lives allows for the reconciling of the current misery of man with the grandeur of his destiny. Cf. Hiriyanna, *Popular Essays in Indian Philosophy*, pp. 47-48.—*BhG.* VI, 40 ff.—

bahūnāṃ janmanām ante jñānavān māṃ prapadyate I
Vāsudevaḥ sarvam iti sa mahātmā sudurlabhaḥ II

Ibid., VII, 19. (*bahūnāṃ janmanāṃ jñānārthasaṃskārāśrayāṇām*, Śaṅkara).—See also below, n. 125; p. 20 and n. 135.

119. *S.* II, p. 17: *lokasamudayaṃ kho, Kaccāyana, yathābhūtaṃ sammappaññāya passato yā loke natthitā sā na hoti; lokanirodhaṃ kho, Kaccāyana, yathābhūtaṃ sammappaññāya passato yā loke atthitā sā na hoti . . . sabbam atthīti kho, Kaccāyana, ayam eko anto; sabbaṃ n' atthīti ayaṃ dutiyo anto. ete te, Kaccāyana, ubho ante anupagamma majjhena Tathāgato dhammaṃ deseti.*—Same text, *ibid.*, III, p. 135. Cf. *MKV.*, pp. 269, 270 and 358; Lamotte, *Traité*, I, p. 72.

Cf. *S.* XLIV, 10 (vol. IV, pp. 400-401; cf. *infra*, p. 25; Appendix VI, pp. 239-240): the Buddha refused to tell the itinerant monk Vacchagotta whether he had an *ātman* or not: if he had told him that he had an *ātman*, he would have been adopting the eternalist point of view (*sassatavāda*); if, on the other hand, he had told him that he did not have one, he would have been adopting the nihilistic point of view (*ucchedavāda*). The truth lies in between: "existence is something between being and not being, that is becoming"

(F. O. Schrader, "On the problem of Nirvāṇa," *loc. cit.*, p. 160). May we be permitted to point out, once and for all, that, contrary to what Oldenberg thought (*LUAB.*[2], p. 309, n. 194; cf. also Frauwallner, *Die Philosophie des Buddhismus,* p. 18), our Sutta has nothing to do with the absolute "ungraspable" *ātman*, with which other Pāli texts are concerned (*supra*, n. 36; *infra*, n. 243). The *ātman* of which it speaks is the empirical *ātman.*

On the subject of "eternalism," cf. *supra*, n. 53.

120. *Infra*, p. 28.

121. Cf. Appendix IV.

122. *iminā nāmarūpena kammaṃ karoti sobhanaṃ vā pāpakaṃ vā, tena kammena aññaṃ nāmarūpaṃ paṭisandahati. aññaṃ māraṇantikaṃ nāmarūpaṃ aññaṃ paṭisandhismiṃ nāmarūpaṃ, api ca tato yeva taṃ nibbattaṃ. dhammasantati sandahati; añño uppajjati añño nirujjhati, apubbaṃ acarimaṃ viya sandahati. tena na ca so na ca añño pacchima-viññāṇasaṅgahaṃ gacchati, Mil.*, pp. 46-48; 40-41. Cf. L. Finot, *Les Questions de Milinda* (Paris, 1923), pp. 87, 90, 80.

Cf. Buddhaghosa, *Visuddhimagga,* XVII, 162 ff. (edition cited). The idea already exists, in embryo, in the *Saṃyutta-Nikāya* (vol. II, pp. 20, 76). Cf. again *Śālistamba-Sūtra*: a text closely related to the passage from the *Milindapañhā* which we have just quoted, and which clarifies it:

kathaṃ na śāśvatataḥ?—yasmād anye māraṇāntikāḥ skandhāḥ, anya aupapattyaṃśikāḥ skandhāḥ. na tu ya eva māraṇāntikāḥ skandhās ta evaupapattyaṃśikāḥ. api tu māraṇāntikāḥ skandhā nirudhyante, tasminn eva ca samaya aupapattyaṃśikāḥ skandhāḥ prādurbhavanti. ato na śāśvatataḥ.

kathaṃ nocchedataḥ?—na ca pūrvaniruddheṣu māraṇāntikeṣu skandheṣu aupapattyaṃśikāḥ skandhāḥ prādurbhavanti, nāpy aniruddheṣu; api tu māraṇāntikāḥ skandhā nirudhyante, tasminn eva ca samaya aupapattyaṃśikāḥ skandhāḥ prādurbhavanti, tulādaṇḍonnāmāvanāmavat, candrabimbapratibimbavat. ato nocchedataḥ. (*MKV.*, p. 569. Cf. *ibid.*, p. 544; La Vallée Poussin, "Dogmatique bouddhique: La négation de l'âme et la doctrine de l'acte," *JA.* 1902 [2], p. 272, n. 2.)

See also Lamotte, *Traité*, II, p. 746, n. 1.

123. Such is not, however, the opinion of Śaṅkara, whose interpretation is manifestly forced (cf. following note). See, e.g., *ṚV.* X, 16, 3.

124. The *ātman* which returns to space (*ākāśa*), would according to Oldenberg, be a part of the psychic and corporeal man,

coordinated with others. Such a conception, as Oldenberg himself emphasizes, is contrary to Yājñavalkya's own doctrine. It must therefore be, Oldenberg thinks, a loose expression, witness to a time when terminology was not yet firmly fixed. "This is obviously an instance of negligent expression understandable at a time when the terminology was at variance." (*LUAB.*[2], p. 94, n. 2.) On this last point, we shall simply remark that the word *ātman* is used in the Upaniṣads, and even later, in several senses. Neither the *ātman* "body," nor even the *ātman* "manas," is the absolute *ātman*; that is the negation of all these *ātman*s (cf. *infra*, n. 245). As for the interpretation of the word in this passage, Śaṅkara would seem to be right in regarding it as meaning that it is the space of the heart (*hṛdayākāśa*), which is the seat of the *ātman* (cf. *BĀU.* IV, 4, 22; *infra*, pp. 191, 195-196, 197 ff.), and which, upon the death of the man, dissolves into the Great Space: *ākāśam ātmety atrātmādhiṣṭhānaṃ hṛdayākāśam ucyate; sa ākāśam apyeti* (*Bṛhadāraṇyakopaniṣad-bhāṣya*, III, 2, 13, p. 418). However, contrary to what Śaṅkara affirms (following on from Bādarāyaṇa), it does not seem to us that this passage speaks in a fashion that is merely "metaphoric" of the absorption of the elements of a man into the macrocosm (according to Śaṅkara, it would, in reality, be the "tutelary deities" [cf. *Muṇḍ.Up.* III, 2, 7] of these elements: Agni, etc., who withdraw their cooperation: *sarvatra hi vāgādiśabdena devatāḥ parigṛhyante, na tu karaṇāny evāpakrāmanti prāṅ mokṣāt* [*Bṛhadāraṇyakopaniṣad-bhāṣya*, III, 2, 13, p. 418].—*ato vāgādyadhiṣṭhātrīṇām Agnyādidevatānāṃ vāgādyupakāriṇīnāṃ maraṇakāla upakāranivṛttimātram apekṣya vāgādayo 'gnyādīn gacchantīty upacaryate* [*Brahmasūtrabhāṣya*, III, 1, 4]).

125. *tau ha yad ūcatuḥ karma haiva tad ūcatuḥ, atha yat praśaśaṃsatuḥ karma haiva tat praśaśaṃsatuḥ: puṇyo vai puṇyena karmaṇā bhavati, pāpaḥ pāpeneti.* [Trans. Senart.]

Yājñavalkya refused to discuss *karman* with Ārtabhāga in public. "Take my hand, Ārtabhāga, my friend; we alone may know of these things; we must not talk about them in public." The doctrine of *karman* is, doubtless, the most irrational of things (cf. *A.* III, 4, 77, vol. II, p. 80: *kammavipāko acinteyyo na cintetabbo*); yet, it is that which allows for the reconciling of the two contradictory sides of man (*supra*, n. 118). Is it by chance that this doctrine is formulated, for the first time, in the Upaniṣads?

126. According to one of the two interpretations of the word *liṅga* given by Śaṅkara, this word is already to be found used in this

sense in *BĀU.* IV, 4, 6 (cf. below): *manaḥpradhānatvāl liṅgasya mano liṅgam ity ucyate.*—Cf. Deussen, *AGPh.* I, 2, p. 254.

127. *Infra*, p. 173, n. 164.

128. H. C. Warren, *Buddhism in Translations* (= *HOS.* 3, Cambridge, Mass., 1896, etc.), p. 234. According to some authors, the *vijñāna/viññāṇa* would play the role of a soul or of a "subtle body, support for rebirth," in Buddhism: Har Dayal, *op. cit.*, pp. 74-75; E. Frauwallner, *Geschichte der indischen Philosophie*, I (Salzburg, 1953), p. 205; *Die Philosophie des Buddhismus*, p. 29; cf. Oldenberg, *Buddha* (ed. 1961), p. 215 (= Oldenberg-Foucher[4], p. 257); *PTS. Dictionary*, s.v. *viññāṇa* (cited by Har Dayal). We are even told that this question is already set forth in the *Bṛhadāraṇyaka-Upaniṣad* (IV, 4, 2): *savijñāno bhavati, savijñānam evānvavakrāmati.* Thus, A. Foucher in Senart, *Bṛhadāraṇyaka-Upaniṣad*, p. xxiii: ". . . the *vijñānam* of the dead (notice the analogy with Buddhist terminology) charged with his science, with his works and experience acquired, enters into a new existence as a caterpillar goes from one blade of grass to the next." See also Keith, *RPhVU.* II, p. 578.—But the opinion according to which the same *viññāṇa* migrates from one existence to the next is formally condemned in the Canon; and the texts which are the supports of our authors—the episodes of Godhika and Vakkali, and the *Mahānidāna-Sutta*—do not, in our opinion, bear the meaning attributed to them. Cf. below, pp. 21 ff.

129. Cf. *supra*, p. 18 and n. 122.

130. IV, 3, 35. (Trans. Senart; passage quoted above, n. 30.)

131. IV, 4, 3.—We have modified here the translation of Senart: *idaṃ śarīraṃ nihatya, avidyāṃ gamayitvā* "shaking off this inanimate body" (Senart: "shaking off the body, stripping away the non-being"). Cf. Śaṅkara: *avidyāṃ gamayitvā: acetanaṃ kṛtvā* [*śarīram*]. See also Oldenberg, *LUAB.*[2], p. 92 and n. 52.

132. See the preceding note.

133. IV, 4, 4.

134. *Supra*, p. 6; *infra*, p. 29.

135. Even though the same *ātman* is everywhere entirely, its presence becomes more and more "actual," as we go from inert matter to plants and trees, to animals, to man, and to superior beings, to culminate in Hiraṇyagarbha. Cf. *Ait.Ār.* II, 3, 2, with the commentary of Sāyaṇa (cf. Śaṅkara, *Brahmasūtra-bhāṣya*, I, 1, 11; *Taittirīyopaniṣad-bhāṣya*, II, 1, p. 57).—*yady apy eka ātmā sarvabhūteṣu sthāvarajaṅgameṣu gūḍhaḥ, tathāpi cittopādhiviśeṣatāratamyād ātmanaḥ*

kūṭasthanityasyaikarūpasyāpy uttarottaram āviṣkṛtasya tāratamyam aiśvaryaśaktiviśeṣaiḥ śrūyate, Śaṅkara, *Brahmasūtra-bhāṣya*, I, 1, 11 (p. 177).—*yathā hi prāṇitvāviśeṣe 'pi manuṣyādistambaparyanteṣu jñānaiśvaryādipratibandhaḥ pareṇa pareṇa bhūyān bhavan dṛśyate, tathā manuṣyādiṣv eva Hiraṇyagarbhaparyanteṣu jñānaiśvaryādyabhivyaktir api pareṇa pareṇa bhūyasī bhavati, ibid.*, I, 3, 30 (p. 335). Cf. also *BĀU.* IV, 3, 32-33; *TU.* II, 8; *Ātmabodha*, 58.

Through the effect of his *karman*, a man may sometimes drop to the level of an inferior species. But no existence is definitive (cf. *supra*, n. 54). The effects of *karman* are exhausted and from one existence we pass on to another. And the seed of good we all carry must one day blossom. "The future of the soul is not finally determined by what it has felt, thought and done in this one earthly life. The soul has chances of acquiring merit and advancing to life eternal. Until the union with the timeless Reality is attained, there will be some form of life or other, which will give scope to the individual soul to acquire enlightenment and attain life eternal . . . as every existing thing has the form of the Divine, it has also the promise of good," Radhakrishnan, *Up.*, p. 115. "Truth will be victorious on earth, and it is the nature of the cosmic process that the finite individual is called upon to work through the exercise of his freedom for that goal through ages of struggle and effort. The soul has risen from the sleep of matter, through plant and animal life, to the human level and is battling with ignorance and imperfection to take possession of its infinite kingdom. It is absolute, not in its actual empirical condition, but in its potentiality, in its capacity to appropriate the Absolute. The historical process is not a mere external chain of events, but offers a succession of spiritual opportunities. Man has to attain a mastery over it and reveal the higher world operating in it," Radhakrishnan, *Eastern Religions and Western Thought*[2], pp. 89-90 (cf. p. 129). "By the constant practice of goodness is finally attained the highest form of existence in which man becomes capable of the experience of union with the universal soul," *ibid.*, p. 103.—Compare with Origen: "As it is God himself who has sown that seed in us, who has imprinted it in us and rendered it connatural with us, one can certainly cover it up and hide it, but never totally destroy it nor extinguish it; it continues endlessly to burn and to shine, to glow and to radiate, and unceasingly it tends to raise itself towards God." (Origen, quoted by Meister Eckhart, "Of noble man," in *Traités et Sermons*, p. 106 [translation quoted].)

The Upaniṣads foreshadow the Jātakas, "the greatest epic in literature of the Ascent of Man" (Mrs. Rhys Davids, "Jātakas and the Man," *Indian Art and Letters* [London], *N.S.*, XV [1941], p. 81). Note, however, that this doctrine should not be confused with that of *saṃsāra-suddhi*, pure determinism, which the Ājīvikas professed, but which is foreign to Buddhist thought, according to which each man is responsible for his actions. As Miss Horner has clearly emphasized, Buddhism avoids, here too, extreme positions, and holds itself to the "middle way" (*majjhimā paṭipadā*: cf. *supra*, p. 18). [I. B. Horner, "The Concept of Freedom in the Pāli Canon," in *Présence du Bouddhisme* (= *France-Asie*, XVI, Saigon, 1959), pp. 343 ff.] It is true that the seed of Good which we all bear is never lost; but we may hasten its blooming, by following the Discipline (otherwise, this would make no sense)—as we may also delay it, if we abandon ourselves to our natural inclinations. In other words, we may *make ourselves*, and, in conformity with our human dignity (cf. *supra*, n. 38 end), we *must* make ourselves, although, in truth, we create nothing new: we do nothing but become that which we truly are. Buddhism, on this point, has sometimes been compared with the philosophy of Sartre; but Buddhism, as we understand it, makes us rather think of the philosophy of Jaspers, where "predestination and liberty are joined" (M. Dufrenne and P. Ricœur, *Karl Jaspers et la Philosophie de l'Existence* [Paris, 1947], p. 121; cf. p. 117, n. 19: "We shall still go part of the way with Sartre, but we shall part company from him when we understand that the self in making itself through its liberty meets itself and *rediscovers* itself").—"I become, it is true, in that I create myself; but if I am truly myself, then I have not created myself," Jaspers, *Philosophie*, II, p. 36. "I create myself in the phenomenal world but have in no way created myself in eternity," *ibid.*, p. 47.—Cf. *infra*, n. 219, and Appendix II (on liberty, Appendix I).

136. Deussen (*Up.*, p. 476, n. 3; *AGPh.* I, 2, pp. 298-299) offers a different interpretation. But it does not seem to us to be very plausible. It is the ritualists who are the target here (cf. *supra*, n. 54; *infra*, p. 180).

137. Cf. *supra*, n. 54; *infra*, p. 95.

138. *prāṇa*: cf. *supra*, n. 29.—*prakaraṇavākyasāmarthyāc ca para evātmātra prāṇaśabdavācyaḥ*, Śaṅkara, *Bṛhadāraṇyakopaniṣad-bhāṣya*, IV, 4, 7 (p. 669). [Cf. *Brahmasūtra-bhāṣya*, I, 1, 23.]

139. *BĀU.* IV, 4, 6-7. (Trans. Senart, modified.)—On the image of the snake shedding its dead skin, cf. *infra*, p. 95; p. 183, n. 6.

140. *Ibid.* IV, 4, 5. (Trans. Senart.)

141. *atho apy anye bandhamokṣakuśalāḥ khalv āhuḥ: satyaṃ kāmādipūrvake puṇyāpuṇye śarīragrahaṇakāraṇam, tathāpi kāmaprayukto hi puruṣaḥ puṇyāpuṇye karmaṇī upacinoti; kāmaprahāṇe tu karma vidyamānam api puṇyāpuṇyopacayakaraṃ na bhavati. upacite api puṇyāpuṇye karmaṇī kāmaśūnye phalārambhake na bhavataḥ. tasmāt kāma eva saṃsārasya mūlam,* Śaṅkara, *Bṛhadāraṇyakopaniṣad-bhāṣya,* IV, 4, 5 (pp. 655-656). Cf. *ibid.*, 6 (p. 657): . . . *kāmo mūlaṃ saṃsārasya . . . ata ucchinnakāmasya vidyamānāny api karmāṇi brahmavido vandhya-prasavāni bhavanti.* See also Radhakrishnan, *Indian Philosophy*[2], II, pp. 623-624.

142. III, 33 and 99 (cf. *supra*, pp. 15-16).—Cf. Lamotte, *Traité*, II, p. 748; Venkata Ramanan, pp. 229-230.

143. Cf. *ChU.* VII, 23-24: *yo vai bhūmā tat sukham. nālpe sukham asti, bhūmaiva sukham . . . yo vai bhūmā tad amṛtam, atha yad alpaṃ tan martyam.*—*BĀU.* III, 4, 2; 5, 1; 7, 23: *ato 'nyad ārtam* (". . . words laden with meaning, a world of experience compressed within them," Deussen, *AGPh.* I, 2, p. 128).

144. Cf. below, pp. 23-24.

145. *A.* III, 99 (*supra*, pp. 15-16).—Cf. the following verse cited in the Buddhist epigraphy of Indonesia:

ajñānāc cīyate karma janmanaḥ karma kāraṇam |
jñānān na cīyate karma karmābhāvān na jāyate ||

(On *ajñāna* [= *avidyā*] and *jñāna*, cf. *infra*, p. 209 and n. 13.)

In the light of the text of the *Aṅguttara*, which we have quoted, the remarks of E. Frauwallner, *Geschichte der indischen Philosophie*, I, p. 193, can doubtless be modified.

146. *patiṭṭhite viññāṇe virūḷhe nāmarūpassa avakkanti hoti, S.* XII, 39 (vol. II, p. 66).

147. *A.* I, pp. 223-224. Cf. *Śālistamba-Sūtra*, cited by La Vallée Poussin, "Dogmatique bouddhique," *loc. cit.*, p. 302, n. 1.

148. Cf. Appendix IV.

149. On the importance of *viññāṇa* in the Pāli Canon, cf. Oldenberg, *Buddha* (ed. 1961), p. 237 (= Oldenberg-Foucher[4], p. 288). Let us recall that, in the Upaniṣads and in classical Vedānta, the expressions *vijñānamaya-ātman, vijñānātman* designate the empirical individual (*TU.* II, 4; *Muṇḍ.Up.* III, 2, 7; *Praśna-Up.* IV, 9, 11).

Vijñāna/viññāṇa is that which binds us; but, well conducted, it is also that which delivers us. It is only when consciousness has removed all the empirical forms that veil Being, that the latter reveals itself to us (cf. *supra*, pp. 9 ff.). It is by consciousness that we must go beyond consciousness to become Consciousness. It is not, therefore, by chance that the *vijñāna* (= *buddhi* = *manas*) is called the "charioteer" of the chariot which is our psycho-physical individuality (*infra*, p. 29). It is *vijñāna/viññāṇa* which makes the finitude of man *open*, unlike that of inferior beings which is closed (*supra*, n. 38 [last paragraph]).—The *Aitareya-Āraṇyaka* (II, 3, 2; cf. above, n. 135) sheds light upon the value of consciousness: *martyenāmṛtam īpsati* "by the mortal [the man endowed with consciousness] desires the Immortal."

150. All this, according to *S.* XXII, 53 (vol. III, pp. 53-54).

151. *seyyathā pi dve naḷakalāpiyo aññamaññaṃ nissāya tiṭṭheyyuṃ, evam eva kho nāmarūpapaccayā viññāṇaṃ, viññāṇapaccayā nāmarūpaṃ . . . tāsaṃ ce naḷakalāpīnaṃ ekaṃ ākaḍḍheyya, ekā papateyya; aparaṃ ce ākaḍḍheyya, aparā papateyya: evam eva kho nāmarūpanirodhā viññāṇanirodho, viññāṇanirodhā nāmarūpanirodho, S.* II, p. 114. Cf. La Vallée Poussin, *Siddhi*, I, pp. 122, 199; *MKV.*, p. 561 (*Śālistamba-Sūtra*); Lamotte, *Somme*, II, 1, pp. 58-59.—*D.* II, pp. 32, 62-63.

152. *M.*, Sutta 38.

153. Lamotte, *Histoire*, p. 40. The quotation is from the *Mahānidāna-Sutta* (*D.* II, p. 63).—Cf. *MKV.*, p. 552; Lamotte, *Somme*, II, 1, p. 55.

154. Lamotte, *Histoire*, p. 661.—Cf. *Visuddhimagga*, already quoted (n. 122). As Oldenberg has also remarked, this text "which seemed to uphold the theory of the passage of knowledge from one being to another, promptly corrects itself: in reality, it says, none of the elements of life migrates from an old existence to a new, but the elements in question rather create themselves anew by way of the causes enclosed in the old existence." (Oldenberg-Foucher[4], p. 257, n. 2.)

155. These are expressions used in scholastic literature. However, the expression *viññāṇa-sota* is met with already in *D.* III, p. 105.

156. *Mil.*, quoted above, n. 122.

157. Cf. *supra*, n. 77; Appendix V.

158. *appatiṭṭhitena viññāṇena Godhiko (Vakkali) kulaputto parinibbuto, S.* I, p. 122; III, p. 124.

159. *M.* I, p. 140 (*supra*, n. 38).

160. *BĀU.* II, 4, 12-13; IV, 5, 13-14. Cf. also the reflection of Indra, in *ChU.* VIII, 11 (*supra*, p. 7 and n. 44). On *saṃjñā*, cf. H. von

Glasenapp, in *Festschrift Nobel*, pp. 59-60. Śaṅkara glosses the word by *viśeṣa-saṃjñā* or *viśeṣa-vijñāna* "specific consciousness." It is said that, in Buddhism, *vijñāna* means "elementary consciousness of the object," and *saṃjñā*, "apperception or distinct idea of the object" (May, nn. 208 and 252, with bibliography). Note, however, that in the Nikāyas this distinction does not yet appear clearly. Thus, *S.* III, p. 87:

saññā: sañjānātīti kho, bhikkhave, tasmā saññā ti vuccati. kiñ ca sañjānāti?—nīlam pi sañjānāti, pītakam pi sañjānāti, lohitakam pi sañjānāti, odātam pi sañjānāti . . .

viññāṇa: vijānātīti kho, bhikkhave, tasmā viññāṇan ti vuccati. kiñ ca vijānāti?—ambilam pi vijānāti, tittakam pi vijānāti, kaṭukam pi vijānāti, madhukam pi vijānāti, khārikam pi vijānāti, akhārikam pi vijānāti, loṇkam pi vijānāti, aloṇakam pi vijānāti . . .

Cf. Mrs. Rhys Davids, *The Birth of Indian Psychology* . . . , p. 320: ". . . *viññāṇa* is, when defined in the Suttas, really nothing more than just *saññā* . . ." Let us recall that the *saññāmaya-attan* of the *Poṭṭhapāda-Sutta* is none other than the *vijñānamaya-ātman* of the *Taittirīya-Upaniṣad* (*supra*, p. 68). See also E. H. Johnston, note on *Buddhacarita*, XII, 85 (translation of *Buddhacarita* = *Panjab University Oriental Publications*, No. 32, Calcutta, 1936).

Another important point: The majority of modern interpreters translate *pretya* "after death." Such is also the opinion of Śaṅkara.[a] However, this hardly seems to accord with what follows immediately in the text (see below), nor with the doctrine, in general, of the Upaniṣads, concerning Deliverance. This has nothing to do with death (cf. *supra*, n. 54; p. 10; *infra*, p. 144). We thus think that the word *pretya* means here, not "after the death" (of a delivered person), but simply "after Deliverance." Literally, *pretya* means: "being gone," whence "after death." Now Deliverance, too, is a "departure," a "death." Only what is in question here is a spiritual attitude, and not a corporeal dissolution. It is, in fact, in this sense that Śaṅkara interprets the word elsewhere: *asmāl lokāt pretya: dṛṣṭādṛṣṭeṣṭaviṣayasamudāyo hy ayaṃ lokaḥ, tasmād asmāl lokāt pretya* pratyāvṛtya nirapekṣo bhūtvā (*Taittirīyopaniṣad-bhāṣya*, II, 8, 5).—*pretya vyāvṛtya mamāhaṃbhāvalakṣaṇād avidyārūpād asmāl lokād uparamya sarvātmaikatvabhāvam advaitam āpannāḥ santo 'mṛtā bhavanti, brahmaiva bhavantīty arthaḥ* (*Padabhāṣya* on *Kena-Up.* II, 5. Cf. *Vākyabhāṣya*[b]: *pretya mṛtvāsmāl lokāc charīrādyanātmalakṣaṇāt, vyāvṛttamamatvāhaṃkārāḥ santa ity arthaḥ, amṛtā amaraṇadharmāṇo nityavijñānāmṛtatvasvabhāvā eva bhavanti.* In his commentaries on the *Kena-Up.* I, 2, Śaṅkara is hesitant). See also *Some Thoughts*, p. 28, n. 80.—When it is said that the Delivered one, "rising from his body," attains his true nature (*asmāc charīrāt samutthāya paraṃ jyotir upasaṃpadya svena rūpeṇābhiniṣpadyate, ChU.* VIII, 3, 4; 12, 3; cf. *MaiU.* II, 2), this is not to say that he really rises out of his body as one rises from a seat: it is not by leaving something other that one attains one's true nature; if it were really a matter of "attaining" to something, it would not be one's true nature (cf. *supra*, n. 36). What is meant is simply that he abandons the false identification of the *ātman* with the body: *asmāc charīrāt samutthāya: śarīrātmabhāvanāṃ parityajyety arthaḥ. na tv āsanād iva samutthāyetīha yuktam. svena rūpeṇeti viśeṣaṇāt. na hy anyata utthāya svarūpaṃ saṃpattavyam. svarūpam eva hi tan na bhavati pratipattavyaṃ cet syāt*, Śaṅkara, *Chāndogyopaniṣad-bhāṣya*, VIII, 3, 4 (cf. *infra*, n. 245). Let us also recall what Śaṅkara writes, regarding the famous passage from the *Bṛhadāraṇyaka-Upaniṣad* (IV, 4, 7; *supra*, p. 20): As the snake abandons its dead skin, as not being itself (*anātmabhāvena*), so the Delivered one (*mukta*) abandons his body as not being himself (*anātmabhāvena*); his body lies as though it were dead (*mṛtam iva*). The text says in fact: "Here below, he attains *brahman*" (*atra brahma samaśnute*). And as Śaṅkara makes clear, in the same commentary: the idea of local separation is foreign to Deliverance (*mokṣo na deśāntaragamanādy apekṣate*; cf. *supra*, p. 57).—Compare with Plotinus, *Enneads*, V, 1, 10: "This is therefore what a being is in itself, exterior and immaterial; it is being isolated from the body and containing nothing of its nature. This is why the demiurge *put the soul outside the world again, and enveloped the world within it*, says Plato apropos the universe; he is indicating the part of the soul which rests in the intelligible; for us, he says that our soul 'comes out through the head mounting right to the heights.' When he recommends that we separate from the body, he is not talking about a local separation (for that separation is established by nature); he intends that there should be no leaning towards the body, even in imagination, and that one should remain a stranger to it . . . " (Trans. Bréhier.)—*etebhyo bhūtebhyaḥ samutthāya tāny evānuvinaśyati*: this sentence from the *Bṛhadāraṇyaka-Upaniṣad* (II, 4, 12, IV, 5, 13) is not necessarily speaking of a material destruction of the "elements" (*bhūta*): these may be "destroyed" simply by Knowledge (cf. *infra*, p. 175, n. 174). The specific consciousness (*viśeṣa-saṃjñā, viśeṣa-vijñāna*; cf. above) finds a point of support in the elements of individuality it "superimposes" upon the Absolute (*kārya-karaṇabhūtabhūtopādhibhyaḥ*, says Śaṅkara); it disappears as soon as that "superimposition" is removed by Knowledge.

---

a. *śarīrāvasthitasyāpi viśeṣasaṃjñā nopapadyate, kim uta kārya-karaṇavimuktasya sarvataḥ* (*Bṛhadāraṇyakopaniṣad-bhāṣya*, II, 4, 12). Note that, according to Ānandajñāna, by *śarīrāvasthita*, Śaṅkara understands simply the state of deep sleep, which he contrasts with total Deliverance (cf. *supra*, p. 67): *suṣuptasyeti yāvat*. This is the interpretation followed by Swāmī Mādhavānanda, in his translation of the *Bṛhadāraṇyakopaniṣad-bhāṣya* (fourth edition, Calcutta, Advaita Ashrama, 1965). It seems forced, however.

b. Cf. Sengaku Mayeda, "On Śaṅkara's authorship of the *Kenopaniṣadbhāṣya*," *IIJ*. X, 1 (1967), pp. 33-55.

161. *M.* I, p. 140 (*supra*, n. 38).

162. *avināśī vā are 'yam ātmānucchittidharmā*, *BĀU.* IV, 5, 14. Cf. Deussen, *Up.*, p. 485, n.; *AGPh.* I, 2, p. 314.—*Supra*, n. 38a (p. 49).

163. *M.* I, p. 140 (*supra*, n. 38).

164. *yad vai tan na vijānāti vijānan vai tan na vijānāti; na hi vijñātur vijñāter viparilopo vidyate, avināśitvāt; na tu tad dvitīyam asti tato 'nyad vibhaktaṃ yad vijānīyāt*, *BĀU.* IV, 3, 30.

165. *yatra hi dvaitam iva bhavati tad itara itaraṃ jighrati, tad itara itaraṃ paśyati, tad itara itaraṃ śṛṇoti, tad itara itaram abhivadati, tad itara itaraṃ manute, tad itara itaraṃ vijānāti; yatra vā asya sarvam ātmaivābhūt tat kena kaṃ jighret, tat kena kaṃ paśyet, tat kena kaṃ śṛṇuyāt, tat kena kam abhivadet, tat kena kaṃ manvīta, tat kena kaṃ vijānīyāt? BĀU.* II, 4, 14 (cf. IV, 5, 15). [Trans. Senart, modified.] See also *supra*, p. 7.

166. *yenedaṃ sarvaṃ vijānāti taṃ kena vijānīyāt? vijñātāram are kena vijānīyāt? BĀU.* II, 4, 14; IV, 5, 15.

167. Śaṅkara writes: Even in the state of ignorance (cf. *supra*, n. 90 end), where one sees the other, the subject of knowledge cannot know himself. It is only possible to know something that is object; the subject, however, can never become an object for himself: fire does not burn itself. Under these circumstances, when all duality is transcended, when only the absolute subject remains, without a second, how will it know itself? *yatrāpy avidyāvasthāyām anyo 'nyaṃ paśyati, tatrāpi yenedaṃ sarvaṃ vijānāti taṃ kena vijānīyāt? yena vijānāti tasya karaṇasya vijñeye viniyuktatvāt. jñātuś ca jñeya eva hi jijñāsā, nātmani. na cāgner iva ātmā ātmano viṣayaḥ, na cāviṣaye jñātur*

jñānam upapadyate. tasmād yenedaṃ sarvaṃ vijānāti taṃ vijñātāraṃ kena karaṇena ko vānyo vijānīyāt? yadā tu punaḥ paramārthavivekino brahmavido vijñātaiva kevalo 'dvayo vartate, taṃ vijñātāram, are, kena vijānīyād iti. (*Bṛhadāraṇyakopaniṣad-bhāṣya*, II, 4, 14. On our passage see also Śaṅkara, *Brahmasūtra-bhāṣya*, I, 4, 22, p. 418; cf. *Chāndogyopaniṣad-bhāṣya*, VII, 24, 1; *Taittirīyopaniṣad-bhāṣya*, II, 1, p. 49; "*Lakṣaṇa, Lakṣaṇā*, and Apophaticism in Śaṅkara's Commentary on *Taittirīyopaniṣad* II, 1," *Le parole e i marmi: Studi in onore di Raniero Gnoli nel suo 70° compleanno* [Roma, 2001: *Serie Orientale Roma* XCII, 1-2], pp. 89-90, n. 22.)

Cf. Deussen: "The source of the whole idea of the unknowability of the Ātman lies in the Yājñavalkya discourses of Bṛhadāraṇyakam. *The boldness and directness with which it is presented there, as well as the originality of its arguments, seem to indicate one single genius as its origi-nator.*" (*AGPh.* I, 2, p. 73; our italics.)

"The subject does now know himself, any more than the fire burns itself": this brings to mind what Wittgenstein writes (after Schopenhauer): "Where in the world is a metaphysical subject to be perceived?—You say, the same relation prevails here as that between the eye and the field of vision. But you do *not* really see the eye." (*Tractatus*, 5. 633 [cf. Gardiner, *op. cit.*, p. 85, n.].)

On *svātmani kriyāvirodha* (or *vṛttivirodha—karma-kartṛ-virodha* or *kartṛ-karma-virodha*), cf. St. Schayer, *Ausgewählte Kapitel aus der Prasannapadā* (W Krakowie, 1931), n. 14; R. Garbe, *op. cit.*, pp. 217, 358; and other references in May, n. 135. See also our translation of the *Vigrahavyāvartanī, loc. cit.*, p. 241, note to v. XXXV.

168. Cf. *supra*, p. 68; *infra*, n. 257.

169. *Supra*, n. 54.

170. *Supra*, p. 21.

171. Such, it seems to us, is the meaning of the Pāli texts cited above. They do not indicate that the *viññāṇa* of a man who has not yet reached Deliverance passes from one existence to the other.—*Supra*, n. 128.

172. *BĀU.* IV, 5, 13 (*vijñānaghana, ibid.*, II, 4, 12).—Senart (*Bṛhadāraṇyaka-Upaniṣad*, p. 88, n. 1) is wrong about the meaning of these passages.

173. *D.* I, p. 223 (ed. Nālandā, p. 190).—Cf. *M.* I, pp. 329-330 (*Brahmanimantaṇika-Sutta*): *viññāṇam anidassanaṃ anantaṃ sabbatopabhaṃ, taṃ paṭhaviyā paṭhavattena ananubhūtaṃ, āpassa āpattena ananubhūtaṃ, tejassa tejattena ananubhūtaṃ, vāyassa vāyattena*

ananubhūtaṃ, bhūtānaṃ bhūtattena ananubhūtaṃ, devānaṃ devattena ananubhūtaṃ, Pajāpatissa Pajāpatattena ananubhūtaṃ, Brahmānaṃ Brahmattena ananubhūtaṃ, Ābhassarānaṃ Ābhassarattena ananubhūtaṃ, Subhakiṇṇānaṃ Subhakiṇṇattena ananubhūtaṃ, Vehapphalānaṃ Vehapphalattena ananubhūtaṃ, Abhibhussa Abhibhattena ananubhūtaṃ, sabbassa sabbattena ananubhūtaṃ. (On the reading *sabbatopabhaṃ* see K. R. Norman, "An Epithet of Nibbāna," *Śramaṇa-Vidyā, Studies in Buddhism: Professor Jagannath Upadhyaya Commemoration Volume,* I [Sarnath, Varanasi, 1987], pp. 23-31 [= *Collected Papers,* III, Oxford, 1992, pp. 183-189].) See also *S.* I, p. 15; *Dhp.* 409 (= *Sn.* 633); *Ud.* I, 10, p. 9 (= *Netti,* p. 150); VIII, 1, p. 80 *(infra,* p. 135); *Sn.* 1037.— Upaniṣadic parallels: *etad vai tad akṣaraṃ, Gārgi, brāhmaṇā abhivadanti: asthūlam anaṇv ahrasvam adīrgham alohitam asneham acchāyam atamo 'vāyv anākāśam . . . , BĀU.* III, 8, 8 (cf. *Subāla-Up.* III [Radhakrishnan, *Up.*, p. 865]).—

na puṇyapāpe mama nāsti nāśo
na janma dehendriyabuddhir asti |
na bhūmir āpo mama vahnir asti
na cānilo me 'sti na cāmbaraṃ ca ||
evaṃ viditvā paramātmarūpaṃ
guhāśayaṃ niṣkalam advitīyam |
samastasākṣiṃ sadasadvihīnaṃ
prayāti śuddhaṃ paramātmarūpam ||

Kaivalya-Up. 23-24 (edition cited).

See also *Nirvāṇadaśaka* and *Nirvāṇaṣaṭka* (attributed to Śaṅkara), in *Bṛhatstotraratnākara* (Bombay, Veṅkaṭeśvara Press, 1885), pp. 63-65; A. Zieseniss, *Studien zur Geschichte des Śivaismus: Die śivaitischen Systeme in der altjavanischen Literatur,* I (= *Bijdragen tot de Taal-, Land- en Volkenkunde van Nederlandsch-Indië,* 98 [1939], pp. 75-223), p. 165.

Cf. R. Kimura, *A Historical Study of the terms Mahāyāna and Hīnayāna and the Origin of Mahāyāna Buddhism* (= *Journal of the Department of Letters* [University of Calcutta], XII [1925], pp. 45-193), pp. 96-97; E. Frauwallner, "Untersuchungen zum Mokṣadharma," *WZKM.* XXXIII (1926), p. 59.

It seems to us impossible to separate the conception we have outlined, from *citta* "without *citta*" of the Mahāyāna (and not only the *Prajñāpāramitās*; cf. *supra,* n. 20).

174. *Sumaṅgalavilāsinī,* II, pp. 393-394. Cf. *Papañcasūdanī,* II, p. 413. See also N. Dutt, *Aspects of Mahāyāna Buddhism and its relation to Hīnayāna* (London, 1930), pp. 148-149 (cf. the unjust remarks by

Mrs. Rhys Davids, *The Birth of Indian Psychology* . . . , p. 246); *Papañcasūdanī*, IV, p. 28.

Modern interpreters are generally wrong about the meaning of the passages of the *Kevaddha-* and of the *Brahmanimantaṇika-Sutta.* Cf. Hajime Nakamura, "Upaniṣadic tradition and the early school of Vedānta as noticed in Buddhist Scripture," *HJAS.* 18 (1955), pp. 78-79; O. H. de A. Wijesekera, "The Concept of Viññāṇa in Theravāda Buddhism," *JAOS.* 84 (1964), p. 258. It is strange that V. Trenckner, editor of the *Majjhima-Nikāya* I, as well as Miss Horner, translator of the same Nikāya, attributes the words of the Buddha to his adversary. Here is what the *Brahmanimantaṇika-Sutta* says in substance (on the account, cf. *S.* I, pp. 142 ff.; *Jāt.* III, pp. 358 ff.): A Brahmā, called Baka, claims that the condition of the Brahmās is the supreme Reality. It is permanent (*nicca*), stable (*dhuva*), eternal (*sassata*), absolute (*kevala*). It is not born, does not grow old and does not die; it does not disappear and does not return to existence (*na jāyati na jīyati na mīyati na cavati na upapajjati*; cf. *supra*, p. 47). There is no issue beyond this (*ito pan' aññaṃ uttariṃ nissaraṇaṃ n' atthi*).[a]—To this pretension of Baka, the Buddha replies: The condition of the Brahmās is but a phenomenal reality, impermanent (*anicca*) and not permanent (*nicca*), unstable (*addhuva*) and not stable (*dhuva*) . . . It is born, it grows old and it dies; it disappears and returns to existence (*jāyati jīyati mīyati cavati upapajjati*). There is another issue, beyond this one (*aññaṃ uttariṃ nissaraṇaṃ*), which surpasses the perception of all empirical realities whatsoever (*sabbassa sabbattena ananubhūtaṃ*).—"But, if you do not perceive it, Sir, by any means, I hope that it be not nothing for you" (*sace kho te, mārisa, sabbassa sabbattena ananubhūtaṃ, mā h' eva te rittakam eva ahosi tucchakam eva ahosi*), retorts Baka.—No, says the Buddha; for the Reality of which he speaks is universal Consciousness. [In the edition of the Pāli Text Society, pp. 329-330, there should be a dash separating, first of all, *Viññāṇaṃ anidassanaṃ*, etc., from the preceding phrase, pronounced by Baka; and next, the words of the Buddha, from *Handa ca hi*, etc., the phrase pronounced by Baka.]

The *Kevaddha-Sutta* gives a similar lesson: The Mahā-Brahmā himself, who passes for omniscient, is incapable of replying to the question: "Where do the four great elements completely cease" (*kattha nu kho ime cattāro mahābhūtā aparisesā nirujjhanti*)? The Buddha, then modifying the question, gives the reply we have quoted above. (On the subject of the Brahmās, cf. *infra*, p. 146, n. 9; Appendix III.)

In support of our interpretation, we have quoted Buddhaghosa, who makes it clear that *viññāṇa*, in these two passages, is a "name of Nirvāṇa." Note, however, that Buddhaghosa does not conceive of Nirvāṇa as universal and absolute Consciousness (contrary to what N. Dutt writes, *loc. cit.*). On the contrary, he refuses to admit such a conception; he thus resorts to a fantastic etymology for the word *viññāṇa*: *viññātabban ti viññāṇaṃ* (*Sumaṅgalavilāsinī*); *viññāṇan ti vijānitabbaṃ* (*Papañcasūdanī*). "*Viññāṇa* (as name of Nirvāṇa) means: 'what must be known'"! —Cf. *infra*, pp. 187 ff. See also *Some Thoughts*, pp. 24 ff.

---

a. Perhaps an allusion should be seen here to the ritualistic belief, in which the "world of Brahmā" (*Brahmaṇo lokaḥ*) is "the most real" (*sattama: Kauṣītaki-Brāhmaṇa* XX, 1 [ed. Lindner, Jena, 1887]). —Cf. Appendix III.

175. Sanskrit *pudgala*, term unknown in the Upaniṣads.

176. *Bhāra(hāra)-Sutta, S.* XXII, 22 (vol. III, pp. 25-26).

177. See below.

178. *ta eva skandhā ye skandhāntarasyotpādāya vartante pūrvakās te bhāra iti kṛtvoktāḥ; ye tūpeṣyante phalabhūtās te bhārahārā ity uktāḥ*, *TSP.*, p. 130 (on 349). Cf. Vasubandhu, *Abhidharmakośabhāṣya*, p. 468; *AK.* IX, p. 257 and n. 2.

179. *nāhaṃ lokena vivadāmi, loko va mayā vivadati*, *S.* XXII, 94, 3 (vol. III, p. 138). Cf. *MKV.*, p. 370.—*D.* I, p. 202; *S.* I, pp. 14-15; Lamotte, *Traité*, I, pp. 67-68.

180. *AK.* IX, p. 265.

181. *Ibid.*, p. 264. Cf. *Abhidharmakośabhāṣya*, p. 470.—*S.* XLIV, 10 (vol. IV, pp. 400-401). Cf. *supra*, n. 119; Appendix VI, pp. 239-240.

182. Of the belief in the soul.

183. *dṛṣṭidaṃṣṭrāvabhedaṃ ca bhraṃśaṃ cāpekṣya*
karmaṇām |
deśayanti jinā dharmaṃ vyāghrīpotāpahāravat ||

verse of Kumāralāta, quoted by Vasubandhu, *Abhidharmakośabhāṣya*, p. 470 (*AK.* IX, p. 265); cf. Kamalaśīla, *TSP.*, p. 129 (on 348), with the reading *cāvekṣya* in *b*. On the name *Kumāralāta*, see H. Lüders, *Bruchstücke der Kalpanāmaṇḍitikā des Kumāralāta* [Leipzeig, 1926], p. 20.

184. *Supra*, p. 9.

185. *buddhānaṃ pana dve kathā: sammutikathā ca paramatthakathā*

ca. tattha satto poso devo Brahmā ti ādikā sammutikathā nāma, Buddhaghosa, *Sumaṅgalavilāsinī*, II, p. 382; cf. *Kathāvatthuppakaraṇa-Aṭṭhakathā* (ed. Minayeff, *JPTS.* 1889), p. 34; *Sāratthappakāsinī*, II, p. 77; *Manorathapūraṇī*, I, pp. 94-95.—*Saṃmuti* = Sanskrit *saṃmati* (root *man-*): Geiger, *Pāli Literature and Language*, II, § 19.2. The form *saṃvṛti* is due to a "hypersanskritism": Edgerton, *Grammar*, p. 17, § 2.30.—For later definitions of *saṃvṛti* (*samantād varaṇa, paraspara-saṃbhavana, saṃketa*), cf. Murti, pp. 244-245. See also P. V. Bapat, "Sammuti, Sammati, Saṃvṛti," in *Some Aspects of Indo-Iranian Literary and Cultural Traditions* (*Commemoration Volume of Dr. V. G. Paranjpe*, Delhi, Ajanta Publications, 1977), pp. 5-8.

186. The passage which follows is from *MKV.*, pp. 356-358, in the (modified) translation by J. W. De Jong, *Cinq chapitres de la Prasannapadā* (Paris, 1949), pp. 15-18. See also Venkata Ramanan, pp. 133 ff. On the comparison of the Buddhas with doctors, cf. *Saddharmapuṇḍarīka-Sūtra* V, 60 ff. (ed. U. Wogihara-C. Tsuchida, Tokyo, 1958).—*Laṅk.* II, 123:

āture āture yadvad bhiṣag dravyaṃ prayacchati |
buddhā hi tadvat sattvānāṃ cittamātraṃ vadanti vai ||

See also *infra*, pp. 194 and 195.—On the subject of the diversity of teaching according to the degree of spiritual advancement of men, cf. J. Daniélou, *Origène* (Paris, 1948), pp. 58-59, 255 ff.

187. Doctrine of the Cārvākas. Cf. De Jong, n. 42.

188. *upapāduka*: cf. De Jong, n. 43. See also Edgerton, *Dictionary*, s.v.; (J. Wackernagel-)A. Debrunner, *Altindische Grammatik*, II, 2 (Göttingen, 1954), p. 481.

189. *sattvadhātu*: cf. Edgerton, *Dictionary*, s.v. *dhātu* (6).

190. *ekajagadbandhubhiḥ*, not translated by De Jong, perhaps because the expression is lacking in the Tibetan.

191. This is a metaphor. Cf. Venkata Ramanan, p. 294: "The thirty-seven factors constitute the Way that leads to Nirvāṇa; faring on this Way one reaches the city of Nirvāṇa. The city has three gates, viz., *śūnyatā, animittatā* and *apraṇihitatā.*" According to Yaśomitra, *nirvāṇapura* means, not "the city of Nirvāṇa," but "the city which is Nirvāṇa" (*nirvāṇam eva puram*), *Abhidharmakośa-vyākhyā*, p. 721 (ed. Wogihara, Tokyo, 1932-1936). See also Oldenberg, *LUAB.*[2], p. 310, n. 200. Let us recall the expressions *brahmaloka* (= *brahmaiva lokaḥ*), *brahmapura* (= *brahmaiva puram*): *supra*, p. 47. See also "Notes bouddhiques," *Indologica Taurinensia*, VII/1979 (*Dr. Ludwik Sternbach Felicitation Volume*), pp. 107-108; *JA.* 1986, p. 294.

192. Cf. *infra*, p. 39 and n. 278.

193. Cf. *MSA*. XVIII, 92.

194. *skandhebhyas tattvānyatvābhyām avācyaḥ*, *BCAP*., p. 215. Cf. *MKV*., pp. 283, 436; *TS*., 336-337; *AK*. IX, pp. 232 ff.

According to La Vallée Poussin (*Le Dogme et la Philosophie du Bouddhisme*[2] [Paris, 1930], p. 108), the Pudgalavādin "sought to reconcile orthodoxy to the necessity for something capable of transmigrating." In fact, it emerges from the *MSA*. XVIII, 93, that even orthodox Buddhists sometimes conceive of the *pudgala* as something "inexpressible" (*avācya*), neither identical to the *skandhas* nor distinct from them:

ekatvānyatvato 'vācyas tasmād doṣadvayād asau |
skandhātmatvaprasaṅgāc ca taddravyatvaprasaṅgataḥ ||

Maintaining equal distance from the two extreme views, Buddhism was, in fact, obliged to adopt such a position. Rejecting nihilism (*ucchedavāda*), it could not identify the *pudgala* with the ephemeral *skandhas*; and, on the other hand, rejecting eternalism (*śāśvatavāda*), it could not accord it an autonomous reality. The entire heresy of the Pudgalavādins, consists therefore in this: while, for the orthodox, the *pudgala* is nothing but a "designation" (*prajñapti*) of a phenomenal series, for the Pudgalavādins, it is a "substance" (*dravya*).—We do not believe that the explanation of the verse given by the commentator (followed by S. Lévi) is correct: *ekatve hi skandhānām ātmatvaṃ prasajyate, pudgalasya ca dravyasattvam* . . . We think on the contrary that, "If it (= the *pudgala*) were one with the *skandhas*, it would have their nature (that is to say, it would be ephemeral); if, on the other hand, it were distinct, it would be a substance." (Cf. *supra*, n. 3.)

(On *avācya/avaktavya*, in this context, cf. E. Frauwallner, *Die Philosophie des Buddhismus*, p. 86: "This inexpressibility does not of course correspond to the ineffability of a highest Being that lies always beyond the grasp of human thought. Rather, it was customary at that time to characterize states that could not be clearly defined, as 'neither this nor that' and to that extent inexpressible.")

195. *TS*. 336.—Cf. La Vallée Poussin, *MKV*., p. 283, n. 4.

196. Cf. E. Conze, *Buddhist Thought in India* (London, 1962; "Ann Arbor Paperbacks," The University of Michigan Press, 1967), pp. 127-128. We may recall that the Naiyāyika Uddyotakara cites the *Bhāra(hāra)-Sūtra* (*supra*, p. 25): *Nyāyavārttika*, III, 1, 1, in *Nyāyadarśanam*, I, edited with Vātsyāyana's *Bhāṣya*, Uddyotakara's *Vārttika*,

Vācaspati Miśra's *Tātparyaṭīkā* and Viśvanātha's *Vṛtti*, by Amarendra Mohan Tarkatīrtha and Taranath Nyāya-Tarkatīrtha, Calcutta, 1936 (*Calcutta Sanskrit Series*, XVIII), p. 703.

197. Cf. *TSP.*, p. 125 (on 336): *te hi . . . pudgalavyājena . . . ātmānaṃ kalpayanti . . . tathāhīdam ātmano lakṣaṇam: yo hi śubhāśubhakarmabhedānāṃ kartā svakṛtakarmaphalasya ceṣṭāniṣṭasya ca bhoktā yaś ca pūrvaskandhaparityāgād aparaskandhāntaropādānāt saṃsarati bhoktā ca sa ātmeti. etac ca sarvaṃ pudgale 'pīṣṭam iti kevalaṃ nāmni vivādaḥ.*

198. *Supra*, p. 6 and n. 30.

199. Pp. 25-28. Cf. *S.* V, 10, 6 (vol. I, p. 135); *Visuddhimagga*, XVIII, 25-28 (edition cited); *Abhidharmakośabhāṣya*, pp. 465-466 (*AK.* IX, p. 249); *MKV.*, p. 346, ll. 1-2; Lamotte, *Traité*, II, p. 749. See also *D.* II, p. 100 (cf. Waldschmidt, *op. cit.*, p. 198; *supra*, n. 83 [p. 75]). *Jāt.* 244 expresses the same idea with a different image: Is there a Ganges (= an individual), independent of the waters, sands and the two banks? No!

200. Cf. *supra*, n. 31.—Coomaraswamy, *Hinduism and Buddhism*, pp. 72-73.—Structural analogy between the account of the *Milindapañhā* and that of the *Chāgaleya-Upaniṣad*, pointed out by Belvalkar-Ranade, p. 132.—*Mil.*, p. 25 (cf. Lamotte, *Traité*, II, p. 735): *vohāro nāmamattaṃ yad idaṃ Nāgaseno ti, na h' ettha puggalo upalabbhati.* Cf. *ChU.* VI, 1, 4-6 (*supra*, p. 12 and n. 91): *vācārambhaṇaṃ vikāro nāmadheyam.*

201. *atha yaiḥ paripūrṇo 'bhibhūto 'yaṃ rathitaś ca tair vaiva muktas tv ātmann eva sāyujyam upaiti, MaiU.* IV, 4.

202. *Kaṭha-Up.* III, 3.

203. *MaiU.* II, 3 ff.; *Chāgaleya-Up.* 7 (edition cited).

204. Cf. *supra*, p. 8 and n. 56.

205. *prapañcāntar anugamyamāno 'pi na tasmin sthitaḥ kiṃ tv asaṅgatayā prapañcātīte svasvarūpe sthita eva san svacaitanyābhāsena prapañcam avabhāsayaṃs tatra sthita iva bhavati, na vastutas tatrāsti*, Rāmatīrtha on *MaiU.* II, 4.

206. Cf. *supra*, p. 59, n. e.; p. 83, n. 107.

207. Cf. *infra*, p. 34 and n. 245.

208. Cf. *infra*, p. 131 and n. 87.

209. *MaiU.* II, 4. 7; III, 2-3.—The Absolute is "beyond good and evil." Cf. *supra*, n. 58; pp. 15-16 and n. 107; *infra*, n. 216; p. 31 and n. 227.

210. In the very first line of the passage we, in fact, read: *kāyo te rathasaññāto manosārathiko lahu.* It is only towards the end that the

word *attā* is substituted for *mano*.—On *ātman* = *manas* (= *citta*), cf. *infra*, n. 245 (last paragraph); p. 183, n. 9. (Wrongly, Coomaraswamy, *Hinduism and Buddhism*, p. 73 and n. 301; see also *infra*, p. 201, n. 12a [p. 202].)

211. Our text distinguishes the "charioteer" from the "master of the chariot." The "charioteer" is engaged in action, whilst the "master of the chariot," the *ātman*, the Absolute, is foreign to all movement. This conception is certainly better than that which has the *ātman* itself as the charioteer (below).—According to the *Kaṭha-Upaniṣad*, *manas* is the "reins" (*pragraha*) used by the *buddhi* (= *vijñāna*). In *MaiU.* II, 6, however, *manas* is the "driver" (*niyantṛ*). In this passage, as in that from the *Jātaka*, *manas* seems to be simply a synonym of *vijñāna*. Let us recall that in the Pāli Canon, *citta*, *manas* and *viññāṇa* are employed as synonyms: cf. Lamotte, *Vimalakīrti*, p. 51. See also *AK.* II, p. 176 and n. 5. (*vijñānaṃ hṛdayaṃ cittaṃ mano buddhiś ca tat samam*, Kāmandaki, I, 30, cited by W. Ruben, *Die Nyāyasūtra's* [= *Abhandlungen für die Kunde des Morgenlandes*, XVIII, 2, Leipzig, Deutsche Morgenländische Gesellschaft, 1928], n. 47). On the position of the Upaniṣads, cf. Deussen, *AGPh.* I, 2, pp. 245-246. Note that, in *TU.* II, 9 (*yato vāco nivartante aprāpya manasā saha*), Śaṅkara glosses *manas* by *vijñāna*.—*tac cātmana upādhibhūtam antaḥkaraṇaṃ mano buddhir vijñānaṃ cittam iti cānekadhā tatra tatrābhilapyate. kvacic ca vṛttivibhāgena saṃśayādivṛttikaṃ mana ity ucyate, niścayādivṛttikaṃ buddhir iti*, *Brahmasūtra-bhāṣya*, II, 3, 32.

Between the *Kaṭha-Upaniṣad* and the *Dhammapada*, we find a striking parallelism:

Kaṭha-Up. III, 5-6:

yas tv avijñānavān bhavaty ayuktena manasā sadā |
tasyendriyāṇy avaśyāni duṣṭāśvā iva sāratheḥ ||
yas tu vijñānavān bhavati yuktena manasā sadā |
tasyendriyāṇi vaśyāni sadaśvā iva sāratheḥ ||

(Cf. *Śvet.Up.* II, 9.—Bhāravi, *Kirātārjunīya*, II, 39: *duṣṭendriyavāji-vaśyatā*.)

Dhp. 94:

yass' indriyāni samathaṃ gatāni
assā yathā sārathinā sudantā |
pahīnamānassa anāsavassa
devāpi tassa pihayanti tādino ||

212. *Buddhaṃ dhammassāmiṃ vītataṇhaṃ dipaduttamaṃ sārathīnaṃ pavaraṃ*, *Sn.* 83.—*dhammāhaṃ sārathiṃ brūmi*, *S.* I, p. 33 (cf. *infra*,

p. 157, n. 60).—*purisadammasārathi* (Buddha), *Vin.* I, p. 35 (and elsewhere).—*sārathivara, M.* I, p. 386.

213. Note 38. Cf. *infra,* p. 111.

214. *yo kho dhammaṃ passati so maṃ passati, yo maṃ passati so dhammaṃ passati; dhammaṃ hi passanto maṃ passati, maṃ passanto dhammaṃ passati, S.* III, p. 120.—Cf. *infra,* ch. II, and p. 200, n. 9.

215. *attadīpā viharatha attasaraṇā anaññasaraṇā, dhammadīpā dhammasaraṇā anaññasaraṇā, D.* II, p. 100 (cf. *supra,* n. 83). Note the expression *anaññasaraṇā* "having none other for refuge," applied at once to the *attan* and to *dhamma.* Cf. M. and W. Geiger, *Pāli Dhamma,* p. 79. Buddhaghosa too recognizes the equivalence *attan* = *dhamma.* But, according to him, the word *dhamma* means *lokiya-lokuttara-dhamma: ko pan' ettha attā nāma?—lokiya-lokuttara-dhammo. ten' evāha: dhammadīpā dhammasaraṇā anaññasaraṇā ti.* (*Sāratthappakāsinī,* II, p. 268; *Sumaṅgalavilāsinī,* III, p. 846).—On the *lokiya-* and *lokuttara-dhamma,* see Geiger, *op. cit.,* p. 102. ("mundane and supramundane states," I. B. Horner, *Milinda's Questions,* II, [= *Sacred Books of the Buddhists,* XXIII, London, 1964], p. 265 [*Mil.,* p. 390]).—Cf. *infra,* p. 160, n. 72; pp. 187 ff.

216. *A.* I, p. 149.—Note that the *kalyāṇātman* is not a moral agent. It is *kalyāṇa* in the absolute sense. As our text indicates, it is above the empirical distinctions of true and of false, and of good and of evil: it is but a "witness" of our acts, good and bad (cf. *infra,* p. 31 and n. 227).—Cf. Appendix I. [Compare the passage from the *Aṅguttara* with *Mbh.* I, 68, 25 (critical edition) and Manu, VIII, 84. See also P. V. Kane, *History of Dharmaśāstra,* II, 1 (Poona, 1941), p. 7.]

217. *Kaṭha-Up.* III, 3 ff.—Cf. *infra,* p. 157, n. 60.

218. The reflexive use of the word *ātman* accords here marvelously with its metaphysical meaning (cf. *supra,* n. 85).

219. Literally: "who has no *ātman*" (*anātman*).—Even though the *ātman* is our true being, it is not yet "actual" for us: it must "be made," be "created," in some way (cf. Appendix II).

220. The idea is this: For the man who has conquered his phenomenal *ātman* by means of the authentic *ātman,* the phenomenal *ātman* has become the means by which the authentic *ātman* "actualizes" ("the lower self has been turned into a willing and ardent ministrant to the purpose of the higher," Hiriyanna, *The Quest after Perfection,* p. 57; cf. *infra,* p. 180). One, on the other hand, who has not realized the *ātman,* considers his phenomenal *ātman* to be his true *ātman;* but this *ātman* is really his enemy, for it prevents him from

becoming that which he *is*, it causes him to "perish" (cf. Śaṅkara, *Upadeśasāhasrī, padya*, XIII, 26: *anyathā hy ātmahā bhavet*; cf. also Commentary on *Īśā-Up.* 3). That is tantamount to saying that the phenomenal *ātman* is thus the enemy of the true *ātman*: it prevents it from "being actualized."—Different interpretation by Radhakrishnan, *Bhagavadgītā*[2]. Cf., however, p. 189: "If we subdue our petty cravings and desires, if we do not exert our selfish will, we become the channel of the Universal Self," and p. 190: "The lower self is not destroyed. It can be used as a helper, if it is held in check."

221. *BhG.* VI, 5-7. Cf. *ibid.*, III, 37 ff. See also *Mbh.* V, 1158-1159. On *ātmanātmānam*, cf. Daniel H. H. Ingalls, in *Festschrift Nobel*, pp. 101 ff.; M. B. Emeneau, "*Bhagavadgītā* Notes," in *Mélanges Louis Renou*, pp. 272 ff. For the logic of our stanzas, cf. Socrates in Plato's *Republic*, IV, 430 e-431a: "Is not 'master of oneself' an absurd expression? A man who was master of himself would presumably be subject to himself, and the subject would be master; for all these terms apply to the same person.—I think, however, the phrase means that within the man himself, in his soul, there is a better part and a worse; and that he is his own master when the part which is better by nature has the worse under its control." (F. M. Cornford, *The Republic of Plato* [New York-London, Oxford University Press, 1945, etc.], p. 124.) Cf. also Patañjali, *Vyākaraṇa-Mahābhāṣya* on Pāṇini, I, 3, 67, *vārttikas* 8-9; III, 1, 87, *vārttika* 10 (ed. F. Kielhorn, third edition by K. V. Abhyankar, Poona, Bhandarkar Oriental Research Institute: Vol. I, 1962; II, 1965).—J. Vialatoux, *L'intention philosophique* (9th edition, Paris, Presses universitaires de France, 1970), p. 36; p. 72, n. 1.

222. The commentator glosses *nātha* by *avassaya, patiṭṭhā* (*Dhammapadaṭṭhakathā*, III, p. 148; IV, p. 117). Cf. the epithet of Buddha: *lokanātha*. See also, on this subject, Rāhula, *op. cit.*, p. 87, n. 19. Note that this meaning of *nātha* is also Vedic.

223. *Dhp.* 160.—Cf. W. Rau, "Bemerkungen und nichtbuddhistische Sanskrit-Parallelen zum Pāli-Dhammapada," in *Festschrift Nobel*, p. 168.

224. *Dhp.* 379-380.—Cf. W. Rau, *loc. cit.*, p. 174.

225. Cf. *MKV.*, p. 354; La Vallée Poussin, "Dogmatique bouddhique," *loc. cit.*, p. 270.

226. Cf. *supra*, n. 58; Appendix I.

227. *ātmā hi ātmano nāthaḥ ko nu nāthaḥ paro bhavet* |
ātmā hi ātmanaḥ sākṣī kṛtasyāpakṛtasya ca ||

verse cited *MKV.*, p. 354. Cf. the texts mentioned above, n. 216.—

Śvet.Up. VI, 11:

eko devaḥ sarvabhūteṣu gūḍhaḥ
sarvavyāpī sarvabhūtāntarātmā |
karmādhyakṣaḥ sarvabhūtādhivāsaḥ
sākṣī cetā kevalo nirguṇaś ca ||

Ibid., IV, 6 = *Muṇḍ.Up.* III, 1, 1 (= *RV.* I, 164, 20).—*BhG.* IX, 18 (*sākṣī prāṇinām kṛtākṛtasya*, Śaṅkara); *Aṣṭāvakra-Gītā*, XV, 4.—Deussen, *Up.*, Index, s.v. "Zuschauer."—Radhakrishnan, *Indian Philosophy*², II, pp. 601-603.—*Supra*, p. 29.

228. *Supra*, n. 60; cf. p. 37.

229. *Supra*, p. 8 and n. 60.

230. *Supra*, p. 6.

231. Thus, *TS.* 349 (cf. *TSP.*, p. 131).

232. *ātmānam anabhyupagacchatā nedaṃ Tathāgatavacanam arthavattāyāṃ śakyaṃ vyavasthāpayitum, yasmād idam uktam: rūpaṃ, bhadanta, nāham . . . eva etad, bhikṣo, rūpaṃ na tvam . . . viśeṣapratiṣedhaś cāyam, na sāmānyapratiṣedhaḥ. ātmānaṃ cānabhyupagacchatā sāmānyenaiva pratiṣeddhavyam: [nāhaṃ] naiva tvam asīti. viśeṣa-pratiṣedhas tv anyavidhināntarīyako bhavati: yathā vāmenākṣṇā na paśyāmīty ukte gamyata eva dakṣiṇena paśyāmīti . . .*, Uddyotakara, cited *TSP.*, pp. 130-131; cf. *Nyāyavārttika*, III, 1, 1, p. 702 (edition cited). [Cf. E. Steinkellner, "Zur Zitierweise Kamalaśīla's," *WZKSO.* VII (1963), pp. 124-125; for *yathā vāmenākṣṇā . . .*, cf. *Nyāyavārttika*, I, 1, 4, p. 127.]

Note, too, the frequent use, in the Pāli texts, of the word *parato* with *anattato* or *no attato*. Thus, *Theragāthā* 1160: *ye pañca khandhe passanti parato no ca attato.* See also *PTS. Dictionary*, s.v. *para*.

What must be concluded? That there is no *ātman*? or that the *khandhas* are not my *ātman*, because they are "foreign" (*para*) to me? (Cf. Śaṅkara, *Upadeśasāhasrī*, *padya*, XIV, 11: *ya ātmā neti netīti* parāpohena *śeṣitaḥ . . .*)

233. *D.* II, pp. 66-67. See also the Note in *Recent Researches in Buddhist Studies: Essays in Honour of Professor Y. Karunadasa* (Colombo-Hong Kong, 1997), pp. 47 ff.; *Some Thoughts*, pp. 27 ff.

234. Here, we may call upon a familiar comparison. This passage actually brings Hume to mind: "For my part, when I enter most intimately into what I call *myself*, I always stumble on some particular perception or other, of heat or cold, light or shade, love or hatred, pain or pleasure. I never can catch *myself* at any time without a perception, and can never observe anything but the perception.

When my perceptions are remov'd for any time, as by sound sleep; so long am I insensible of *myself*, and may truly be said not to exist. And were all my perceptions remov'd by death, and cou'd I neither think, nor feel, nor see, nor love, nor hate after the dissolution of my body, I shou'd be entirely annihilated, nor do I conceive what is farther requisite to make me a perfect non-entity. If any one, upon serious and unprejudic'd reflection, thinks he has a different notion of *himself*, I must confess I can reason no longer with him. All I can allow him is, that he may be in the right as well as I, and that we are essentially different in this particular. He may, perhaps, perceive something simple and continu'd, which he calls *himself*; tho' I am certain there is no such principle in me.

"But setting aside some metaphysicians of this kind, I may venture to affirm of the rest of mankind, that they are nothing but a bundle or collection of different perceptions, which succeed each other with an inconceivable rapidity, and are in a perpetual flux and movement." (*A Treatise on Human Nature*, edited, with preliminary dissertations and notes, by T. H. Green and T. H. Grose, London, 1874, vol. I, p. 534.)

But the Buddha had gone further than Hume!

235. *etena hi rūpādayaḥ skandhā ahaṃkāraviṣayatvena pratiṣiddhāḥ . . . tadvilakṣaṇo 'sty ātmeti sūcitaṃ bhavati, TSP.*, pp. 130-131; cf. *Nyāyavārttika*, III, 1, 1, p. 702 (edition cited).

236. Pp. 7 ff., 14-15; p. 78, n. 90. See also below, p. 111 (*Saptaśatikā Prajñāpāramitā*).

237. Edition-translation by S. Lévi, "Encore Aśvaghoṣa," *JA*. 1928 (2), pp. 209 ff. Cf. Sujitkumār Mukhopādhyāya, *Nairātmyaparipṛcchā*, Viśvabhāratī, Śāntiniketan, 1931; P. L. Vaidya, *Mahāyāna-Sūtra-Saṃgraha*, I, pp. 174-176. See also Biswanath Bhattacharya, "A critical appraisal of the *Nairātmya-paripṛcchā* ascribed to Aśvaghoṣa," *WZKSO*. X (1966), pp. 220-223.

238. Cf. below, p. 109.

239. That is to say: subject (*grāhaka*) and object (*grāhya*).

240. *Viṃśatikā-vṛtti*, p. 6, ll. 17-18. (Trans. S. Lévi, where we substitute, however, "phenomenon" [*dharma*] for "Essence.")—Cf. La Vallée Poussin, *Siddhi*, I, p. 427. See also *MSA*. XI, 47, Commentary; "Notes bouddhiques," *Indologica Taurinensia*, VII/1979 (*Dr. Ludwik Sternbach Felicitation Volume*), pp. 109-110.

241. *Ud.* VIII, 3 (trans. Oldenberg-Foucher[4], p. 320).—Cf. *supra*, n. 38.

242. *Supra*, n. 38; p. 58 and p. 59, n. d; pp. 22-23.

243. *M.* I, p. 141. Cf. *S.* XXII, 33 (vol. III, p. 34); XXXV, 101 (vol. IV, p. 82).—La Vallée Poussin, *Dogme et Philosophie* . . . , p. 100.

Commenting on this passage, the celebrated Buddhist scholar writes (*ibid.*, p. 101):

"In the light of this text, which really is quite straightforward, we may understand several sermons, and notably the sermon of Benares, not as the negation of the *ātman* as do the Buddhists—but as the affirmation of an *ātman* distinct from the *skandhas*." In a note (p. 197) the author remarks: "It seems obvious that the celebrated sermon: 'Sensation is not the *attā*, the "Self," for one will have the sensations one wants . . . the body is not the *attā*, for the body will be what one wants it to be,' contrasts sensation (and other psycho-physical data) with an *attā* = Absolute, not a *pudgala* or *jīva*, vital principle, soul in the western sense of the word; and does not deny the existence of an *attā* = Absolute." He adds however: "But the Vedanticist indications do not show the general direction of Buddhist speculation." He translates the passage from the *Majjhima-Nikāya* (I, p. 138), which we have quoted above (n. 36), as follows: "If my I existed, there would be something belonging to my I; if something belonging to my I existed, there would be my I. The existence neither of an I nor of a Mine, can be observed. . . . " [Cf. *Kathāvatthu*, I, 1, 242.]

The whole question is to know what should be understood by *anupalabbhamāna* (or *anupalabbhiyamāna*). The controversy between Oldenberg and La Vallée Poussin appears meaningless, for it takes place on two distinct levels. Oldenberg translates *anupalabbhamāna/ anupalabbhiyamāna* by "nicht zu erfassen" (not to be grasped), and opts for the transcendence of the *ātman*, whilst La Vallée Poussin translates the expression by "not perceived, observed" and opts for the non-existence of the *ātman* (cf. La Vallée Poussin, *Nirvāṇa* [Paris, 1925], p. 104, n. 1). It is quite true that, according to the Pāli texts, the individual (*satta, puggala*) is non-existent because "not perceived, observed" (*na upalabbhati*: *S.* I, p. 135; *Mil.*, p. 25 [*supra*, n. 200]; cf. *MSA.* XVIII, 92). Yet, in the passage of the *Majjhima-Nikāya*, as well as in that of the *Saṃyutta*, quoted above, p. 47 (Oldenberg, *Buddha* [ed. 1961], p. 262, and p. 388, n. 77; cf. also Frauwallner, *Geschichte der indischen Philosophie*, I, pp. 228-229), the contexts preclude such an interpretation. What they are saying is this: the *ātman*, the Absolute, cannot be an object of grasping. We may recall that, according to the Mahāyānic texts, the Absolute is *anupalambha* (cf. *ASP.*, p. 89; *Laṅk.* III, 29; *MK.* XXV, 24; *MSA.* XI, 47; *Triṃśikā,* 29; also Gauḍapāda, *Māṇḍ.Kār.* IV, 88). But what escapes "grasping" is not "non-existent"; its objective non-existence is, on the contrary, its metaphysical existence par excellence; its "non-grasping" is its "grasping" par excellence. In other words, it is "grasped" beyond the subject-object split:

yāvidyamānatā saiva paramā vidyamānatā |
sarvathānupalambhaś ca upalambhaḥ paro mataḥ ||

(*MSA.* IX, 78. Cf. *ibid.*, 79:

bhāvanā paramā ceṣṭā bhāvanām avipaśyatām |
pratilambhaḥ paraś ceṣṭaḥ pratilambhaṃ na paśyatām ||.)

Against Oldenberg: "in truth and in certitude," La Vallée Poussin remarks: "The 'ablatives' *satyatas, sthitatas* [Pāli *saccato, thetato*] mean: 'as true, as durable.'" In support of this interpretation may be cited *Puggalapaññatti,* III, 17 (cf. *Kathāvatthu,* I, 1, 243): *attānaṃ saccato thetato paññāpeti—na paññāpeti* (*attan,* in this passage, is a synonym of *satta* = *puggala*).—But this objection in no way weakens Oldenberg's conclusion: the *ātman* that can only be "grasped" objectively, cannot be "true" nor "durable." It is not "true," since the *ātman*-object is, in fact, a non-*ātman;* and is not "durable," since, like all objects, it is exterior to me, and thus, I am always threatened with its loss. This is clearly explained in the very passage of the *Majjhima-Nikāya,* which immediately precedes the one we are considering here: *taṃ, bhikkhave, pariggahaṃ pariganheyyātha yvāssa pariggaho nicco dhuvo sassato avipariṇāmadhammo, sassatisamaṃ tath' eva tiṭṭheyya,* etc. (*M.* I, p. 137).

Whether *saccato thetato* is interpreted here as "in truth and in certitude" or as "as true, as durable," it comes to the same thing: the *ātman* cannot be an object of grasping; if it is only "grasped," it is no longer the *ātman.*

The same term, *anupalabbhamāna/anupalabbhiyamāna,* may be employed apropos the individual and apropos the *ātman,* in two opposite senses, since the individual and the *ātman* belong to two opposite domains. The individual belongs to the domain of the thinkable. If it exists, it must therefore by graspable by thought (*upalabdhir nāma buddhyā pratipattiḥ, MSA.*, p. 155, Commentary; cf. *Nyāyasūtra,* I, 1, 15). Now, in whatsoever manner it is considered, it is not grasped (cf. *supra,* p. 32). Thence it is concluded that it does not exist. The *ātman,* on the other hand, is the Unthinkable. Its grasping by thought is thus a non-grasping. It is grasped only in the immediate consciousness: "it is" (*astīty evopalabdhavyaḥ*), beyond all thought, and thus, beyond the subject-object split (*Kaṭha-Up.* VI, 12-13, with Deussen, *Up.*, p. 286). However, from the objective point of view, this "grasping" is but a "non-grasping." Thus the term *anupalabbhamāna/anupalabbhiyamāna* takes on an entirely positive meaning, when it is applied to the *ātman.* "It is only known to one who does not know it; one who knows it, does not know it" (*Kena-Up.*, II, 3). The commentators on Jaspers, Dufrenne and Ricœur, could write (*op. cit.*, p. 52): "By an invincible paradox, I am assured of that being at the moment when I understand that I cannot grasp it nor name it, and I identify it as it is not identifiable. This is the sole decisive step."

What we have been saying is formally confirmed in a passage of the *Saptaśatikā Prajñāpāramitā* (= *Mañjuśrīparivarta*). Our text, just like the *Saṃyutta-Nikāya*, XXII, 85, identifies the *ātman* with the Buddha (*Tathāgataṃ, bhadanta Śāradvatīputra, paryeṣitukāmena ātmā paryeṣitavyaḥ, ātmeti, bhadanta Śāradvatīputra, Buddhasyaitad adhivacanam*). And it brings out the "ungraspable," "ineffable" nature,—the objective non-existence,—of the *ātman*-Buddha: *yathā ātmā atyantatayā na saṃvidyate nopalabhyate, tathā Buddho 'py atyantatayā na saṃvidyate nopalabhyate. yathā ātmā na kenacid dharmeṇa vacanīyaḥ, tathā Buddho 'pi na kenacid dharmeṇa vacanīyaḥ. yatra na kācit saṃkhyā, sa ucyate Buddha iti. na caitad, bhadanta Śāradvatīputra, sukaram ājñātum ātmeti yad adhivacanam; evam etad, bhadanta Śāradvatīputra, na sukaram ājñātuṃ Buddha iti yad adhivacanam.* (*Mahāyāna-Sūtra-Saṃgraha*, edited by P. L. Vaidya, part I, p. 347.) "Just as the *ātman* absolutely does not exist, is not grasped, so the Buddha absolutely does not exist, is not grasped. Just as the *ātman* cannot be expressed by any empirical reality (*dharma*), so the Buddha cannot be expressed by any empirical reality. Where there is absolutely no name, that is what is called 'Buddha.' Bhadanta Śāradvatīputra, it is not easy to know the meaning of the designation '*ātman*'; even so, Bhadanta Śāradvatīputra, it is not easy to know the meaning of the designation 'Buddha.'" (Cf. a little further above, on the same page: *apadādhivacanam etad yad idam ucyate Buddha iti . . . apadasyaitad, bhadanta Śāradvatīputra, adhivacanaṃ yad uta Buddha iti* "'Buddha' is the designation of that which is beyond words" [*apada*; cf. above, p. 60, n. 61: *anakṣara, akṣaravarjita*].—"There is no word which is identical" [that is to say: which designates the Buddha exactly by coinciding with him]: *nāpy atra kiṃcit padam abhedam.*) [See also "The Ātman in two Prajñāpāramitā-Sūtras," *Our Heritage*, 150th Anniversary Volume, Sanskrit College, Calcutta, 1979, pp. 39-45.]

Whatever the name attributed to the Absolute at the level of empirical knowledge,—*ātman, brahman, buddha, nirvāṇa, tathatā,*— it can only *indicate* it, without expressing it directly. The Absolute cannot be an object of grasping; consequently, it cannot be named. As an object, the Absolute is no longer the Absolute, but an empirical reality,—no longer Being itself, but only a determined being, related, on the one hand, to the thinking subject and, on the other, to other objects. It is in this sense that the *Aṣṭasāhasrikā Prajñāpāramitā* states: Buddha and Nirvāṇa, in the same way as other empirical realities, are similar to illusions, to dreams; if there were a higher reality than Nirvāṇa itself, it would also be similar to an illusion, to a dream (*yadi nirvāṇād apy anyaḥ kaścid dharmo viśiṣṭataraḥ syāt, tam apy ahaṃ māyopamaṃ svapnopamam iti vadeyam*), *ASP.*, p. 20; cf. *MKV.*, pp. 449-450. See also *MKV.*, pp. 540-541.

Cf. *infra*, pp. 132, 188, 240-241.

244. *Supra*, p. 7.

245. *Supra*, p. 5.—Cf. *Mbh.* III, 13986: *dṛṣṭvātmānaṃ nirātmānam.* —*Ibid.*, XII, 192, 122 (critical edition) [cf. G. C. Pande, *Studies in the Origins of Buddhism* (University of Allahabad, 1957), p. 488, n. 209]:

amṛtāc cāmṛtaṃ prāptaḥ śītībhūto nirātmavān |
brahmabhūtaḥ sa nirdvandvaḥ sukhī śānto nirāmayaḥ ||

(On *brahmabhūta*, cf. ch. II.)

Śaṅkara glosses *anātmya*[a] (*TU.* II, 7) by *aśarīra* "incorporeal." Cf. *BĀU.* I, 4, 17; 6, 3; *Kaṭha-Up.* III, 4; IV, 12; *BhG.* IV, 21; V, 7; VI, 10, with Śaṅkara's commentaries; also Śaṅkara, *Upadeśasāhasrī, padya,* XV, 35; XVI, 19: *ātman* = body, reflecting a more ancient conception (cf. L. Renou, "On the word Ātmán," *loc. cit.*, p. 157, n. 8). In this sense, the word is also attested to in literary works: thus, Kālidāsa, *Raghuvaṃśa*, I, 14 (*ātmā jīve dhṛtau dehe svabhāve paramātmanīti Viśvaḥ,* Mallinātha [ed. S. P. Pandit, Bombay, 1869-1874]). Neither should we forget that *TU.* II, 1 ff. uses the word *ātman* in the sense of "trunk," in an image borrowed from the ritualist tradition (cf. A. Minard, *Trois énigmes sur les Cent Chemins*, I [= *Annales de l'Université de Lyon*, troisième série, Lettres, fascicule 17, Paris, 1949], p. 46, § 129 a): a sense which Śaṅkara also recognizes.—*ChU.* VIII, 3, 4 (cf. 12 3; *MaiU.* II, 2): *atha ya eṣa saṃprasādo 'smāc charīrāt samutthāya paraṃ jyotir upasaṃpadya svena rūpeṇābhiniṣpadyate, eṣa ātmeti hovāca, etad amṛtam abhayam, etad brahmeti; tasya ha vā etasya brahmaṇo nāma satyam iti.—asmāc charīrāt samutthāya* = *śarīrātmabhāvanāṃ parityajya, dehādi-vailakṣaṇyam ātmano rūpam avagamya, dehātmabhāvanāṃ hitvā*, Śaṅkara; *tad vismṛtya, tadabhimānaṃ parityajya*, Rāmatīrtha on *MaiU.* II, 2. [Cf. *supra*, p. 95; *infra*, n. 253 (*Brahmasūtra-bhāṣya*, I, 3, 19).]—By *śarīra*, in these passages, should be understood, not only "gross body" (*sthūla-śarīra*), but also "subtle body" (*sūkṣma-* or *liṅga-śarīra*). This term therefore designates the psycho-physical complex. *śarīram ity atra sahendriyamanobhir ucyate*, Śaṅkara on *ChU.* VIII, 12, 1. Cf. also *Brahmasūtra-bhāṣya*, I, 3, 19, quoted below, n. 253; Rāmatīrtha on *MaiU.* II, 2 and III, 2; *Brahmasūtra-bhāṣya*, I, 2, 6 (*para evātmā dehendriyamanobuddhyupādhibhiḥ paricchidyamāno bālaiḥ śārīra ity upacaryate*). [Cf. Vātsyāyana on *Nyāyasūtra* III, 1, 4: *śarīra-grahaṇena śarīrendriyabuddhivedanāsaṃghātaḥ prāṇibhūto gṛhyate.*]

Rāmatīrtha on *MaiU.* II, 4, glosses *nirātman* by *manorahita* (*atrātmeti mana ucyate, manorahitaḥ saṃkalpādhyavasāyādidharmarahita ity arthaḥ*): an explanation suggested by the Upaniṣad itself (VI, 20): *yadātmanātmānam aṇor aṇīyāṃsaṃ dyotamānaṃ manaḥkṣayāt paśyati, tadātmanātmānaṃ dṛṣṭvā nirātmā bhavati.*—Rāmatīrtha: *nirātmā bhavati, nirmanasko bhavati, jīvabhāvān nivartate; eṣāvasthā yogibhir unmanīty ucyate.—nirātmaka* = *nirindriyamanaska* = *nirliṅga*, Rāmatīrtha on *MaiU.* VI, 21. (*manas* = *ātman, BĀU.* I, 4, 17; cf. *supra*, p. 29 and n. 210; *infra*, p. 183, n. 9.)

---

a. The form *anātmya* also figures in a passage (omitted in the Tibetan) of the *Mahāyāna-Sūtrālaṃkāra* (p. 91, l. 5).

246. *Supra*, pp. 1 ff.

247. Cf. Śaṅkara, various commentaries, for example, *Brahma-sūtra-bhāṣya*, Introduction, pp. 39 ff. (cf. pp. 16-17: *mithyājñāna-nimittaḥ satyānṛte mithunīkṛtya "aham idam," "mamedam" iti naisargiko 'yaṃ lokavyavahāraḥ*); I, 3, 2 (p. 274): *dehādiṣv anātmasv aham asmīty ātmabuddhir avidyā* (cf. *Sarvopaniṣatsāra*, 1 [*Ānandāśrama Sanskrit Series*, 29 (1895), p. 587]: *anātmāno dehādīn ātmatvenābhimanyate, so 'bhimāna ātmano bandhaḥ, tannivṛttir mokṣaḥ, tam abhimānaṃ kārayati yā sāvidyā, so 'bhimāno yayābhinivartate sā vidyā*). [Cf. *infra*, p. 36 and n. 255.]—Śaṅkara, *Upadeśasāhasrī, padya*, XVII, 46.—*Vivekacūḍāmaṇi*, 2, 47, 49, 71 ff., 122-123, 137, 140, 146, 152 ff., 203, 268-269, 275, 379, 533.—Abhinavagupta, *Paramārthasāra*, 31 (edition cited). Cf. also *BhG.* VI, 6 (*supra*, p. 30).—*Mbh.* V, 1299:

calaccittam anātmānam indriyāṇāṃ vaśānugam |
arthāḥ samativartante haṃsāḥ śuṣkaṃ saro yathā ||

The term *anātman* is already met with, *ŚB.* II, 2, 2, 8 (S. Lévi, *La Doctrine du Sacrifice dans les Brāhmaṇas* [Paris, 1898; reprinted: 1966], pp. 42-43). Oldenberg writes on this subject: "What a distance separates the primitive, mythologically coloured representation of the Brāhmaṇa and the abstract clarity of Buddhist thought! But both lie on the same path of development." (*WBT.*, p. 87.)

". . . the self which is denied [in the Advaita] is the narrow or egoistic self, and that which is affirmed in its place is the universal one," Hiriyanna, *Popular Essays in Indian Philosophy*, p. 87.—See also *infra*, p. 211, n. 18.

248. *BĀU.* IV, 4, 12. Cf. *supra*, n. 87.

249. Murti, p. 17, and n. 3. In an analogous manner, V. Bhattacharya, *The Basic Conception of Buddhism*, pp. 64 ff. K. Venkata Ramanan, however, recently rightly said, ". . . by this '*ātman*' he [Śaṅkara] did not mean the *ātman* of the Vaiśeṣikas and the Mīmāṃsakas or even of the Sāṅkhyas; for him it meant the true nature, the essential nature (*pāramārthikasvarūpa*) of the individual.

". . . one can say that the one accepts or denies *ātman* as much as the other; both [the Mādhyamika and the Advaita Vedānta] deny *ātman* as a separate substantial entity inhabiting the body of each individual, and both accept *ātman* in the sense of the essential nature, the *svarūpa* or the *svabhāva*, of the individual as well as of all things . . . in regard to the ultimacy of the unconditioned, which is what the equation, *ātman* = *brahman* means,[a] there is hardly any difference between the two," Venkata Ramanan, p. 320. Cf. *infra*, p. 164, n. 95. See also *supra*, pp. 1-2 (*MSA.*).

With regard to the doctrine of the Buddha, the same author writes (p. 171): "To cut at its root the tendency to cling to the specific as ultimate is the deepest truth of the denial of self which the Buddha taught. It is a denial not of the self itself but of the falsely imagined self-hood in regard to the body-mind complex. The basic meaning of self is underivedness, unconditionedness. The self-being (*svabhāva*) is the independent, unconditioned being which does not depend on anything to come into existence. Even the 'coming into existence' is not relevant in regard to it, for it never goes out of existence. That which was not existent before, is existent now, and will cease to be later is not self-being. But arising and perishing are the very nature of the elements that constitute the body-mind complex. So the Buddha declared that the entities that are subject to arising and perishing are not fit to be considered as the self, for they are devoid of the nature of self, viz. self-being. It is this imagination of self-being or absoluteness in regard to the conditioned and contingent that is the root of error and suffering. It is this that the Buddha exhorts everyone to dispel. In its general form this is the error of misplaced absoluteness."

---

a. Let us recall, for example, Śaṅkara, *Brahmasūtra-bhāṣya*, III, 2, 21 (p. 713): *brahma . . . jīvasya svarūpam, jīvatvaṃ tv avidyākṛtam eva.*

250. Cf. *supra*, p. 13 and n. 97. See also Murti, pp. 223-224, where he summarizes thus the Vedāntic position: "The abandonment of the particular standpoint of the ego and identification with the universal Being (Brahman) makes passions (attachment and aversion) impossible; there is no other which you can like or hate. Freedom is the consequence of the attainment of universality (sarvātmatva)."

251. Thus, M. Walleser, criticizing F. O. Schrader and H. Oldenberg:

"We should take into consideration the fact that the Brahman of the Upaniṣads is fully identical with the I, the ātman. Indeed this is distinctive of that great world vision: *the concept of an Absolute as an essence distinct from the ground-of-being of the living is quite unknown to it.* On the contrary, it is based upon the immediate identification of the individual subject, the soul, with the universal subject. Hence, from this point of view, an absolute Brahman cannot be postulated without there being a simultaneous acknowledgement of a self, ātman; and conversely, it is not possible, presuming the intrinsic identity of ātman and Brahman, to deny the individual self without concomitantly denying this Self as the absolute. The denial of ātman is, however, the most basic tenet of Buddhist teaching; from which it follows with inescapable logic that the concept of an absolute self in the sense of the Brahman must necessarily have been perceived by Buddhists as an incomprehensible contradiction within their own system." (*Prajñāpāramitā* [Göttingen-Leipzig, 1914], p. 9; our italics.)

252. *ChU.* VI, 8, 7 ff.—*aitadātmya* is glossed thus by Śaṅkara: *etat sad ātmā yasya sarvasya tad etadātma, tasya bhāva aitadātmyam. etena sadākhyenātmanātmavat sarvam idaṃ jagat.* Cf. Deussen, *Up.*, p. 157, n. 1: "*aitadātmyam*, unnecessarily weakened by Böhtlingk to *etad-ātmakam*; *etad-ātman* adj. 'having this as self,' from which the abstract noun *aitadātmyam* 'the That-selfness.' The world is not a substance as would possess *etadātman* as an attribute; rather it is *solely this quality* (the world does not merely exist through *ātman*, but is utter *ātman*-being), and otherwise an insubstantial appearance. Thus *aitadātmyam* is the result of a self-surpassing power of abstraction which—in strictly logical terms—transcends its own objective."

253. *vikārānṛtādhikṛtajīvātmavijñānanivartakam evedaṃ vākyaṃ tat tvam asīti siddham*, Śaṅkara, *Chāndogyopaniṣad-bhāṣya*, VI, 16, 3, at end. Cf. *Brahmasūtra-bhāṣya*, I, 3, 19 (p. 303): *yāvad eva hi sthāṇāv iva puruṣabuddhiṃ dvaitalakṣaṇām avidyāṃ nivartayan kūṭasthanitya-dṛksvarūpam ātmānam ahaṃ brahmāsmīti na pratipadyate, tāvaj jīvasya jīvatvam. yadā tu dehendriyamanobuddhisaṃghātād vyutthāpya śrutyā pratibodhyate, nāsi tvaṃ dehendriyamanobuddhisaṃghātaḥ, nāsi saṃsārī, kiṃ tarhi tad yat satyaṃ sa ātmā caitanyamātrasvarūpas tat tvam asīti, tadā kūṭasthanityadṛksvarūpam ātmānaṃ pratibudhyāsmāc charīrādy-abhimānāt samuttiṣṭhan sa eva kūṭasthanityadṛksvarūpa ātmā bhavati.*—In the *Upadeśasāhasrī* (*padya*, XVIII), Śaṅkara gives an exegesis of *tat tvam asi.* See also P. Hacker, *op. cit.*, pp. 73 (1979) ff. (The relationship, on this point, between Śaṅkara's *Upadeśasāhasrī* and Sureśvara's *Naiṣkarmyasiddhi* [which P. Hacker analyzes, *loc. cit.*] was first noticed by J. A. B. van Buitenen, *Rāmānuja's Vedārthasaṃgraha* [= *Deccan College Monograph Series* 16, Poona, 1956], p. 63 and n. 175).—See also *Chāndogyopaniṣad-bhāṣya*, V, 11, 1: *ātma-brahma-śabdayor itaretara-viśeṣaṇa-viśeṣyatvam: brahmety adhyātmaparicchinnam ātmānaṃ nivartayati, ātmeti cātmavyatiriktasyādityādibrahmaṇa upāsyatvaṃ nivartayati.*

254. *S.* III, p. 46, 130. Cf. Buddhaghosa, *Papañcasūdanī*, III, p. 141: *asmimāno ti rūpādisu asmīti māno.*—Nāgārjuna, *Ratnāvalī*, V, 10 (edition cited).

255. *ahaṃdhīr idamātmotthā vācārambhaṇagocarā* |
niṣiddhātmodbhavatvāt sā na punar mānatāṃ vrajet ||
Upadeśasāhasrī, padya, II, 2. (On *vācārambhaṇa*, cf. *supra*, p. 12 and

n. 91).—*dehādāv anātmany ātmabuddhir ahaṃdhīr ity ucyate,* Rāmatīrtha. Our interpretation of the second half of the verse differs from that of Rāmatīrtha, however.

256. *Infra,* pp. 121 ff.

257. *asmimāno samucchinno, S.* III, p. 83 (*gāthā*).—Cf. Sureśvara, *Naiṣkarmyasiddhi,* II, 29: *brahmāsmīti dhiyāśeṣā hy ahaṃbuddhir nivartyate* (ed. Colonel G. A. Jacob, revised edition with Introduction and Explanatory Notes by M. Hiriyanna, Poona, Bhandarkar Oriental Research Institute, 4th edition, 1980; cf. Notes, p. 238). See also, on the question, P. Hacker, *op. cit.*, pp. 46 (1952) ff.

In actuality, one who has "become *brahman,*" does not say: "I am *brahman.*" Cf. Śaṅkara, *Upadeśasāhasrī, padya,* XII, 13-14. Have we not to do, here, with an ineffable "certitude?" (*supra,* p. 23). The fact of having become the *brahman* translates itself into deeds rather than into words. A Mahātmā is only a Mahātmā for another person. Gandhi often said: "I must reduce myself to zero!"

258. P. 17.

259. *kaṃcid dhi paramārtham ālambyāparamārthaḥ pratiṣidhyate, yathā rajjvādiṣu sarpādayaḥ* (*Brahmasūtra-bhāṣya,* III, 2, 22, p. 719).—Coomaraswamy, *Hinduism and Buddhism,* p. 76, n. 175.

260. *S.* III, p. 46 (*supra,* p. 58).

261. *seyyathā pi, bhikkhave, mahāsamuddo ekaraso loṇaraso, evam eva kho, bhikkhave, ayaṃ dhammavinayo ekaraso vimuttiraso, Cullavagga,* IX, 1, 4 (*Vin.* II, p. 239). Cf. Lamotte, *Histoire,* p. 156.

262. *M.* III, pp. 18-19; *S.* XXII, 71-72, 91-92, 124-125. Cf. Venkata Ramanan, pp. 98 ff.—The Deliverer "who sees himself in all beings and all beings in himself," is *nirmama* and *nirahaṃkāra*: *BhG.* II, 71; XII, 13 (*supra,* p. 82); *Aṣṭāvakra-Gītā,* XV, 6.

263. *yo nu kho dukkhaṃ allīno dukkhaṃ upagato dukkhaṃ ajjhosito dukkhaṃ: etaṃ mama, eso 'ham asmi, eso me attā ti samanupassati, api nu kho so sāmaṃ vā dukkhaṃ parijāneyya, dukkhaṃ vā parikkhepetvā vihareyya? M.* I, p. 233.—Cf. *MaiU.* III, 2 and VI, 30.—*duḥkham eva hi ta ātmatvenopagacchanti,* Śaṅkara, *Bṛhadāraṇyakopaniṣad-bhāṣya,* IV, 4, 14.

264. "Hier wird doch, was nicht das Selbst ist, gedacht an dem Massstab eines eigentlichen Selbst," Jaspers, *Die grossen Philosophen,* I (München, 1957), p. 139.

265. *Supra*, n. 60.

266. *Supra*, p. 9.

267. See below, p. 39.

268. Cf. Kimura, *op. cit.*, p. 97, n. 2: "From a perusal of such identical expressions as we come across in both [the Pāli texts and the Upaniṣads], we may hold that in a certain sense Buddha's Ontological perception . . . does not surpass the ideas of the Upanishads. But the difference between them is the different way of realization; that is to say, the way of realization of the Upanishads is philosophical, while Buddha's way is a religious one."

269. Radhakrishnan, *Indian Philosophy*², I, p. 387.

270. *Ibid.*, p. 683.—Cf. on the question, *infra*, pp. 208 ff.

271. *Supra*, p. 11 and n. 83; pp. 29-30; *infra*, p. 127.

272. Cf. *supra*, n. 83; n. 215; *infra*, p. 156, n. 50.

273. "Experience teaches that there is nearly always a metaphysical shipwreck at the origin of these great sorrows, and, in our time, it is good in the aftermath of the crumbling of the great idealistic systems that we see similar strong ideas spreading amongst us. When speculation, having undermined the concept of the real in the sensible object, is obliged to admit that the transcendent object escapes in its turn, there remains only the alternative of scepticism or the philosophy of despair: one is cārvāka or Buddhist. It is thus in an idealistic doctrine, in primitive Vedānta, but in a Vedānta that has lost faith in brahman, that we should, it would seem, be seeking the departure point for Buddha's ideas. It is necessary to believe in the Absolute to experience profoundly enough the inanity and imperfection of finite things: it is necessary to have believed in it and to have found that belief vain to ignore it with a sufficiently calm and inflexible resolution." *Œuvres*, I, p. 110.)—But whereas, for Barth, it is the Buddha who suffered a "shipwreck," we, on the contrary, think that it is the Buddhists who suffered one. ". . . this is as if one were to come aboard asking for the captain and, rejecting boatswain and purser as being 'not he,' were to go away saying: 'there is no captain'!" Mrs. Rhys Davids, "The Self: an overlooked Buddhist Simile," *JRAS.* 1937, p. 260.

274. *AK.* IX, pp. 252-253. Cf. *Abhidharmakośabhāṣya*, p. 467.

275. *A.* II, p. 52; cf. *supra*, n. 81.

276. *S.* III, p. 46; cf. *supra*, pp. 37, 58.

277. *Supra*, pp. 2 and 3.

278. *Supra*, pp. 2 ff.—Cf. *MKV.*, p. 469: *yadā caivam anātmādikaṃ na saṃbhavati tadā tad api svarūpato 'vidyamānatvād ātmādivat kathaṃ na viparyāsaḥ syāt? tasmāj jātijarāmaraṇasaṃsāracārakāgārabandhanān mumukṣubhir aṣṭāv apy ete viparyāsās tyājyāḥ.*—*Vimalakīrtinirdeśa*, VIII, 15.26 (Lamotte, *Vimalakīrti*, pp. 308, 314). See also *MK.* XIII, 8, and *Ratnakūṭa* (= *Kāśyapaparivarta*), cited *MKV.*, pp. 248-249 (cf. *supra*, n. 62); *Bodhisattvabhūmi*, cited by La Vallée Poussin, "Śūnyatā," *IHQ.* IV (1928), p. 162 (ed. Wogihara [Tokyo, 1930-1936], p. 46).—In the Mahāyānic *Mahāparinirvāṇa-Sūtra*, the Great Nirvāṇa is "defined as permanence, bliss, self (*ātman*) and purity; the 'self' of this definition is conceived as a 'great self' (*ta-wo, mahātman*), which transcends at once the 'self' of the non-buddhists and the 'without-self' (*nairātmya*) of the Buddhists of the Lesser Vehicle" (P. Demiéville, chapter on "Les sources chinoises," in Renou-Filliozat, *L'Inde classique*, II [Paris-Hanoi, 1953], p. 435; cf. Suzuki, *Outlines . . .*, p. 348; Kimura, *op. cit.*, p. 103; *infra*, pp. 198-199).

CHAPTER TWO

Brahman = Ātman = Dharma = Buddha = Nirvāṇa

If Buddhism has recognized the Upaniṣadic *ātman*, can it be said that it has equally recognized the *brahman*, with which the Upaniṣads identify the *ātman*? Buddhologists claim that this is not so. Thus Rhys Davids wrote long ago: "The neuter Brahman is, so far as I am aware, entirely unknown in the Nikāyas."[1] That opinion still seems to be prevalent today.[2]

Under these circumstances, however, how should we interpret this phrase which is often repeated:

> *so anattantapo aparantapo diṭṭhe va dhamme nicchāto nibbuto sītibhūto sukhapaṭisaṃvedī brahmabhūtena attanā viharati*?[3]

Brahmabhūta is usually translated by "become Brahmā."[4] Buddhaghosa glosses this expression by *seṭṭhabhūta*; but for him the word *seṭṭha* simply means Brahmā.[5] He writes, for instance, in the *Visuddhimagga* (IX, 106 = *Atthasālinī*, § 428):

> *seṭṭhaṭṭhena tāva niddosabhāvena c' ettha Brahmavihāratā veditabbā. sattesu sammāpaṭipattibhāvena hi seṭṭhā ete vihārā; yathā ca Brahmāno niddosacittā viharanti, evam etehi sampayuttā yogino Brahmasamā hutvā viharantīti seṭṭhaṭṭhena niddosabhāvena ca Brahmavihārā ti vuccanti.*

> It must be understood that the *Brahmavihāras* are thus named because they represent the best of spiritual exercises and because they are exempt from defects. These exercises are, in fact, the best (*seṭṭha*), because they consist in perfect

behaviour towards beings. Moreover, just as the Brahmās live, with mind pure, so do the *yogins*, who become like the Brahmās,[6] by devoting themselves to these exercises. It is for these reasons that these exercises are called *Brahmavihāra.* In this way it is understood that they are the best exercises and that they are exempt from defects.

It is impossible, however, to compare the state of the Brahmās,—Buddhism recognizes several,—with that of a man whose individual existence is extinguished, who enjoys Supreme Bliss (*nicchāto nibbuto sītibhūto sukhapaṭisaṃvedī*), in other words, who has attained Nirvāṇa.[7] "The *Rūpa-* and the *Ārūpyadhātu* are inhabited by the gods of Brahmaloka. These Brahmās are freed from desire and immersed in the joys of meditation which constitute their sole and unique nourishment. They are not, however, exempt from errors and they often wrongly think themselves to be the creators of the universe; but, just like the rest of the world, they are subject to the law of *karman* and destined to be reborn."[8] The *Mahāgovinda-Suttanta* puts the following words into the mouth of the Buddha:

> In those days, I was the brahmin Mahāgovinda. I showed these disciples the way which leads to communion [with Brahmā] in *Brahmaloka.* But, Pañcasikha, that *brahmacariya* does not lead to indifference, detachment, cessation and appeasement, to Knowledge, Awakening and to Nirvāṇa, but only to rebirth in *Brahmaloka.* On the other hand, Pañcasikha, this *brahmacariya,* which I profess, leads to total indifference, to detachment, to cessation, appeasement, to Knowledge, Awakening, and to Nirvāṇa; and this *brahmacariya* is the noble eightfold path.[9]

The expressions *brahmabhūta, °bhūya,* etc., are well known in Vedāntic literature. We read thus in the *Bhagavadgītā*:

> *yo 'ntaḥsukho 'ntarārāmas tathāntarjyotir eva yaḥ* |
> *sa yogī brahmanirvāṇaṃ brahmabhūto 'dhigacchati* || (V, 24).

praśāntamanasaṃ hy enaṃ yoginaṃ sukham uttamam |
upaiti śāntarajasaṃ brahmabhūtam akalmaṣam || (VI, 27).

māṃ ca yo 'vyabhicāreṇa bhaktiyogena sevate |
sa guṇān samatītyaitān brahmabhūyāya kalpate || (XIV, 26).

ahaṃkāraṃ balaṃ darpaṃ kāmaṃ krodhaṃ parigraham |
vimucya nirmamaḥ śānto brahmabhūyāya kalpate ||

brahmabhūtaḥ prasannātmā na śocati na kāṅkṣati |
samaḥ sarveṣu bhūteṣu madbhaktiṃ labhate parām ||
(XVIII, 53-54).

One who finds happiness, joy and light only within, that yogin, becomes *brahman* (*brahmabhūta*), attains to *brahma-nirvāṇa.*[10]

The yogin whose mind is at peace, whose passions are calmed and who is without stain, who has become *brahman*, attains to the supreme Bliss.

And one who serves me with faultless devotion, that one, going beyond these *guṇa*s, is on the way to becoming *brahman.*

If, freed from egoism, violence, insolence, desires, anger and possession, one is without 'mine' and at rest, he is on the way to becoming *brahman.*[11]

The man who has become *brahman* has a serene soul; he is exempt from chagrin and desires. Seeing all beings with an equal eye,[12] he attains to supreme devotion towards me.

Do these stanzas not bring to mind, in some measure, the Pāli texts which we have quoted above?[13] And, nevertheless, there is no question in the *Gītā* of "becoming Brahmā!"[14]

The expression *brahmabhūta* is used, in the Pāli Canon, not only for the Arahants, but also for the Buddha himself.[15] Another synonymous expression is used at the same time: *dhammabhūta.*[16] We thus read in the *Aggañña-Suttanta*:[17]

tumhe khv attha, Vāseṭṭha, nānā-jaccā nānā-nāmā nānā-gottā nānā-kulā agārasmā anagāriyaṃ pabbajitā. "ke tumhe" ti puṭṭhā samānā, "samaṇā sakya-puttiy' amhā" ti paṭijānātha. yassa kho pan' assa, Vāseṭṭha, Tathāgate saddhā niviṭṭhā mūla-jātā patiṭṭhitā daḷhā asaṃhāriyā samaṇena vā brāhmaṇena vā devena vā Mārena vā Brahmunā vā kenaci vā lokasmiṃ, tass' etaṃ kallaṃ vacanāya: "Bhagavato 'mhi putto oraso mukhato jāto dhammajo dhammanimmito dhammadāyādo" ti.—taṃ kissa hetu?—Tathāgatassa h' etaṃ, Vāseṭṭha, adhivacanaṃ: Dhamma-kāyo iti pi Brahma-kāyo iti pi, Dhamma-bhūto iti pi Brahma-bhūto iti pi.

O Vāseṭṭha, you, who have different births, different names, and who belong to different lines and to different families,—you have left your hearths to set out on a life of wandering. And when someone asks you: 'Who are you?' you reply: 'We are Samaṇas who follow the son of Sakya.'[18] But, one, Vāseṭṭha, whose faith in the Tathāgata is founded, rooted, established and firm and cannot be shaken by a Samaṇa or by a Brāhmaṇa, by Deva or by Māra, by Brahmā or by anyone in the world,—that one has the right to say: 'I am a true son of Bhagavant, born of his mouth, born of the Dhamma, made of Dhamma, heir to Dhamma.'—Why so?—Because, Vāseṭṭha, the following designations are applied to the Tathāgata: 'He who has the Dhamma for his body' (*Dhamma-kāya*), or 'He who has the Brahman for his body' (*Brahma-kāya*); 'He who has become the Dhamma' (*Dhamma-bhūta*), or 'He who has become Brahman' (*Brahma-bhūta*).[19]

Apropos this passage again, Buddhaghosa writes: *Dhammo hi seṭṭhaṭṭhena Brahmā ti vuccati.*[20] Nevertheless, our text makes it clear that *brahma°*, in *brahmabhūta,* is not a Brahmā: *yassa kho pan' assa, Vāseṭṭha, Tathāgate saddhā niviṭṭhā . . . asaṃhāriyā samaṇena vā brāhmaṇena vā devena vā Mārena vā Brahmunā vā kenaci vā lokasmin . . .* The aim of this Sutta is to establish the superiority of Dhamma in relation to the brahmins.[21] These claim that their class (*vaṇṇa*) is the best (*seṭṭha*), because they are "the true sons of Brahmā, born of his mouth, created by Brahmā, heirs to Brahmā."[22] But the "true sons of Bhagavant

(Tathāgata)," who belong to no social class, are superior to brahmins because they are "born of Dhamma (= *brahman* = Buddha), made of Dhamma, heirs to Dhamma." This, in our opinion, is the true meaning of the text: there is no question here of a simple parallelism between brahminic pretensions and Buddhist doctrine, as has sometimes been thought.[23]

Buddhism[24] naturally could not accept the brahminic interpretation of the origin of social classes, which does nothing but consecrate the hierarchy existing amongst them: the brahmin issuing from the mouth of Brahmā, the Kṣatriya from his arms, the Vaiśya from his thighs, and the Śūdra from his feet.[25] The *Aggañña-Sutta*[26] thus sets out a cosmogony which takes account of the origin of the world and of the human race, as well as of the "natural" evolution of the four classes (*vaṇṇa*), according to men's occupations:[27] in the first place figure the Kṣatriya/Khattiya, "masters of the fields" (*khettānaṃ patīti kho Khattiyo*), chosen by the people, desirous of order and justice; then the brahmins, dedicated to meditation and to teaching,[28] next the Vaiśya/Vessa, given over to husbandry, to commerce and to other occupations of that sort,[29] lastly the Śūdra/Sudda, occupied in hunting (?).[30] It is not, therefore, a cosmic Being who has emitted the four classes from different hierarchized portions of his body but rather one same people which has split up. There is no real hierarchy amongst the four classes; they are distinguished, one from another, only by the qualities and the functions to which they correspond. In spite of their apparent differences, they discover their equality when brahmins, Kṣatriyas, Vaiśyas and Śūdras, "disavowing their own *dhamma*" (*sakaṃ dhammaṃ garahamāno*), become Samaṇa. Our text ends by saying that the *bhikkhu* Arahant, who has attained to supreme Perfection, who has, in other words, become Dhamma, *brahman* (*dhammabhūta, brahmabhūta*), is superior to all social classes.

This attitude is not foreign to Hinduism. *Cāturvarṇyaṃ mayā sṛṣṭaṃ guṇakarmavibhāgaśaḥ*, says the *Gītā*.[31] "There was originally, O Yudhiṣṭhira, but one class in the world; the four classes were instituted following upon the differentiation of functions."[32] Is this particular verse from the *Mahābhārata*? We cannot know. The idea is, however, found in the *Śānti-parvan.*[33] Let us not, on the other hand, forget that Buddhism has never repudiated the ideal of the brahmin. According to the *Aggañña-Sutta* itself, the word *brāhmaṇa* means: "one who removes evil."[34] In the *Dhammapada* there is an entire chapter entitled *Brāhmaṇavagga* (ch. XXVI). According to our text, however, "it is neither by tuft, lineage nor by birth that one is a brahmin. One in whom reside Truth and Dhamma, such a one is happy and is a brahmin."[35] In other words, it is neither by birth nor by outward signs of a holy life that one becomes a brahmin: it is inner purity which makes a brahmin.[36] The *Chāndogya-Upaniṣad* (IV, 4) had already stated this ideal in the well-known episode of Satyakāma:

> Satyakāma Jābāla one day said to Jabālā, his mother: 'I want, O my Mother, to make my novitiate as a *brahmacārin.* What is my line (*gotra*)?'
>
> She answered him: 'I do not know, my child, which line you belong to. I wandered around a good deal as a servant in my youth, when I conceived you.[37] Thus, I don't know which your line is. But I am called Jabālā, you are called Satyakāma. Therefore, call yourself Satyakāma Jābāla.'
>
> Going therefore to Hāridrumata Gautama, he said to him: 'I would like, Lord, to make my novitiate as a *brahmacārin* with you. Will you accept me, Lord?'
>
> He replied: 'Well, from what line are you, my friend?'—The other said: 'I do not know, Lord. I asked my mother. She replied: "I wandered about a great deal as a servant in my youth, when I conceived you. Thus I do not know which your line is. But I am called Jabālā, you are called Satyakāma." I am thus Satyakāma Jābāla.'
>
> Gautama replied: 'Only a brahmin could speak so candidly. Carry the firewood. I will initiate you. You have not departed from Truth.'

According to the *Dhammapada*,[38] the brahmin or Arahant[39] is one who is liberated from all the bondages of existence, who is "appeased" (*sītibhūta*), "extinguished" (*nibbuta*), free of all individuality (*nirupadhi*),[40]—who is "awakened" (*buddha*), "who knows the Uncreated" (*akataññu*),[41] "who is immersed in the Immortal" (*amatogadham anuppatta*), beyond good and evil (*puññañ ca pāpañ ca ubho saṅgaṃ upaccagā*),[42]—in other words, who knows *brahman*, who has become *brahman*. Now, is it not the definition of the word *brāhmaṇa* given by the *Bṛhadāraṇyaka-Upaniṣad*?[43]

Whatever may have been the attitude, at a lower level, of Hinduism, towards classes and castes (*varṇa* and *jāti*),[44]—this is no place to speak of that,—it is certain that one who became *brahman* and who, consequently, "regarded all beings with an equal eye,"[45]—brahmin, cow, elephant, dog, Cǎṇḍāla,[46]—was considered as superior to all other social categories. One who has become *brahman* "is my *guru*, whether he be Cāṇḍāla or brahmin," wrote the author of the *Manīṣā-pañcaka* (attributed to Śaṅkara).[47]

The Pāli Canon thus recognizes the Upaniṣadic Absolute, in identifying Dhamma with *brahman*: *Dhammakāyo iti pi Brahmakāyo iti pi, Dhammabhūto iti pi Brahmabhūto iti pi.* The *Saṃyutta-Nikāya*, as we have seen, has the Buddha say: "Who sees the Dhamma sees me, and who sees me sees the Dhamma."[48] We know now that the Buddha is also identified with the *brahman*. In conformity with Upaniṣadic thought, the Pāli texts identify, on the other hand, the Dhamma-*brahman*-Buddha with the *ātman*. We have already spoken above of the texts which indicate sometimes the equivalence of the Tathāgata and the *ātman*, sometimes that of the Dhamma and the *ātman*.[49] Here is a text which says that all the Buddhas—past, present and future—venerated, venerate and will venerate the Dhamma, and that all those who wish to know the *ātman*, that is, who aspire to the "Great Ātman,"[50] must do the same:

ye ca atītā sambuddhā ye ca buddhā anāgatā |
yo c' etarahi sambuddho bahūnaṃ sokanāsano ||
sabbe saddhammagaruno vihaṃsu viharanti ca |
atho pi viharissanti esā buddhāna dhammatā ||
tasmā hi attakāmena mahattam abhikaṅkhatā |
saddhammo garukātabbo saraṃ buddhāna sāsanam[51] ||

Aside from the Pāli texts cited above, there are still others, concerned with the *brahman*. The Buddha is "one who has attained the *brahman*" (*brahmapatta*).[52] This term is but a synonym of *brahmabhūta*, already met with above. To attain the *brahman* is, in fact, to become it: *brahmaiva san brahmāpyeti*.[53] Again, it is said that Deliverance consists in attaining to *brahman*: *brahmapatti*;[54] and the discipline which must be followed in order to reach it is called *brahmacariya* (= Sanskrit °*carya*).[55] A verse attributed to Thera Udāyin also contains the expression *brahmapatha*, designating the way which leads to Deliverance;[56] and one of the manuscripts of the *Aṅguttara-Nikāya* inserts the gloss *amatapathe* after *brahmapathe*. As Geiger[57] remarks, this clearly proves the equivalence of *brahman* and Nirvāṇa (= *amata*).[58]

The term *brahman* again replaces *dhamma*, and vice versa. Thus, in place of the formula *dhammacakkaṃ pavatteti*, we often find: *brahmacakkaṃ pavatteti*.[59] One of our texts uses the expression *brahma-yāna* as a synonym of *dhamma-yāna*.[60] In *Suttanipāta*, 274: *dhammacariyaṃ brahmacariyaṃ etad āhu vasuttamaṃ*, the expression *brahmacariya* seems to gloss *dhamma-cariya*. *Suttanipāta*, 696: *sambodhipatto vicarati dhammamaggaṃ*, brings to mind *Theragāthā*, 689 (already cited above): *sambuddhaṃ . . . iriyamānaṃ brahmapathe*.[61] It would, moreover, seem that this verse establishes a parallelism between (b) *vicarati dhammamaggaṃ* and (d) *carassu . . . brahmacariyaṃ*.[62] In place of Manu *brahmadāna*,[63] we find *dhammadāna* in the Pāli texts.[64] In a list of *gaṇa* or human groups, the *Milinda-pañhās* put the *dhammagiriyā* and the *brahmagiriyā* side by side.[65] Lastly, the *Brahmajāla-Sutta* of *Dīgha-Nikāya* is also called *Dhammajāla-Sutta*.[66]

The equivalence *dharma* (Pāli *dhamma*) = *brahman* is not without Upaniṣadic antecedent. We read thus in the *Bṛhadāraṇyaka-Upaniṣad* (II, 5, 11):

> *ayaṃ dharmaḥ sarveṣāṃ bhūtānāṃ madhu, asya dharmasya sarvāṇi bhūtāni madhu. yaś cāyam asmin dharme tejomayo 'mṛtamayaḥ puruṣaḥ, yaś cāyam adhyātmaṃ dhārmas tejomayo 'mṛtamayaḥ puruṣaḥ ayam eva sa yo 'yam ātmā, idam amṛtam, idaṃ brahma, idaṃ sarvam.*

In another passage, that same Upaniṣad says that there is nothing above *dharma* (*dharmāt paraṃ nāsti*).[67] The *Mahānārāyaṇa-Upaniṣad* says, for its part, that *dharma* is the "foundation of the whole Universe."[68] Manu expressedly recognizes the equivalence *dharma* = *brahman*, when he says:

> *utpattir eva viprasya mūrtir dharmasya śāśvatī* |
> *sa hi dharmārtham utpanno brahmabhūyāya kalpate*[69] ||

The word *dharma*—meaning that which "sustains" all things, that which constitutes their foundation[70]—was, in actual fact, destined to become a synonym of *brahman.* There was even perhaps, in the minds of our authors, an etymological connection between these two words.[71] What then does the word *dhamma,* in the Pāli Canon, exactly signify when it is identified with *brahman*?

According to Buddhaghosa, it would simply refer to the teaching of the Buddha, as it is expressed in the *Tipiṭaka*:

> *kasmā Tathāgato Dhammakāyo ti vutto?—Tathāgato hi tepiṭakaṃ Buddhavacanaṃ hadayena cintetvā vācāya abhinīhari; ten' assa kāyo Dhammamayattā Dhammo va; iti Dhammo kāyo assā' ti Dhammakāyo.*[72]

Such too is the opinion of the author of the *Milindapañhā*:

yo dhammaṃ passati so Bhagavantaṃ passati, dhammo hi, Mahārāja, Bhagavatā desito (p. 71);
dhammakāyena pana kho, Mahārāja, sakkā Bhagavā nidassetuṃ, dhammo hi, Mahārāja, Bhagavatā desito (p. 73).

In the Nikāyas themselves, we find passages which present the teaching (*dhamma*) of the Buddha as a "guide" (*satthar*), and as a "refuge" (*paṭisaraṇa*):

yo vo, Ānanda, mayā dhammo ca vinayo ca desito paññatto, so vo mam' accayena satthā.[73]
na kho mayaṃ, brāhmaṇa, appaṭisaraṇā; sappaṭisaraṇā mayaṃ, brāhmaṇa, dhammapaṭisaraṇā.[74]

The *Theragāthā* 491 has the same to say apropos earlier Buddhas:

yeh' ayaṃ desito dhammo dhammabhūtehi tādihi.

Let us not forget that, according to the *Aggañña-Sutta* itself, the "true son of Bhagavant," who is "born of Dhamma, made of Dhamma and heir to Dhamma," is equally "born from the mouth" (*mukhato jāto*) of the Bhagavant.[75]

There is, however, no reason to consider, as is sometimes claimed, that the word *dhamma* in the Pāli Canon, has no metaphysical meaning.[76] If, in the passages we have quoted, the word does designate the teaching of the Buddha, that teaching can be identified with *brahman* only in that it reveals the true nature of things, the Emptiness (*suññatā*):

suttantā Tathāgata-bhāsitā gambhīrā gambhīratthā lokuttarā suññatā-paṭisaṃyuttā.[77]

*Suttanta*s, spoken by the Tathāgata, which are profound, which have profound meaning, which are supramundane,—which concern Emptiness.

Elsewhere we read:

> *yo paṭiccasamuppādaṃ passati so dhammaṃ passati; yo dhammaṃ passati so paṭiccasamuppādaṃ passati.*[78]

> One who sees the *paṭicca-samuppāda* (Sanskrit *pratītya-samutpāda*) sees the *dhamma*; one who sees the *dhamma* sees the *paṭicca-samuppāda.*

The *dhamma* is thus identified with the *paṭicca-samuppāda.* But what is the *paṭicca-samuppāda,* if not the timeless Truth, the immutable Reality (*ṭhitā dhātu, dhammaṭṭhitatā, dhamma-niyāmatā, tathatā*)?[79]

These passages already foreshadow the Mahāyāna. The latter, as we know, designates the Absolute by the names *dharmadhātu, dharmakāya, śūnyatā, tathatā* . . . But it also uses the terms *ātman, mahātman, paramātman,* as we have seen.[80] The term *brahman* seems rarely attested to.[81] Perhaps our authors preferred terms semantically more precise. However this may be, the *brahman,* whatever may have been its original meaning,[82] too often tended to be confused with Brahmā.[83] The old commentators made that confusion,[84] and some modern Buddhist scholars continue to perpetrate it.[85] The Pāli Canon, it seems to us, represents, in this movement, a transitional stage. It still uses the term *brahman*; however, another term, whose etymology is transparent, appears uppermost: *dhamma* (= Sanskrit *dharma,* from the root *dhṛ-* "to bear, to sustain").[86]

What is *śūnyatā/suññatā*?—The Absolute of the Upaniṣads and of Buddhism is empty (*śūnya/suñña*)[87] of all objective content. From the objective point of view, it is a "non-being" (*asant*).[88] Yet, this "non-being" is the authentic Being, the foundation of all beings (*satyasya satyam, dharmāṇāṃ dharmatā*),[89] their essential nature (*svabhāva, svarūpa, prakṛti*). It is the *tathatā,* the Reality in itself and by itself, beyond all objective determination:

yadi khalu tad adhyāropād bhavadbhir astīty ucyate, kīdṛśaṃ tat?—yā sā dharmāṇāṃ dharmatā nāma, saiva tat svarūpam.—atha keyaṃ dharmāṇāṃ dharmatā?—dharmāṇāṃ svabhāvaḥ.—ko 'yaṃ svabhāvaḥ?—prakṛtiḥ.—kā ceyam prakṛtiḥ?—yeyaṃ śūnyatā.—keyaṃ śūnyatā?—naiḥsvābhāvyam.—kim idaṃ naiḥsvābhāvyam?—tathatā. —keyaṃ tathatā?—tathābhāvo 'vikāritvam, sadaiva sthāyitā. sarvadānutpāda eva hy agnyādīnāṃ paranirapekṣatvād akṛtrimatvāt svabhāva ity ucyate.[90]

In other words, individual phenomena, as such, are not in themselves and by themselves. Born dependent upon causes and conditions (*pratītya-samutpanna*),[91] they have no nature of their own. Now it is this absence of own-nature, it is this Emptiness (*śūnyatā*), which is the true nature of phenomena; for, once the veils of their individual appearances, subject to birth, death, and to all sorts of changes in time, have been parted, they are nothing but the universal and immutable Reality.[92]

The philosopher thus strives to express the Reality, which is ineffable, negatively. The "own-nature" (*svabhāva*) of the phenomena, which is not subject to becoming (*anutpādātmaka*),[93] is not itself an objectively determinable entity (*akiṃcit*). From the objective point of view, it is merely a "non-existence" (*abhāvamātra*), a "non-own-nature" (*asvabhāva*). Thus then it is once more impossible to speak of the "own-nature" of phenomena.[94] This is the object of the most intimate experience of sages.[95]

The Absolute has no name. We give it names to designate it for ourselves as best we may. All these names, however, serve only to express the way in which *we* conceive of it, they do not express it *itself.* "If absolute Truth has genuinely been realized, by body, speech and thought, let the name 'Absolute Truth' be not uttered, for then only empirical truth would be designated."[96] The very fact of saying that it "is" (*asti*) is a "superimposition" (*samāropa, adhyāropa*).[97]—Under these circumstances, how can the Absolute be identified with the teaching of the Buddha? Does not the parable of the boat[98] run counter to this assimilation? The word *dhamma*, insofar as it is a synonym of *brahman*, cannot, therefore, designate the teaching of the Master, as it can be seen developed through the texts, but it designates, beyond speech, the profound Truth of which this teaching is but a reflection: timeless (*akālika*) Truth, which the Buddha has *discovered*, and which he invites each of us to "verify" for ourselves.[99]

Let us recall the text which we have already evoked, in part, above:[100]

> Shortly after his awakening, the Buddha asked himself to whom he could render homage. But, searching the three worlds, he found no one superior to himself. So, he said to himself: "Suppose I render homage to Dhamma to which I am awakened?"[101] At that moment, Brahmā Sahampati[102] descends from the skies and agrees with the Buddha. He says to him: All previous Buddhas have rendered homage to Dhamma, and all future Buddhas will do the same; the current Buddha must therefore venerate the Dhamma.[103]

Another text from the Pāli Canon says that the Buddha discovered the Dhamma as though it had been an old city buried in a forest, following a path already trodden by the ancients:

> *seyyathā pi, bikkhave, puriso araññe pavane caramāno passeyya purāṇaṃ maggaṃ purāṇañjasaṃ pubbakehi manussehi anuyātaṃ. so tam anugaccheyya. tam anugacchanto passeyya purāṇaṃ nagaraṃ purāṇaṃ rājadhāniṃ pubbakehi manussehi ajjhāvutthaṃ . . . evam eva khvāhaṃ, bhikkhave, addasaṃ purāṇaṃ maggaṃ purāṇañjasaṃ pubbakehi sammāsambuddhehi anuyātaṃ. . . .*[104]

Lastly, the *Itivuttaka*, where we find again the words of the Master: "One who sees Dhamma sees me" (*dhammaṃ passanto maṃ passati*),[105] explains this in the following manner:

One who has seen Dhamma (that is to say, who has become it), is liberated from all the impulses of phenomenal existence. He is peaceful "as a lake which is not agitated by the wind" (*rahado va nivāto*).[106] He is thus comparable with the Buddha, who has also seen Dhamma and who is thus liberated from all impulses:

> *yo ca dhammam abhiññāya dhammaṃ aññāya paṇḍito* |
> *rahado va nivāto ca anejo vūpasammati* ||
> *anejo so anejassa nibbutassa ca nibbuto* |
> *agiddho vītagedhassa passa yāvañ ca santike*[107] ||

Would we be stepping too far outside our text were we to add: He who sees the Dhamma sees the *ātman-brahman*, the "Great Ātman" (*mahātman*), and, consequently, he sees the Tathāgata?[108]

It is true, however, that *dharma/dhamma* designates, in the popular imagination, the teaching of the Buddha, materially represented by the Scriptures. "Ancient *stūpa*s, in Indochina, as well as in India have frequently yielded fragments of texts of the Buddhist Canon, of Dharma, in the guise of relics. One such text, found in Burma, is a résumé of the essential elements of the Buddhist doctrine, quite analogous with a Pāli text from Cambodia with the significant title of *Dhammakāya*: it begins with a table of equivalences between the various elements of *dhamma* and the different parts of the body of the Buddha. The holy Scriptures constitute a genuine relic of Buddha who has said: 'One who sees the *dhamma*, sees me.' Thus, when a résumé or a fragment of the Canon is placed in a *stūpa*, it is a fragment of the 'Body of the Law' of the Buddha, of the *Dharmakāya*, which is introduced. Moreover, it is not purely by chance, that, in Siam, the chests of religious manuscripts meant to contain that holy relic and called *hip p'ră th'ăm* 'chest of the holy *dharma*,' are of a shape strikingly similar to that of *hem* caskets (less the points of the lid), and to that of stone pools found at Aṅkor."[109]

The identification of the *brahman-ātman* with the Buddha is quite normal in the Upaniṣadic perspective. To know the *brahman-ātman* is, in fact, to become it, and to become the *brahman-ātman* is to be "awakened" to that which one really is. Even the term *pratibuddha* is used in the *Bṛhadāraṇyaka*:

> *yasyānuvittaḥ pratibuddha ātmāsmin saṃdehye gahane praviṣṭaḥ* ।
> *sa viśvakṛt sa hi sarvasya kartā tasya lokaḥ sa u loka eva*[110] ॥

Numerous authors have, on the other hand, emphasized the comparison between the *brahman* and Nirvāṇa. The point of departure was no doubt the *Bhagavadgītā*, which uses the expression *brahmanirvāṇa.*[111] We have, however, seen that the oldest Buddhist tradition gives formal support to this subject. Other texts from the Pāli Canon make this relationship even more clear:

> *atthi, bhikkhave, tad āyatanaṃ, yattha n' eva paṭhavī na āpo na tejo na vāyo na ākāsānañcāyatanaṃ na viññāṇānañcāyatanaṃ na ākiñcaññāyatanaṃ na nevasaññānāsaññāyatanaṃ nāyaṃ loko na paraloko na ubho candimasuriyā. tad ahaṃ, bhikkhave, n' eva āgatiṃ vadāmi, na gatiṃ na ṭhitiṃ na cutiṃ na upapattim. appatiṭṭhaṃ appavattaṃ anārammaṇam eva taṃ. es' ev' anto dukkhassa.*[112]
>
> *atthi, bhikkhave, ajātaṃ abhūtaṃ akataṃ asaṃkhataṃ. no ce taṃ, bhikkhave, abhavissa ajātaṃ abhūtaṃ akataṃ asaṃkhataṃ, na-y-idha jātassa bhūtassa katassa saṃkhatassa nissaraṇaṃ paññāyetha. yasmā ca kho, bhikkhave, atthi ajātaṃ abhūtaṃ akataṃ asaṃkhataṃ, tasmā jātassa bhūtassa katassa saṃkhatassa nissaraṇaṃ paññāyati.*[113]

Long ago, whilst commenting upon these passages, Oldenberg wrote: "On the face of it, these words sound to the ear as if we were hearing the Upaniṣadic philosophers speaking of the Brahman, the Being without beginning or end, which is neither large nor small, and which is called 'Not not,' since no word can encompass its nature.[114] And in fact, we have here reached the point where the old concept of Brahman appears, inasfar as it may so, in the totality of

Buddhist speculation. There is no doubt that the concept of Nirvāṇa derived from that of Brahman."[115]

It is to F. O. Schrader, however, that we owe the most important contribution to this subject:[116]

> A further argument [for the existence of an absolute reality] can be derived from the simile of the flame applied early and frequently to the passing away of the enlightened one. 'As the flame,' the *Suttanipāta* (1074) tells us, 'blown down by the vehemence of the wind goes out, and can be named no more, even so the sage, liberated from individuality, goes out and can be named no more.'[117] In the *Aggi-Vacchagotta-Sutta* of the *Majjhima-Nikāya* (I.487) we have a complete working out of the idea; the flame ceases to appear when the fuel is consumed; similarly, when the different constituents of the enlightened one disappear, the fuel of the Tathāgata's fire is consumed. But the Tathāgata, liberated from these constituents of spirit and material form, is deep, unmeasurable, difficult to fathom, like the great ocean. The comparison is indeed significant, for there is no doubt that the Indian idea of the extinction of fire was not that which occurs to us of utter annihilation, but rather that the flame returns to the primitive, pure invisible state of fire in which it existed prior to its manifestation in the form of visible fire. This view is expressly attested to in the *Śvetāśvatara-Upaniṣad,* which can reasonably be regarded as good evidence for the period of the coming into existence of the Canon. The same Upaniṣad contains, also, the comparison of the supreme self with a fire, the fuel of which has been consumed, showing emphatically that the extinction of the fuel has nothing to do with the destruction of the fire, though it ceases to be visible,[118] and the *Maitreyī-Upaniṣad* (older than *Maitri-Upaniṣad*), a text of the yoga philosophy, with which Buddhism has much in common, applies the simile to the action of the thinking principle: 'As fire for want of fuel comes to rest in its own place of birth, so, through the cessation of its motions, the thinking principle comes to rest in its own birthplace.'[119]

In the course of the present work, we have met with still more proofs of the equivalence between Nirvāṇa and *brahman.*[120] According, however, to H. von Glasenapp, these two conceptions are "entirely distinct" ("durchaus verschieden"). The *brahman,* he writes, " . . . is . . . the *ens realissimum,* the divine source from which all being arises and through which all beings exist. Nirvāṇa, however, is *not* the substance of the world, in which all existence is rooted; rather it is the very opposite of all which is . . . the wholly other, the total negation of all troubled and transitory existence."[121]

This interpretation, however, hardly seems to accord with the Canonical texts. According to these, Nirvāṇa consists in attaining to that which truly *is*: the "unborn, unproduced, uncreated, unformed" (*ajātaṃ abhūtaṃ akataṃ asaṃkhataṃ*), beyond the evanescent reality of the empirical world, "the born, the produced, the created, the formed" (*jāta, bhūta, kata, saṃkhata*);[122] and it is "immediatized" in this very life[123] —as if it were something which exists throughout all eternity in ourselves,[124] but of which we had no knowledge, in the manner of those ignorant ones who walk every day in a field where a treasure is hidden without finding it.[125] Nirvāṇa can thus not be a reality exterior to ourselves, "das ganz andere" of H. von Glasenapp.[126] We consider as entirely authentic the Mahāyānic doctrine according to which there is, in the transcendent sense, no distinction between *saṃsāra* and *nirvāṇa.*[127] "*Nirvāṇa* is the reality of *saṃsāra* or conversely, *saṃsāra* is the falsity (*saṃvṛti*) of *Nirvāṇa. Nirvāṇa* is *saṃsāra* without birth and decay. The difference between them is in *our way of looking at them*; it is epistemic not metaphysical."[128] Or again:

> The transcendence of the Absolute must not be understood to mean that it is an other that lies outside the world of phenomena. There are not two sets of the real. The Absolute is *the reality* of the apparent (*dharmāṇāṃ dharmatā*); it is their real nature (*vāstavikaṃ rūpam*). Conversely, phenomena are the veiled form or false appearance of the Absolute (*sāṃvṛtaṃ rūpam*).[129] If this position is discountenanced and two reals

are accepted, there would be no point in calling one of them the absolute and the other appearance. Both would be equally, unconditionedly, real. The absolute, as lacking determinations and without any recognisable content, would even be less real than the empirical.[130]

To study the word *upadhi* may help us to throw light on this problem.[131]

This word appears frequently in the *Suttanipāta*. The sorrows of existence, says our text, belong to the *upadhi*, and to the ignorance which creates the *upadhi*, undergo suffering without end; the sage must therefore not bring into being the *upadhi*:

upadhīnidānā pabhavanti dukkhā
ye keci lokasmiṃ anekarūpā |
yo ve avidvā upadhiṃ karoti
punappunaṃ dukkham upeti mando |
tasmā pajānaṃ upadhiṃ na kayirā
dukkhassa jātippabhavānupassī[132] ||

The Delivered, again according to the *Suttanipāta*, is he who has surpassed the *upadhi*s, for whom all the *upadhi*s are destroyed:

upadhī te samatikkantā āsavā te padālitā |
sīho si anupādāno pahīnabhayabheravo[133] ||
aññāya padaṃ samecca dhammaṃ
vivaṭaṃ disvāna pahānam āsavānaṃ |
sabbūpadhīnaṃ parikkhayā
sammā so loke paribbajeyya[134] ||

Nirvāṇa/Nibbāna is *anupadhika, nirupadhi.*[135]

What then does the word *upadhi* mean? One of the stanzas of the *Suttanipāta* (364) seems to indicate this:

na so upadhīsu sāram eti
ādānesu vineyya chandarāgaṃ |

so anissito anaññaneyyo
sammā so loke paribbajeyya ||

"He sees no substance in the *upadhi*s": this phrase recalls the texts of the Pāli Canon, which say that the psycho-physical elements of our phenomenal existence—the *khandhas*—are empty of all substance.[136] It is, in fact, in this sense that the *Paramatthajotikā* interprets in this passage the word *upadhi*: *upadhīsū 'ti khandhūpadhīsu.*[137]

The word *upadhi* does not, however, designate simply the individual, but also that which belongs to the individual. According to the *Majjhima-Nikāya,* I, p. 162, the *upadhi*s are wife, children, servants, cattle, gold and silver (*puttabhariyaṃ, dāsidāsaṃ, ajeḷakaṃ, kukkuṭasūkaraṃ, hatthigavāssavaḷavaṃ, jātarūparajataṃ*). Cf. again *Suttanipāta,* 33-34 (= *Saṃyutta-Nikāya,* I, p. 6 = pp. 107-108):

nandati puttehi puttimā
iti Māro pāpimā
gomiko gohi tath' eva nandati |
upadhī hi narassa nandanā
na hi so nandati yo nirūpadhi ||

socati puttehi puttimā
iti Bhagavā
gomiko gohi tath' eva socati |
upadhī hi narassa socanā
na hi so socati yo nirūpadhi ||

The word *upadhi* therefore designates empirical individuality in the most complete sense. *Nirupadhi*[138] is one who is liberated from his individuality. That individuality is, as we know, impermanent (*anicca*) and sorrowful (*dukkha*), *anattā.*[139] Now, according to the Vedānta, through the force of ignorance (*avidyā,* Pāli *avijjā,*[140] we attribute to the Absolute the *upādhi*s (literally, the word means "apposition"), by virtue of which it appears in the forms of personal god, of the world and of individual souls; but, in reality, it is not affected by these *upādhis*: crystal is not altered by the color with which it is coated.[141] As long as we are attached to these *upādhis*, thinking: "I am this, this is mine," we are subject to phenomenal becoming. But, when that ignorance is dissipated by intuition of the Truth, when all the "superimpositions" (*adhyāsa, adhyāropa*) are negated (*apavāda, niṣedha, pratiṣedha*), we find our true being, the *ātman-brahman*, which is eternally free.

Buddhism, which says that Deliverance consists in the destruction or the rejection[142] of the *upadhis*, and that Nirvāṇa is *anupadhika, nirupadhi*,[143] manifestedly adopts the same conception.[144] The role of the concept of *upādhi*—writes P. Horsch, with justification—"is to make the bridge between the absolute and the relative; and, in fact, the term is well suited to this mediatory task, given the bivalent and very relative meaning it comprises, for *upādhi* designates the external, superficial envelope, but at the same time implies a true content, profound and pure."[145]

The Pāli Canon has yet another term: *upādi*. This appears only in the compound *upādisesa*. According to Oldenberg,[146] this would be nothing but "a written form of the word *upadhi*, belonging to our modern Pāli manuscripts" ("eine . . . unsern modernen Pāli-Manuscripten eigenthümliche Schreibung des Wortes *upadhi*"). He writes:

> The genesis of this spelling is not far to find if we consider the significant circumstance that *upādi* only appears in combination with *sesa*. Just as the name of the god Skanda is written *khanda* in the Pāli manuscripts, obviously influenced by the form *khandha*[147]—Sanskrit *skandha*, or as the Sanskrit *smṛti* is written *sammuti* under the influence of the word *sammuti* (naming, appointing), it would appear to me that the Pāli manuscript tradition has made the word *anupadhisesa* resemble the word *saṃghādisesa* which was very familiar to all scribes of sacred texts; this, perhaps in conjunction with the influence of *anupādāya*, has led to the word-formation *anupādisesa*.

The word *upādi* may equally be considered as a middle-Indian form of *upādhi,*[148] from which *upadhi* differs only in the absence of the prefix *ā-*.[149]

Such an interpretation is, however, contrary to a canonical text: the *Sunakkhatta-Suttanta* of the *Majjhima-Nikāya.*[150] It is true that Oldenberg[151] supports his proposal of the equivalence of *upādi* = *upadhi* on this very text. According to him the text is saying:

> A man, so the parable relates, is struck by a poisoned arrow. A doctor treats his wound, 'apaneyya visadosaṃ saupādisesaṃ anupādiseso ti maññamāno.' He presumes that the poison has been overcome, while, in fact, a portion of the poisonous substance still remains. This case is then contrasted with another in which the danger has been entirely vanquished: 'apaneyya visadosaṃ anupādisesaṃ anupādiseso ti jānamāno.' The first man considers himself cured, lives heedlessly and eventually succumbs to the wound. The man in the second example lives circumspectly and achieves a complete cure. When the spiritual significance of this parable is then presented, the expression *nirupadhi* replaces the word *anupādiseso.* About the successfully aspiring monk, with whom the second of the two men is compared, it is said: *so vata Sunakkhatta bhikkhu chasu phassāyatanesu saṃvutakārī upadhi dukkhassa mūlan ti iti viditvā nirupadhi upadhisaṃkhaye vimutto upadhismiṃ vā kāyaṃ upasaṃharissati cittaṃ vā anuppadassati: n' etaṃ ṭhānaṃ vijjati.*

This interpretation is inexact, however. Our text applies the expressions *sa-upādisesa* and *anupādisesa,* not to men affected by poison (*visadosa* = *avijjā*), but to poison itself, as is clearly shown in the sentences: *apanīto visadoso anupādiseso, asuci visadoso apanīto anupādiseso* (or *sa-upādiseso*). What is in question here is a specific usage of *sa-upādisesa* and of *anupādisesa.*[152]

In a formula which often comes up in our texts, the expression *upādisesa* designates the condition of the Anāgāmin, distinct from that of the Arahant: *diṭṭhe va dhamme aññā, sati vā upādisese anāgāmitā.*[153] According to Buddhaghosa, the word *upādi*, in this formula, is synonymous with *upādāna*:[154] *sati vā upādisese ti upādānasese vā sati, aparikkhīṇe.*[155] It may thus be said, in accordance with A. O. Lovejoy,[156] that the expression *upādisesa* designates the Anāgāmin "as one who has just fallen short of the religious perfection of the Arahat by reason of slight residuum of *upādāna*." Such may equally be the meaning of the word *upādi* in a passage of the *Suttanipāta* where, after the death of Nigrodhakappa-Thera, his disciple Vaṅgīsa asks the Buddha if his *upajjhāya* has attained *nibbāna* or if he is still *sa-upādisesa: nibbāyi so ādu sa-upādiseso.*[157]—An Anāgāmin, it is said, is one who, being free of the five "inferior" (*orambhāgiya*) fetters (*saṃyojana*), does not return here below; but, since he is not yet delivered entirely, he will be reborn—"spontaneously" (*opapātika*)—in *Brahmaloka*, from whence he will attain Nirvāṇa.[158] Now, the word *saṃyojana* appears in some texts as a synonym of *upādāna*.[159]

The word *upādi* is therefore distinct from *upadhi*. The conception that we are studying here is, however, very close to that which we have met with above apropos *upadhi*. According to the *Paṭicca-samuppāda*, *upādāna* "attachment" is the cause of becoming (*bhava*). But all attachments, whatever they may be, spring from that primordial attachment, which is attachment to our empirical individuality, composed of the five *khandha*s. These last are also called *upādānakkhandha*, since they are, as a passage in the *Saṃyutta-Nikāya* makes clear, *upādāniyā dhammā.*[160] One of our texts has a sage say: "If I attached myself to the *rūpa* (and to the other *khandha*s), by reason of this attachment becoming would appear."[161] Now, what is our empirical individuality, if not the blind attachment we devote to it?[162] When we have transcended it, we have destroyed all our impulses (*āsava*), we no longer attach ourselves to anything (*anupādāna*),[163] and, as a result, we are delivered from phenomenal becoming.[164]

But, the verb *upādā-* means, literally, "to grasp, to assume." The derivatives *upādāna* and *upādi*[165] would therefore signify "action of assuming, that which is assumed"; and *sati vā upādisese* may be translated by "if he must again assume [the *khandhas*]," that is to say, if he must be reborn again. Cf. *Paramatthajotikā,* II, 2, p. 504: *upādisesan ti punabbhavavasena upādātabbakkhandhasesaṃ vuccati.*

From this point of view, too, the concept expressed by *upādi/upādāna* is very close to that expressed by *upadhi.* In fact, the borderline between "to appose" (*upă-dhā-*) and "to assume" (*upā-dā-*) is difficult to draw here, for the two levels, objective and subjective, are confused. It may equally be said: through the power of ignorance, we "appose" to the Absolute individual determinations which are foreign to it; or else: we "assume" individual determinations which are foreign to us —for the Absolute is ourselves.

There are at least two texts which seems to suggest the equivalence *upadhi* = *upādāna.* One of these texts is *Saṃyutta-Nikāya,* XII, 66 (vol. II, pp. 107 ff.), from which we have already quoted a passage above,[166] and on which Oldenberg lays stress.[167] According to our text, from *taṇhā* comes *upadhi,* and from *upadhi* old-age and death (*jarāmaraṇa*). According to the *Paṭicca-samuppāda,* as is well known, the *taṇhā* conditions the *upādāna,* the *upādāna* the *bhava,* the *bhava* the *jāti,* and the *jāti* the *jarāmaraṇa.* The other text is *Udāna,* III, 10, p. 33 (= *Nettippakaraṇa,* p. 157):

> *upadhī hi paṭicca dukkham idaṃ sambhoti,*
> *sabbūpādānakkhayā n' atthi dukkhassa sambhavo.*

In this last passage it is clear that the words *upadhi* and *upādāna* designate the same thing.

Whatever may be the original meaning of the word *upādi,* it is often used in the Pāli Canon to designate the *khandhas*: in practice, thus, it is confused with *upadhi.* It is remarkable, in this regard, that the Sanskrit texts use the expressions *sopadhiśeṣa-* and *anupadhiśeṣa-* (or *nirupadhiśeṣa-*) *nirvāṇa,* in place of *sa-upādisesa-* and of *anupādisesa-nibbāna* in the Pāli texts.

According to this last conception, the Nirvāṇa that is attained whilst one is alive is incomplete, since the *upādi/upadhi*, that is, the *skandha/khandhas*,[168] still remain; true Nirvāṇa is that attained at death. The *sa-upādisesa-nibbāna* is, in some way, the precursor of perfect Nirvāṇa: when one speaks of the death of the Buddha or of an Arahant, one says: *anupādisesāya nibbānadhātuyā parinibbuto.*[169]

We are in the presence here of a concept of Nirvāṇa which seems new. According to the texts which we have examined above—and which appear to be the oldest—one who has freed himself from the *upadhi*s has attained to complete Nirvāṇa, even if he is still alive.[170] Such, too, is the Upaniṣadic conception of Deliverance.[171] One who knows the *brahman* becomes the *brahman*; the continuity or cessation of existence, like all that pertains to the phenomenal world, is thus indifferent: death adds nothing to what has already been obtained and removes nothing from which one has not already been separated.[172]—But classical Vedānta introduces a distinction between "deliverance acquired in this life" (*jīvanmukti*) and "deliverance acquired by death" (*videhamukti*),—a distinction which corresponds exactly to that which Buddha makes between *sa-upādisesa* (*sopadhiśeṣa*)- and *anupādisesa* (*anupadhiśeṣa*)-*nibbāna* (*nirvāṇa*). Just as the potter's wheel (*kulāla-cakra*) continues to turn for a time after the pot is finished, so the phenomenal existence of the Delivered may be prolonged[173] if he has not yet worn out his past actions, effects of which have already begun to manifest (*ārabdhakārya, pravṛttaphala*), in bringing about his present existence.[174] He lives in the *upadhi*s, but is not sullied by their properties.[175] When they disappear, that is, when the Delivered breathes his last, he is identified with the Absolute, as water mixes with water, ether with ether and fire with fire.[176]

Here we see, once more, how close Buddhism is to Vedānta. It seems to us that both doctrines have evolved in the same direction. We recognize, however, in modified form, the ancient fundamental idea: Deliverance does not consist in becoming something different from what we are, but, simply, in *rediscovering* our true being by transcending our phenomenal existence.

Notes to Chapter Two

1. T. W. Rhys Davids, *Dialogues of the Buddha,* I (= *Sacred Books of the Buddhists,* edited by F. Max Müller, vol. II, London, 1899 [reprint: 1956]), p. 298.

2. Cf. E. J. Thomas, *The History of Buddhist Thought*[2] (London, 1951 [reprint: 1953]), p. 87; Hajime Nakamura, "Upaniṣadic tradition and the early school of Vedānta as noticed in Buddhist Scripture," *HJAS.* 18 (1955), p. 77.—See, however, M. and W. Geiger, *Pāli Dhamma* (1920), pp. 7-8, 76 ff.; W. Geiger, *Dhamma und Brahman* (1921). [We have borrowed numerous references from Geiger here; however, we do not view the problem in the same manner as he does (cf. *infra,* n. 86).]

H. von Glasenapp rightly criticizes J. G. Jennings (cf. *infra,* p. 192), who sees in the *Tevijja-Sutta* of the *Dīgha-Nikāya* an allusion to the *brahman* (while the text speaks of *Brahmā*; cf. *infra,* n. 158); but he seems to be unaware of the numerous passages in the Canon which undoubtedly refer to the *brahman.* (H. von Glasenapp, *Vedānta und Buddhismus* [= *Abhandlungen der Akademie der Wissenschaften und der Literatur in Mainz: Geistes- und Sozialwissenschaftlichen Klasse,* 1950, NR. 11], pp. 12-13 [1022-1023].)

3. *D.* III, pp. 232-233; *M.* I, pp. 341, 411-412; II, p. 159; *A.* II, p. 206; *Puggalapaññatti,* p. 56. Cf. *A.* I, p. 197.—*S.* III, p. 83 (cf. *supra,* p. 36 and n. 257): *loke anupalittā te [arahanto] brahmabhūtā anāsavā.*—Geiger, *Pāli Dhamma,* p. 77; *Dhamma und Brahman,* p. 5.

4. "Literally, become as Brahmā," T. W. and C. A. F. Rhys Davids, *Dialogues of the Buddha,* III (= *Sacred Books of the Buddhists,* IV, London, 1921 [reprint: 1957]), p. 223, n. 5.—"he dwells with self that has become Brahmā," F. L. Woodward, *The Book of the Gradual Sayings,* II (= *Pāli Text Society Translation Series,* No. 24, London, 1933 [reprint: 1952]), p. 218.—*Ibid., The Book of Kindred Sayings,* III (= *Pāli Text Translation Series,* No. 13, London, 1925 [reprint: 1954]), p. 69: "These god-like beings."—Cf. *PTS. Dictionary,* p. 336a, l. 20 from the bottom.

5. Wrongly, Geiger, *Pāli Dhamma*, p. 77, n. 3; *Dhamma und Brahman*, p. 8. See "Some Thoughts on Ātman-Brahman in Early Buddhism," *Dr. B. M. Barua Birth Centenary Commemoration Volume* (Calcutta, Bauddha Dharmankur Sabha [Bengal Buddhist Association], 1989), pp. 63-83.

6. Cf. Appendix III.

7. In a parallel passage *(A.* V, p. 65), in fact, we read: *diṭṭhe va dhamme nicchāto nibbuto sītibhūto anupādāparinibbānaṃ paññāpemi.* (On *anupādā-parinibbāna*, cf. *infra*, p. 142 and n. 163.)

8. Lamotte, *Histoire*, p. 761.

9. *ahaṃ tena samayena Mahāgovindo brāhmaṇo ahosiṃ. ahaṃ tesaṃ sāvakānaṃ Brahmaloka-sahavyatāya maggaṃ desesiṃ. taṃ kho pana, Pañcasikha, brahmacariyaṃ na nibbidāya na virāgāya na nirodhāya na upasamāya na abhiññāya na sambodhāya na nibbānāya saṃvattati, yāvad eva Brahmalokūpapattiyā. idaṃ kho pana me, Pañcasikha, brahmacariyaṃ ekantanibbidāya virāgāya nirodhāya upasamāya abhiññāya sambodhāya nibbānāya saṃvattati, ayam eva ariyo aṭṭhaṅgiko maggo* . . . , *D.* II, p. 251. (*Brahmalokasahavyatāya* = *Brahmaloke Brahmunā saha-bhāvāya*, Buddhaghosa, *Sumaṅgalavilāsinī*, II, p. 670. On *sahavyatā*, see also *infra*, p. 226, n. 11.)—The true *brahmacariya* (= Sanskrit *brahmacarya*) is that which leads, not to the condition of the Brahmās, but to the *brahman* (= *nirvāṇa*) [cf. *infra*, p. 128 and n. 55]. See also *supra*, p. 47.

See also *S.* I, p. 181 (cf. *infra*, n. 54). In *M.*, Sutta 97 (vol. II, pp. 195-196), Sāriputta establishes the brahmin Dhānañjāni in *Brahmaloka*, which is inferior (*hīna*), whereas there is a higher task to be accomplished (*sati uttarikaraṇīye*); and he thereby incurs the reproach of the Buddha. Let us also recall that, according to *M.*, Sutta 52, the *Brahmavihāras* are, like the meditations (*jhāna*), "conditioned" (*abhisaṃkhata*) and, consequently, they are impermanent (*anicca*) and must, in keeping with their inherent nature, come to an end (*nirodhadhamma*). [Cf. *supra*, p. 51, n. 54.] On the attitude of the Nikāyas towards the pretensions of the Brahmās, see *supra*, p. 99.—Cf. Coomaraswamy, *The Living Thoughts of Gotama the Buddha* (London, 1948), p. 26.

10. On *brahmanirvāṇa*, cf. *infra*, p. 128 and n. 58.

11. Translation (modified) by S. Lévi and J.-T. Stickney (*Bhagavadgītā*, Paris, 1938).

12. Cf. *supra*, p. 13.

13. See also Mrs. Rhys Davids, *The Birth of Indian Psychology and*

its Development in Buddhism (= *Buddhist Psychology*[3], London, 1936), p. 231.

14. Cf. *brahmabhūta, Vivekacūḍāmaṇi*, 224, 568; *brahmībhūta, ibid.*, 556 (cited below, n. 174; see also Śaṅkara, *Brahmasūtra-bhāṣya*, I, 3, 15). —Manu, I, 98 (cited below, n. 43; p. 129); XII, 102.—*Mbh.*, cited above, p. 112, n. 245.—*kalpate brahmabhūyase, ibid.*, XII, 8751.—

atrātmavyatirekeṇa dvitīyaṃ yo na paśyati |
brahmabhūtaḥ sa eveha vedaśāstra udāhṛtaḥ ||

verse cited by Śaṅkara (?), *Śvetāśvataropaniṣad-bhāṣya*, Introduction, p. 17.

The idea is found, needless to say, in the ancient Upaniṣads. Cf. *supra*, p. 7 and n. 52; *infra*, p. 128 and n. 53.

15. Originally, Buddhism does not seem to have made the distinction between the Buddha and the Arahants. Cf. Oldenberg, *Buddha* (1961 edition), p. 394, n. 111 (= Oldenberg-Foucher[4], p. 364, n. 3); Rhys Davids, *Dialogues of the Buddha*, II (= *Sacred Books of the Buddhists*, III, London, 1910, fifth edition, 1966), pp. 2, 89, n. 1; III (= *Sacred Books of the Buddhists*, IV), p. 6.

16. Cf. also *infra*, n. 60.

17. *D.* III, p. 84.

18. Cf. *Vin.* II, p. 239 (*Cullavagga*, IX, 1, 4), *infra*, p. 232, n. 15.

19. Cf. *M.* I, p. 111; III, pp. 195, 224; *S.* IV, p. 94; *A.* V, pp. 226, 256; *It.*, p. 57; *Sn.* 561, 563 (=*Theragāthā* 831, 833); *Paṭisaṃbhidāmagga*, II, p. 194.—Geiger, *Pāli Dhamma*, p. 78; *Dhamma und Brahman*, p. 7.

20. *Sumaṅgalavilāsinī*, III, p. 865, cited by Geiger, *Pāli Dhamma*, p. 78. According to Geiger, *Dhamma und Brahman*, p. 8 (cf. *Pāli Dhamma*, p. 77, n. 3), Buddhaghosa also speaks of *brahman* and not of Brahmā. But this interpretation is incorrect. Cf. *supra*, pp. 121-122.

21. According to our text, the Dhamma is the supreme Principle (*"das höchste Prinzip,"* Geiger): *dhammo hi seṭṭho jan' etasmiṃ diṭṭhe yeva dhamme abhisaṃparāyañ ca.* The Buddha and the Arahants are superior to all, since they represent its most perfect accomplishment ("*vollkommenste Verwicklichung,*" Geiger). But, also, from another point of view, the Dhamma is superior to the brahmins, etc. The brahmins are only brahmins by virtue of the Dhamma which is proper to them. The same is true of the other social classes, as well as for the Samaṇas (see below): *tesaṃ ñeva sattānaṃ anaññānaṃ sadisānaṃ ñeva no asadisānaṃ dhammen' eva no adhammena.* Geiger points out: "The *dh.* that is operative in each of these instances is

thus a conditioned, limited *dh.*, a fragment of the great World-Order, or its application to specific cases and relations." (*Pāli Dhamma*, pp. 79-80; on *dhammā* in the plural, cf. *ibid.*, pp. 8-9).—Cf. *infra*, p. 131 and n. 89. (On the locutions *dhammen' eva no adhammena* and *sadisānaṃ ñeva no asadisānaṃ*, cf. Geiger, p. 79, n. 3.)

22. *Brahmuno puttā orasā mukhato jātā Brahmajā Brahmanimmitā Brahmadāyādā*, *D.* III, p. 81. Cf. *M.* II, pp. 84, 148.

23. "Just as a *brāhmaṇa* would say that he is born of Brahmā, through his mouth—*Brahmuno putto oraso mukhato jāto brahmajo brahmanimmito brahmadāyādo*—so a *Sakyaputtiya-samaṇa* may say that he is born of Bhagavā, through his mouth, born of his doctrine, made of his doctrine, etc. Though in this passage Dhamma is equated with Brahmā (sic!), the context shows that there is no metaphysical sense in it; it is only to draw a parallel between a *brāhmaṇa* and a *Sakyaputtiya-samaṇa* that *Dhammakāya* is equated with *Brahmakāya*," N. Dutt, *Aspects of Mahāyāna Buddhism and its relation to Hīnayāna* (London, 1930), p. 99. Cf. also Geiger, *Pāli Dhamma*, p. 78: "The replacement of the Brahman-concept by *dhamma*, however, appears most distinctly in the following formula in which the follower of the Tathāgata is described as being his spiritual son. It reads: *bhagavato putto oraso mukhato jāto dhammajo dhammanimmito dhammadāyādo* . . . This formula reposes upon the wording of the one by which the brahmins substantiate their caste superiority: *brahmuno puttā orasā mukhato jātā brahmajā brahmanimmitā brahmadāyādā* . . . *Dhamma* (or *bhagavant*) has been substituted for the concept *brahman*.—Cf. *infra*, n. 86.

24. On the social attitude of Buddhism, cf. also W. Rāhula, *History of Buddhism in Ceylon* (Colombo, 1956), pp. 233 ff.—"The Buddhist counter-assertions are that in freedom as against freedom members of each caste are on an exact level, for it is not caste in itself that is undesirable or to be done away with (which Gotama never tried to do), but the arrogant brahman claims," I. B. Horner, *The Middle Length Sayings*, II (*Pāli Text Society Translation Series*, No. 30, London, 1957), p. xxii.

25. *ṚV.* X, 90, 12; Manu, I, 31, 87, 93. Cf. *Viṣṇu-Purāṇa*, I, 6 (Jīvānanda Vidyāsāgara edition, Calcutta, 1882); *Bhāgavata-Purāṇa*, II, 1, 37; XI, 17, 13; *Praśastapādabhāṣya*, p. 64 (ed. Jitendra S. Jetly, with the *Kiraṇāvalī* of Udayanācārya, Baroda, 1971 = *Gaekwad's Oriental Series*, No. 154); H. Brunner, "Analyse du *Suprabhedāgama*," *JA*. 1967, p. 42.—J. Muir, *Original Sanskrit Texts*, I (London, 1858), pp. 5 ff.

This is perhaps not the original meaning of the myth. Society is an organism composed of various members, and the four parts of the body may symbolize merely the various functions attributed to the four social classes (mouth: brahmin [teacher]; arms: Kṣatriya [warrior]; thighs [which are the seat of effort, *īhāśraya*, according to Śaṅkara, *Bṛhadāraṇyakopaniṣad-bhāṣya*, I, 4, 6, p. 107]: Vaiśya [farmer, etc.]; feet: Śūdra [servant]). Just as the body cannot function without the cooperation of all its members, so society cannot function without the cooperation of all its classes. Cf. Gandhi: "The four Varṇas have been compared in the Vedas to the four members of the body, and no simile could be happier. If they are members of one body, how can one be superior or inferior to another? If the members of the body had the power of expression and each of them were to say that it was higher and better than the rest, the body would go to pieces." (*In Search of the Supreme*, compiled and edited by V. B. Kher, Ahmedabad, Navajivan Publishing House, vol. III, 1962, p. 128.) See also D. M. Datta, *The Philosophy of Mahātmā Gandhi* (Madison, The University of Wisconsin Press, 1953), p. 104; Radhakrishnan, *The Hindu View of Life*, pp. 76-77 (American edition: Macmillan, New York, n.d.); *Eastern Religions and Western Thought*[2] (Oxford University Press, 1940), pp. 355 ff.

Perhaps it is permissible to think that the division of Indian society into four classes may have preceded the *Puruṣa-Sūkta*. Such divisions also existed in other Indo-European communities. The *Puruṣa-Sūkta*, in making the four social classes emanate from the universal Principle, the cosmic Man, was no doubt declaring, for the first time, their essential identity.—See also P. Mus, "Où finit Puruṣa?", in *Mélanges Louis Renou*, pp. 539 ff.

26. On this text, see also U. Schneider, "Acht Etymologien aus dem Aggañña-Sutta," in *Asiatica: Festschrift Friedrich Weller* (Leipzig, 1954), pp. 575 ff.; "Ein Beitrag zur Textgeschichte des *Aggañña-Suttanta*," *IIJ*. I (1957), no. 4, pp. 253 ff.; A. Mette, *Indische Kulturstiftungsberichte und ihr Verhältnis zur Zeitaltersage* (= *Abhandlungen der Akademie der Wissenschaften und der Literatur in Mainz: Geistes- und Sozialwissenschaftlichen Klasse*, 1973, NR. 1), pp. 30 ff.; G. von Simson, "Etymologie als Mittel ideologischer Auseinandersetzung: Bemerkungen zum Aggaññasutta des Dīghanikāya," in *Studia indogermanica et slavica: Festgabe für Werner Thomas zum 65. Geburtstag* (München, 1988), pp. 87-98; S. Collins, "The Discourse on What is Primary (Aggañña-Sutta), *An Annotated Translation*," *Journal of*

Indian Philosophy, 21, 4 (December 1993), pp. 301 ff.

27. This theory of the evolution of the social classes (without the cosmogony) is taken up again in the *Śārdūlakarṇāvadāna* (ed. Sujitkumār Mukhopādhyāya, Viśvabhāratī, Śāntiniketan, 1954, pp. 32-33). See also the *Sūtra* cited by Vasubandhu, *Abhidharmakośa-bhāṣya*, III, 97-98, pp. 186-187 (*AK.* III, pp. 204-206).

28. Our text makes a distinction between contemplatives (*jhāyaka*) and teachers (*ajjhāyaka*). When, it says, they were unable to sustain meditation in their huts made of leaves in the depths of the forest, certain brahmins went and settled near villages and towns and composed books (the Vedas): *tesaṃ ñeva kho, Vāseṭṭha, sattānaṃ ekacce sattā araññāyatane paṇṇa-kuṭīsu taṃ jhānaṃ anabhisambhuṇamānā gāma-sāmantaṃ nigama-sāmantaṃ osaritvā ganthe karontā acchanti.* (*ganthe karontā ti tayo vede abhisaṃkharontā c' eva vācentā ca*, Buddhaghosa, *Sumaṅgalavilāsinī*, III, p. 870).—The teachers thus represented only a degenerate section of the brahmins. Our text explains the word *ajjhāyaka*, "teacher" (*Śārdūla-karṇāvadāna: adhyāpaka*), in the sense of "he who doesn't meditate" (*a-jjhāyaka*: a linguistic joke which no doubt hides a deep feeling!): *na dān' ime jhāyantīti kho, Vāseṭṭha, "Ajjhāyakā, Ajjhāyakā" tv eva tatiyaṃ akkharaṃ upanibbattaṃ.*—According to Buddhism, the brahmin is "he who removes evil." See *infra*, p. 126 and n. 34. [Cf. Index: "Etymologies."]

29. *vissuta-kammante = gopakamma-vāṇijakammādike vissute uggate kammante*, Buddhaghosa, *Sumaṅgalavilāsinī*, III, p. 871.

30. *luddācārā khuddācārā ti kho, Vāseṭṭha, "Suddā, Suddā" tv eva akkharaṃ upanibbattaṃ.*—Doubtful interpretation. Buddhaghosa is of no help. The *Śārdūlakarṇāvadāna* omits *luddācārā* (= Sanskrit *raudrācārāḥ*? cf. H. Lüders, *Beobachtungen über die Sprache des buddhistischen Urkanons*, aus dem Nachlass herausgegeben von E. Waldschmidt [= *Abhandlungen der Deutschen Akademie der Wissenschaften zu Berlin: Klasse für Sprachen, Literatur und Kunst*, 1952, Nr. 10, Berlin, 1954, § 77]): *athānyatame sattvāḥ kṣudreṇa karmaṇā jīvikāṃ kalpayanti sma; teṣāṃ śūdrā iti saṃjñā udapādi.* (*Śārdūlakarṇāvadāna*, p. 33, Sujitkumār Mukhopādhyāya edition, already cited.) On *sudda* = *khudda* (<*kṣudra*), cf. U. Schneider, "Acht Etymologien . . . ," *loc. cit.*, p. 580.

31. *BhG.* IV, 13. Cf. XVIII, 41 ff. (P. V. Kane, *History of Dharma-śāstra*, V, 2 [Poona, 1962], pp. 1635-1636). Regarding "natural" occupations (*svabhāvaja, sahaja, BhG.* XVIII, 42-44, 48; cf. also

Kālidāsa, *Śakuntalā*, VI, 1 [Pischel-Cappeller, editors, *HOS.* 16]), cf. Socrates in Plato, *Republic*, II, 370 a-b: ". . . no two people are born exactly alike. There are innate differences which fit them for different occupations . . . more things will be produced and the work be more easily and better done, when every man is set free from all other occupations to do, at the right time, the one thing for which he is naturally fitted." (F. M. Cornford, *The Republic of Plato* [New York-London, Oxford University Press, 1945, etc.], pp. 56-57.)

Socrates said besides: "It is true, we shall tell our people in this fable, that all of you in this land are brothers; but the god who fashioned you mixed gold in the composition of those among you who are fit to rule, so that they are of the most precious quality; and he put silver in the Auxiliaries, and iron and brass in the farmers and craftsmen. Now, since you are all of one stock, although your children will generally be like their parents, sometimes a golden parent may have a silver child or a silver parent a golden one, and so on with all the other combinations. So the first and chief injunction laid by heaven upon the Rulers is that, among all the things of which they must show themselves good guardians, there is none that needs to be so carefully watched as the mixture of metals in the souls of the children. If a child of their own is born with an alloy of iron or brass, they must, without the smallest pity, assign him the station proper to his nature and thrust him out among the craftsmen or the farmers. If, on the contrary, these classes produce a child with gold or silver in his composition, they will promote him, according to his value, to be a Guardian or an Auxiliary. They will appeal to a prophecy that ruin will come upon a state when it passes into the keeping of a man of iron or brass." (*Ibid.*, III, 415 a-c: Cornford, pp. 106-107.)

It seems to us that a similar principle originally guided social organization in India. There was thus a compromise between heredity and social mobility. See also the notes by Radhakrishnan, *Bhagavadgītā*² (London, 1949, etc.), pp. 364 ff.—Wrongly, Edgerton, *Bhagavadgītā*, pp. 161-162 ("Harper Torchbooks," New York, 1964).

32. *ekavarṇam idaṃ pūrvaṃ viśvam āsīd Yudhiṣṭhira* |
karmakriyāviśeṣeṇa cāturvarṇyaṃ pratiṣṭhitam ||

verse cited in the *Vajrasūcī*: A. Weber, "Über die *Vajrasūcī* (Demantnadel) des *Aśvaghoṣa*," *Philologische und historische Abhandlungen der Königlichen Akademie der Wissenschaften zu Berlin*, 1859, p. 226, v. 40;

Sujitkumār Mukhopādhyāya, *The Vajrasūcī of Aśvaghoṣa* (Viśva-bhāratī, Śāntiniketan, second edition, 1960), p. 10, v. 41.

It still seems impossible to clarify the relations existing between the *Vajrasūcī*, attributed sometimes to Aśvaghoṣa, sometimes to Dharmakīrti (E. H. Johnston, translation of the *Buddhacarita* [= *Panjab University Oriental Publications* No. 32, Calcutta, 1936], p. xxii; against the attribution to Dharmakīrti, cf. Sujitkumār Mukhopādhyāya, *op. cit.*, pp. xi-xiii), and the *Vajrasūcī* (or *°sūcikā*) *-Upaniṣad*, sometimes attributed to Śaṅkara. (Generally, the Upaniṣad is considered as an adaptation of the *Vajrasūcī* by a Hindu author.) However, the identical titles and the similarity of the contents (the first paragraphs of the two texts say roughly the same thing, and sometimes in the same terms) prove that certain Hindu and Buddhist milieux reacted in the same way against the absurd pretensions of the brahmins. The whole significance of the *Vajrasūcī*, moreover, resides in the fact that it combats these pretensions with the aid of Hindu texts.

33. *Mbh.* XII, ch. 181 (critical edition). Cf. E. W. Hopkins, *Ethics of India* (New Haven, Yale University Press, 1924), p. 131; P. V. Kane, *History of Dharmaśāstra*, II, 1 (Poona, 1941), p. 101; V, 2 (1962), p. 1636.

34. *pāpake akusale dhamme bāhentīti kho, Vāseṭṭha, "Brāhmaṇā, Brāhmaṇā" tv eva paṭhamaṃ akkharaṃ upanibbattaṃ.* Cf. *Vin.* I, p. 3 (*Mahāvagga*, I, 2, 3, = *Ud.* I, 4, p. 3 = *Netti*, p. 150):

yo brāhmaṇo bāhitapāpadhammo
nihuhuṅko nikasāvo yatatto |
vedantagū vusitabrahmacariyo
dhammena so brāhmaṇo brahmavādaṃ vadeyya || [*dhammena so brāhmaṇo brahmavādaṃ vadeyya* = *"brāhmaṇo ahan" ti etaṃ vādaṃ dhammena ñāyena vadeyya*, Dhammapāla, *Paramatthadīpanī: Udānaṭṭhakathā*, p. 55; cf. Buddhaghosa, *Samantapāsādikā*, V, p. 958. This interpretation is entirely in accord with the context; one should not see in *brahmavāda*, as, after Mrs. Rhys Davids (cf. I. B. Horner, *The Book of the Discipline*, IV [= *Sacred Books of the Buddhists*, XIV, London, 1951], p. 4, n. 3), Radhakrishnan does (*Up.*, p. 679), a synonym of *brahmavidyā* (*provāca tāṃ tattvato brahmavidyām, Muṇḍ.Up.* I, 2, 13). The word *vedānta*, in *vedantagū*, on the other hand, does not refer to a particular doctrine. According to the interpretation that is already to be found in the ancient texts (cf. *Sn.* 529, with *Paramatthajotikā*, II, 2, pp. 430-431), the word *veda*, in *vedantagū* (or *vedagū*), means "knowledge" (*ñāṇa*, according to the commentaries)

or "sensation" (= *vedanā*). *Vedagū* or *vedantagū* thus means: "he who has attained Knowledge" (or "who has reached the end, *anta*, of Knowledge"), or again: "He who has gone beyond all specific knowledge" (*sabbaṃ vedam aticca vedagū so, Sn.* 529), or "who has gone beyond all sensations," (*sabbavedanāsu vītarāgo, ibid.*). The commentators add yet another meaning: "he who, by means of Knowledge, has reached the end (of birth, old age and death, in other words, Nirvāṇa)." Thus, *Mahāniddesa*, I, p. 93 (cf. pp. 204-205): *vedehi jāti-jarā-maraṇassa antagato . . . nibbānagato . . . vedānaṃ vā antagato ti vedagū, vedehi vā antagato ti vedagū.*—Buddhaghosa, *Samantapāsādikā*, V., p. 958: *vehehi vā antaṃ, tiṇṇam* (?) *vedānaṃ vā antaṃ gatattā vedantagū.* Perhaps should be seen here, as in the expressions *tisso vijjā* and *tevijja* (epithet of a true brahmin, in other words of a Buddha or an Arhat [below]), the "Buddhist antithesis to the authority of the Veda" (*PTS. Dictionary*, s.v. *veda*; cf. *ibid.*, article *vijjā*, regarding *tisso vijjā* and *tevijja*). See also "Some Thoughts on Ātman-Brahman in Early Buddhism," *loc. cit.*, n. 103. In the commentaries, *veda* is often glossed by *catu-magga-ñāṇa*. Thus, *Mahāniddesa*, I, p. 93: *vedā vuccanti catūsu maggesu ñāṇaṃ.* There are four Vedas! (On the attitude of the Upaniṣads and of Buddhism towards vedic knowledge, cf. *infra*, pp. 181-182.) Let us note, however, that the expression *vedāntaga* (= Pāli *vedantagū*) is encountered in the *Mahābhārata* (for example, XIII, 1749 = XIII, 25, 63), where Nīlakaṇṭha glosses it by *jñātatattva.* (Cf. Index IV.)—See also Edgerton, *Dictionary*, s.v. *vedaka.*]

See also *S.* I, p. 141; *Dhp.* 388; *Ud.* I, 5, p. 4 (= *Netti*, p. 150); *Sn.* 519 (cf. *infra*, p. 224); *Abhidharmakośa-vyākhyā*, cited by La Vallée Poussin, *AK.* VI, p. 244, n. 3 (Wogihara edition [Tokyo, 1932-1936], p. 578); *TSP.* 3589.—*kundendudhavalaṃ hi brāhmaṇatvaṃ nāma sarvapāpasyāpakaraṇam, Vajrasūcī* (Weber, p. 221; Mukhopādhyāya, p. 4). The *Śārdūlakarṇāvadāna* gives a different interpretation: *atha teṣāṃ grāmavāsināṃ sattvānām etad abhavat: duṣkarakārakā vata bhoḥ sattvā ye svakaṃ parigraham utsṛjya grāmanigamajanapadebhyo bahir nirgatāḥ, teṣāṃ* bahirmanaskā brāhmaṇā *iti saṃjñā udapādi.* (*Śārdūlakarṇāvadāna*, p. 32, edited by Sujitkumār Mukhopādhyāya, already cited.) Cf. *Abhidharmakośabhāṣya*, III, 98, p. 187, l. 16 (*tatra ye gṛhebhyo* bahirmanasaḥ *saṃvṛttās teṣāṃ* brāhmaṇā *iti saṃjñotpannā*) [naturally, this "etymology" does not appear in the translation, *AK.* III, p. 206]. See also Candrakīrti, *Catuḥśatakavṛtti*, in V. Eltschinger, *"Caste" et philosophie bouddhique* (Wien, 2000: *Wiener Studien zur*

Tibetologie und Buddhismuskunde, herausgegeben von E. Steinkellner, Heft 47), p. 77. [On *bāhayati, bāheti*, cf. Edgerton, *Dictionary*, s.v. See also on the question, J. Brough, *The Gāndhārī Dharmapada* (London, 1962), p. 178.]

35. *na jaṭāhi na gottena na jaccā hoti brāhmaṇo* |
yamhi saccañ ca dhammo ca so sukhī so ca brāhmaṇo || *Dhp.* 393; translation (modified) of Dhammārāma, *BEFEO.* LI, 2 (1963), p. 315.

36. Cf. also *Dhp.* 141-142; *S.* IV, pp. 117-118; *Sn.* 136 ff., 462 (= *S.* I, p. 168), 249; *Vin.* I, p. 3 (above, n. 34); *Ud.* I, 9, p. 6 (= *Netti*, p. 151); *Soṇadaṇḍa-Sutta* (*D.* I, pp. 111 ff.).—*Mbh.* III, 13454 ff. (W. Rau, "Bemerkungen und nicht- buddhistische Sanskrit-Parallelen zum Pāli-Dhammapada," in *Festschrift Nobel*, p. 167).—*Vajrasūcī*, vv. 13 ff., with notes by Sujitkumār Mukhopādhyāya. See also Radhakrishnan, *Eastern Religions and Western Thought*[2], p. 375; *Up.*, p. 938; *The Hindu View of Life*, p. 86 (edition cited); Kshiti Mohan Sen, *Hinduism* ("Penguin Books," 1961), ch. 4; Hopkins, *op. cit.*, p. 131; Kane, *op. cit.*, II, 1, pp. 100-101; V, 2, pp. 1636-1637.

37. *bahv ahaṃ carantī paricāriṇī yauvane tvām alabhe.* Senart translates differently (cf. also Śaṅkara's commentary).

38. Cf. also *Sn.* 620 ff. (*Vāseṭṭha-Sutta* = *M.*, Sutta 98).

39. On the *Brāhmaṇa* = *Arhant* equivalence, cf. also *Avadānaśataka*, cited by P. Mus, "Le sourire d' Angkor," *Artibus Asiae*, XXIV, 3/4 (1961) [*Felicitation Volume presented to Professor George Cœdès on the occasion of his Seventy-fifth Birthday*], pp. 366-367; "Où finit Puruṣa?", *loc. cit.*, p. 562.

40. Cf. *infra*, p. 139.

41. Cf. *supra*, p. 46, n. 38; *infra*, pp. 181-182.

42. Cf. *supra*, p. 53, n. 58; Appendix I.

43. *BĀU.* III, 5; 8, 10; IV, 4, 23. Cf. also *Vajrasūcī* (°*sūcikā*)-*Upaniṣad* (Radhakrishnan, *Up.*, pp. 935 ff.); *ChU.* IV, 1, 7. (*brāhmaṇa* = *brahmavid*, Śaṅkara).

utpattir eva viprasya mūrtir dharmasya śāśvatī |
sa hi dharmārtham utpanno brahmabhūyāya kalpate || *Manu*, I, 98 (cf. *infra*, p. 129).

japyenaiva tu saṃsidhyed brāhmaṇo nātra saṃśayaḥ |
kuryād anyan na vā kuryān maitro brāhmaṇa ucyate || *Ibid.*, II, 87: verse cited by Śaṅkara, *Brahmasūtra-bhāṣya*, III, 4, 38. Cf. *Mbh.* XII, 60, 12 (critical edition):

parinisṭhitakāryas tu svādhyāyenaiva brāhmaṇaḥ |

kuryād anyan na vā kuryān maitro brāhmaṇa ucyate || See also *supra*, p. 83, n. 100.—*brāhmaṇo brahmaṇaḥ saṃbandhī brahmaṇi līyata ity āgameṣūcyate*, Kullūka on Manu, II, 87.

According to the *Bṛhadāraṇyaka-Upaniṣad*, I, 4, 11 ff., while the Kṣatriyas, the Vaiśyas, and the Śūdras are emanations of the One (the *brahman*), the brahmin is the *brahman* itself. Cf. Gandhi: "A Brāhmaṇa who considers himself superior to any single creature of God ceases to be a knower of Brahma" (*In Search of the Supreme*, compiled and edited by V. B. Kher, Ahmedabad, Navajivan Publishing House, vol. I, 1961 p. 115 [cf. vol. III, 1962, p. 131]).

See also J. Gonda, *Notes on Brahman* (Utrecht, 1950), ch. V, pp. 50 ff.; Radhakrishnan, *The Hindu View of Life*, pp. 83-84 (edition cited).—Appendix III, and Index IV, s.v. *brāhmaṇa.*

44. The terms *varṇa* and *jāti* are often confused: cf. Kane, *op. cit.*, II, 1, p. 55; V, 2, p. 1633.

45. *samaḥ sarveṣu bhūteṣu, BhG.* XVIII, 54 *(supra,* p. 123). Cf. Manu, XII, 125:

evaṃ yaḥ sarvabhūteṣu paśyaty ātmānam ātmanā |
sa sarvasamatām etya brahmābhyeti paraṃ padam ||

See also *supra*, p. 13 and nn. 99 and 101.

46. *BhG.* V, 18 (cf. *Mbh.* XII, 8752). [*Supra*, p. 81, n. 99.] See also *ChU.* V, 24, 4, with Śaṅkara.—"The whole system of caste and untouchability is undermined by the perception of the Indwelling Self in all," Radhakrishnan, *Up.*, p. 445.

Cf. Meister Eckhart: "A gnat considered as it is in God is nobler than the highest angel as he is in himself. In God all things are equal and God Himself." (*Traités et Sermons*, translated from the German by F. A. and J. M. with an introduction by M. de Gandillac, Paris, 1942, p. 178 [cf. p. 256].)

47. *brahmaivāham idaṃ jagac ca sakalaṃ cinmātravistāritaṃ*
sarvaṃ caitad avidyayā triguṇayāśeṣaṃ mayā kalpitam |
itthaṃ yasya dṛḍhā matiḥ sukhatare nitye pare nirmale
cāṇḍālo 'stu sa tu dvijo 'stu gurur ity eṣā manīṣā mama ||

Manīṣā-pañcaka, 2 (*Minor Works of Śrī Śaṅkarācārya*, edited by H. R. Bhagavat [= *Poona Oriental Series* No. 8, second edition, 1952], p. 364).

Cf. also *BĀU.* IV, 3, 22. The *ātman-brahman* is beyond distinctions between brahmin, Kṣatriya, etc. (*apetabrahmakṣatrādibheda*): Śaṅkara, *Brahmasūtra-bhāṣya*, Introduction, p. 43 (cf. II, 3, 43, with Durgamohan Bhattacharyya, "An Inkling of Philosophic Material in the *Paippalādasaṃhitā,*" in *Brahma-vidyā, The Adyar Library Bulletin,* XXVIII, parts 1-2 (May 1964), pp. 133-134; "New Materials for Atharvavedic Study," *Mélanges Louis Renou,* p. 103). See also Śaṅkara, *Upadeśasāhasrī, padya,* XV, 5; XVII, 45.—*Ātmabodha,* 11; *Aṣṭāvakra-Gītā,* I, 5.—Sureśvara, *Saṃbandha-vārttika,* 292-293, 363 (edited and translated by T. M. P. Mahadevan = *Madras University Philosophical Series,* No. 6, 1958); *Naiṣkarmyasiddhi,* II, 88.—Cf. P. Hacker, *Untersuchungen über Texte des frühen Advaitavāda,* 1. *Die Schüler Śaṅkaras (= Abhandlungen der Akademie der Wissenschaften und der Literatur in Mainz: Geistes- und Sozialwissenschaftlichen Klasse,* 1950, NR. 26), p. 11 (1917) and n. 1.

48. *Supra,* p. 29 and n. 214.

49. *Supra,* p. 47 (cf. p. 111); pp. 29-30 and n. 215.

50. *attakāmena mahattam abhikaṅkhatā.* Cf. *supra,* pp. 1 ff., 14 ff., 21; p. 119, n. 278.—*ātmakāmāḥ* = *ātmajñānakāmāḥ,* Rāmatīrtha on *MaiU.* VII, 10.—Buddhaghosa considers *mahatta* as an abstract noun, derived from *mahant: mahattam abhikaṅkhatā ti mahanta-bhāvaṃ patthayamānena* (*Sāratthappakāsinī,* I, p. 204; *Manoratha-pūraṇī,* III, p. 26). Concerning our interpretation, however, cf. Geiger, *Pāli Literature and Language,* II, § 92. 2.

51. *S.* I, p. 140 (p. 141 of the Nālandā edition); *A.* II, p. 21 (p. 24 of the Nālandā edition). [The *Aṅguttara* adds a passage on the Saṃgha, which is missing in the *Saṃyutta.*]—Quotation (in agreement with Buddhaghosa, it seems [preceding note]), *A.* IV, p. 91 (III, p. 222 of the Nālandā edition).—See also *infra,* p. 133.

52. *M.* I, p. 386. Cf. *brahmaprāpta, Kaṭha-Up.* VI, 18.—The expression *brahmappatta,* which *A.* II, p. 184 employs in connection with the *brahmavihāras,* refers to Brahmā (cf. Appendix III).

53. *BĀU.* IV, 4, 6 (taken up again in *Subāla-Up.* III: Radhakrishnan, *Up.,* p. 866). Śaṅkara, in commenting on this passage, employs the expression *brahmabhūta.* Cf. also Śaṅkara on *BhG.* XVIII, 54 *(supra,* p. 123): *brahmabhūta* = *brahmaprāpta* (= Pāli *brahma-patta*).

54. *cittaṃ ca susamāhitaṃ vippasannam anāvilaṃ* |
akhilaṃ sabbabhūtesu so maggo brahmapattiyā ||

S. IV, p. 118.—*Maggo brahmapattiyā:* cf. *brahmapatha,* below.—Geiger, *Pāli Dhamma,* p. 77.—The *brahmapatti* of *S.* I, p. 181, which the Buddha rejects, refers to Brahmā (cf. *supra,* n. 9).

55. *S.* I, p. 169 (PTS edition and Nālandā edition). Cf. *ChU.* VIII, 4, 3; 5.—"Its [*brahmacarya*] root meaning may be given thus:

that conduct which puts one in touch with God," Gandhi, quoted by D. M. Datta, *op. cit.*, p. 101. See also *supra*, n. 9.

56. *manussabhūtaṃ sambuddhaṃ attadantaṃ samāhitaṃ* |
iriyamānaṃ brahmapathe cittass' upasame rataṃ || *Theragāthā*, 689 = *A.* III, p. 346. Cf. *maggo brahmapattiyā*, above, n. 54. See also below. On *manussabhūta*, cf. *infra*, p. 185, n. 35, and on *attadanta*, *supra*, pp. 30-31; *infra*, p. 180.—In *S.* I, p. 141 (as in the *Chāndogya-Upaniṣad*, cf. below, n. 58), the expression *brahmapatha* refers to Brahmā (cf. Appendix III).

57. *Dhamma und Brahman*, pp. 4-5. Cf. *Pāli Dhamma*, p. 77.

58. Cf. V. V. Gokhale, "The Vedānta Philosophy described by Bhavya in his *Madhyamakahṛdaya*," *IIJ.* II (1958), no. 3, p. 177.—*BhG.* II, 72; V, 24.25.26: *brahmanirvāṇa* (cf. VI, 15: *śāntiṃ nirvāṇaparamām* [*amataṃ santiṃ nibbānapadam accutaṃ, Sn.* 204]). See also *infra*, p. 226, n. 7.—The expression *brahmapatha* is to be found in the *Chāndogya-Upaniṣad* (IV, 15, 5), but there it is a question of Brahmā (Geiger, *Pāli Dhamma*, p. 77; *Dhamma und Brahman*, p. 5; cf. *infra*, n. 158). Cf. however *MaiU.* VI, 30 (with Rāmatīrtha's commentary): *eṣātra brahmapadavī . . . eṣo 'tra brahmapathaḥ*; *BhG.* VI, 38: *vimūḍho brahmaṇaḥ pathi* (*brahmaṇaḥ pathi* = *brahmaprāptimārge*, Śaṅkara; cf. *maggo brahmapattiyā*, above, n. 54).—On Nirvāṇa (or *brahman-ātman*) = *amṛta/amata*, cf. *supra*, p. 46, n. 38.

59. *M.* I, pp. 69 ff.; *S.* II, p. 27; *A.* II, p. 9 (the prose text reads: *brahmacakkaṃ pavatteti*; but in the *gāthās* we find: *yo dhammacakkaṃ . . . pavattayi*); *A.* II, p. 24 (= *It.*, p. 123); III, pp. 9, 417; V, p. 33; *Paṭisaṃbhidāmagga*, II, p. 174.—Geiger, *Pāli Dhamma*, pp. 77-78; *Dhamma und Brahman*, p. 6.—The expression *brahmacakra* is found in the *Śvetāśvatara-Upaniṣad* (I, 6 and VI, 1), but in a different context.

The *Abhidharmakośa* and the *Bodhisattvabhūmi* interpret *brahma-cakra* in these terms: "because it is set in motion by Brahmā": La Vallée Poussin, *AK.* VI, pp. 244-245 and n. 2 on page 245. (Brahmā = *brāhmaṇa, anuttarabrāhmaṇyayogāt, Abhidharmakośa*: cf. Appendix III.)

60. *brahmayānam iti pi dhammayānam iti pi anuttaro saṃgāma-vijayo iti pi, S.* V, p. 5.—Geiger, *Pāli Dhamma*, p. 78; *Dhamma und Brahman*, p. 6.—Compare the passage of the *Aggañña-Sutta*, cited above, p. 124: *dhammakāyo iti pi brahmakāyo iti pi, dhammabhūto iti pi brahmabhūto iti pi.*—When *dhamma°* and *brahma°* are thus employed side by side, "the one is intended, as it were, to comment on and

elucidate the other" ("*der eine den anderen gewissermassen zu erläutern und zu verdeutlichen bestimmt ist*"), Geiger, *Dhamma und Brahman*, p. 6.—At the end of the *Saṃyutta-Nikāya* passage there is a series of verses describing the *brahma* (= *dhamma*) *-yāna*, in other words, the vehicle which takes one to Deliverance. The last of these verses is (according to the Pāli Text Society edition):

etad attaniyam bhūtaṃ brahmayānam anuttaraṃ |
niyyanti dhīrā lokamhā aññadatthu jayaṃ jayaṃ ||

Geiger (*Dhamma und Brahman*, pp. 6-7; cf. *Pāli Dhamma*, pp. 78-79), proposes the following translation:

"That is the true *ātman*-teaching, the unsurpassable vehicle of Brahma; verily the sages go forth out of this world only to victory, to victory."

And he adds: ". . . If this is correct, we have here a reference to the pre-Buddhist doctrine of *ātman-brahman*, which was replaced by the doctrine of *Dhamma*. This would then be one of the very few passages in the Canon in which the synonymity of *ātman* and *brahman* is still remembered."

But the true reading is the one given by the Nālandā edition (vol. IV, p. 7; cf. already the note of the PTS edition!):

etad attani sambhūtaṃ brahmayānaṃ anuttaraṃ |
niyyanti dhīrā lokamhā aññadatthu jayaṃ jayaṃ ||

The meaning is clear: "the vehicle which takes one to *brahman*" (*brahmayāna*) is not something outside ourselves. (Let us recall the words of Plotinus, *Enneads*, I, 6, 8, cited above, p. 57.) This vehicle "has its origin in ourselves" (*attani sambhūtaṃ*).[a] As our text makes clear, its different elements are made up out of what we are ourselves as individuals—while raising us however to a higher level (this condition is what distinguishes it from the psycho-physical "vehicles" that are ordinary individuals, *supra*, p. 28)—: *saddhā, paññā, hirī, manas, sati, sīla, jhāna, viriya, upekkhā, anicchā, avyāpāda, avihiṃsā, viveka, titikkhā*. And it leads to the plenitude of our being, to the *ātman-brahman*.

Cf. again *S.* I, p. 33, where the "chariot" that leads to Nirvāṇa is described somewhat in the same terms as here and where it is said, moreover, that the *dhamma* (= *ātman-brahman*) is the "charioteer" (*sārathi*; cf. *supra*, p. 29); *Dhp.* 369-370 (cf. *Sn.* 771), where the *bhikkhu* is asked to empty the boat that is his individuality of the water that has infiltrated into it, namely: the "five bonds" (*rāga, dosa, moha, māna* and *diṭṭhi*),—that he might sail lightly on the ocean of *saṃsāra* and reach easily Nirvāṇa; *S.* IV, pp. 291-292 (cf. *Ud.* VII, 5, p. 76), where the Arhant is compared to a marvellous chariot; finally, *Jāt.* VI, pp. 252-253 (cf. *supra*, p. 29), where the virtuous and disciplined man is compared to a chariot whose charioteer is the *manas.*

As can be seen, the word *attan*, in our stanza, is not, contrary to what Geiger writes (*Pāli Dhamma*, p. 79), "Bezeichnung für das 'höchste Prinzip,'" "designation of the Supreme Principle," rather it designates the phenomenal *ātman.* Nonetheless, our text indirectly indicates the identity of the *brahman* and the *ātman*: the *brahman* to which the "vehicle" leads is our true being (*ātman*), which we must attain in the very depths of ourselves, through our sublimated existence (cf. *supra*, p. 30).

Cf. *supra*, p. 46, n. 38 (last paragraph).

---

a. *attano purisākāraṃ nissāya laddhattā attani sambhūtaṃ nāma hoti*, Buddhaghosa, *Sāratthappakāsinī*, III, p. 122. (*etad attaniyaṃ bhūtan ti* must be an error. Cf. Siam edition, III, p. 202.)

61. Cf. Geiger, *Pāli Dhamma*, p. 77. As the commentator makes clear, the word *dhamma* here designates Nibbāna, "supreme Dhamma": *dhammamaggan ti paramadhammassa nibbānassa maggaṃ* (*Paramatthajotikā*, II, 2, p. 489).—Cf. Geiger, *Pāli Dhamma*, pp. 67, 98.

62. *"Buddho" ti ghosaṃ yada parato suṇāsi*
"sambodhipatto vicarati dhammamaggaṃ" |
gantvāna tattha samayaṃ paripucchiyāno
carassu tasmiṃ Bhagavati brahmacariyaṃ || *Sn.* 696.

63. *sarveṣām eva dānānāṃ brahmadānaṃ viśiṣyate*, Manu, IV, 233.

64. *A.* I, p. 91; IV, p. 364; *Dhp.* 354; *It.*, p. 98; *Mil.*, p. 167. Cf. Geiger, *Pāli Dhamma*, pp. 72 and 78.

65. *Mil.*, p. 191. Cf. Geiger, *Pāli Dhamma*, p. 78.

66. Geiger, *Pāli Dhamma*, p. 78; *Dhamma und Brahman*, p. 6.

67. *BĀU.* I, 4, 14.

68. *dharmo viśvasya jagataḥ pratiṣṭhā, Mahānārāyaṇa-Upaniṣad*, 524 (edited by J. Varenne = *Publications de l'Institut de Civilisation indienne*, fascicule 11, Paris, 1960). Cf. also *ibid.*, 510: *dharmeṇa sarvam idaṃ parigṛhītam.*—*BĀU.* I, 5, 22-23 (cf. *infra*, n. 82).—Geiger, *Pāli Dhamma*, p. 8; *Dhamma und Brahman*, p. 4; Coomaraswamy, *Hinduism and Buddhism*, p. 85, n. 299; Radhakrishnan, *Up.*, p. 204.

brahman = *ṛta* = *satya*, *TU.* I, 1 (cf. 12): *tvam eva pratyakṣaṃ brahmāsi, tvām eva pratyakṣaṃ brahma vadiṣyāmi, ṛtaṃ vadiṣyāmi, satyaṃ vadiṣyāmi.*—*dharma* = *satya*, *BĀU.* I, 4, 14.—*brahman-ātman* = *satya*, *BĀU.* V, 4; *ChU.* VI, 8-16 (*tat satyam, sa ātmā, tat tvam asi*); VIII, 3, 4 (cf. *TU.* II, 1: *satyaṃ jñānam anantaṃ brahma*) [*brahman-ātman* = *satyasya satyam* (*supra*, p. 12); cf. the Buddhist formula: *dharmāṇāṃ dharmatā* (*infra*, p. 131)]. Cf. again *TU.* I, 11: *satyaṃ vada, dharmaṃ cara . . . satyān na pramaditavyam, dharmān na pramaditavyam.*—*Dhp.* 217:

sīladassanasampannaṃ dhammaṭṭhaṃ saccavādinaṃ |
attano kamma kubbānaṃ taṃ jano kurute piyaṃ ||

S. I, p. 169:

saccaṃ dhammo saṃyamo brahmacariyaṃ
majjhesitā brāhmaṇa brahmapatti |

69. Manu, I, 98. Cf. *supra*, n. 43.

70. On the notion of *dharma*, cf. J. Gonda, "*Het begrip dharma in het Indische denken*," *Tijdschrift voor Philosophie* (Louvain), 20 (1958), pp. 213-266. See also L. Renou, "Sur deux mots du *Ṛgveda*," I, *JA.* 1964, pp. 159 ff.

71. *Infra*, n. 82.

72. *Sumaṅgalavilāsinī*, III, p. 865. Cf. *Papañcasūdanī*, II, p. 76; *Sāratthappakāsinī*, II, p. 389.—Different interpretation in the *Sāratthappakāsinī* (II, p. 314: on *S.* III, p. 120, quoted above, p. 105, n. 214; cf. *Sāratthappakāsinī*, III, p. 204): *navavidho hi lokuttaradhammo Tathāgatassa kāyo nāma.* Likewise, Dhammapāla, *Paramatthadīpanī: Itivuttakaṭṭhakathā*, II, p. 116 (on *It.*, p. 91, cited below, p. 133). Cf. *supra*, p. 105, n. 215. See also Dhammapāla, *Paramatthadīpanī: Theragāthā-Aṭṭhakathā*, II, p. 205 (on *Theragāthā* 491, below).

73. *D.* II, p. 154; cf. *Mil.*, p. 99.

74. *M.* III, pp. 9-10.

75. *Supra*, p. 124.—Cf. *M.* III, p. 29; *S.* II, p. 221; *It.*, p. 101.

76. Cf. N. Dutt, *op. cit.*, pp. 98 ff.

77. *S.* II, p. 267; V, p. 407; *A.* I, p. 72; III, p. 107. Cf. *Mil.*, p. 16: *gambhīrāya abhidhammakathāya lokuttarāya suññatāpaṭisaṃyuttāya.*—*Bodhisattvabhūmi*, cited by La Vallée Poussin, "Sūnyatā," *IHQ.* IV (1928), p. 161 (Wogihara, editor [Tokyo, 1930-1936], p. 46; cf. p. 303): *durvijñeyān sūtrāntān mahāyānapratisaṃyuktān gambhīrān śūnyatāpratisaṃyuktān . . .*

78. *M.* I, pp. 190-191.

79. *uppādā vā tathāgatānaṃ anuppādā vā tathāgatānaṃ ṭhitā va sā dhātu dhammaṭṭhitatā dhammaniyāmatā idappaccayatā. taṃ Tathāgato abhisambujjhati abhisameti; abhisambujjhitvā abhisametvā ācikkhati

deseti paññāpeti paṭṭhapeti vivarati vibhajati uttānīkaroti, "passathā" 'ti cāha: jātipaccayā, bhikkhave, jarāmaraṇaṃ . . . iti kho, bhikkhave, yā tatra tathatā avitathatā anaññathatā idappaccayatā, ayaṃ vuccati, bhikkhave, paṭiccasamuppādo, S. II, pp. 25-26.

Scholasticism, it is true, sees no metaphysical meaning in this passage (*Kathāvatthu,* VI, 2; *Visuddhimagga,* XVII, 5-6 [edited by Warren-Kosambi, *HOS.* 41; cf. *Sāratthappakāsinī,* II, pp. 40-41]; *Abhidharmakośabhāṣya,* III, 28, p. 137 [*AK.* III, pp. 77-78]). Cf. however, among others, *Laṅk.*, quoted below, n. 104.—The Buddhist schools, with which the *Kathāvatthu* and the *Abhidharmakośa* take issue, were mistaken in considering the *pratītya-samutpāda/paṭicca-samuppāda* as an *asaṃskṛta-dharma.* In reality, this only brings out the "absence of self-nature" (*niḥsvabhāvatva, naiḥsvābhāvya*) in the phenomena which arise, all of them dependent upon causes and conditions (*hetu-pratyaya*). It is in this way that the Mahāyānists understood it:

idaṃ pratītyedaṃ bhavatīty evam abhidhānena bhagavatā Tathāgatena niḥsvabhāvatvam eva sarvadharmāṇāṃ spaṣṭam āveditam, MKV., p. 159.

Cf. the stanza of the *Anavataptahradāpasaṃkramaṇa-Sūtra,* cited *ibid.*, pp. 239, 491, 500 and 504:

yaḥ pratyayair jāyati sa hy ajāto
no tasya utpādu sabhāvato 'sti |
yaḥ pratyayādhīnu sa śūnya ukto
yaḥ śūnyatāṃ jānati so 'pramattaḥ ||

Laṅk., cited *ibid.*, p. 504 (cf. p. 262): *svabhāvānutpattiṃ saṃdhāya, Mahāmate, sarvadharmāḥ śūnyā iti mayā deśitāḥ.*—Murti, pp. 122, 178, 194-195; and still other references, in Lamotte, *Vimalakīrti,* pp. 41-42, nn.—Nāgārjuna, *Vigrahavyāvartanī* (cf. our translation in *Journal of Indian Philosophy,* I, 3 [November 1971], pp. 217 ff.).

Now, it is this "absence of own-nature," it is this "Vacuity" (*śūnyatā*) of phenomena as such, which unveils their essential nature: the Unconditioned. The *pratītya-samutpāda/paṭicca-samuppāda* is thus only a negative expression of the *dharma/dhamma.* See below, p. 132. Cf. also *tathatta = nibbāna*: *PTS. Dictionary,* s.v. (= *tathatva*: Edgerton, *Dictionary,* s.v. *tathatā,* etc.).

80. *Supra,* pp. 1 ff., and the references given at the end of note 20 on page 41.

81. Cf. *Laṅk.* III, 26:
mātrā svabhāvasaṃsthānaṃ pratyayair bhāvavarjitam |
niṣṭhābhāvaḥ paraṃ brahma etāṃ mātrāṃ vadāmy aham ||

See also *infra*, p. 226, n. 7.

82. The question is much disputed. We may, however, for our present purpose, take note of the following: in the same way that, in *BĀU.* I, 5, 23, the *vāyu/prāṇa* (cf. *supra*, p. 41, n. 29) is the *dharma* of the *devas* (*taṃ devāś cakrire dharmam*), in I, 6, 1 ff., speech (*vāc*) is the *brahman* of names (*nāman*), the eye (*cakṣus*), the *brahman* of forms (*rūpa*), and the body (*ātman*: cf. *supra*, p. 112, n. 245), the *brahman* of acts (*karman*). [Cf. Appendix IV.] This last text derives the word *brahman* from the root *bhṛ-* "to bear, to sustain": *etad eṣāṃ brahma, etad dhi sarvāṇi nāmāni (rūpāṇi, karmāṇi) bibharti* (= *dhārayati*, Śaṅkara). In the mind of the author, there was then a close etymological link between *brahman* and *dharma* (from the root *dhṛ-* "to bear, to sustain": below).—Through this diversity, one grasps limited aspects (cf. *supra*, n. 21) of *brahman-dharma*, sole support of all supports. (Cf. *supra*, p. 79, n. 91.)

83. Cf. J. Gonda, *Notes on Brahman*, ch. VII, pp. 62 ff. See also Appendix III.

84. Cf. *supra*, pp. 121, 124.

85. Cf. N. Dutt, *op. cit.*, pp. 87, 99 (passage cited above, n. 23). Cf. also Barth, *Œuvres*, II, p. 372: "It is, I believe, almost certain that the confusion made by M. Leclère between the impersonal brahman, the absolute Being of Hindu philosophy, and the Brahmās of the celestial worlds . . . is made in Cambodia by the Buddhists themselves, by the most literate and, in other respects, most orthodox bonzes."—Likewise, the term *ātman* tended to be confused with *pudgala*: here, it seems to us, is the reason for which this term is rather rarely employed to designate the Absolute.

86. Here we part company with Geiger (cf. also J. Gonda, "Het begrip dharma in het Indische denken," *loc. cit.*, p. 251). According to Geiger, when the Buddha utilized the term *brahman*, he did not give it exactly the meaning that it has in the Upaniṣads. "It (the traditional concept of Brahman) receives a particular shading . . . is seen in a new light," *Dhamma und Brahman*, p. 4. The very term *dhamma* (Sanskrit *dharma*), which the Buddha borrowed from the past, and which was destined to replace that of *brahman*, would, Geiger thinks, be none other than "the traditional receptacle that he filled with a new content," (*ibid.*). Geiger sums up his thinking in these terms: "*Dhamma* is to the Buddhist what *brahman* is to the brahmanic philosopher. Quite deliberately, Buddha substituted the concept of *dhamma* for that of *brahman*; in place of the eternal,

immutable World-Soul was posited the idea of eternal genesis and dissolution; instead of the idea of substance, that of non-substance," *Pāli Dhamma*, p. 7. In both the preceding and following pages, we have endeavored to show that such an opposition between the Upaniṣads and Buddhism is fictive (cf. *supra*, n. 60).

87. The term *śūnya*, it is true, appears for the first time only in the *Maitri-Upaniṣad* (cf. *supra*, p. 29); but we have seen that the *neti neti* of Yājñavalkya expresses the same idea (*supra*, p. 8).

88. Cf. *supra*, p. 46, n. 37.

89. On *dhammatā* in the Pāli Canon, cf., in general, Geiger, *Pāli Dhamma*, A II 2d, p. 19; A IV la, p. 28. *Theragāthā* 712 already seems to herald the Mahāyānic usage:

> *uttamaṃ dhammataṃ patto sabbaloke anatthiko* |
> *ādittā va gharā mutto maraṇasmiṃ na socati* ||

Cf. *supra*, nn. 21, 68, 82. This problem would be worth going into in depth and perhaps we shall do so some day.

90. Candrakīrti, *MKV.*, pp. 264-265 (cf. J. W. De Jong, "Text-critical Notes on the Prasannapadā," *IIJ.* 20 [1978], p. 58: read *sarvaśo 'nutpāda?*). Cf. Murti, p. 235. The rest of this passage is reproduced and translated in Lamotte, *Vimalakīrti*, p. 48; however, we must point out that this translation is inaccurate (cf. below).

91. Cf. above, n. 79.

92. Cf. *ASP.*, p. 170: *yathā, Subhūte, tathatā tathā gambhīraṃ rūpam. evaṃ vedanā saṃjñā saṃskārāḥ. yathā, Subhūte, tathatā tathā gambhīraṃ vijñānam. tatra, Subhūte, yathā rūpatathatā tathā gambhīraṃ rūpam. yathā vedanātathatā saṃjñātathatā saṃskāratathatā. tatra, Subhūte, yathā vijñānatathatā tathā gambhīraṃ vijñānam. yatra, Subhūte, na rūpam, iyaṃ rūpasya gambhīratā. yatra, Subhūte, na vedanā na saṃjñā na saṃskārā na vijñānam, iyaṃ vedanāsaṃjñāsaṃskārāṇām, iyaṃ vijñānasya gambhīratā.*—"To be devoid of (all determinate) essence is itself to be identical with *dharma-dhātu, tathatā, bhūtakoṭi* (i.e. the ultimate reality)," Venkata Ramanan, p. 88. See also *ibid.*, p. 256; *Bodhisattvabhūmi*, cited by La Vallée Poussin, "Śūnyatā," *loc. cit.*, pp. 162-163 (edited by Woghihara, pp. 47-48).—Compare with Jaspers: "Das Nichtsein allen uns zugänglichen Seins, das sich im Scheitern offenbart, ist das Sein der Transzendenz—(The non-being of all being approachable by us, which reveals itself in the shipwreck, is the being of Transcendence)." (*Philosophie* III [Berlin, 1932], p. 234.)

On the subject of the identity of the Absolute and the phenomena, of *nirvāṇa* and *saṃsārā*, cf. *infra*, pp. 137-138. On *śūnyatā* = *nairātmya* = *tathatā* = *dharmakāya* = *ātman*, see *supra*, pp. 1 ff.

93. Cf. *MKV.*, pp. 263-264: *kālatraya 'py avyabhicāri nijaṃ rūpam akṛtrimam.* See also *infra*, p. 200, n. 9 (p. 201).

94. *sa caiṣa bhāvānām anutpādātmakaḥ svabhāvo 'kiṃcittvenābhāvamātratvād asvabhāva eveti kṛtvā nāsti bhāvasvabhāva iti vijñeyam, MKV.*, p. 265.—Cf. *ASP.*, p. 96: . . . *prakṛtyaiva na te dharmāḥ kiṃcit. yā ca prakṛtiḥ sāprakṛtiḥ, yā cāprakṛtiḥ sā prakṛtiḥ sarvadharmāṇām; ekalakṣaṇatvād yad utālakṣaṇatvāt.*—". . . that nature of things which is unconditioned is not anything specific; there all things are of one nature, *ekalakṣaṇa*, viz., of no specific nature, *alakṣaṇa*," Venkata Ramanan, p. 359 a, n. 1 of ch. VII. See also our translation of the *Vigrahavyāvartanī*, *loc. cit.*, pp. 237-238, n. 2 in v. XXIX.

Cf. the three kinds of *niḥsvabhāvatā* spoken of by the Vijñānavādins: *Saṃdhinirmocana-Sūtra*, VII, 3 ff. (E. Lamotte, *Saṃdhinirmocana-Sūtra: L'Explication des Mystères*, Louvain-Paris, 1935); Asaṅga, *Abhidharmasamuccaya*, p. 84 (P. Pradhan, editor, Viśvabhāratī, Śāntiniketan, 1950); Vasubandhu, *Triṃśikā*, 23-25, with Sthiramati's commentary. Cf. La Vallée Poussin, *Siddhi*, II, pp. 556 ff.

95. *avidyātimiraprabhāvopalabdhaṃ bhāvajātaṃ yenātmanā vigatāvidyātimirāṇām āryāṇām adarśanayogena viṣayatvam upayāti, tad eva svarūpam eṣāṃ svabhāva iti vyavasthāpyate, MKV.*, p. 265.—Unlike the "ignorant," the Āryas do not see the totality (*jāta*) of phenomena (*bhāva*), because they see their "essential nature." In reality, they "see" nothing at all: theirs is the highest vision, where there is no longer any division between subject and object.—On the subject of the locution *adarśanayogena viṣayatvam upayāti*, cf. *supra*, p. 5 and n. 20. See also *supra*, p. 109, n. 243, and cf. *MK.* V, 8.—*Ātman* = *svarūpa*? Cf. *supra*, pp. 1-2 (*MSA.*); p. 114, n. 249.

96. *yadi hi, devaputra, paramārthataḥ paramārthasatyaṃ kāyavāṅmanasāṃ viṣayatām upagacchet, na tat paramārthasatyam iti saṃkhyāṃ gacchet, saṃvṛtisatyam eva tad bhavet, Satyadvayāvatāra-Sūtra*, cited *BCAP.*, p. 177.—Cf. *supra*, p. 109, n. 243. Compare with Plotinus, *Enneads*, V, 5, 6: "One doubtless employs the word *one* to begin the research with the word designating the maximum of simplicity; but finally even this attribute of it must be negated, as it is no more worthy than the others to designate a nature which cannot be grasped by the hearing nor understood by one who hears it named, but only by one who sees it. And still, if he who sees sought to

contemplate its form, he would not know it." (Trans. Bréhier.)

97. Candrakīrti, *MKV.*, p. 264 (cf. the passage quoted above).—Cf. Plotinus, *Enneads*, VI, 8, 8: "Let us suppress even the word *it is*, and with this word its connection with beings." (Trans. Bréhier.)

98. *Supra*, p. 9.

99. *saṃdiṭṭhiko ayaṃ dhammo akāliko ehipassiko opanayiko paccattaṃ veditabbo viññūhi*, passim. On *ehipassika*, see *PTS. Dictionary*, s.v. *ehi*. Cf. also *S.* II, pp. 25-26, cited above, n. 79.—See *supra*, p. 61, n. 62; p. 9 and n. 66; *infra*, pp. 181-182.

100. Pp. 127-128.

101. *yaṃ nūnāhaṃ yvāyaṃ dhammo mayā abhisaṃbuddho tam eva dhammaṃ sakkatvā garukatvā upanissāya vihareyyaṃ.*

102. Cf. Appendix III.

103. *S.* I, pp. 138-140 (pp. 139-141 in the Nālandā edition); *A.* II, pp. 20-21 (pp. 22-24 in the Nālandā edition).—The text ends with a verse enjoining all those who aspire to the "Great Ātman" to venerate the Dhamma (*supra*, p. 128).

104. *S.* II, pp. 105-106.—Sanskrit version: C. Tripāṭhī, *Fünfundzwanzig Sūtras des Nidānasaṃyukta*, Berlin, 1962 (*Sanskrittexte aus den Turfanfunden VIII*), Sūtra 5. On the importance of this text in the Buddhist world, see S. Lévi, "Documents de l'Asie Centrale (Mission Pelliot): Textes sanskrits de Touen-Houang," *JA.* 1910, pp. 435-436.—The image reappears in the *Laṅkāvatāra-Sūtra*, pp. 143-144, along with that of the hidden treasure; there, moreover, are found again the terms in *S.* II, pp. 25-26, cited above, n. 79:

tatra paurāṇasthitidharmatā katamā?—yad uta paurāṇam idaṃ, Mahāmate, dharmatāvartma. hiraṇyarajatamuktākaravan, Mahāmate, dharmadhātusthititā. utpādād vā tathāgatānām anutpādād vā tathāgatānāṃ sthitaivaiṣā dharmāṇāṃ dharmatā, dharmasthititā, dharmaniyāmatā. paurāṇanagarapathavan, Mahāmate. tadyathā, Mahāmate, kaścid eva puruṣo 'ṭavyāṃ paryaṭan paurāṇaṃ nagaram anupaśyed avikalapathapraveśam. sa taṃ nagaram anupraviśet. tatra praviśya pratiniviśya nagaraṃ nagarakriyāsukham anubhavet. tat kiṃ manyase, Mahāmate: api nu tena puruṣeṇa sa panthā utpādito yena pathā taṃ nagaram anupraviṣṭaḥ, nagaravaicitryaṃ ca?—āha: no Bhagavan.—Bhagavān āha: evam eva, Mahāmate, yan mayā taiś ca tathāgatair adhigatam, sthitaivaiṣā dharmatā, dharmasthititā, dharmaniyāmatā, tathatā, bhūtatā, satyatā. (To *paurāṇasthitidharmatā*, compare *pūrvadharmasthititā*, *Laṅk.*, p. 241, l. 14.)

105. *Supra*, p. 29.

106. Concerning this image, cf. A.-J. Festugière, *Épicure et ses dieux* (Paris, 1946), pp. 123, 125.

107. *It.*, pp. 91-92.

108. Cf. *supra*, p. 127.

109. G. Cœdès, "La destination funéraire des grands monuments khmèrs," *BEFEO.* XL, pp. 329-330, with bibliography.

We will go back over the *Dharmakāya* in a subsequent study on the "Bodies of the Buddha" in the Mahāyāna.

110. *BĀU.* IV, 4, 13. Cf. Oldenberg, *LUAB.*[2], p. 113, n. 1. On this stanza, see also *supra*, p. 13.—Cf. also *BĀU.* I, 4, 10: *tad yo yo devānāṃ pratyabudhyata sa eva tad abhavat. tatharṣīṇāṃ tathā manuṣyāṇām* (cf. Oldenberg, *LUAB.*[2], p. 114 and n. 2).

111. *Supra*, n. 58.

112. *Ud.* VIII, 1, p. 80.

113. *Ibid.*, VIII, 3, pp. 80-81; *It.*, p. 37; *Netti*, p. 62. Cf. *supra*, p. 46, n. 38, and pp. 33-34.

114. Cf. *supra*, p. 8.—*BĀU.* III, 8, 8: *etad vai tad akṣaraṃ, Gārgi, brāhmaṇā abhivadanti: asthūlam anaṇv ahrasvam adīrgham alohitam asneham acchāyam atamo 'vāyv anākāśam asaṅgam arasam agandham acakṣuṣkam aśrotram avāg amano 'tejaskam aprāṇam amukham amātram anantaram abāhyam.* See also *supra*, p. 97, n. 173.

115. Oldenberg-Foucher[4], pp. 320-321. Cf. also E. Frauwallner, *Geschichte der indischen Philosophie*, I (Salzburg, 1953), p. 234.

116. F. O. Schrader, "On the problem of Nirvāṇa," *JPTS.* 1904-1905, pp. 165-168. We reproduce here the passage as it is summarized by A. B. Keith, *Buddhist Philosophy in India and Ceylon* (Oxford, 1923), pp. 65-66. It is regrettable that the credit for this important discovery is often attributed to Keith himself: cf. La Vallée Poussin, *Nirvāṇa* (Paris, 1925), p. 146; Radhakrishnan, *Indian Philosophy*[2], I, p. 689, n. 5; N. Dutt, *op. cit.*, p. 148 and n. 1.

117. *accī yathā vātavegena khitto*
atthaṃ paleti na upeti saṃkhaṃ |
evaṃ munī nāmakāyā vimutto
atthaṃ paleti na upeti saṃkhaṃ || (Cf. *Mil.*, p. 73.)

Cf. *ibid.*, 1076:

atthaṃgatassa na pamāṇam atthi
yena naṃ vajju taṃ tassa n' atthi |
sabbesu dhammesu samūhatesu
samūhatā vādapathā pi sabbe ||

Ud. VIII, 10, p. 93:

ayoghanahatass' eva jalato jātavedassa |
anupubbūpasantassa yathā na ñāyate gati ||
evaṃ sammāvimuttānaṃ kāmabandhoghatārinaṃ |
paññāpetuṃ gati n' atthi pattānaṃ acalaṃ sukhaṃ ||

Dhp. 179: *taṃ buddhaṃ anantagocaraṃ apadaṃ kena padena nessatha*; *ibid.*, 92 (cf. *Theragāthā*, 92): *ākāse va sakuntānaṃ gati tesaṃ durannayā*; *ibid.*, 420 (= *Sn.* 644).—Cf. *Mbh.* XII, 5953; 6763; 8756-57 (cf. XIII, 5570); 12156 (W. Rau, *loc. cit.*, pp. 164, 175); Śaṅkara on *Muṇḍ.Up.* III, 2, 6, and on *Māṇḍ.Kār.* IV, 95; *Samādhirāja-Sūtra*, XXXII, 48; XXXVI, 67 (P. L. Vaidya, editor, Darbhanga, 1961 [= *Buddhist Sanskrit Texts*, No. 2]).—*M.* I, p. 140, cited above, p. 46, n. 38 (cf. p. 22); *S.* I, pp. 12 and 23; *ibid.*, p. 122, and III, p. 124 (cf. *supra*, p. 22); *D.* I, p. 46.—*M.* I, p. 141; *S.* XXII, 56-57: *vaṭṭaṃ tesaṃ n' atthi paññāpanāya.*—*A.* II, p. 9 (Nālandā, II, p. 11): *vādapathātivatta.*

Muṇḍ.Up. III. 2, 8 (cf. *Praśna-Up.* VI, 5):

yathā nadyaḥ syandamānāḥ samudre
'staṃ gacchanti nāmarūpe vihāya |
tathā vidvān nāmarūpād vimuktaḥ
parāt paraṃ puruṣam upaiti divyam ||

(Cf. *infra*, p. 230. For the image, cf. also Venkata Ramanan, p. 259.)

BĀU. II, 4, 12, and IV, 5, 13; *ChU.* VI, 9 and 10 (cf. *supra*, p. 7).

118. *vahner yathā yonigatasya mūrtir na dṛśyate naiva ca liṅganāśaḥ* | *sa bhūya evendhanayonigṛhyas* . . . *Śvet.Up.* I, 13.—

niṣkalaṃ niṣkriyaṃ śāntaṃ niravadyaṃ nirañjanam |
amṛtasya paraṃ setuṃ dagdhendhanam ivānalam || *Ibid.*, VI, 19.

Cf. *Mil.*, p. 327: *yathā pana, Mahārāja, atthi aggi nāma, n' atthi tassa sannihitokāso, dve kaṭṭhāni saṅghaṭṭento aggiṃ adhigacchati, evam eva kho, Mahārāja, atthi nibbānaṃ, n' atthi tassa sannihitokāso, sammāpāṭipanno yoniso-manasikārena nibbānaṃ sacchikaroti.*

119. *yathā nirindhano vahniḥ sva-yonāv upaśāmyati* |
tathā vṛtti-kṣayāc cittaṃ sva-yonāv upaśāmyati ||

Maitreya(ī)-Upaniṣad, I, 3 (F. O. Schrader, *The Minor Upaniṣads*, I [*Saṃnyāsa-Upaniṣads*], Madras, Adyar Library, 1912, p. 110) = *MaiU.* VI, 34.

The idea appears in the *Mahābhārata* as well: cf. Frauwallner, *op. cit.*, p. 226; G. C. Pande, *Studies in the Origins of Buddhism* (University of Allahabad, 1957), p. 480, n. 177 (*Śāntiparvan*, ch. 187, vv. 2-6). Cf. also *Ahirbudhnya-Saṃhitā*, IV, 76-77 (M. D. Rāmānujācārya, editor, Madras, Adyar Library, 1916):

indhanābhāvato jvālā vahnibhāvaṃ yathā gatā ||
brahmabhāvaṃ vrajaty evaṃ sā śaktir vaiṣṇavī parā |

(The relation between the Absolute and its *śakti* [by whom it manifests itself] is compared to that which exists between fire and flame, or again, between the moon and its light. Thereby it is shown that there is an invisible fire, independent of the visible fire, and an invisible moon, independent of the visible moon.—See *Les Religions brahmaniques dans l'ancien Cambodge, d'après l'épigraphie et l'iconographie* [= *Publications de l'École française d'Extrême-Orient*, XLIX, Paris, 1961], p. 63.)

120. Cf. *supra*, pp. 121-122. See also *infra*, p. 226, n. 7.

121. H. von Glasenapp, in Oldenberg, *Buddha*, 1961 edition, p. 435. Cf. *Vedānta und Buddhismus*, p. 4 (1914).

122. *Supra*, p. 46, n. 38; pp. 33, 135.

123. *diṭṭhe va dhamme sayaṃ abhiññā sacchikatvā upasaṃpajja viharati*, passim. Cf. *supra*, pp. 121-122 (and n. 7); *infra*, n. 170.

124. This, in fact, is what a Mahāyānic text says:

na nirvāsi nirvāṇena nirvāṇaṃ tvayi saṃsthitam |

(*Laṅkāvatāra-Sūtra*, II, 7, *supra*, p. 56).

125. *ChU.* VIII, 3, 2 (*supra*, p. 59, n. f).

126. Nirvāṇa, the Absolute, is, to be sure, the "Wholly-Other"; but, as in the Upaniṣads, is not the farthest at the same time the nearest? Cf. *supra*, p. 43, n. 31; pp. 47-48. By his "ganz andere," H. von Glasenapp distorts, at once, the Absolute of the Upaniṣads and that of Buddhism.

127. *Supra*, pp. 47-48; p. 54, n. 60; p. 157, n. 60; Appendix VI.

128. Murti, pp. 162-163. Cf. *MK.* XXV, 9, with Candrakīrti's commentary.—Compare with Śaṅkara: . . . *idaṃ jagad utpatti-vināśātmakam iti kevalajagadvyapadeśaḥ*, . . . *"mahān aja ātmā," "asthūlo 'naṇuḥ," "sa eṣa neti neti" ityādi kevalātmavyapadeśaḥ.* (*Bṛhad-āraṇyakopaniṣad-bhāṣya*, I, 4, 7, p. 118.)

129. Cf. Venkata Ramanan, p. 122: ". . . the mundane is itself (in its real nature) the transmundane and the transmundane is itself (what appears as) the mundane."

130. Murti, pp. 232-233.—Conversely, the immanence of the Absolute does not exclude its transcendence. On the contrary, the transcendence of the Absolute is the very condition of its genuine immanence. See *supra*, p. 43, n. 31, and *infra*, p. 241, n. 3.

131. There exists, to our knowledge, but a single important study on this word: that of Oldenberg, *Buddha*[1] (1881), pp. 432 ff. ("dritter

Excurs"; these "Excurses" have not been included in subsequent editions of the work [cf. Oldenberg, *Buddha*², Berlin, 1890, p. viii]; nor have they been translated by Foucher). This study—in part outdated today—contains a considerable number of citations (according to manuscripts, particularly) which have been very useful to us for the present exposition.—Cf. also *"Upadhi-, upādi-* et *upādāna-* dans le Canon bouddhique pāli," *Mélanges Louis Renou*, pp. 81 ff.

132. *Sn.* 728. Cf. *ibid.*, 1049-1051; *Theragāthā*, 152.—*yaṃ kho idaṃ anekavidhaṃ nānappakāraṃ dukkhaṃ loke uppajjati jarāmaraṇaṃ, idaṃ kho dukkhaṃ upadhinidānaṃ upadhisamudayaṃ upadhijātikaṃ upadhipabhavaṃ; upadhismiṃ sati jarāmaraṇaṃ hoti, upadhismim asati jarāmaraṇaṃ na hoti, S.* II, p. 108.—*upadhi dukkhassa mūlaṃ, M.* I, p. 454; II, pp. 260-261 (cf. *infra*, p. 141). See also *M.* III, p. 70; *S.* I, p. 117.

133. *Sn.* 546 and 572 (= *Theragāthā*, 840).

134. *Sn.* 374. Cf. *ibid.*, 992 (= *S.* I, p. 134 = *A.* II, p. 24 = *It.*, p. 123): *vimutto upadhisaṃkhaye.—nirupadhi upadhisaṃkhaye vimutto, M.* I, p. 454; II, pp. 260-261.—*sabbūpadhīṇaṃ parikkhayā buddho soppati, kin tav' ettha Māra, S.* I, p. 107.

135. *sukittitaṃ Gotam' anūpadhīkaṃ, Sn.* 1057, 1083.—*disvā padaṃ santam anupadhīkaṃ akiñcanaṃ kāmabhave asattaṃ, Vin.* I, p. 36 (*Mahāvagga*, I, 22, 5; cf. *Mahāvastu*, III, p. 445 [E. Senart, editor, Paris, 1897]: *dṛṣṭvā muniṃ śāntam anūpadhīkam akiñcanaṃ sarvabhaveṣu asaktaṃ*).—*kāyena amataṃ dhātuṃ phassayitvā nirūpadhiṃ* | *upadhippaṭinissaggaṃ sacchikatvā anāsavo* | *deseti sammāsambuddho asokaṃ virajaṃ padaṃ* || *It.*, pp. 46 and 62.

D. III, pp. 112-113, speaks of *anāsavā anupadhikā ariyā iddhi* (opp. *sāsavā sa-upadhikā no ariyā*). The *Mahācattārīsaka-Sutta* of the *Majjhima-Nikāya* (Sutta 117, vol. III, pp. 71 ff.), in turn, speaks of two kinds of *sammā-diṭṭhi*, of *sammā-saṃkappa*, of *sammā-vācā*, of *sammā-kammanta* and of *sammā-ājīva*. The first, which is *sāsava*, leads to merit (*puññabhāgiya*) and to *upadhi* (*upadhivepakka*); while the second, which is *ariya, anāsava* and *lokuttara*, forms part of the *Magga* (*maggaṅga*), in other words, leads to Nirvāṇa. [The word *opadhika*, always associated with *puñña* (*S.* I, p. 233; *A.* IV, p. 292; *It.*, pp. 20, 78; *Vimānavatthu*, XXXIV, 21; 24), and which the commentators gloss by *upadhi-vipāka, upadhi-vepakka*, seems to have a different meaning: cf. Edgerton, *Dictionary*, s.v. *upadhi, upadhika, upadhi-vāra, upadhi-vāraka (°vārika), aupadhika.*]

See also *Vin.* I, pp. 5, 42, 197 (*Mahāvagga*, I, 5, 2; 24, 3 [cf. *S.* I, p. 124; *A.* III, p. 382; and below, n. 170]; V, 13, 10 [= *Ud.* V, 6, p. 59]);

II, p. 156 (*Cullavagga*, VI, 4, 4 = *S.* I, p. 212 = *A.* I, p. 138); *S.* I, pp. 194-195; IV, p. 158 (= *It.*, p. 58); *A.* I, p. 80; *It.*, pp. 21, 50; *Sn.* 642 (= *Dhp.* 418); *Theragāthā*, 1216 (= *S.* I, p. 186), 1250; *Therīgāthā*, 320; Geiger, *Pāli Dhamma*, p. 98 and n. 8.

136. *sāro ettha na vijjati*, *S.* III, p. 143. Cf. *supra*, p. 11 and n. 82.

137. *Paramatthajotikā*, II, 1, p. 363. Cf. also *S.* I, p. 107 (IV, 1, 6), with *Sāratthappakāsinī*, I, p. 174.—According to the commentaries, there are three or four kinds of *upadhi: (kāmupadhi), khandhupadhi, kilesupadhi,* and *abhisaṃkhārupadhi.* For a different classification, cf. *Cullaniddesa*, 157; *Paramatthajotikā*, II, 2, p. 590. See also *PTS. Dictionary*, s.v. *upadhi.*

138. Sometimes *nirupadhika*, cf. *S.* I, p. 141 (on the likening of the Arhat to Brahmā, which this text does, cf. Appendix III).

139. Cf. *It.*, p. 69: *sabbe upadhī aniccā dukkhā vipariṇāmadhammā.*

140. Cf. *infra*, p. 209 and n. 13.

141. Deussen, *Das System des Vedānta* (Leipzig, 1883), p. 327. The term *upādhi* does not yet appear in the ancient Upaniṣads, even though the idea is already present there (cf. *infra*, p. 229).

142. *upadhippaṭinissagga*: n. 135. Cf. *sabbupadhipaṭinissagga*, passim.

143. *Supra*, p. 138.

144. Cf. *Vivekacūḍāmaṇi*, 554:

jīvann eva sadā muktaḥ kṛtārtho brahmavittamaḥ |
upādhināśād brahmaiva san brahmāpyeti nirdvayam ||

The *ātman-brahman* is *anupādhi(ka), nirupādhi(ka)*: Śaṅkara, passim.

145. P. Horsch, *La notion* d'upādhi *dans la philosophie de Śaṅkara* (University thesis in Paris in 1951), p. 7.

146. *Buddha*[1], pp. 441-442.

147. *Khanda*, in the text, must be a printer's error.

148. Cf. E. Müller, *A Simplified Grammar of the Pāli Language* (London, 1884), p. 36.—On the deaspiration, see also Geiger, *Pāli Literature and Language*, II, § 40.2.

149. The Vedāntins do not seem to make any distinction between *upa-dhā-* and *upā-dhā-*. We read, thus, in Padmapāda: *citsvabhāva evātmā tena tena prameyabheden*opadhīyamāno *'nubhavābhidhānīyakaṃ labhate, avivakṣit*opādhir *ātmādiśabdair abhidhīyate* (*Pañcapādikā*, ed. Rāmaśāstrī Bhāgavatācārya, Benares, 1891 [= *Vizianagram Sanskrit Series*, No. 3], p. 19). We find, too, in Vedānta, *upadhāna* = *upādhi* (cf. Śaṅkara, *Upadeśasāhasrī, padya*, XV, 15), and the participle *upahita.* Note that *upādhi* and *upadhi* are both used in Sanskrit in the sense of "deception." See also "Notes bouddhiques," *JA.* 1986, p. 295.

150. Sutta 105, vol. II, pp. 252 ff.

151. *Buddha*[1], p. 441.

152. The poison is *anupādisesa* when it is completely removed; it is *sa-upādisesa* when it is incompletely removed. According to Buddhaghosa, the word *upādi* means here "what must be removed." Literally, the expressions *anupādisesa* and *sa-upādisesa*, therefore, mean: "without residue of that which must be removed," "with residue of that which must be removed": *sa-upādisesan ti sa-gahaṇasesaṃ, upādātabbaṃ gaṇhitabbaṃ hi idha upādīti vuttaṃ . . . ettha sa-upādāna-salluddhāro viya appahīno avijjāvisadoso daṭṭhabbo.* (*Papañcasūdanī*, IV, p. 55.)

153. Cf. Geiger, *Pāli Dhamma*, p. 100.

154. Cf. also Sthiramati, *Triṃśikā-bhāṣya*, p. 19, l. 11: *upādānam upādiḥ.*

155. *Sumaṅgalavilāsinī*, III, p. 805; *Papañcasūdanī*, I, pp. 301-302. Cf. *Manorathapūraṇī*, IV, pp. 40, 174.

156. "The Buddhistic technical terms *upādāna* and *upādisesa*," *JAOS.* 19 (1898), second half, pp. 126-136.

157. *Sn.* 354 (= *Theragāthā*, 1274).—*anupādisesa* = *nibbāna*, *ibid.*, 876.

158. Cf. *D.* I, p. 156, with Buddhaghosa, *Sumaṅgalavilāsinī*, I, p. 313.—Perhaps it should be considered that the *Tevijja-Sutta* of *Dīgha-Nikāya* (Sutta XIII, vol. I, pp. 235 ff.) is also envisaging the condition of Anāgāmin when, in criticizing the pretensions of ritualist brahmins (cf. Appendix III), it says that the *bhikkhu*, practising the *Brahmavihāras*, will obtain after his death, the "company of Brahmā" (*Brahma-sahavyatā*). Let us also recall that the ancient Upaniṣads seem to speak already of a Deliverance that is attained in the "world of Brahmā" (*Brahmaloka*, distinct from *brahmaloka* "world that is the *brahman*"; *supra*, p. 47): *BĀU.* VI, 2, 15; *ChU.* IV, 15, 5; V, 10, 2 (on the confusion between Brahmā and *brahman* which these last two passages make, cf. Appendix III); VIII, 6, 6 (= *Kaṭha-Up.* VI, 16); 15, 1: texts from which originated the theory of the *kramamukti* "gradual Deliverance," in later Vedānta. See also *Muṇḍ.Up.* I, 2, 11, with Śaṅkara; *ibid.*, III, 2, 6 (differently, Śaṅkara; cf., however, Śaṅkarānanda on *Kaivalya-Up.* 3, in *Thirty-Two Upaniṣads* [= *Ānandāśrama Sanskrit Series*, 29, Poona, 1895], p. 103; Nārāyaṇa on *Mahānārāyaṇa-Up.* 10, 6 [ed. Colonel Jacob = *Bombay Sanskrit Series*, XXXV, 1888]); *Praśna-Up.* V, 5 (cf. Śaṅkara, *Brahmasūtra-bhāṣya*, I, 3, 13); *BhG.* VIII, 24, with Śaṅkara; *MaiU.* VI, 30, with Rāmatīrtha.—Cf. Rhys Davids, *Dialogues of the Buddha*, I,

p. 201, n. 4: "It is impossible to ignore a reference here to the view expressed in the Bṛhad Āraṇyaka Upaniṣad (VI, 2, 15)...."

159. See Oldenberg, *Buddha*[1], p. 435, n. 2, and cf. the following note.

160. *katame ca, bhikkhave, upādāniyā dhammā, katamaṃ upādānaṃ?—rūpaṃ*—pe—*upādāniyo dhammo; yo tattha chandarāgo, taṃ tattha upādānaṃ, S.* XXII, 121 (vol. III, p. 167).—Cf.:

ime pana, bhante, pañcupādānakkhandhā kiṃmūlakā?—ime kho, bhikkhu, pañcupādānakkhandhā chandamūlakā.—taṃ yeva nu kho, bhante, upādānaṃ te pañcupādānakkhandhā udāhu aññatra pañcupādānakkhandhehi upādānaṃ?—na kho, bhikkhu, taṃ yeva upādānaṃ te pañcupādānakkhandhā, na pi aññatra pañcupādānakkhandhehi upādānaṃ. yo kho, bhikkhu, pañcupādānakkhandhesu chandarāgo, taṃ tattha upādānaṃ, M. III, p. 16 (= *S.* III, pp. 100-101; cf. *M.* I, pp. 299-300).

S. XXII, 48 (vol. III, pp. 47-48) makes clear that it is when they are "accompanied by impulses" (*sāsava*) and are thus "objects of attachment" (*upādāniya*), that the five *khandhas* become *upādānakkhandha: pañca, bhikkhave, khandhe desissāmi, pañcupādānakkhandhe ca . . . yaṃ kiñci, bhikkhave, rūpaṃ atītānāgatapaccuppannaṃ ajjhattaṃ vā bahiddhā vā oḷārikaṃ vā sukhumaṃ vā hīnaṃ vā paṇītaṃ vā, yaṃ dūre santike vā, ayaṃ vuccati rūpakkhandho.* (The same goes for the other *khandhas*.) . . . *yaṃ kiñci, bhikkhave, rūpaṃ . . . sāsavaṃ upādāniyaṃ, ayaṃ vuccati rūpupādānakkhandho.* (The same goes for the other *khandhas*.)

In place of *upādāna* and *upādāniya* [*dhamma*], *S.* XXII, 120 (vol. III, pp. 166-167) uses the expressions *saṃyojana* and *saṃyojaniya* [*dhamma*]. Elsewhere, it is the twelve *āyatanas*—"bases of knowledge"—which are considered to be the *saṃyojaniyā* or *upādāniyā dhammā*, and it is the attachment to the *āyatanas* which constitutes the *saṃyojana* or *upādāna*: *katame ca, bhikkhave, saṃyojaniyā* (or *upādāniyā*) *dhammā, katamañ ca saṃyojanaṃ* (or *upādānaṃ*)?—*cakkhuṃ*—pe—*saṃyojaniyo* (or *upādāniyo*) *dhammo; yo tattha chandarāgo, taṃ tattha saṃyojanaṃ* (or *upādānaṃ*), *S.* XXXV, 109-110; 122-123 (vol. IV, pp. 89, 107-108); cf. *ibid.*, XLI, 1 (vol. IV, pp. 281-283).—See also *S.* II, pp. 84 ff.

The *khandhas* or the *āyatanas* thus do not constitute, by themselves, the *upādāna* (or *saṃyojana*); but there is no *upādāna* (or *saṃyojana*) apart from them. Analogous, *S.* III, p. 130: the *khandhas*, by themselves, do not constitute an "I"; but the idea of "I" cannot arise unless one is attached to them. (Cf. *supra*, p. 36.)

The doctrine is familiar to us (*supra*, p. 11 and n. 80).

161. *ahaṃ hi rūpaṃ*—pe—*yeva upādiyamāno upādiyeyyaṃ, tassa me assa upādānapaccayā bhavo, S.* III, p. 94. Cf. also *M.* I, p. 511.

According to the interpretation in the Nikāyas themselves, and which Buddhist scholasticism voluntarily adopts, by *upādāna,* cause of becoming, should be understood the four *upādāna*s, that is: the *kāmupādāna,* the *diṭṭhupādāna,* the *sīlabbatupādāna* and the *attavādupādāna* (cf. *supra*, p. 8 and n. 60): *D.* II, pp. 57-58; *M.* I, pp. 50-51, 67; *S.* II, p. 3. Oldenberg ("Buddhistische Studien," *ZDMG.* LII [1898], p. 692, n. 4) thinks that what is in question here is a "subsequent, purely scholastic interpolation of terms that originated in another context." We should say, rather, that the four *upādāna*s are simply various aspects of attachment to individuality: behind all these "attachments," lies the attachment to an "I." This is, in short, what Buddhaghosa says:

kamato ti ettha pana tividho kamo: uppattikkamo pahānakkamo desanākkamo ca. tattha, anamattagge saṃsāre imassa paṭhamaṃ uppattīti abhāvato kilesānaṃ nippariyāyena uppattikkamo na vuccati; pariyāyena pana yebhuyyena ekasmiṃ bhave attagāhapubbaṅgamo sassatucchedābhiniveso, tato, sassato ayaṃ attā ti gaṇhato attavisuddhatthaṃ sīlabbatupādānaṃ, ucchijjatīti gaṇhato paralokanirapekkhassa kāmupādānan ti evaṃ paṭhamaṃ attavādupādānaṃ tato diṭṭhi-sīlabbatakāmupādānānīti ayam etesam ekasmiṃ bhave uppattikkamo. (*Visuddhimagga,* XVII, 244 [edition cited].)

162. *Supra*, p. 21.

163. Cf. also the expressions *anupādā(ya) vimutto, anupādāparinibbāna,* etc.; and the expression *anādāna* (often associated with *akiñcana*). [Cf. *Sn.* 364, above, p. 138.]

164. To illustrate this thought, some texts of the Pāli Canon use the image of fire (or of the lamp) and the fuel, or again, that of the tree and the sap contained in the earth (*M.* I, p. 487; *S.* II, pp. 84 ff.). In all these texts, the word *upādāna* means something like "support of existence." Cf. Oldenberg, "Buddhistische Studien," *loc. cit.*, p. 691, n. 2. For the individual, this "support of existence" is the attachment to the elements of his sensible existence (*upādāniyā* or *saṃyojaniyā dhammā,* cf. above, n. 160). One who has transcended this is delivered from becoming, as fire or a lamp cease to burn when the fuel is used up, or as a tree ceases to live, for want of sap, when it is uprooted.—One of our texts (*S.* IV, pp. 399-400) uses the term *upādāna* apropos of wind, which carries the fire from one

place to another: *yasmiṃ kho, Vaccha, samaye acci vātena khittā dūraṃ pi gacchati, tam ahaṃ vātupādānaṃ vadāmi, vāto hi 'ssa, Vaccha, tasmiṃ samaye upādānaṃ hoti.* Just as, thanks to the wind, fire moves from one place to another, so, because of its "thirst" (*taṇhā*), the being transmigrates[a] from one body to another: "thirst" is therefore the *upādāna* of the being in that circumstance: *yasmiṃ kho, Vaccha, samaye imañ ca kāyaṃ nikkhipati satto ca aññataraṃ kāyaṃ anupapanno hoti, tam ahaṃ taṇhupādānaṃ vadāmi, taṇhā hi 'ssa, Vaccha, tasmiṃ samaye upādānaṃ hoti.*

---

a. Contrary to the doctrine presented above, p. 19.

165. For the form *upādi* (and *upădhi*), cf. Pāṇini, III, 3, 92; (J. Wackernagel-)A. Debrunner, *Altindische Grammatik*, II, 2 (Göttingen, 1954), p. 299.

166. P. 169, n. 132.

167. *Buddha*[1], p. 437.—Cf. also Geiger, *Saṃyutta-Nikāya*, II (München-Neubiberg, 1925), p. 149, n. 3.

168. *upādi* = *khandha*: Buddhaghosa, *Visuddhimagga*, XVI, 68; 73 (edition cited). Cf. Candrakīrti, *MKV.*, p. 519: *upadhiśabdenātmaprajñaptinimittāḥ pañcopādānaskandhā ucyante.* See also Edgerton, *Dictionary*, s.v. *upadhi.*

169. Cf. *D.* II, pp. 108, 136; III, p. 135; *A.* II, p. 120; IV, pp. 74 ff.; *Vin.* II, p. 239.—*It.*, pp. 38-39:

ekā hi dhātu idha diṭṭhadhammikā
sa-upādisesā bhavanettisaṃkhayā |
anupādisesā pana samparāyikā
yamhi nirujjhanti bhavāni sabbaso ||

According to an erroneous, but very widespread opinion, of Rhys Davids, the term *parinibbāna* would designate complete Nirvāṇa, attained through death, whilst the term *nibbāna* would designate Nirvāṇa attained in this life; each of the terms, *nibbāna* and *parinibbāna* would thus correspond to *sa-upādisesa-* and *anupādisesa-nibbāna.* Cf. however Oldenberg, *Buddha*[1], pp. 448-449; E. J. Thomas, "Nirvāṇa and Parinirvāṇa," in *India Antiqua: A Volume of Oriental Studies presented by his friends and pupils to J. Ph. Vogel, on the occasion of the fiftieth anniversary of his doctorate* (Leyden, 1947), pp. 294-295. See also Nyānatiloka, *Buddhistisches Wörterbuch* (Konstanz, 1954), s.v. *parinibbāna.*

170. It is not death but Knowledge (*ñāṇa*) which destroys the *upadhis*, and there is nothing beyond that destruction (*anuttara*):

gambhīre ñāṇavisaye anuttare upadhisaṃkhaye vimutte, Vin. I, p. 42 (*Mahāvagga,* I, 24, 3). [*gambhīra-ñāṇa-visaye*? L. Alsdorf, *Die Āryā-Strophen des Pāli-Kanons* (= *Abhandlungen der Akademie der Wissenschaften und der Literatur in Mainz: Geistes- und Sozialwissenschaftlichen Klasse,* 1967, NR. 4), p. 69 (311).]

171. Cf. *BĀU.* IV, 4, 6-7 and 14.—*Supra,* p. 51, n. 54; p. 93, n. 160.

172. Deussen, *AGPh.* I, 2, p. 321.

173. Deliverance may also coincide with death. Cf. Nyānatiloka, *op. cit.,* s.v. *nibbāna* and *samasīsī.*

174. Śaṅkara, *Brahmasūtra-bhāṣya,* IV, 1, 15; 19. Cf. *Chāndogyopaniṣad-bhāṣya,* V, 24, 3; VI, 14, 2; *Muṇḍakopaniṣad-bhāṣya,* II, 2, 8; *Bhagavadgītā-bhāṣya,* IV, 37; XIII, 23; *Bṛhadāraṇyakopaniṣad-bhāṣya,* I, 4, 10 (pp. 173-175); IV, 4, 22 (pp. 698-699); *Upadeśasāhasrī, padya,* IV. —Deussen, *Das System des Vedānta,* p. 459. (Dhammapāla, *Paramatthadīpanī: Itivuttakaṭṭhakathā,* I, p. 166: *tassa arahato carimabhavahetubhūtaṃ kammaṃ yāva na khīyati . . .*)

On the other hand, acts which have not yet begun to bear fruit (*anārabdhakārya, apravṛttaphala*) are "burnt" (cf. *A.* III, 33) by the fire of Knowledge. These acts may belong as much to the present existence as it was led before "Awakening" (*prabodha*), as to the innumerable earlier existences. The acts which the Delivered accomplishes during the rest of his existence no longer affect him, for they are not accompanied by egoistic desires. Cf. *supra,* pp. 20-21.

According to the *Vivekacūḍāmaṇi,* the doctrine of *prārabdhakarman* is simply a concession made to popular opinion (cf. *infra,* pp. 235-236); it in no way indicates that the psycho-physical existence of the Delivered is real:

> *jñānenājñānakāryasya samūlasya layo yadi* |
> *tiṣṭhaty ayaṃ kathaṃ deha iti śaṅkāvato jaḍān* ||
> *samādhātuṃ bāhyadṛṣṭyā prārabdhaṃ vadati śrutiḥ* |
> *na tu dehādisatyatvabodhanāya vipaścitām* ||

Vivekacūḍāmaṇi, 462-463.

In fact, the Delivered is not conscious of his individual existence: it has already been destroyed by Knowledge:

brahmībhūtasya yateḥ prāg eva tac cidagninā dagdham, ibid., 556 (cf. *upādhināśa,* v. 554, cited above, n. 144).

How, moreover, can the origin and the destruction of that which is merely "superimposed" be conceived?

> *śarīrasyāpi prārabdhakalpanā bhrāntir eva hi* |
> *adhyastasya kutaḥ sattvam asattvasya kuto janiḥ* |

ajātasya kuto nāśaḥ prārabdham asataḥ kutaḥ || *Ibid.*, 461.

May it not be thought, without a great deal of temerity, that the idea of *prārabdha-karman* was introduced simply to stay the rush towards suicide, permitted, theoretically, to the Deliverer (*supra*, p. 72, n. 77)? This is the intention that seems to be manifested by Manu, VI, 45, and *Mbh.* XII, 237, 15 (critical edition):

nābhinandeta maraṇaṃ nābhinandeta jīvitam |
kālam eva pratīkṣeta nirveśaṃ bhṛtako yathā ||

(On the reading *nirveśam*, cf. G. Buhler, *The Laws of Manu* [= *Sacred Books of the East*, edited by F. Max Müller, vol. XXV, Oxford, 1886], p. 207, n.)

Cf. *Mil.*, p. 45 (and *Theragāthā*, 606-607, 654-655, 685-686, 1002-1003; cf. also *It.*, p. 69):

nābhinandāmi maraṇaṃ nābhinandāmi jīvitaṃ |
kālañ ca paṭikaṅkhāmi nibbisaṃ bhatako yathā ||
nābhinandāmi maraṇaṃ nābhinandāmi jīvitaṃ |
kālañ ca paṭikaṅkhāmi sampajāno patissato ||

—*kālaṃ nayethāḥ sati karmabandhe, Vivekacūḍāmaṇi*, 320.

See also Appendix V.

175. *upādhistho 'pi taddharmair alipto vyomavan muniḥ, Ātmabodha*, 52. Cf. *Vivekacūḍāmaṇi*, 450.—*katamā, bhikkhave, sa-upādisesā nibbānadhātu?—idha, bhikkhave, bhikkhu arahaṃ hoti khīṇāsavo vusitavā katakaraṇīyo ohitabhāro anuppattasadattho parikkhīṇabhavasaṃyojano sammadaññāvimutto. tassa tiṭṭhant' eva pañc' indriyāni yesam avighātattā manāpāmanāpaṃ paccanubhoti, sukhadukkhaṃ paṭisaṃvediyati. tassa yo rāgakkhayo dosakkhayo mohakkhayo, ayaṃ vuccati, bhikkhave, sa-upādisesā nibbānadhātu, It.*, p. 38.

176. *upādhivilayād viṣṇau nirviśeṣaṃ viśen muniḥ* |
jale jalaṃ viyad vyomni tejas tejasi vā yathā ||

Ātmabodha, 53. [*viṣṇau* = *sarvavyāpake parabrahmaṇi*, Commentary. —"'Viṣṇu' etymologically means the Pervasive One and . . . it is used in this sense by advaitins," S. S. Suryanarayana Sastri, "Paramārthasāra," *NIA*. I, 1 (April 1938), p. 41.]

For the image, cf. *Kaṭha-Up.* IV, 15:

yathodakaṃ śuddhe śuddham āsiktaṃ tādṛg eva bhavati |
evaṃ muner vijānata ātmā bhavati Gautama ||

Vivekacūḍāmaṇi, 566:

kṣīraṃ kṣīre yathā kṣiptaṃ tailaṃ taile jalaṃ jale |
saṃyuktam ekatāṃ yāti tathātmany ātmavin muniḥ ||

Chapter Three

Reaction Against Vedic Ritualism

Up to this point, we have seen how close is the agreement (on fundamental points) between Buddhism and the Upaniṣads. Moreover, they reacted in the same manner against Vedic ritualism.[1]

The reaction against ritualism was already foreshadowed in the more recent sections of the Brāhmaṇas. Let us listen to S. Lévi:

> The *Śatapatha* is familiar with the classical division of the sacrifices into five major categories. 'There are five great sacrifices; these are the great ritual sessions: sacrifice to beings, sacrifice to men, sacrifice to the Fathers, sacrifice to the gods, sacrifice to the *brahman*. Each day, sustenance is offered to beings; this is the sacrifice to beings. Each day, alms are given, including the pot of water; this is the sacrifice to men. Each day, the funeral offerings are made, including the pot of water; this is the sacrifice to the Fathers. Each day, the offering to the gods is made, including wood for burning; this is the sacrifice to the gods. And the sacrifice to the *brahman*? The sacrifice to the *brahman* is sacred study.'[2]

Kane writes:

> It will be noticed . . . that they [*pañca mahāyajñāḥ*] are distinguished from the solemn *śrauta* sacrifices in two respects. In these five the chief agent is the honourable householder himself, he does not need the help and ministration of a professional priest, while in the *śrauta* sacrifices the priests occupy the most prominent place and the householder is

> more or less a passive spectator or agent in the hands of the priests who direct everything. In the second place, in the five *yajñas* the central point is the discharge of duties to the Creator, to the ancient sages, to the Manes, and to the whole universe with myriads of creatures of various grades of intelligence. In the *śrauta* sacrifices the mainspring of action is the desire to secure Heaven or some object such as prosperity, a son, etc. Therefore the institution of the five sacrifices is morally and spiritually more progressive and more ennobling than that of the *śrauta* sacrifices.[3]

These "sacrifices" thus have nothing to do with the true Vedic sacrifices; all the same, they are called "great sacrifices" (*mahāyajña*), "great ritual sessions" (*mahāsattra*), both to evoke "traditional typology"[4] and to demonstrate their superiority to ancient Vedic rites. The *Śatapatha* again compares the different elements of *brahmayajña* (the most important of these "great sacrifices") with the different elements of ordinary sacrifice.[5] That is not all however:

> . . . the enthusiastic exaltation of the sacrifice to *brahman,* which concludes this enumeration, attests to a new orientation of thought, foreign, or rather in opposition, to the Brāhmaṇas. The doctrine, in accordance with the composition, leads towards the Upaniṣad which concludes the *Śatapatha.* The spirit of the Upaniṣads is expressed more clearly still in another classification of sacrifices. 'It is said: who does best? One who sacrifices to the self (*ātman*)? One who sacrifices to the gods? The reply must be: One who sacrifices to the self. One who sacrifices to the self is one who knows thus: By this all my members are purified; by this all my members are put in place. As a snake sloughs off its dead skin, so he rids himself of this mortal body which is evil; made of *ṛc,* made of *yajus,* made of *sāman,* made of oblations, he takes possession of the heavenly world. And one who sacrifices to the gods is one who knows thus: To the gods I sacrifice this,

to the gods I offer this. As an inferior who brings tribute to a greater, or as a *vaiśya* who brings tribute to a king, such is he, and he does not win such a high place as the other.'[6]

On the *ātmayajña*,[7] which has just been considered, we find an echo in the Pāli Canon too. We read in the *Saṃyutta-Nikāya* (I, p. 169):

mā brāhmaṇa dāru samādahāno
suddhiṃ amaññi bahiddhā hi etaṃ |
na hi tena suddhiṃ kusalā vadanti
yo bāhirena parisuddhim icche ||

hitvā ahaṃ brāhmaṇa dārudāhaṃ
ajjhattam eva jalayāmi jotiṃ |
niccagginī niccasamāhitatto
arahaṃ ahaṃ brahmacariyaṃ carāmi ||

māno hi te brāhmaṇa khāribhāro
kodho dhūmo bhasmani mosavajjaṃ |
jivhā sujā hadayaṃ jotiṭṭhānaṃ
attā sudanto purisassa joti ||

Do not think, O Brahmin, that you obtain purity by putting wood in the fire.[8] That is only exterior. Experts do not speak of the purity of someone who aspires to obtain purity by exterior means.

I have renounced, O Brahmin, the burning of wood. It is within that I light the flame. With a fire permanently burning and the mind[9] constantly concentrated, I follow, as an Arahant, the way which leads to *brahman*.[10]

Your pride, O brahmin, is a heavy burden to you.[11] Your anger is the smoke, and in the ashes rest your lies.[12] The tongue is the sacrificial spoon,[13] and the heart the fire altar. The (phenomenal) *ātman*, perfectly controlled, is, for man, his light.[14]

Let us recall, further, the enumeration of the "sacrifices" (*yañña*), in order of their value, in the *Kūṭadanta-Suttanta* of the *Dīgha-Nikāya*.[15] The best "sacrifice," according to our text, is the achievement of the *arahatta*.

Thus we see how Buddhism is in agreement with the Upaniṣads in exalting spiritual knowledge and inner purification, in opposition to Vedic ritualism. Vedic sacrifice procures only temporary, even illusory, fruits. The sacrificer rises to the heavenly world; but, as soon as his merit is exhausted, he comes down to earth again.[16] It is thus not by sacrifice that happiness is obtained.[17] True happiness is supreme Bliss, which transcends all the antinomies of the empirical world[18]; and this happiness is none other than the "integral experience"[19] of the *ātman-brahman*, our true being. Sacrifice does not lead to this experience: "The Uncreated cannot be obtained by that which is created."[20] On the contrary, sacrifice, carried out for egoistic ends, serves only to "reinforce our I,"[21] and thus to bind us indefinitely to phenomenal becoming.

"It is within that I light the flame"; "the perfectly controlled *ātman* is, for man, his light": these phrases remind us of the Upaniṣadic and Buddhist texts which compare *ātman* with light.[22] The *ātman*, say the Upaniṣads, is the "inner light" (*antarjyotis*).[23] It is not, however, that *ātman* that has to be controlled: it has no need to be controlled for it is eternally pure. The *ātman* that has to be controlled is our phenomenal *ātman*, which obscures our true *ātman* "as smoke obscures fire, or as dust obscures a mirror."[24] But it is only by making the authentic *ātman* triumph,—which is the *ātman* of all things,—that we are able to control our phenomenal *ātman*. Spiritual knowledge and inner purification go therefore together. Our phenomenal *ātman* does not disappear when it is controlled: it becomes the vehicle, a genuine "support" (*adhiṣṭhāna*),[25] by which the authentic *ātman* manifests in all its clearness. As the *Bhagavadgītā* says, our phenomenal *ātman* becomes "the friend of our authentic *ātman*."[26]

It is appropriate, in this context, to emphasize the analogous usage of the word *yajña* by Gandhi:

> . . . *yajña* has a deeper meaning than the offering of ghee and other things in the sacrificial fire. *Yajña* is sacrifice of one's all for the good of humanity, and to me these offerings of *āhutis* have a symbolic meaning. We have to offer up our weaknesses, our passions, our narrowness into the purifying fire, so that we may be cleansed.[27]

In this passage, Gandhi seems to have in mind two aspects of the *ātmayajña*. On the one hand, it is a matter of sacrificing to our Great I all our weaknesses, which belong to the small I; in other words, of overcoming our small I by our Great I.[28] On the other hand, it is a matter of sacrificing ourselves for the good of humanity, not conceived objectively, but as identical to ourselves. It may be recalled that, according to Manu, the *ātmayājin* is one who "sees himself in all beings and all beings in himself."[29]

Again, it is in identical terms that the Upaniṣads and ancient Buddhism attack Vedic knowledge. A man versed in the Vedas may boast about his science; but what he knows is only exterior, he has not verified it by personal experience. This knowledge is transmitted from generation to generation, from master to disciple, in a mechanical fashion; but not a single master has *seen* the Truth, whether at the beginning, in the middle or at the end. Thus the *Muṇḍaka-Upaniṣad* compares this succession of ritualists to a series of blind men led by a blind man (*andhenaiva nīyamānā yathāndhāḥ*).[30] We find the same comparison in the Pāli Canon (*andha-veṇi-paramparā*).[31]

The "knower of mantras" (*mantravid*),[32] that is to say, the ritualist, may perhaps, thanks to the faith he has in received truth, contribute to the "conservation" of that truth (*saccānurakkhanā*); but he does not awaken to the Truth (*saccānubodha*), he does not attain it (*saccānupatti*).[33] In order to attain spiritual knowledge, faith (*śraddhā/saddhā*) is necessary only at the beginning, when the disciple submits to the authority of the master, whom he has voluntarily chosen after having thoroughly examined him.[34] The "knower of the uncreated" (*akataññu*) has made the Truth his own, and, as a result, is beyond faith (*assaddha*).[35]

We have no intention whatsoever of arguing that the Upaniṣads are equivalent to Buddhism. The Upaniṣads have relegated Vedic knowledge and sacrifice to an inferior level; nevertheless, they have not rejected them. K. N. Jayatilleke seems to be justified in writing:[36]

> The significant difference [between the Upaniṣads and Buddhism] . . . is that the Upaniṣads as part of the Vedic tradition generally did not directly attack yajña and are careful, even when advocating ahiṃsā, to make the single exception of the sacrifice.[37] The reason for this exception is obvious. To deny the sacrifice was to deny the authority of the injunctive assertions of the Veda and to deny the sacred authority of the Vedic tradition itself. This the Buddha did but the Upaniṣads never dared to do; however much of their speculation may have been at variance with orthodoxy.

—It is, all the same, surprising that we find no allusion to the Upaniṣads in the Pāli Canon—if Buddhism is really their enemy.[38] All the texts, on the contrary, lead us to think that Buddhist opposition to Vedic tradition, though inspired by the Upaniṣadic opposition, was *more radical* than the latter. Thus Deussen writes, with reference to the effort to reassert the importance of the sacrifice, to which three Upaniṣads bear witness, that is the *Kaṭha*, the *Śvetāśvatara* and the *Maitri*:

> Brahminism, in view of the consequences which the stance of the earlier Upaniṣads had entailed in Buddhism and similar manifestations, draws back to its original underlying principles.[39]

Notes to Chapter Three

1. On the attitude of the Upaniṣads towards the Veda, cf. in general, Deussen, *AGPh.* I, 2, pp. 51 ff.—The Pāli Canon knows the distinction between *yañña-patha* "way of sacrifice" (= *karma-mārga* "way of ritual") and *ñāṇa-patha* (= *jñāna-mārga*) "way of knowledge." Cf. *Sn.* 868 and 1045.

2. S. Lévi, *La doctrine du sacrifice dans les Brāhmaṇas* (Paris, 1898 [reprint: 1966]), p. 78.—*ŚB.* XI, 5, 6. 1-3.

3. P. V. Kane, *History of Dharmaśāstra,* II, 1 (Poona, 1941), p. 697.

4. On this question, cf. "Le 'védisme' de certains textes hindouistes," *JA.* 1967, pp. 199 ff.

5. *ŚB.* XI, 5, 6, 3 ff. Cf. Kane, *op. cit.*, pp. 700-701.

6. S. Lévi, *op. cit.*, pp. 78-79.—*ŚB.* XI, 2, 6, 13-14. The *Bṛhad-āraṇyaka-Upaniṣad* (IV, 4, 7) will take up again the image of the snake abandoning its dead skin, rejecting, however, the (ritualistic) idea of local separation (*supra*, pp. 20, 95; cf. p. 45, n. 36). Closer to this passage of the *Śatapatha-Brāhmaṇa* is *Praśna-Up.* V, 5. Let us not forget that this last passage speaks of the *kramamukti* (*supra*, p. 171, n. 158).

7. Cf. A. K. Coomaraswamy, "Ātmayajña: Self-Sacrifice," *HJAS.* VI (1942), pp. 358 ff.

8. *samādahāna*: cf. W. Geiger, *Saṃyutta-Nikāya,* I (München-Neubiberg, 1930), p. 264, n. 2.

9. As in a great many similar cases, the word *attan* here means "mind" (*citta, manas*). Cf. *supra*, p. 29 and n. 210; p. 112, n. 245 (last para.).—*niccasamāhitatto ti niccaṃ sammāṭhapita-citto,* Buddhaghosa, *Sāratthappakāsinī,* I, p. 236; *attā ti cittaṃ, ibid.*, p. 237.

10. Such is the real meaning of *brahmacariya* (= Sanskrit °*carya*): see *supra*, p. 128 and n. 55.—The *Chāndogya-Upaniṣad* (VIII, 5) also attempts to establish the equivalence *yajña = brahmacarya.*

11. *khāribhāra*: "The thought is this: You want to ascend with your sacrifice to heaven, but your pride of birth and lineage weighs upon you, like a heavy burden on your shoulders, pressing you down to the earth," Geiger, *op. cit.*, p. 265, n. 1.

12. "The smoke of anger and the ash of falsehood prevent the sacrificial fire from burning brightly," *ibid.*, p. 265, n. 2.

13. The idea is the following: It is with a spoon that the oblations are poured into the fire. In the same way it is with the tongue

that the true words are spoken. Now, it is with truth that one controls one's psycho-physical *ātman* (*saccena danta*, *S.* I, p. 168), and *ātman* perfectly controlled is the light for a man,—the real sacrificial fire. Cf. the following note.

14. The strophe means: It is not an outer fire that must be maintained, but the inner fire, the spiritual *ātman*, transcending the psycho-physical *ātman* (which is only a non-*ātman*), which must be made to shine with all its clearness. Cf. below.

15. *D.* I, pp. 127 ff.

16. *BĀU.* I, 4, 15; III, 8, 10; IV, 4, 6-7; *ChU.* VIII, 1, 6 (cf. VII, 25, 2); II, 23, 1-2; *Muṇḍ.Up.* I, 2; *BhG.* IX, 20-21 (cf. II, 42-44). Cf. *Sn.* 1043 ff.

17. Cf. *supra*, p. 51, n. 54.

18. *Supra*, p. 10 and n. 71.

19. *Supra*, p. 62.

20. *nāsty akṛtaḥ kṛtena, Muṇḍ.Up.* I, 2, 12.

21. Cf. *supra*, p. 53, n. 55.

22. *Supra*, p. 74, n. 83.

23. *Supra*, p. 6 and n. 32.

24. *BhG.* III, 38.

25. Cf. *supra*, p. 5.

26. *Supra*, p. 30.—On *attā sudanto*, cf. *Dhp.* 160 (*supra*, p. 31).

27. Gandhi, *In Search of the Supreme*, compiled and edited by V. B. Kher, Ahmedabad, Navajivan Publishing House, vol. I, 1961, p. 276.

28. *BhG.* VI, 5-7; *supra*, p. 30.

29. *sarvabhūteṣu cātmānaṃ sarvabhūtāni cātmani* |
samaṃ paśyann ātmayājī svārājyam adhigacchati ||
Manu, XII, 91. Cf. *supra*, p. 13 and n. 99.

30. *Muṇḍ.Up.* I, 2, 8. The verse also figures in the *Kaṭha* (II, 5), but apropos materialists (cf. also *MaiU.* VII, 9).—Cf. *Chāgeleya-Upaniṣad* (edition-translation of L. Renou, Paris 1959). [On subsequent usages of the image, cf. L. Renou, *Śaṅkara: Prolégomènes au* Vedānta (Paris, 1951), p. 37, n. 2; R. Garbe, *Die Sāṃkhya-Philosophie*[2] (Leipzig, 1917), p. 199.]

31. *M.* II, p. 170. Cf. *ibid.*, p. 200; *D.* I, p. 239. ("[The Pharisees] are the blind who lead the blind," *Matthew*, XV, 14.)

The *Subha-Sutta* of the *Majjhima-Nikāya* (Sutta 99, vol. II, pp. 196 ff.) brings in an important precision. Ritualistic brahmins blindly practise the five virtues: truth (*sacca*), austerity (*tapa*), chastity (*brahmacariya*), study (*ajjhena*) and donation (*cāga*),—without "immediatizing" their consequences through personal experience (*sayaṃ abhiññā sacchikatvā*). To them, they are ends in themselves. For the Buddha, on the contrary, they are nothing but means, "equipments" (*parikkhāra*) of the mind, which lead to *spontaneous* morality, where the mind is free of enmity and ill-will (*ye te, māṇava, brāhmaṇā pañca dhamme paññāpenti puññassa kiriyāya, kusalassa ārādhanāya, cittassāhaṃ ete parikkhāre vadāmi, yad idaṃ cittaṃ averaṃ abyāpajjhaṃ tassa bhāvanāya, M.* II, pp. 205-206).—Cf. *supra*, p. 53, n. 58; Appendix I.

This same Sutta reproduces the opinion of a brahmin, Pokkharasāti: it is impossible for a simple human being (*manussabhūta*) to have access to knowledge and vision surpassing the human condition (*uttari manussadhammā alamariyañāṇadassanavisesaṃ*, pp. 200-201). This, there can be no doubt, emphasizes the fundamental difference there is between ritualism and a spiritual doctrine, such as that of the Buddha: the former rests upon a superhuman authority whilst the latter insists upon personal experience.—See also Jayatilleke, p. 181, and cf. the discussion between the Mīmāṃsaka and the Buddhist, in *TS.*, ch. XXVI.

32. *ChU.* VII, 1, 3; cf. *D.* I, pp. 88, 114 (*mantadhara*), 238; *M.* II, p. 170.

33. *M.* II, pp. 171 ff. (*Caṅkī-Sutta* = Sutta 95).

34. *Ibid.*—On the choice of master, see also *Vīmaṃsaka-Sutta* (*M.* I, pp. 317 ff., Sutta 47).

The various stages of spiritual knowledge which the *Caṅkī-Sutta* describes bring to mind *śravaṇa* "hearing" (cf. *dhammaṃ suṇāti, M.* II, p. 173), *manana* "reasoning" (cf. *dhāritānaṃ dhammānaṃ atthaṃ upaparikkhati, ibid.*), *nididhyāsana* "continuous meditation" (which implies personal certitude) [cf. *kāyena c' eva paramasaccaṃ sacchikaroti, ibid.*] and *darśana* "vision" (cf. *paññāya ca taṃ ativijjha passati, ibid.*) of the Vedāntic tradition (cf. *supra*, p. 76, n. 86 end). [Cf. *M.* I, p. 480.]

35. *assaddho akataññū ca sandhicchedo ca yo naro* |
hatāvakāso vantāso sa ve uttamaporiso || *Dhp.* 97.

uttamaporiso (cf. *uttamapuriso paramapuriso paramapattipatto, S.* III, p. 116; IV, p. 380; cf. also the expressions *aggapuggala, uttamapuggala, dipaduttama*, etc.) = *uttamaḥ puruṣaḥ, ChU.* VIII, 12, 3. It may be recalled that the Buddha and the Arahants are not "superior men" except to other men; in reality, they are simply *men who have realized their condition as men,* by becoming that which they truly are: *manussabhūtaṃ sambuddhaṃ, Theragāthā,* 689 = *A.* III, p. 346 (cf. *supra,* p. 157, n. 56).

On the subject of *saddhā,* to be surpassed in *paññā,* cf. Jayatilleke, pp. 396-399. The author also cites Nāgārjuna, *Ratnāvalī,* I, 5 (G. Tucci, "The Ratnāvalī of Nāgārjuna," *JRAS.* 1934, p. 309):

śrāddhatvād bhajate dharmaṃ prājñatvād vetti tattvataḥ ǀ
prajñā pradhānaṃ tv anayoḥ śraddhā pūrvaṃgamāsya tu ǀǀ

"Through *śraddhā* one is associated with *dharma;* but it is by *prajñā* that one truly knows. *Prajñā* is the more important of the two; it is *śraddhā* that comes first, however."

Plotinus has an analogous conception: cf. Bréhier, *Ennéades,* VI² (coll. Budé), p. 177, in note.—See also *supra,* p. 61, n. 62; p. 9 and n. 66; p. 133 and n. 99.

36. P. 189.

37. *ChU.* VIII, 15: *ahiṃsan sarvabhūtāny anyatra tīrthebhyaḥ.*

38. Cf. Mrs. Rhys Davids, *Sakya or Buddhist Origins* (London, 1931), p. 187.

39. *AGPh.* I, 2, p. 60.

Chapter Four

On some ancient and modern theories relating to the Anattā

Buddhaghosa

Amongst ancient authors a special place must be given to Buddhaghosa who, as is well known, is greatly esteemed in the Theravāda.

Unfortunately the effect of the "metaphysical shipwreck" to which we have earlier alluded,[1] makes itself felt in his case too. We have already mentioned his incorrect usage, not only of the terms *attan* and *viññāṇa*, but of *brahman* and *dhamma* as well.[2] Here is yet another example of "metaphysical shipwreck." Buddhaghosa is uncertain of the meaning of this passage from the *Majjhima-Nikāya:*[3] *diṭṭhe vāhaṃ, bhikkhave, dhamma Tathāgatam ananuvejjo ti vadāmi.* The word *ananuvejja,* he says, means here either "non-existent" (*asaṃvijjamāna*) or "unknowable" (*avindeyya*). If *Tathāgata* is taken to mean "individual" (*satta*), he must be said to be "non-existent"; but if the word is understood as meaning "supreme man whose impulses have been destroyed" (*uttamapuggalo khīṇāsavo*),[4] then he must be said to be "unknowable": *Tathāgatassā 'ti ettha satto pi Tathāgato ti adhippeto, uttamapuggalo khīṇāsavo pi, ananuvejjo ti asaṃvijjamāno vā avindeyyo vā; Tathāgato ti hi satte gahite asaṃvijjamāno ti attho vaṭṭati; khīṇāsave gahite avindeyyo ti attho vaṭṭati.*[5]

A Śaṅkara, had he had to comment upon this passage, would have expressed himself differently; he would, for example, have recalled the passage from the *Taittirīya-Upaniṣad: yato vāco nivartante aprāpya manasā saha,* "From whence words as well as thoughts turn back without attaining it."[6] We have no need of Śaṅkara here however; it is enough to read Nāgārjuna:

ghanagrāho gṛhītas tu yenāstīti Tathāgataḥ[7] |
nāstīti sa vikalpayan nirvṛtasyāpi kalpayet ||
svabhāvataś ca śūnye 'smiṃś cintā naivopapadyate |
paraṃ nirodhād bhavati Buddho na bhavatīti vā ||
prapañcayanti ye Buddhaṃ prapañcātītam avyayam |
te prapañcahatāḥ sarve na paśyanti Tathāgatam ||

Whoever is attached to the gross error of thinking that the Tathāgata exists, must also think that, when he has passed away he no longer exists.

As the Buddha is void of own-nature,[8] it is impossible to think that he either exists or does not exist after death.

All those who speak of the Buddha, who is beyond all words and is imperishable, do not see the Tathāgata; they are undone by [their own] words.[9]

The Tathāgata (= *tathatā* = *śūnyatā*) of the Mādhyamikas is, in fact, none other than the *ātman-brahman* of the Upaniṣads.[10] The *Saṃyutta-Nikāya* (XXII, 85) already established this equivalence as we have seen above.[11] Buddhaghosa, again with reference to this text, is mistaken. Contrary to his approach in the *Papañcasūdanī*, he here allows for no choice. He categorically declares: the word Tathāgata means *satta* "individual" who does not exist.[12]

It is true that whenever a negation of the *ātman* is in question in the Pāli Canon, Buddhaghosa specifies: the *ātman* negated is the individual *ātman*. Thus, this sentence: *suññam idaṃ attena vā attaniyena vā*[13] is glossed in the *Papañcasūdanī* as follows: *attabhāva-posa-puggalādi-saṃkhātena attena suññaṃ*.[14] Nonetheless, Buddhaghosa seems to be unaware of any *ātman* other than that "imaginary *ātman*" (*kalpita ātmā*).[15]

The result is that he is led into terrible contradictions. There is no *ātman*, in the sense of "individual": all Buddhists, with the exception of the Pudgalavādins[16] are in agreement on this point. But Buddhaghosa cannot fail to take into account the texts which speak of the transcendent *ātman*. How does he interpret them? Whilst negating the *ātman* which everyone—wrongly—believes he possesses, he is led to acknowledge another one, greater and more sublime, it is true, but nonetheless not unrelated to the former. Thus, the *attan-dhamma*, according to him, is composed of "mundane and supramundane states" (*lokiya-lokuttara-dhamma*).[17] The Tathāgata, he further states, is identified with Dhamma because he incarnates the nine *lokuttara-dhammas*.[18] He is "profound" (*gambhīra*), not, as might be concluded from the texts being commented on, because he is the transcendent Reality, beyond all conceptual grasp, but by virtue of his "qualities" (*guṇagambhīra*).[19] Similarly, as he sees it, it is not because one has realized one's unity with universal Being that one is *mahattā*,[20] but "by the greatness of one's qualities" (*guṇamahantatāya*).[21]

Buddhaghosa seems to have no sense of Transcendence as it is envisaged in the Upaniṣads and, as we believe, by the Buddha as well.[22]

Rhys Davids

Modern Buddhist scholars have, in general, only made an already confused situation more so. We have already examined above[23] the opinions of certain authors on this subject. Given the immense influence exercised by T. W. Rhys Davids, not only over Buddhological science, but over Buddhists themselves, his opinion merits careful consideration.

If, as we have tried to show, the so-called doctrine of *anattā* most often rests upon either a misunderstanding[24] or upon ignorance of the true spiritual *ātman* of the Upaniṣads, Rhys Davids is no exception to the rule. Thus he writes:

> . . . it is certain that all the religions and all the philosophies, the existing records show to have existed in India, in

> the time when Buddhism arose, are based on the belief in a subtle but material 'soul' inside the body, and in shape like the body. It would scarcely be going too far to say that all religions, and all philosophies, then existing in the world, were based upon it. Buddhism stands alone among the religions of India in ignoring the soul. The vigour and originality of this new departure are evident from the complete isolation in which Buddhism stands, in this respect, from all other religious systems then existing in the world. And the very great difficulty which those European writers, who are still steeped in animistic preoccupations, find in appreciating, or even understanding the doctrine, may help us to realize how difficult it must have been for the originator of it to take so decisive and so far-reaching a step in religion and philosophy, at so early a period in the history of human thought.[25]

In the preceding pages we have tried to show that the Buddha was in no way an "isolated" figure; on the contrary, he was continuing the Upaniṣadic tradition. There is, however, a difference between the Buddha and the Upaniṣads: the Buddha condemns from the outset any animistic representation of the *ātman*, whilst the Upaniṣads provisionally admit the utility of the crudest animistic representations, as a starting point for the *ongoing pursuit* of the Absolute.[26] "The general method for spiritual direction traditionally employed (in India) recommends accepting the disciple, along with his dispositions, just as he is, to make him become aware first of the sacred and divine, through his present state, his present conceptions, however confused and murky they may be, and to proceed to purify the spiritual feeling he manifested in coming to seek the master, only after having somehow loaded him at this first level. The same procedure, moreover, will be repeated at the following stage, and so on up to the ultimate one."—"To guide his disciple, progressively, to the redeeming intuition," "the master of perfection" proposes "increasingly transparent symbols for his meditation, each destined to be withdrawn one after the other." He "superimposes on the Absolute less and less limiting forms, repudiated one after the other until, finally, all veils being down, the infinite truth shines alone."[27]

It is true that the Upaniṣads sometimes use terms that seem shocking to designate the *ātman-brahman*: *prāṇa, jīva.* In fact, the word *ātman* itself, if we refer to the generally accepted interpretation, seems simply a vestige of the old animistic tradition.[28] Nonetheless, the Upaniṣads give a new significance to all these words; in this way they demonstrate what separates them from the earlier tradition. The essence of the individual is no more located in the vital breath nor in any other psychic or corporeal element which can be fixed objectively; in his most profound essence, the individual *is not an individual* but is the universal and absolute Being.[29] "From animism to idealism there is direct development, and it is for this reason that we meet with primitive terminologies invested with a new significance."[30]

Not only are there primitive terms in the Upaniṣads, there are also primitive ideas. "But this does not mean that the highest of these thoughts is primitive, it means only that the historical continuity of thought is preserved in the final system, and that system remains adapted to the intelligence of various minds. Śaṅkara, writing long afterward . . . very clearly perceived this complexity of thought in the Upaniṣads, and explained their inconsistencies and contradictions by the brilliant generalization in which the scriptural teachings are divided into absolute or esoteric truth (*parā vidyā*), and relative or exoteric truths (*aparā vidyā*). With this clue in our hands we are able to regard the whole Aupanishadic literature as a process of thought, culminating in certain well-defined formulae, and we can distinguish the poetic and symbolic nature of many other passages which do not the less refer to truth because they speak in parables."[31]

This, it seems to us, is the proper attitude to adopt with regard to the Upaniṣads. In all great thought there is a central point around which all the rest turns. If we miss the essential, the meaning of the surface inevitably eludes us.

The difference between the Upaniṣads and Buddhism must not however be exaggerated; the idea of "gradual teaching" also exists in the latter, which admits, provisionally, the belief in the soul.[32]

Partisans of the Opposite Opinion

Are we then forced to take the side of authors such as Mrs. Rhys Davids, J. G. Jennings and H. Günther, who have tried to prove that the Buddha did not repudiate the *ātman*?

Each of these authors had a valid intuition but they went astray in their proofs. We will not speak here of Jennings and Günther: H. von Glasenapp has ably pointed out their errors.[33] Here we will speak only of Mrs. Rhys Davids.

Mrs. Rhys Davids has, incontestably, contributed a great deal towards the clarification of the problem which concerns us; but it is also incontestable that her viewpoint is highly individualistic. According to her, the *ātman* was the central point in the Buddha's Buddhism, and the monks, "editors" of the Suttas, sometimes have difficulties themselves in concealing this fact; however, they have, on the whole, betrayed the Master.[34]

To our mind, there is nothing to justify such an opinion. The Buddha no doubt did not say everything that has been attributed to him and it may also be conjectured that he did say things which have not been reproduced in the Suttas. However, we find no trace there of a negation of the Upaniṣadic *ātman*. Despite her valid intuition, Mrs. Rhys Davids has, in this way, rendered the worst possible service to her cause. There would be little purpose in giving a point by point demonstration here to show that she was mistaken but we would like to draw attention to the famous passage from the *Majjhima-Nikāya*, which she, in company with most other authors, interprets as a negation of the *ātman*.[35] The actual meaning of it is, as we have seen, quite different.[36] Neither should it be forgotten that Mrs. Rhys Davids' research goes astray in the confusion she makes, again along with most other Buddhist scholars, between the Upaniṣadic *ātman* and the *pudgala*. In these circumstances, it is not surprising that she is regarded as a modern representation of the Great Heresy.[37]

Two Mahāyānic Texts

I. Laṅkāvatāra-Sūtra

We have already seen how the Mahāyāna reacts against the scholastics to the end of restoring Buddhism to its orig-inal purity.[38] To return, once again, to the words of Vasubandhu, *nairātmya* is only the negation of the "imaginary *ātman*" (*kalpita ātmā*) and not of the true spiritual *ātman*, which is ineffable (*anabhilāpya*), and the "domain of the Buddhas" (*buddhānāṃ viṣayaḥ*).[39]

The position of the *Laṅkāvatāra-Sūtra* merits special study, since it has often been misunderstood. We shall not lay stress upon the *Sagāthaka*, which virulently attacks those who repudiate the *ātman*:[40] the problem of its relationship to the *Laṅkāvatāra-Sūtra* does not yet seem to have been resolved.[41] We should like to speak here of the well-known and oft-cited passage which denies a particular concept of the *ātman*:[42]

atha khalu Mahāmatir bodhisattvo mahāsattvo Bhagavantam etad avocat: tathāgatagarbhaḥ punar Bhagavatā sūtrāntapāṭhe 'nuvarṇitaḥ. sa ca kila tvayā prakṛtiprabhāsvaraviśuddhyādi-viśuddha eva varṇyate, dvātriṃśallakṣaṇadharaḥ sarvasattvadehā-ntargataḥ. mahārghamūlyaratnaṃ malinavastupariveṣṭitam iva skandhadhātvāyatanavastuveṣṭito rāgadveṣamohābhūtaparikalpa-malamalino nityo dhruvaḥ śivaḥ śāśvataś ca Bhagavatā varṇitaḥ. tat katham ayaṃ, Bhagavaṃs, tīrthakarātmavādatulyas tathāgata-garbhavādo na bhavati? tīrthakarā api, Bhagavan, nityaḥ kartā nirguṇo vibhur avyaya ity ātmavādopadeśaṃ kurvanti.

Bhagavān āha: na hi, Mahāmate, tīrthakarātmavādatulyo mama tathāgatagarbhopadeśaḥ. kiṃ tu, Mahāmate, tathāgatāḥ śūnyatābhūtakoṭinirvāṇānutpādānimittāpraṇihitādyānāṃ, Mahā-mate, padārthānāṃ tathāgatagarbhopadeśaṃ kṛtvā tathāgatā arhantaḥ samyaksaṃbuddhā bālānāṃ nairātmyasaṃtrāsapada-vivarjitārthaṃ nirvikalpanirābhāsagocaraṃ tathāgatagarbha-

mukhopadeśena deśayanti. na cātra, Mahāmate, anāgatapraty-utpannair bodhisattvair mahāsattvair ātmābhiniveśaḥ kartavyaḥ. tadyathā, Mahāmate, kumbhakāra ekasmān mṛtparamāṇurāśer vividhāni bhāṇḍāni karoti hastaśilpadaṇḍodakasūtraprayatna-yogāt, evam eva, Mahāmate, tathāgatās tad eva dharmanairātmyaṃ sarvavikalpalakṣaṇavinivṛttaṃ vividhaiḥ prajñopāyakauśalyayogair garbhopadeśena vā nairātmyopadeśena vā kumbhakāravac citraiḥ padavyañjanaparyāyair deśayante. etasmāt kāraṇān, Mahāmate, tīrthakarātmavādopadeśatulyas tathāgatagarbhopadeśo na bhavati.

evaṃ hi, Mahāmate, tathāgatagarbhopadeśam ātmavādā-bhiniviṣṭānāṃ tīrthakarāṇām ākarṣaṇārthaṃ tathāgatagarbho-padeśena nirdiśanti, kathaṃ vatābhūtātmavikalpadṛṣṭipatitāśayā vimokṣatrayagocarapatitāśayopetāḥ kṣipram anuttarāṃ samyaksaṃ-bodhim abhisaṃbudhyerann iti. etadarthaṃ, Mahāmate, tathāgatā arhantaḥ samyaksaṃbuddhās tathāgatagarbhopadeśaṃ kurvanti. ata etan na bhavati tīrthakarātmavādatulyam. tasmāt tarhi, Mahā-mate, tīrthakaradṛṣṭivinivṛttyarthaṃ tathāgatanairātmyagarbhā-nusāriṇā ca te bhavitavyam.

Then Mahāmati, the Bodhisattva-Mahāsattva, said to Bhaga-vant: 'In a Sūtra,[43] the Tathāgatagarbha is described by you as naturally luminous, originally pure, residing in the bodies of all beings, endowed with the thirty-two marks (bodily marks peculiar to the Buddha). It is also described as permanent, stable, blessed and eternal, but clothed in the garment[44] composed of the aggre-gates (*skandha*), the elements (*dhātu*), and the bases of knowledge (*āyatana*), tainted by the stain of concupiscence, hatred, infatuation and false imaginings, like a precious gem wrapped in a dirty garment. Under these conditions, Lord, is not this doctrine of the Tathāgatagarbha similar to that of the *ātman* professed by the *tīrthakaras*?[45] The *tīrthakaras* also, Lord, teach that the *ātman* is per-manent, agent, without qualities, omnipresent, imperishable.'

Bhagavant said: 'No, Mahāmati, my teaching concerning the Tathāgatagarbha is not similar to the doctrine of the *ātman* professed by the *tīrthakaras*. The Tathāgatas teach, by way of Tathāgatagarbha, things such as *śūnyatā, bhūtakoṭi, nirvāṇa, anutpāda, ānimitta* and *apraṇihita*. It is so as to avoid the terror that the doctrine of *nairātmya* inspires in children (*bāla*)[46] that the Tathāgatas, who are Arhants and perfectly awakened, teach as being the Tathāgatagarbha, [the Absolute] whose domain surpasses all thought and all imagery. O Mahāmati, the Bodhisattva-Mahāsattvas, present and future, should not see the *ātman* here. Just as a potter, Mahāmati, fashions different vessels out of a single mass of clay, by the skill of his hands, the rod, the water and the effort he puts in, in the same way, Mahāmati, the Tathāgatas, applying diversely their skillfulness in means, issued from the Supreme Wisdom, teach the same *dharmanairātmya*,[47] which is devoid of all sign of thought, in making use of various expressions: now as Tathāgatagarbha, now as *nairātmya*. That is why, Mahāmati, the teaching relative to the Tathāgatagarbha is not similar to that of the *tīrthakaras* as regards the doctrine of *ātman*.

'Thus, Mahāmati, [the Tathāgatas] teach the doctrine of the Tathāgatagarbha in order to win over the *tīrthakaras*, who cling to their doctrine of the *ātman*. [Their compassionate thought goes out to them:] "They have fallen into the false view of the *ātman*. How will they manage to concentrate their thought on that which is accessible only to the three *vimokṣas*,[48] and rapidly attain thereby the Supreme Awakening?" It is to this end, Mahāmati, that the Tathāgatas, who are Arhants and perfectly awakened, teach the Tathāgatagarbha. This teaching is thus not similar to the doctrine of the *ātman* professed by the *tīrthakaras*. Consequently, Mahāmati, you must conform to [the idea of] the Embryo of the Tathāgata,[49] which consists of *nairātmya* (*tathāgatanairātmyagarbha*), to the end of renouncing the point of view of the *tīrthakaras*.'

It has not been useless to quote this long passage which brings up so many interesting ideas. The image of the Tathāgatagarbha is only an expedient, made use of by the Tathāgatas to win over the *tīrthakaras* who believe in the *ātman*. The Tathāgatas make use of this expedient, only to lead the "children," in whom the doctrine of *nairātmya* inspires the greatest dread,[50] *swiftly*[51] to the Supreme Awakening, that is, to the full blossoming of their consciousness.

The image of the Tathāgatagarbha thus belongs to empirical truth (*vyavahāra-* or *saṃvṛti-satya*), not to Absolute Truth (*paramārtha-satya*). The Upaniṣads too employ such images with regard to the *ātman-brahman*,[52] and these belong to the same level of truth as the image of the Tathāgatagarbha. Some Mahāyānic texts, such as the *Mahāparinirvāṇa-Sūtra*, even identify the Tathāgatagarbha with the *ātman*, which appears to be none other than the Upaniṣadic *ātman*.[53] At bottom, though, what is this *ātman*, if not a negation of the empirical *ātman*, which people generally take to be the authentic *ātman*? As the *Laṅkāvatāra-Sūtra* itself puts it, the Tathāgatagarbha is, in fact, none other than the *tathāgata-nairātmya-garbha* (and not the *tathāgatātmagarbha*, if by *ātman* is meant empirical individuality). There is no conflict here between the Upaniṣadic doctrine and that of the *Laṅkāvatāra-Sūtra*.

Why then does it say that the Tathāgatagarbha is not the *ātman*, or rather that it is but a semblance of the *ātman*, which attracts those who believe in the *ātman*, and which will lead them beyond their initial belief when it will be truly understood? Even according to an author as acute as S. N. Dasgupta, what is referred to there would be "the Vedāntic *ātman*."[54] Nonetheless, taking a closer look at the text, we cannot fail to notice that the *ātman* it speaks of is not the *ātman-brahman* of the Upaniṣads. The latter is not an agent (*kartṛ*).[55] The description of the *ātman* given in our text makes us think rather of the *ātman* of the *Nyāya-Vaiśeṣika*.[56]

Let us not forget that the *Laṅkāvatāra-Sūtra* recognizes the *paraṃ brahma* as the absolute Reality.[57]

II. Mahāprajñāpāramitā-Śāstra (Upadeśa)

In the *Mahāprajñāpāramitā-Śāstra* we read:

> . . . There are people for whom the idea of Ātman arises relative to something other [than themselves]: thus the heretical

contemplatives (*tīrthikadhyāyin*),[58] employing the global view of the Earth (*pṛthivīkṛtsnāyatana*), see the Earth as being the Ātman and the Ātman as being the Earth. And likewise also (for other things): water, fire, wind and void. But it is through error (*viparyāsa*) that the idea of Ātman is conceived of in relation to others.

Some say that the Ātman resides in the thought (*citta*) and that it is as thin (*sūkṣma*) as a mustard seed (*sarṣapa*); pure, (*viśuddha*), it is called subtle matter body (*prasādarūpakāya*). According to different opinions, it would be like a grain of wheat (*yava*), like a bean (*māṣa, masūra*), half the height of a thumb (*ardhāṅguṣṭha*), the height of a thumb (*aṅguṣṭha*).[59]

Commenting on the second passage, E. Lamotte writes:[60]

We have here a very clear-cut allusion to the speculations of the Upaniṣads, in which Brahman, soul of the world, is often contrasted with the brahman, psychic principle: as such, the Being dwells in the citadel of the body (*puriśayaḥ puruṣaḥ*: Praśna Up. V, 5), in the heart lotus (*daharaṃ puṇḍarīkaṃ veśma*: Chāndogya Up. VIII, 1, 1). It is dwarf-like (*vāmana*: Kaṭha Up. V, 3), the height of a span (*pradeśamātra*: Chāndogya Up. V, 18, 1), the height of a thumb (*aṅguṣṭha-mātra*: Kaṭha Up. IV, 12), smaller than . . . a grain of millet, than the kernel of a grain of millet (*aṇīyān vrīher vā yavād vā sarṣapād vā śyāmākād vā śyāmākataṇḍulād vā*: Chāndogya Up. III, 14, 3), no bigger than the point of a needle (*ārāgramātra*: Śvetāś. Up. V, 8). It is vital breath (*prāṇa*: Kauṣītaki Up. III, 2), the witness (*sākṣin*), the man who appears in the pupil (*ya eṣo 'kṣaṇi puruṣo dṛśyate*: Chāndogya Up. IV, 15, 1).

Such clear cut references to the wild imaginings of the Upaniṣads are rarely found in Buddhist texts.

It would appear that a number of ideas, not all of which belong to the same level, have been confused here. We have already spoken of the animistic ideas contained in the

Upaniṣads.[61] But does the passage in the *Mahāprajñāpāramitā-Śāstra* really amount to a polemic against the Upaniṣads?

Hajime Nakamura, in his article entitled "Upaniṣadic Tradition and the Early School of Vedānta as Noticed in Buddhist Scripture,"[62] cites the (Mahāyānic) *Mahāparinirvāṇa-Sūtra,*

> which describes an *ātma*-theory stated to be different from that taught by the Tathāgata: 'Ordinary persons (*pṛthagjana*) and foolish men (*bāla*) speak of the *ātmā* thus: some say it is the size of a thumb (*aṅguṣṭhamātra*); some say it is like a grain of mustard-seed; some say it is the size of an atom. But the [*mahān*]-*ātmā* taught by the Tathāgata is not such as this.'
>
> Another passage in the same *sūtra* refers to similar ideas: 'Laymen hold various opinions concerning the *ātmā*—that it is like a grain of Deccan-grass or like a grain of rice or a bean, or like a thumb. They hold several false conceptions of such a kind, which are not true at all.'
>
> Again, it is said that when a *śrāvaka* and a *pratyekabuddha* asked some ordinary folk the nature of the *ātmā,* the latter answered that it was the size of a thumb. 'And some say it is like a grain of rice; some that it is like a grain of Deccan-grass. Some say it dwells in the heart of men, and is brilliant like the sun.'

The "ordinary people" (*pṛthagjana*) and the "children" (*bāla*), to whom our text attributes these conceptions of the *ātman,* are they the adepts of the Upaniṣads? Perhaps. These conceptions, however, most certainly do not represent the *higher doctrine* of the Upaniṣads. We are aware of no Upaniṣad with them as sole content.

Then where did these ideas come from? They were certainly not the creation of the Upaniṣads: they were *found* by the Upaniṣads, in popular belief. When, for example, the *Mahābhārata* says that Yama tugged fiercely at the body of Satyavant, "the man no taller than a thumb," whom he had first bound,[63] must we see an Upaniṣadic conception here? We do not think so.[64]

If the two texts we have quoted really are directed at the Upaniṣads,[65] we are forced to conclude that they miss the *essential* of which we were just speaking.[66] Is it not making a caricature out of Upaniṣadic thought to want to confine it to these images? "The words of the Vedānta," Śaṅkara writes, "have two things in view: sometimes they clarify the nature of the supreme *ātman*, sometimes they teach the identity of the individual *ātman* (*vijñānātman*)[67] with the supreme *ātman*. Here (in the passage which speaks of the "man no higher than a thumb"), it is the identity of the individual *ātman* with the supreme *ātman* that is being taught, and not the size of anything whatsoever."[68]

We do not wish to accuse the Buddhist authors of a lack either of understanding or honesty. We thus believe them to be focusing, not upon the Upaniṣads, but only upon certain popular conceptions relating to the *ātman*, the conceptions of the "crowd" (*pṛthagjana*). At the very most, we may believe them to be concerned with certain caricatures of Upaniṣadic thought, current during the epoch in which they lived, and not with the Upaniṣads themselves.

Be that as it may, the *Mahāparinirvāṇa-Sūtra* does accept a *mahān ātmā*, which would seem to be none other than the true spiritual *ātman* of the Upaniṣads.[69]

As for the first passage of the *Mahāprajñāpāramitā-Śāstra*: "it is with people that the idea of the Ātman arises relative to something other [than themselves] . . . ," it refers, as the text itself suggests ("thus the heretical contemplatives," etc.), to a yogic exercise.

Notes to Chapter Four

1. *Supra*, p. 38 and n. 273.
2. *Supra*, p. 98, n. 174 end; p. 105, n. 215; pp. 121, 124, 129.—See also p. 46, n. 38 end.
3. I, p. 140 (*supra*, p. 46, n. 38).
4. Re: *uttamapuggala*, cf. *supra*, p. 185, n. 35.
5. *Papañcasūdanī*, II, p. 117, . . . Buddhaghosa clarifies his thought in this way: *tattha purimanaye ayam adhippāyo: Bhikkhave, ahaṃ diṭṭhe va dhamme dharamānakaṃ yeva khīṇāsavaṃ, Tathāgato satto puggalo ti na paññāpemi; appaṭisandhikaṃ pana parinibbutaṃ khīṇāsavaṃ satto ti vā puggalo ti vā kiṃ paññāpessāmi? ananuvejjo Tathāgato. na hi paramatthato satto nāma koci atthi. tassa avijjamānassa idaṃ nissitaṃ viññāṇan ti anvesantā pi kiṃ adhigacchissanti? kathaṃ paṭilabhissantīti attho.—dutiyanaye ayam adhippāyo: Bhikkhave, ahaṃ diṭṭhe va dhamme dharamānakaṃ yeva khīṇāsavaṃ viññāṇavasena Indādīhi avindiyaṃ vadāmi. na hi sa-Indā devā sa-Brahmakā sa-Pajāpatikā anvesantā pi khīṇāsavassa vipassanācittaṃ vā maggacittaṃ vā phalacittaṃ vā, idaṃ nāma ārammaṇaṃ nissāya vattatīti jānituṃ sakkonti. te appaṭisandhikassa parinibbutassa kiṃ jānissantīti.* (*Ibid.*)
6. *Supra*, p. 60, n. 61; etc.
7. For the reading see J. W. De Jong, "Textcritical Notes on the Prasannapadā," *IIJ*. 20 (1978), p. 237.
8. Cf. *supra*, p. 132.
9. *MK.* XXII, 13-15; cf. J. W. De Jong, *Cinq chapitres de la Prasannapadā* (Paris, 1949), pp. 83-84.

"Words are linked to objects but the Tathāgata is not an object" (*vastunibandhanā hi prapañcāḥ syuḥ, avastukaś ca Tathāgataḥ*), Candrakīrti on *MK.* XXII, 15 (*MKV.*, p. 448). Candrakīrti quotes the passage from the *Vajracchedikā Prajñāpāramitā* (cf. *Mahāyāna-Sūtra-Saṃgraha*, edited by P. L. Vaidya, part I [= *Buddhist Sanskrit Texts*, No. 17, Darbhanga, 1961], p. 87), which states: It is not in his individual appearance that the Buddha is to be seen. The Buddha is the *dharma/dharmatā*, the Absolute. (Cf. *supra*, p. 29, and ch. II; see also *ASP.*, pp. 48, 253.) Now, the Absolute cannot be "known" objectively (*dharmatā ca na vijñeyā na sā śakyā vijānitum*).—Cf. *Niraupamya-stava*, 17 (G. Tucci, "Two Hymns of the Catuḥ-stava of Nāgārjuna," *JRAS*, 1932, p. 318):

na ca rūpeṇa dṛṣṭena dṛṣṭa ity abhidhīyase |
dharme dṛṣṭe sudṛṣṭo 'si dharmatā na ca dṛśyate || See also "Notes

bouddhiques," *Indologica Taurinensia*, VII/1979 (*Dr. Ludwik Sternbach Felicitation Volume*), p. 109.

The Tathāgata is "imperishable" (*avyaya*), because he is not subject to becoming: *anutpādasvabhāvāc ca svabhāvāntarāgamanād avyayaḥ*, Candrakīrti, *loc. cit.* (Cf. *Saptaśatikā Prajñāpāramitā* [= *Mañjuśrīparivarta*]: *Buddha iti paramārthato 'nutpādasyaitad adhivacanam* [*Mahāyāna-Sūtra-Saṃgraha*, I, p. 345]; *anutpādasyaitat . . . adhivacanaṃ yad uta ātmeti . . . yasyaitad adhivacanam ātmeti, tasyaitad adhivacanaṃ Buddha iti* [*ibid.*, pp. 346-347; cf. *supra*, p. 111].)

10. Cf. *supra*, p. 114, n. 249; p. 164, n. 95.—We have seen (p. 111; cf. also the preceding note) that the *Saptaśatikā Prajñāpāramitā* expressly identifies the *ātman* with the Buddha.

11. *Supra*, p. 47; cf. pp. 109 ff., n. 243.

12. *Tathāgato ti satto . . . diṭṭhe va dhamme saccato thirato satte anupalabbhiyamāne ti*, *Sāratthappakāsinī*, II, p. 311. (By *anupalabbhiyamāna*, Buddhaghosa means "nonexistent." Cf., two lines further: *yaṃ dukkhaṃ taṃ niruddhan ti: yaṃ dukkhaṃ tad eva niruddhaṃ, añño satto nirujjhanako nāma n' atthi.* See also Nyānatiloka, *Buddhistisches Wörterbuch* [Konstanz, 1954], under *Tathāgata.*—Cf., however, *supra*, pp. 109 ff., n. 243.)

It is true that those who ask what happens to the Tathāgata, perfect being, after the dissolution of his mortal body, see him as an individual, a "soul." In this context, Buddhaghosa and his successor, Dhammapāla, ably interpret the word in this way: Buddhaghosa, *Sumaṅgalavilāsinī*, I, p. 118: *satto Tathāgato ti adhippeto*; Dhammapāla, *Paramatthadīpanī: Udānaṭṭhakathā*, p. 340: *Tathāgato ti attā, taṃ hi diṭṭhigatiko kāraka-vedakādi-saṃkhātaṃ nicca-dhuvādi-saṃkhātaṃ vā Tathāgata-bhāvaṃ gato ti Tathāgato ti voharati.*[a] The Tathāgata has, however, transcended his empirical individuality. He can thus no longer be spoken of an as individual. Buddhaghosa says so himself, with regard to *S.* XLIV, 1: *tassa evaṃ guṇagambhīrassa sato sabbaññu-Tathāgatassa yaṃ upādāya satta-saṃkhāto Tathāgato ti paññatti hoti, tadabhāvena tassā paññattiyā abhāvaṃ passantassa ayaṃ satta-saṃkhāto hoti Tathāgato paraṃ maraṇā ti idaṃ vacanaṃ na upeti, na yujjati; na hoti Tathāgato paraṃ maraṇā ti ādi vacanaṃ pi na upeti, na yujjatīti attho.* (*Sāratthappakāsinī*, III, p. 113 [reading modified according to the Siamese edition, III, p. 192]; cf. below, p. 189 and n. 19.) Up to this point Buddhaghosa is sound. But our texts say something more, which eludes him completely: the Tathāgata is Being itself; consequently, he is "ungraspable," even in this existence (*diṭṭhe va dhamme saccato thetato Tathāgato anupalabbhiyamāno*, *S.* XXII, 85-86; XLIV, 2 [vol. III, pp. 112, 118; IV, p. 384]); how then can one pretend to define his future state?—Cf. Nāgārjuna, *MK.* XXV, 17-18:

paraṃ nirodhād Bhagavān bhavatīty eva nājyate |
na bhavaty ubhayaṃ ceti nobhayaṃ ceti nājyate ||
tiṣṭhamāno 'pi *Bhagavān bhavatīty eva nājyate* |
na bhavaty ubhayaṃ ceti nobhayaṃ ceti nājyate || (For the reading *nājyate* see J. W. De Jong, "Textcritical Notes on the Prasannapadā," *IIJ.* 20 [1978], p. 246; also "Once More, *ajyate*," *JAOS.* 118.1 [1998], pp. 69-70.)

---

a. The word *attan*, in this passage, is a synonym of *satta* = *puggala*; it does not designate the Upaniṣadic *ātman.*—Wrongly, Coomaraswamy, *Hinduism and Buddhism* (New York, n.d.), p. 73; *The Living Thoughts of Gotama the Buddha* (London, 1948), p. 27. (Cf. *supra*, p. 103, n. 210 [p. 104].) Note also that Coomaraswamy is mistaken when he sees in *buddhattā* (*buddhattā buddho, Visuddhimagga*, p. 209) "one whose Self is awake" (as if Buddhaghosa were thinking of *BĀU.* IV, 4, 13 [*supra*, p. 135]!), and in *ajātattā* (. . . *nibbānaṃ, taṃ hi ajātattā na jiyyati na miyyati. . . , Dhammapadaṭṭhakathā*, I, p. 228; cf. *supra*, p. 51, n. 53) "the unborn Self that neither ages nor dies" (*Living Thoughts* . . . , p. 27 and n. 1).

13. *M.* I, p. 297.

14. *Papañcasūdanī*, II, p. 353.

15. Cf. *supra*, p. 33.

16. *Supra*, pp. 28 ff.

17. *Supra*, p. 105, n. 215.

18. *Supra*, p. 160, n. 72.

19. *Sāratthappakāsinī*, III, p. 113 (cf. above, n. 12). Cf. *Papañcasūdanī*, III, p. 199 (on *M.* I, p. 487: *Aggi-Vacchagotta-Sutta* [cf. *supra*, p. 136]).

20. *Supra*, pp. 15, 21.

21. *Manorathapūraṇī*, II, p. 361. Cf. also the gloss of *mahattam abhikaṅkhatā: mahantabhāvaṃ patthayamānena* (*supra*, p. 156, n. 50).

22. Buddhaghosa is also unaware of the conception which holds that the Absolute is beyond the empirical distinction between good and evil (*supra*, p. 53, n. 58; Appendix I). Thus he writes,

commenting on the sentence: *puññañ ca pāpañ ca ubho saṅgaṃ upaccagā* (*supra*, p. 127): *puññaṃ hi sagge laggāpeti apuññaṃ apāye, tasmā ubhayam p' etaṃ saṅgan ti āha.* (*Papañcasūdanī*, III, p. 439.)

23. Pp. 34 ff.

24. Or, if one prefers, a *literal* interpretation.

25. *Dialogues of the Buddha*, I (= *Sacred Books of the Buddhists*, II), pp. 242-243.

26. *ChU.* VIII, 7-12; *TU.* II and III.

27. O. Lacombe, "La direction spirituelle selon les traditions indiennes," in *Direction spirituelle et Psychologie* ("Études Carmélitaines," Bruges, 1951), pp. 163 and 165. See also Coomaraswamy, *The Buddha and the Gospel of Buddhism*, pp. 188-189 (Harper Torchbooks, New York, etc., 1964).—Cf. *supra*, pp. 9-10.

28. See *supra*, p. 41, n. 29.

29. *Supra*, pp. 7, 35.

30. Coomaraswamy, *Buddha and the Gospel of Buddhism*, p. 207 (edition cited).

31. *Ibid.*—Cf. *infra*, pp. 196, 197 ff.

32. *Supra*, pp. 25 ff.

33. *Vedānta und Buddhismus* (= *Abhandlungen der Akademie der Wissenschaften und der Literatur in Mainz: Geistes- und Sozialwissenschaftlichen Klasse*, 1950, NR. 11). This is a review of J. G. Jennings, *The Vedāntic Buddhism of the Buddha* (London, 1947), and of H. Günther, *Das Seelenproblem im älteren Buddhismus* (Konstanz, 1949; the author has since published *Der Buddha und seine Lehre*, Zürich, 1956).—As regards H. von Glasenapp's own position, cf. *supra*, p. 45, n. 36; p. 145, n. 2; pp. 37-38; *infra*, pp. 238-239.

34. Cf. *The Birth of Indian Psychology and its Development in Buddhism* (= *Buddhist Psychology*[3], London, 1936), ch. XI.

35. *Ibid.*, pp. 216-217.

36. *Supra*, p. 45, n. 36; p. 51, nn. 53, 54; p. 109, n. 243.—See also, regarding *viññāṇa*, *supra*, p. 98, n. 174.

37. Cf. E. Conze, *Buddhist Thought in India* (London, 1962; Ann Arbor Paperbacks, University of Michigan Press, 1967), pp. 122 and 280.

38. In a subsequent work we will study the position of other Mahāyānic texts with regard to the problem with which we are here concerned, as well as the attitude of Vedānta towards Buddhism.

39. *Supra*, p. 33.

40. Vv. 765 ff.

41. Cf. D. T. Suzuki, *The Laṅkāvatāra Sūtra* (London, 1932), pp. xliv ff.

42. *Laṅk.*, pp. 77-79.

43. *Tathāgatagarbha-Sūtra* (cf. P. Demiéville, *Le Concile de Lhasa*, [Paris, 1952], pp. 116-117, note; Lamotte, *Vimalakīrti*, p. 55).

44. For *vastu* = *vastra*, cf. Edgerton, *Dictionary*, s.v.

45. We consider *tīrthakara* to be an abbreviation of **anya-tīrthakara*, **para-tīrthakara*, or **ku-tīrthakara*, "master of another doctrine, of a faulty doctrine" (*tīrtha* = doctrine).—Cf. "Supplément aux Recherches sur le Vocabulaire des inscriptions sanskrites du Cambodge," I, *BEFEO.* LIII, 1 (1966), pp. 274-275. See also *supra*, p. 4; *infra*, n. 58.

46. Cf. *supra*, p. 44, n. 34.

47. Cf. *supra*, pp. 3 and 4-5, 33; *infra*, pp. 240-241.

48. On the three *vimokṣa*s (or *samādhi*s), cf. Lamotte, *Traité*, I, pp. 321 ff.

49. Cf. Lamotte, *Vimalakīrti*, pp. 54-56.

50. Cf. *supra*, p. 68.—Candrakīrti, *MKV.*, p. 264 (cf. *supra*, p. 132): *śrotṝṇām uttrāsaparivarjanārthaṃ saṃvṛtyā samāropya tad astīti brūmaḥ.* See also Vidhuśekhara Bhaṭṭācārya, *Gauḍapādīyam Āgama-śāstram* (University of Calcutta, 1950), pp. 142 ff. (commentary on IV, 42).

51. Even without the help of the Tathāgatas, they are bound to attain the Supreme Awakening, thanks to their natural evolution (cf. *supra*, p. 89, n. 135). The Tathāgatas only hasten the process.

52. *Supra*, p. 87, n. 124; p. 191. Cf. *infra*, pp. 197 ff.—P. Demiéville, (*op. cit.*, p. 117, n.) has noticed the parallelism between the Tathāgatagarbha, "seen concretely" (endowed with the thirty-two signs, etc.), and the "inner *puruṣa* of the Upaniṣads."

53. *Infra*, pp. 198-199.

54. S. N. Dasgupta, *Indian Idealism* (Cambridge University Press, 1933 [reprint: 1962]), p. 93.

55. *Supra*, p. 29.—The *ātman* is neither an "agent" (*kartṛ*) nor an "enjoyer" (*bhoktṛ*). It is only due to the *upādhi*s, contingent "appositions" (*supra*, pp. 139-140), which are "superimposed" on it by "ignorance," that it appears as such. Cf. Śaṅkara, *Brahmasūtra-bhāṣya*, II, 3, 40. Cf. also the close of the celebrated Introduction to the *Brahmasūtra-bhāṣya*: *evam ayam anādir ananto naisargiko 'dhyāso mithyāpratyaya-rūpaḥ kartṛtvabhoktṛtvapravartakaḥ sarvalokapratyakṣaḥ. asyānartha-hetoḥ prahāṇāya ātmaikatvavidyāpratipattaye sarve vedāntā ārabhyante.*

See also *Upadeśasāhasrī, padya,* XI and XII.—"Note sur le Vedānta dans l'inscription de Prè Rup (Cambodge)," *JA.* 1971, p. 101.

56. It must perhaps be assumed that our text associates the Sāṃkhya with the Nyāya, as is indicated by the term *nirguṇa* (the *ātman-puruṣa* of the Sāṃkhya is, in effect, *nirguṇa;* all the other terms in our text are applicable to the *ātman* of the Nyāya-Vaiśeṣika). Let us bear in mind that it is the Sāṃkhya that Candrakīrti is aiming at:

ātmā tīrthyaiḥ kalpyate nityarūpo
'kartā bhoktā nirguṇo niṣkriyaś ca |
kaṃcit kaṃcid bhedam āśritya tasya
bhedaṃ yātā prakriyā tīrthikānām ||

Madhyamakāvatāra, VI, 121, cited in *MKV.,* p. 344. Cf. Murti, p. 203.

57. *Supra,* p. 161, n. 81.

58. The translation of *tīrthika* by "heretic" has become customary. It is inexact however. It should be "adept of another doctrine, of a faulty doctrine" (*tīrthika = anya-tīrthika, para-tīrthika,* or *ku-tīrthika*).—Reference, above, n. 45.

59. Lamotte, *Traité,* II, pp. 738, 744.

60. *Ibid.,* p. 744, n. 1.

61. *Supra,* p. 191.

62. *HJAS.* XVIII (1955), pp. 86-87.

63. *tataḥ Satyavataḥ kāyāt pāśabaddhaṃ vaśaṃ gatam* |
aṅguṣṭhamātraṃ puruṣaṃ niścakarṣa Yamo balāt ||

Mbh. III, 281, 16 (critical edition); also cited by Śaṅkara, *Brahmasūtra-bhāśya,* I, 3, 24.

64. See also Oldenberg, *Die Religion des Veda* (Berlin 1894), p. 526.

65. Note that Kamalaśīla, who cites the conceptions that have just been under consideration (*TSP.,* p. 93, line 6 from the bottom), does not attribute them expressly to the *Upaniṣadvādin,* who are named a little further on the same page.

66. *Supra,* p. 191.

67. Cf. *supra,* p. 92, n. 149.

68. *dvirūpā hi vedāntavākyānāṃ pravṛttiḥ: kvacit paramātmasvarūpanirūpaṇaparā, kvacid vijñānātmanaḥ paramātmaikatvopadeśaparā. tad atra vijñānātmanaḥ paramātmanaikatvam upadiśyate, nāṅguṣṭhamātratvaṃ kasyacit,* Śaṅkara, *Brahmasūtra-bhāṣya,* I, 3, 25.

69. Cf. Lamotte, *Vimalakīrti,* p. 56. See also *supra,* p. 59, n. f; p. 119, n. 278.

Conclusion

We have endeavored to determine whether the author of the Bàt Cũṃ inscription,—which was the point of departure for this study,—understood the teachings of the Buddha properly, when he wrote: "The Buddha taught the doctrine of *nairātmya* as the means (*sādhana*) of attaining to *paramātman.*" We have come to a positive conclusion. This author, in all probability, remembered what he had read in Mahāyānic texts such as the *Mahāyāna-Sūtrālaṃkāra* and the *Ratnagotra-vibhāga.* He had not, however, gone deeply into this teaching. He therefore committed the grave error of adding that the idea of *paramātman* is contradictory (*viruddha*) to that same doctrine of *nairātmya*![1]

The Buddha certainly denied the *ātman.* That *ātman,* however, is not the Upaniṣadic *ātman.* Better still: the true spiritual *ātman,* for the Upaniṣads as for the Buddha, is the negation of that which men generally consider to be the *ātman,* that is, the psycho-physical individuality.

In actual fact, our controversy is nothing but an argument over words. The authentic *ātman,* being the negation of the empirical *ātman,* is *anātman*; and *anātman* is a negative expression which *indicates* the authentic *ātman,* which is ineffable and—from the objective point of view—"non-existent."[2] There is no contradiction between *ātman* and *anātman.* The *ātman,* which is denied, and that which is affirmed, through that negation itself, pertains to two different levels. It is only when we have not succeeded in distinguishing between them, that the terms *ātman* and *anātman* seem to us to be opposed.

But, if the Buddha entirely admitted the Upaniṣadic doctrine of *ātman-brahman,* wherein lies his originality?

The word "originality" is not appropriate to the Buddha. Did he not say that he had but "discovered" the Dhamma, as an old city buried in a forest, by following a road already trodden by the ancients?[3] It should, nonetheless, be recognized that Gotama succeeded in doing that which the ancient Buddhas were not able to do: in elaborating a teaching method, adapted to the needs of the greatest number (*bahujanahitāya*).[4]

The authors of the Upaniṣads knew that the Absolute could not be expressed in definable concepts. *Neti, neti . . . , Yato vāco nivartante aprāpya manasā saha.*[5]—They tried to express it all the same, by means of myths and images. The Buddha, on the other hand, never seems to have had recourse to such procedures. He affirmed the *ātman*, when he was dealing with those who were capable of understanding it; but, more often, he said what the *ātman* is not, so as to bring men to a sense of the Real, through an *internal revolution.*[6]

It cannot be said that the Buddha was opposed to all speculative processes of thought. "The Tathāgata has gone beyond the domain of the *diṭṭhi*s."[7] But how can one pretend to have gone beyond something, if one has never used it?[8] The Buddha did not condemn the *diṭṭhi*s, but only the blind attachment to these (*diṭṭhupādāna*), as he condemned also the blind attachment to moral and ritual practices (*sīlabbatupādāna*).[9]

In that also, the Buddha was faithful to the spirit of the Upaniṣads. However, he knew, better than anyone, that the danger was great, for men not prepared, to fall into dogmatism and to carry all their lives on their shoulders what was to be only a "boat of passage."[10] He also knew that one human life was not enough to attain to the supreme knowledge. Did it not take Indra more than one hundred years to attain to it, under the direction of Prajāpati?[11] And these were gods! We thus understand why the Buddha attached so much importance to the "Four Noble Truths" (*Cattāri Ariyasaccāni*) which he taught: Sorrow (*dukkha*), Arising of Sorrow (*dukkha-samudaya*), Cessation of Sorrow (*dukkha-nirodha*), and the Way that leads to the Cessation of Sorrow (*dukkha-nirodha-*

gāminī paṭipadā). The Upaniṣads, too, had said: what is finite is painful;[12] however, this pain is only adventitious, for it has its origin in our "ignorance," that is, in our imperfect consciousness;[13] consequently, it has its end in Knowledge, that is, in the full blooming of our consciousness; and there is an intellectual and moral discipline which one must follow to achieve this end. But, while the Upaniṣads placed the emphasis on the Beatitude (*ānanda*) of the Infinite, the Buddha places it on the sorrow (*dukkha*) of the finite. How can one attain the Infinite, if one is not yet conscious of the finiteness of the finite? The Infinite is not outside of the finite, it is not another world: it is the ultimate Reality, the farthest and yet the nearest. To attain it, one does not, therefore, quit the finite. However, one must transcend the finiteness of the finite.[14] Now, how to transcend it, if one is not even conscious of it? Only he who knows the world can attain the "end of the world," says one of our texts.[15]

Let us understand sorrow and its cause, let us follow the Way: we will see, some day or other, thanks to the purification accomplished in the course of existences,[16] the end of sorrow, in the intuition of the Ultimate Truth. Such must have been the thought of the Buddha. As has been well said by Walpola Rahula, the fourth Truth, that of the Way, contains practically the entire teaching of the Buddha.[17] In the mind of the Buddha, the Way counts more than the goal. Aspiring to the *ātman*, is it not making of it an *object*, and, in consequence, getting far away from it?[18]

Of this Way also the Buddha says that he has "discovered" it.[19] It must therefore have existed before him.[20] No one seems, however, to have interpreted it as well as he did.

In the final analysis, the difference between the Upaniṣads and Buddhism seems to be simply a difference in emphasis. The authors of the Upaniṣads, who are philosophers before they are saviours, speak much more of the Infinite than of the finite, much more of the Goal than of the Way, whilst the Buddha, who is more saviour than philosopher,[21] speaks more of the finite than of the Infinite, more of the

Way than of the Goal. The goal of the saviour is, however, also that of the philosophers: Deliverance through Knowledge or, rather, Knowledge which is Deliverance.

Notes to the Conclusion

1. *Supra*, pp. 1 ff.
2. *Supra*, p. 109, n. 243.
3. *Supra*, p. 133.
4. *Supra*, p. 86, n. 113.
5. *Supra*, p. 8; p. 60, n. 61; etc.
6. On the diversity of teachings, cf. *supra*, pp. 25 ff.
7. *Supra*, p. 54, n. 60.
8. Cf., in this respect, the *Māgandiya-Sutta* of the *Suttanipāta* (vv. 835 ff.).
9. *Supra*, p. 8.
10. *Supra*, p. 9.—We are in agreement here with F. O. Schrader, *Über den Stand der indischen Philosophie zur Zeit Mahāvīras und Buddhas* (Inaugural-Dissertation Strassburg, Leipzig, 1902), p. 40: "Buddha knew only too well that this insight would not only be unobtainable for the multitude, but even difficult to impart to the schooled philosophers; that, should his teaching be invested *ex professo* with this basis, it would necessarily be misunderstood, viewed as *diṭṭhi* (speculation, fantasy) and would forfeit its ethical character."
11. *ChU.* VIII, 7 ff. Cf. *supra*, pp. 5, 7; p. 65, n. 71. In another context, see Patañjali, *Mahābhāṣya, Paspaśā*: Kshitish Chandra Chatterji, *Patañjali's Mahābhāshya* (Calcutta, 1972, 4th edition), pp. 45-46.
12. Cf. *supra*, p. 21 and n. 143.
13. Cf. *supra*, p. 78, n. 90, and *passim*.—For Buddhism, it is said, "ignorance is ignorance of the four sacred truths, ignorance of the origin and of the disappearance of the *skandhas*, the fourfold misapprehension (*viparyāsa*) which consists in the taking for eternal that which is transitory, for happy that which is sorrowful, for pure that which is impure (the body), for an I, that which is deprived of 'self' (the five *skandhas*)" [Lamotte, *Histoire*, p. 39; on the *viparyāsa/vipallāsa*, cf. *supra*, pp. 2-4; p. 74, n. 81; p. 39 (and n. 278)]. So be it. But are not all these "ignorances" simply diverse expressions of that imperfect consciousness, which "superimposes" (*supra*, pp. 139 ff.)?

According to *M.* I, pp. 54-55, the *āsava*s and the *avijjā* condition each other (*āsavasamudayā avijjāsamudayo, āsavanirodhā avijjānirodho; avijjāsamudayā āsavasamudayo, avijjānirodhā āsavanirodho*). The relationship between the *nāmarūpa* and the *viññāṇa* comes to mind (*supra,* p. 21). But the *āsava*s can be considered to be "causes" or "conditions" of the *avijjā* only inasmuch as they "cover" Knowledge (cf. *BhG.* III, 38 ff.), and as they supply "food" (*āhāra*) to the *avijjā* (cf. Lamotte, *loc. cit.*). They would not exist themselves if there were no *avijjā.*

14. Cf. *supra,* p. 43, n. 31; p. 46, n. 38 (last paragraph); pp. 9 ff., 12 ff.

15. *lokavidū . . . lokantagū, S.* I, p. 62 (*gāthā*). Cf. *supra,* p. 46, n. 38 (last paragraph); p. 9 and n. 68.

16. Cf. *supra,* p. 18 and n. 118.

17. "Practically the whole teaching of the Buddha, to which he devoted himself during 45 years, deals in some way or other with this Path. He explained it in different ways and in different words to different people, according to the stage of their development and their capacity to understand and follow him. But the essence of those many thousand discourses scattered in the Buddhist Scriptures is found in the Noble Eightfold Path." (*What the Buddha Taught*[2] [London, 1967], pp. 45-46; cf. *L'enseignement du Bouddha* [Paris, 1961], pp. 70-71.)

18. Cf. *supra,* pp. 7-8; p. 109, n. 243. Śaṅkara has said, at the end of a discussion on the *ātman*'s "not being an object" (*aviṣayatva*): "Therefore, one should not make an effort for knowledge [of the *ātman*] but solely for the cessation of the notion of *ātman* in what is non-*ātman*" (*tasmāj jñāne yatno na kartavyaḥ, kiṃ tv anātmany ātmabuddhinivṛttāv eva*): *Bhagavadgītā-bhāṣya,* XVIII, 50. See also "Notes bouddhiques," *JA.* 1986, p. 295.

19. *S.* II, p. 106. Cf. *supra,* p. 133.

20. Cf. *BĀU.* IV, 4, 8: *aṇuḥ panthā vitataḥ purāṇaḥ.*

21. Cf. *supra,* pp. 37-38. See also "Unity in Diversity: Anattā revisited," *Sanskrit Studies Centre Journal* (Silpakorn University, Bangkok), II (2006), pp. 1-7.

Appendices

APPENDIX I

Beyond good and evil

We have seen that, according to the Upaniṣads and the Pāli texts, the Absolute is beyond good and evil.[1] Even though such a conception is not only found in India,[2] it has not always been understood aright by modern interpreters. One of these writes: "... the primitive Hindus ... had not yet considered the relation between Being and the Good."[3]

This interpretation is incorrect. There is an absolute Good, beyond empirical good.[4] In fact, our empirical good cannot be true good. It only exists when opposed to evil (just as evil exists only in opposition to good); it is, therefore, not *good in itself.* From the point of view of absolute Good, which transcends the empirical distinction between good and evil, it too is evil.[5]

To this logical reason can be added a psychological reason. "Saint Augustine knew the endlessly recurring perversion that our finitude renders inevitable, that of contentment with self: to do good, it is necessary for me to discern and recognize my action as good. But, at the very moment when I become aware of it, my pride already begins to arise. Without that knowledge, I cannot become good; with it, I do not remain perfectly so. And humility conscious of it ceases to be humble, and quickly becomes pride in humility."[6]

It is then interesting to note that the Upaniṣads often use the words *pāpa* and *pāpman* (which ordinarily designate evil) to designate both good and evil.[7]

The empirical distinction between good and evil is made by our finite consciousness, which moves within dualities,—whereas absolute Good is infinite Consciousness. It is beyond all moral rule, for it is pure liberty. "... the action of the seer ... is creative living where external authority gives place to inward freedom."[8] We have already spoken of the liberty which consists in tending towards the Good, our true being, by detaching ourselves from the constraint of our natural inclinations.[9] That freedom is not yet perfect however. Liberty, in the highest degree, does not consist in choosing between good and evil. "Where I choose, and could act otherwise, I am not free."[10] "Liberty is one with necessity"[11]—if, by "necessity," is understood, not the necessity born of external constraint, but the inner necessity, that I experience invincibly at the very depths of my being, once I have become myself.[12]

Such, in fact, is the behavior of the Mahātman, of Infinite Being.[13] He is incapable of evil. The focus of evil resides in the ego. Now the Mahātman is one who has transcended the ego. How then could he do evil? "One who sees himself in all beings and all beings in himself," "does not wound himself by himself."[14] Not only does he not wound himself by himself but, spontaneously, he "works for the good of all,"[15] in the manner of Spring and of moonlight, which spontaneously rejoice the world.[16] Is not the good of each his own good too?[17]

Transcending good and evil does not therefore mean that one may do evil, while being exempt from sin oneself; on the contrary, it is impossible for one who has transcended that distinction to do evil. "He goes beyond the ethical, though rooted in it."[18] The Mahātman is absolutely good. His entire Being is Goodness, there is no place in him for evil. We read in the *Mahāprajñāpāramitā-Śāstra* (*Upadeśa*):[19]

> (The farer on the Great Way), the bodhisattva, comprehends the (ultimate) sameness of all deeds; and he does not take the good deed as meritorious and the evil deed as devoid of merit. (For, in the ultimate truth there is not this distinction of good and bad.) In the ultimate truth there are no deeds, good or evil. This is the true *prajñā*. But this is itself also the right deed (for it issues in the deed that is done with the right understanding) . . . Having achieved the true understanding of deeds, one neither does deeds nor desists from them (for one is devoid of clinging and so one does not

consider oneself as the doer of deeds). And such a wise man always does the right deeds and never any wrong ones. This is the right deed of the bodhisattva.

It is true that the Mahātman may perform deeds contrary to the articles of moral law. The Upaniṣads give several examples of this.[20] But are these acts really bad? They are bad according to our finite point of view, our "worldly point of view" (*laukikī dṛṣṭi*), as Śaṅkara puts it.[21] But all that the Mahātman does, he does for the love of All; and true love "guarantees the moral authenticity of his behaviour."[22]

The Law ceases to be law when it has attained its goal, Love, the "fundamental actualization of the Eternal in man."[23] All the rules enjoined by ordinary morality remain valid; they are, however, no longer "rules," for the practices they prescribe have become spontaneous.[24] On the other hand, the moral rules, at this transcendent level, have value only in relation to Love, and not in themselves. That is why no act performed in the name of Love can be bad, even if it appears to be so according to our "worldly point of view."

In the final analysis, "Good" and "Love" are simply conventional designations. We give a thing a name only so long as effort is required to obtain it. When for us it has become spontaneous, it has no more name. To be and to will are one and the same thing here. Not even the category of liberty applies; there is neither liberty nor non-liberty. Yet, since we are here, at the level of language, we may say: Good is one with infinite Being. Consequently, only one who has realized the *ātman-brahman*, who has become infinite Being, may truly incarnate Good.

According to Vedānta and to Buddhism, moral perfection consists in the integral gift of oneself.[25] It is not, however, possible to give oneself totally without transcending the level of the self and the other. Thus, only the Mahātman is a perfect being, by virtue of the "intuition of the identity (of the self and the other)" [*samatā-jñāna*], the intuition upon which rest *maitrī* and *karuṇā*.[26]

Notes to Appendix I

1. *Supra*, p. 53, n. 58.

2. Cf. Jaspers, *Von der Wahrheit* (München, 1947 and 1958), p. 599:

"Jesus is beyond good and evil. Kierkegaard recognizes absolute truth in the realm of religion, from which the suspension of ethical judgement might proceed. Nietzsche also provisionally had this genuine 'beyond good and evil' in mind (then to retrogress into a theoretical amorality and distort the meaning)."

3. R. C. Zaehner, *Mysticism, Sacred and Profane* (Oxford University Press, 1961), p. 118.

4. In a Pāli text, the *ātman*, which would seem to be elevated above empirical distinctions of true and false, of good and bad, is called, at the same time, *kalyāṇa* "good" (*A.* I, p. 149; cf. *supra*, p. 105 and n. 216).

5. Cf. F. H. Bradley, *Appearance and Reality: A Metaphysical Essay* (second edition with an introduction by Richard Wollheim, Oxford University Press, 1969), p. 355: "And viewed from the ground of what is higher—of what they fail to reach or even oppose—the lower truth and lower goodness become sheer error and evil."

6. Jaspers, *Les grands philosophes* (Paris, 1963), pp. 333-334.

7. Cf. *BĀU.* IV, 3, 8; 3, 21; 4, 23; *ChU.* V, 24, 3; VIII, 1, 5; 4, 1; 6, 3; 13, 1; *Kena-Up.* IV, 9; *Īśā-Up.* 8; *Muṇḍ.Up.* III, 2, 9, with Śaṅkara's commentaries (*pāpmaśabdena dharmādharmāv ucyete*; *pāpmā puṇyapāpalakṣaṇaḥ*; etc.). See also *Brahmasūtra-bhāṣya*, IV, 1, 14 (p. 956).

8. Radhakrishnan, *Eastern Religions and Western Thought*[2] (Oxford University Press, 1940), p. 102.

9. *Supra*, p. 89, n. 135 (p. 91).

10. Jaspers, *Les grands philosophes*, p. 803 (chapter on Spinoza). Cf. J. F. Staal, *Advaita and Neoplatonism: A Critical Study in Comparative Philosophy* (= *Madras University Philosophical Series*, No. 10, 1961), pp. 226 ff.

11. Jaspers, *Les grands philosophes*, p. 802.—Cf. the formulae of the *Philosophie* (II, p. 196): ". . . the individual would choose that which seemed necessary, but this is not to be understood as 'free' choice; absolute freedom would be absolute necessity; the highest determination for the Right would leave no choice."

12. "Freedom is a being-delivered unto oneself out of Transcendence. This freedom is . . . a volition liberated from all

coercion, which is a *transcendent must.*" Jaspers, *Der philosophische Glaube* (Zürich, 1948), p. 153 (our italics).

13. Cf. *supra*, pp. 15-16 and n. 108.

14. *na hinasty ātmanātmānam, BhG.* XIII, 28. Cf. *supra*, p. 81, n. 99.

15. *sarvabhūtahite ratāḥ, BhG.* V, 25; XII, 4. Cf. *supra*, p. 81, n. 99.

16. *Vivekacūḍāmaṇi*, 37-38 (*supra*, p. 84, n. 108).

17. Cf. Schopenhauer, *Le Monde comme Volonté et comme Représentation* (translation by A. Burdeau, new edition, revised and corrected by R. Roos, Paris, 1966), p. 471.

18. Radhakrishnan, *Up.*, p. 120.

19. Venkata Ramanan, p. 190. (This part of the *Mahāprajñāpāramitā-Śāstra* [of which only the Chinese translation is available] has not been translated by E. Lamotte. [Cf. *infra*, p. 245, fn.])

20. *BĀU.* IV, 3, 22; *Kauṣ.Up.* III, 1. Cf. Zaehner, *op. cit.*, pp. 116-117, 187.

21. *Bhagavadgītā-bhāṣya*, XVIII, 17.

22. Jaspers, *Introduction à la Philosophie* (translation by J. Hersch, ed. 10/18, Paris, 1965), p. 63. The author makes a cross-reference to Saint Augustine: "Love and do what you will." See also *Les grands Philosophes*, pp. 341-342.

23. "Grundwirklichkeit des Ewigen im Menschen," Jaspers, *Der philosophische Glaube*, p. 95 (edition cited).

24. Cf. the verse by Sureśvara (*Naiṣkarmyasiddhi*, IV, 69), often quoted:

utpannātmaprabodhasya tv adveṣṭṛtvādayo guṇāḥ |
ayatnato bhavanty asya na tu sādhanarūpiṇaḥ ||

"For one who is awakened to the *ātman*, virtues such as the absence of enmity are realized without effort; they are no longer the means." (Cf. P. Hacker, *Untersuchungen über Texte des frühen Advaitavāda*, 1. *Die Schüler Śaṅkaras* [= *Abhandlungen der Akademie der Wissenschaften und der Literatur in Mainz: Geistes- und Sozialwissenschaftlichen Klasse*, 1950, NR. 26], p. 105 [2011].)

sīlavā hoti, no ca sīlamayo, M. II, p. 27. "When you have gone across the great temporal river of death to where there is the perfection of the Undying, you can be right without being righteous, *sīlavā no ca sīlamayo*, because you are no longer in the making, no longer becoming what you ought to be, but you have done what was to be done, and are the finished product, finished both in its sense of made and in its sense of perfect and complete, whole and entire.

You are *evaṃ-dhammo,* of the very stuff of your being," I. B. Horner, "Early Buddhist Dhamma," *Artibus Asiae,* XI, 1/2 (1948), p. 123.—Cf. *supra,* p. 184, n. 31.

25. Bergson is wrong when he writes, quoting "a historian of religions": [Buddhism] "remained unaware of 'the total and mysterious gift of oneself.'" (*Les deux sources de la Morale et de la Religion* [one hundred and fortieth edition, Paris, Presses universitaires de France, 1965], p. 239.)

26. *Supra,* pp. 13-16.

Appendix II

bhāvitatta, kṛtātman

In the Pāli Canon, the word *bhāvitatta* is often used apropos the Arahants and the Buddha. It may, in general, be thought, that this word does not comprise a precise metaphysical meaning.[1] It would, however, seem to be otherwise when the same word is associated with *brahmabhūta*.[2]

What does it mean? We think that, in the context we have indicated, it can only mean "one who has realized his *ātman*" (literally, "one who has made his *ātman* be"). The *ātman* is the *brahman*. One who has "become the *brahman*" (*brahmabhūta*), or "whose *ātman* has become the *brahman*" (*brahmabhūtena attanā viharati*),[3] is also one who has "made be" his *ātman*, that is to say, one who has become that which he truly is.

The Pāli text which associates this word with *brahmabhūta* makes us think, on the other hand, of the passage from the *Chāndogya-Upaniṣad* (VIII, 13) which we have already cited above:[4] *akṛtaṃ kṛtātmā brahmalokam abhisaṃbhavāmi.*

What does this word *kṛtātman* mean? Śaṅkara glosses it by *kṛtakṛtya* "one who has accomplished his task, one who has attained his goal." What, however, would "accomplishing his task" and "attaining his goal" mean to the sage who is speaking here, if not liberating himself from his contingent finitude to become the Infinite which he is in the depths of his being?[5] *aśva iva romāṇi vidhūya pāpam, candra iva rāhor mukhāt pramucya dhūtvā śarīram akṛtaṃ kṛtātmā brahmalokam abhisaṃbhavāmi.*—"Shaking off good and evil,[6] as the horse sheds its coat, shaking off the body[7] as the moon frees itself from the jaws of Rāhu,[8] I attain the uncreated[9] world which is the *brahman*,[10]—I, who am *kṛtātman*." (*ChU.* VIII, 13.)

Let us recall that the Pāli Canon often uses the expressions *katakicca* (= Sanskrit *kṛtakṛtya*) and *katakaraṇīya* (= Sanskrit *kṛtakaraṇīya*), as epithets for an Arahant who has attained the "supreme goal" of his existence, that is, Nirvāṇa.[11]

But the word *kṛtātman* means: "one who has created his *ātman.*" It is, obviously, not a question of "creating the *ātman*" in the literal sense of the word: "The uncreated cannot be obtained by that which is created."[12] In his commentary on the *Muṇḍaka-Upaniṣad,* Śaṅkara clarifies this: "*Kṛtātman* is one who, through Knowledge (*vidyā*), has created his *ātman* in the transcendent form (*para*) proper to it, after having separated it from its inferior form (*apara*), which has 'ignorance' (*avidyā*) for its characteristic."[13] Or again: "*Kṛtātmānaḥ* are those who are *accomplished* in the form of *paramātman,* which is proper to them."[14]

This idea may be expressed, as well, by the word *bhāvitātman/bhāvitatta.* One who has "created his *ātman,*" has, in fact, created nothing: he has done nothing but become what he truly is. In other words, he has "made being his *ātman.*"[15]

Notes to Appendix II

1. On the various meanings of the Sanskrit *bhāvitātman,* cf. Apte, *Sanskrit-English Dictionary,* s.v. (revised and enlarged edition, Poona, 1957-1959).

2. *bhāvitattaññataraṃ brahmabhūtaṃ tathāgataṃ, It.*, p. 57. Cf. also *M.* I, p. 386: *brahmapattassa . . . bhāvitattassa pattipattassa.*

3. *Supra,* pp. 121 ff.

4. *Supra,* p. 47.

5. Cf. Śaṅkara, *Upadeśasāhasrī, padya,* XIII, 26.

6. *pāpaṃ dharmādharmākhyam,* Śaṅkara: cf. *supra,* p. 215 and n. 7.

7. *dhūtvā śarīram*: cf. *supra*, p. 112, n. 245 (p. 113).

8. Cf. *Sn.* 465.

9. *Akṛta* = Pāli *akata* = Nirvāṇa: cf. *supra*, p. 47.

10. *Brahmaloka.*—Senart (*Chāndogya-Upaniṣad* [Paris, 1930], p. 120, n. 2) confuses, in an unexpected manner, the *brahmaloka* of

Chāndogya, VIII, 13, which is called *akṛta,* with the *brahmaloka* of *Muṇḍaka,* I, 2, 6, which is called *sukṛta.* In actual fact, the second of these two *brahmalokas* (= *svarga,* according to Śaṅkara),—which is the fruit of the sacrifice, of "the liturgical act,"—is "the world of Brahmā" (cf. *supra,* p. 98, n. 174 a [p. 100]; *infra,* p. 226 and n. 11), whilst the first is "the world which is the *brahman*" (*brahmaiva lokaḥ*) [*supra,* p. 47]. Otherwise expressed, the *brahmaloka* of the *Muṇḍaka,* I, 2, 6, is "time extended," and that of the *Chāndogya,* VIII, 13, is "time transcended" (cf. *supra,* p. 52). The first is evanescent (cf. *Muṇḍ.Up.* I, 2, 7: *plavā hy ete adṛḍhā yajñarūpāḥ* . . .), whereas the second is permanent.

11. Cf. *Dhp.* 386: *katakiccaṃ anāsavaṃ uttamatthaṃ anuppattaṃ.*

12. *nāsty akṛtaḥ kṛtena, Muṇḍ.Up.* I, 2, 12.

13. *kṛtātmano 'vidyālakṣaṇād apararūpād apanīya svena pareṇa rūpeṇa kṛta ātmā vidyayā yasya, Muṇḍakopaniṣad-bhāṣya,* III, 2, 2.

14. *kṛtātmānaḥ paramātmasvarūpeṇaiva niṣpannātmānaḥ, ibid.,* III, 2, 5.

15. Cf. *supra,* p. 89, n. 135 (p. 91).

Appendix III

Buddha = Brahmā

The Buddha, as we have seen,[1] is "one who has become *brahman*" (*brahma-bhūta*). He is sometimes, however, also called Brahmā. Thus, *Aṅguttara-Nikāya*, I, p. 207:

> *idha, Visākhe, ariyasāvako Tathāgataṃ anussarati:—iti pi so Bhagavā arahaṃ sammāsambuddho vijjācaraṇasampanno sugato lokavidū anuttaro purisadammasārathi satthā devamanussānaṃ Buddho Bhagavā ti. tassa Tathāgataṃ anussarato cittaṃ pasīdati, pāmojjaṃ uppajjati, ye cittassa upakkilesā te pahīyanti. ayaṃ vuccati, Visākhe, ariyasāvako Brahmūposathaṃ upavasati, Brahmunā saddhiṃ saṃvasati, Brahmañ c' assa ārabbha cittaṃ pasīdati pāmojjaṃ uppajjati, ye cittassa uppakkilesā te pahīyanti.*

Geiger, who indicates this passage,[2] writes:

> Apparently, no distinction is made between the neuter *brahman* and the masculine *Brahman.*[3]

Must we then side with this eminent scholar? We think not. In the passage which we have just quoted, it is not a question of one of the gods known by the name of Brahmā;[4] rather, as in Sanskrit, the word *Brahmā* is nothing but a synonym of *brāhmaṇa.* The *Suttanipāta,*[5] in fact, has the Buddha say, in reply to the question: *kiṃpattinaṃ āhu brāhmaṇaṃ?* (518)—:

> *bāhetvā sabbapāpakāni*[6]
> *vimalo sādhusamāhito ṭhitatto* |
> *saṃsāram aticca kevalī so*
> *asito tādi pavuccate sa Brahmā* || (519). (*so Brahmā so brāhmaṇo ti, Paramatthajotikā,* II, 2, p. 427.)

Cf. also *Sn.* 293; *Jāt.* II, p. 346; IV, p. 288; VI, p. 524, etc.; *Petavatthu,* I, 12, 9.

Now the Buddha may certainly be called Brahmā, since, having "become the *brahman,*" he is a true brahmin.[7]

It is true that the Buddha and the Arahants are sometimes likened to Brahmā.[8] But there is no question at all of any confusion between *brahman* and Brahmā. This comparison belongs to another level of Buddhism than the one with which we are concerned here: it indicates simply a concession made to popular belief and especially to that of the ritualistic brahmins.[9] These brahmins, who claimed to have issued from the mouth of Brahmā,[10] aspired to rejoin him by means of sacrifice, and to live in his company.[11] Buddhism, as well as the Upaniṣads, in rejecting the pretension of the Brahmās to Unconditionality,[12] did not reject the Brahmās themselves. It is Brahmā Sahampati who intervenes to make the Buddha decide to teach the Truth. This mystification was no doubt necessary to the propagation of the doctrine. The Brahmās are moreover praised for their perfect conduct which is presented here below as a model to emulate. Now the Buddha and the Arahants practise the *Brahmavihāras*. They are thus "like unto Brahmā."[13] Here too, it is easy to discern "the skill in methods" (*upāyakauśalya*) of the propagators of the doctrine: demonstrably, their aim was to turn the attention of the crowd from the invisible Brahmās, living in a distant world and draw it towards the terrestrial Brahmās, accessible to all.[14]—It is also a concession which texts make when they speak of the Anāgāmins who attain to Deliverance in *Brahmaloka*: this conception, as we have seen, is not peculiar to Buddhism, for it is also to be found in the Upaniṣads.[15]

The Pāli Canon seems to be exempt from those confusions between *brahman* and Brahmā which the Upaniṣads themselves indicate.[16] It is only at the level of the commentaries that, in Buddhism, *brahman* becomes purely and simply Brahmā.[17]

Notes to Appendix III

1. Ch. II.
2. Cf. also *Sn.* 1065.
3. M. and W. Geiger, *Pāli Dhamma,* p. 77.—Differently, I. B. Horner, "Early Buddhist Dhamma," *Artibus Asiae,* XI, 1/2 (1948), p. 118. Buddhaghosa is content to say: *Brahmā vuccati sammāsambuddho* (*Manorathapūraṇī,* II, p. 322).—*Brahmā ti seṭṭhavacanaṃ, Paramatthajotikā,* II, 2, p. 592 (on *seṭṭha,* see *supra,* p. 121).
4. Cf. *supra,* p. 122.
5. Cf. *Mahāvastu,* III, p. 396 (ed. Senart, Paris, 1897).
6. Cf. *supra,* p. 126 and n. 34.
7. *Supra,* p. 127 and n. 43. Cf. Coomaraswamy, *The Living Thoughts of Gotama the Buddha* (London, 1948), p. 26.—*brahmavid brāhmaṇo Brahmā brahmanirvāṇam āptavān . . . , Nāmasaṃgīti,* cited by La Vallée Poussin, *Nirvāṇa* (Paris, 1925), p. 73, n. 1. See also *AK.* VI, p. 245 and n. 2 (citing *Bodhisattvabhūmi*) [cf. *supra,* p. 157, n. 59].
8. Cf. *S.* I, p. 141; *Sn.* 479, 508.
9. Cf. ch. III.
10. *Supra,* p. 124.
11. Cf. *Tevijja-Sutta, D.* I, pp. 235 ff.—*ime kho brāhmaṇā Brahmalokādhimuttā, M.* II, pp. 194, 196. The term *sahavyatā,* used by the Pāli texts, recalls the *sāyujya* of the ritualist tradition. Cf. *Kauṣītaki-Brāhmaṇa,* XXI, 1 (ed. B. Lindner, Jena, 1887): *Brahmaṇaḥ salokatāṃ sāyujyam.* Let us recall that, according to the same Brāhmaṇa (XX, 1; cf. *supra,* p. 98, n. 174 a [p. 100], the "world of Brahmā" (*Brahmaṇo lokaḥ,* and not *brahmaiva lokaḥ* "world which is the *brahman*": *supra,* p. 47; p. 222, n. 10) is "the most real" (*sattama*) of all. The *Abhidharmadīpa* actually employs the expression *Brahmasāyujya* in connection with the *Brahmavihāras*: *Abhidharmadīpa with Vibhāṣāprabhāvṛtti,* critically edited with Notes and Introduction by Padmanabh S. Jaini, Patna, K. P. Jayaswal Research Institute, second edition, 1977 (*Tibetan Sanskrit Works Series,* Vol. IV), p. 428; cf. "Notes bouddhiques," *Indologica Taurinensia,* VII/1979 (*Dr. Ludwik Sternbach Felicitation Volume*), pp. 108-109.
12. *Supra,* p. 98, n. 174. Cf. p. 146, n. 9.
13. *Supra,* pp. 121-122. Cf. *A.* II, p. 184; III, pp. 224-225; *Sn.* 508 (below, n. 14, p. 227).
14. *dūre ito brāhmaṇi Brahmaloko*
    yassāhutiṃ pagganhāsi niccaṃ |

n' etādiso brāhmaṇi Brahmabhakkho
kiṃ jappasi Brahmapathaṃ ajānantī ||
eso hi te brāhmaṇi Brahmadevo . . . , *S.* I, p. 141.

"Far from here, O Brāhmaṇī, lies Brahmaloka, towards which you regularly send your offerings. The Brahmās do not eat such food. What are you muttering,[a] not knowing the way that leads to the Brahmās? Here, O Brāhmaṇī, is your Brahmadeva . . . "

Brahmadeva is the name of the Arahant, son of the *brāhmaṇī*; but the word signifies: "the god Brahmā." There is, demonstrably, a double meaning here. Note that it is Brahmā Sahampati himself who thus exhorts the *brāhmaṇī*!

Cf. *Sn.* 479 and 508: *Brahmā hi sakkhi paṭigaṇhātu me Bhagavā* [*pūraḷāsam*]; *Bhagavā hi me sakkhi Brahm' ajja diṭṭho.*—Why is the Buddha Brahmā "before the eyes" (*sakkhi* = *paccakkhaṃ, Paramatthajotikā,* II, 2, p. 411)?—Because he practises the *Brahmavihāras: sutaṃ m' etaṃ, bhante: Brahmā mettāvihārīti. taṃ me idaṃ, bhante, Bhagavā sakkhi diṭṭho, Bhagavā hi, bhante, mettāvihārī, sutaṃ m' etaṃ, bhante: Brahmā upekhāvihārīti. taṃ me idaṃ, bhante, Bhagavā sakkhi diṭṭho, Bhagavā hi, bhante, upekhāvihārī, M.* I, pp. 369 and 370.

15. *Supra,* p. 171, n. 158.

16. Cf. *BĀU.* II, 6, 3; IV, 6, 3; VI, 1, 7; 5, 4 (as opposed to *ChU.* III, 11, 4; VIII, 15); *ChU.* IV, 15, 5; V, 10, 2; VIII, 5, 3-4; and especially, the "apocalyptic" description in the *Kauṣ.Up.* I (cf. R. Antoine, "Religious Symbolism in the Kauṣītaki Upaniṣad," *Journal of the Oriental Institute* [Baroda], IV, 4 [June, 1955], pp. 330-337).—These confusions are even more common amongst modern interpreters.

17. *Supra,* pp. 121, 124. Cf. p. 131 and n. 85. See on this question "Some Thoughts on Ātman-Brahman in Early Buddhism," *Dr. B. M. Barua Birth Centenary Commemoration Volume* (Calcutta, Bauddha Dharmankur Sabha [Bengal Buddhist Association], 1989), pp. 63-83.

---

a. *jappasi.* This concerns mantras which are recited during the course of a religious ceremony. Cf. Geiger, *Saṃyutta-Nikāya,* I (München-Neubiberg, 1930), p. 221, n. 2.

Appendix IV

Nāmarūpa

In the preceding pages, we have several times had occasion to cite the expression *nāmarūpa.* This also is an expression common to Buddhism and to Vedānta. Even though it is not possible—as far as the Absolute is concerned—to draw, from that resemblance, a conclusion as certain as that which we believe we have been able to draw from the use of the expression *upădhi,*[1] it nevertheless merits a study. While the term *upādhi* is known only to classical Vedānta, the expression *nāmarūpa* (in compound) already appears in the Upaniṣads, and the words *nāman* and *rūpa* are found juxtaposed as early as the Saṃhitās and the Brāhmaṇas.[2] The name (*nāman*) and the form (*rūpa*) together constitute the "principle of individuation": it is by their agency that the One appears in the form of the Multiple:

tad dhedaṃ tarhy avyākṛtam āsīt. tan nāmarūpābhyām eva vyākriyata, asaunāmāyam, idaṃrūpa iti, BĀU. I, 4, 7.

seyaṃ devatemās tisro devatā anenaiva jīvenātmanānupraviśya nāmarūpe vyākarot, ChU. VI, 3, 3.

ākāśo vai nāma nāmarūpayor nirvahitā; te yadantarā tad brahma, tad amṛtam, sa ātmā, ChU. VIII, 14. (*ākāśo vā ityādi brahmaṇo lakṣaṇanirdeśārtham ādhyānāya. ākāśo vai nāma śrutiṣu prasiddha ātmā. ākāśa ivāśarīratvāt sūkṣmatvāc ca. sa cākāśo nāmarūpayoḥ svātmasthayor jagadbījabhūtayoḥ salilasyeva phenasthānīyayor nirvahitā nirvoḍhā vyākartā. te nāmārūpe yadantarā yasya brahmaṇo 'ntarā madhye vartete . . .* , Śaṅkara, *Chāndogyopaniṣad-bhāṣya,* VIII, 14.—Cf. *Brahmasūtra-bhāṣya,* II, 1, 14 [p. 462]; *Upadeśasāhasrī, gadya,* §§ 18-19.)

Cf. also *ŚB.* XI, 2, 3, 1 ff., *TB.* II, 2, 7, 1.

According to *BĀU.* I, 6, 3 (cf. *supra,* p. 77, n. 88), the *nāman* and the *rūpa* are those which obscure the One:

> *tad etad amṛtaṃ satyena cchanam; prāṇo vā amṛtam, nāmarūpe satyam; tābhyām ayaṃ prāṇaś channaḥ.*

It may be seen that the idea of *upādhi* is already present here, even though the term is not used.

The *Bṛhadāraṇyaka-Upaniṣad* (I, 6, 1 ff.; cf. I, 4, 7: *tāny asyaitāni karmanāmāny eva*) adds acts (*karman*) to name and form as the third element making up the empirical individual. This last conception makes us think of the assertions of the *Milindapañhā*.[3] The word *nāma*, in the Buddhist text, does not, however, have the same value as in the Upaniṣads, as we shall shortly see.

What is the *nāman* in the thought of the Brāhmaṇas and of the Upaniṣads? What is the *rūpa*? What is the relationship between the *nāman* and the *rūpa*? It would be vain to expect uniform replies to all these question. The most advanced ideas are mixed, in our texts with the most primitive ideas.[4]

> . . . the name is indeed more that mere name. Especially is the name for a thing which is current among the gods, to a greater extent than to mortal designation, indicative of the essence of the thing.[5]

On its side, the *rūpa* "form" is not identical with the material body: a corpse is a mass without form.[6]

Just as the name expresses the essential character of a person or thing, so the form corresponds to the name.[7]

According to the *Śatapatha-Brāhmaṇa* (XI, 2, 3, 5-6), the *nāman* is itself a *rūpa*; the *rūpa*, therefore, is superior to the *nāman*.[8] The *rūpa*, says our text, is thought (*manas*), for it is by thought that one knows: This is a form. The *nāman* is speech (*vāc*), for it is by speech that the name is grasped.[9] Now, elsewhere in the same Brāhmaṇa we read: the *manas* is superior to the *vāc*, for the *vāc* merely follows and imitates the *manas*.[10] Perhaps this is a rough draft of a first step towards idealism.[11]

We read, *BĀU.* III, 2, 12, that the name (*nāman*) of a person does not leave him when he dies, for the name is "infinite" (*ananta*). This conception is only explicable in relation to the primitive mentality:[12]

> The name of a person is his very soul—let us say his 'name-soul'—i.e. his reason for living, his life as far as it has any personality . . . the name of the dead man given to the newly-born child is justified. What survives of the man is not his apparition, shadow, or any other of these more or less fluid multiple survivals, which move in the abodes of the dead; it is above all his 'name-person,' his 'name-soul.'[13]

According to Śaṅkara, the *upādhi*s of the individual soul,—the psycho-physical elements which constitute the empirical individual,—are "made" (*kṛta*), "issued" (*nirvṛtta*), "formed" (*racita*) from *nāman* and from *rūpa*. The *nāman* and the *rūpa*, for their part, rest upon "ignorance" (*avidyākṛta, °pratyupasthāpita, °kalpita, °adhyasta, °adhyāropita, °ātmaka*). Sometimes, the *nāman* and the *rūpa* are themselves considered as *upādhi*s.[14]

Buddhism simply constitutes itself the heir to the Upaniṣadic tradition when it designates the empirical individual by the expression *nāmarūpa*. It is significant that we find in one Upaniṣad and in the Pāli Canon an identical formula: "delivered from *nāmarūpa*" (or *nāmakāya*).[15]

Buddhism has, however, elaborated another analysis of the individual: the individual would be composed of five "aggregates" (*khandhas*), that is: *rūpa, vedanā, saññā, saṃkhārā* and *viññāṇa*. We shall not discuss the problem of determining whether this analysis goes back to the earliest teaching, for we shall never know the answer. It is, in any case, certain that the identification *nāmarūpa = skandha/khandha* rests upon a confusion, simply:[16] as the two groups had in common the element *rūpa*, they were identified with one another; then in the element *nāma* of the compound *nāmarūpa* was seen a universal designation of the psychic or "noncorporeal" (*arūpin*) *khandhas*.[17] In *nāmarūpa*, sometimes the five *khandhas* are counted and sometimes only four of them, the fifth *khandha*, the *viññāṇa,* being the *raison d'être* of our empirical individuality.[18] Here is yet another interpretation of *nāmarūpa:*

> *vedanā saññā cetanā phasso manasikāro, idaṃ vuccati nāmaṃ. cattāri ca mahābhūtāni catunnañ ca mahābhūtānaṃ upādāya-rūpaṃ, idaṃ vuccati rūpaṃ. iti idañ ca nāmaṃ idañ ca rūpaṃ, idaṃ vuccati nāmarūpaṃ, M.* I, p. 53; *S.* II, pp. 3-4.

Cf. also *Netti,* p. 15.—*Mil.,* p. 49: *yaṃ tattha, mahārāja, oḷārikaṃ etaṃ rūpaṃ, ye tattha sukhumā cittacetasikā dhammā etaṃ nāmaṃ.*—Oldenberg, *Buddha*[1], pp. 450-451.

Notes to Appendix IV

1. *Supra,* pp. 138 ff.

2. "The juxtaposition *nắman/rūpá* exists only in a crude state in the *RV.* III. 38, 4 and 7, V. 43, 10, VII. 103, 6[a]; in a more precise way, *AV.* XI. 7, 1, XII. 5, 9," L. Renou, *Études védiques et pāṇinéennes,* II (= *Publications de l'Institut de Civilisation indienne,* fascicule 2, Paris, 1956), p. 56, n. 2. See also Oldenberg, *WBT.,* p. 102, n. 2; E. H. Johnston, *Early Sāṃkhya* (London, 1937), p. 22; J. Gonda, *Notes on Names and the Name of God in Ancient India* (Amsterdam-London, 1970: *Verhandelingen der Koninklijke Nederlandse Akademie van Wetenschappen,* Afd. Letterkunde, Nieuwe Reeks, Deel 75, No. 4), p. 45.

---

a. L. Renou's addition.

3. *Supra,* p. 18.

4. On this point, cf. also *supra,* p. 191.

5. Oldenberg, *WBT.,* p. 103.—*ŚB.* I, 1, 4, 4.

6. *tad atha yadā prāṇa utkrāmati dārv eveva bhūto 'narthyaḥ pariśiṣyate, na kiṃcana rūpam, JUB.* III, 32, 3. Cf. Oldenberg, *WBT.,* pp. 104-105.

7. *ŚB.* VI, 1, 3, 10 ff. Cf. Oldenberg, *WBT.,* pp. 103-104.

8. *tayor anyataraj jyāyo rūpam eva, yad dhy api nāma rūpam eva tat.*

9. *mano vai rūpam, manasā hi vededaṃ rūpam iti . . . vāg vai nāma, vācā hi nāma gṛhṇāti.*—Cf. *BĀU.* III, 9, 20: *kasmin nu rūpāṇi pratiṣṭhitānīti hṛdaya iti hovāca, hṛdayena hi rūpāṇi jānāti, hṛdaye hy*

eva rūpāṇi pratiṣṭhitāni bhavantīti. (*hṛdayam iti buddhimanasī ekīkṛtya nirdeśaḥ*, Śaṅkara.)

10. *ŚB.* I, 4, 5, 8-11.

On all this, see S. Lévi, *La doctrine du Sacrifice dans les Brāhmaṇas* (Paris, 1898 [reprinted: 1966]), pp. 30-31; Keith, *RPhVU.* II, p. 455.

11. M. Walleser, *Die philosophische Grundlage des älteren Buddhismus*[2] (Heidelberg, 1925), p. 33, n. 1.

12. Cf. F. Edgerton, *The Beginnings of Indian Philosophy* (London, 1965), p. 22.—A different interpretation by Deussen, *Up.*, p. 431, and *AGPh.* I, 2, p. 314.

This conception should not be confused with *Sn.* 808: *nāmam evāvasissati akkheyyaṃ petassa jantuno.* Cf. *Paramatthajotikā* (II, 2, p. 534): *sabbaṃ rūpādidhammajātaṃ pahīyati, nāmamattam eva tu avasissati, Buddharakkhito, Dhammarakkhito ti evam akkhātuṃ kathetuṃ.*

13. *ERE.* IX, p. 135a. Cf. *ibid.*, p. 151b: "The Egyptian name is so definitely a soul—a living being existing by itself—that the most important and oldest liturgical texts make it the essential element in their magical operations.—*Ibid.*, p. 154a: "Every 'resemblance' of a person may become his exact equivalent by having his name inscribed on it (the name, of course, being pronounced during the operation)—e.g., the statues, figures, and figurines of temples and tombs, and the figures of the servants of the dead in the frescoes and bas-reliefs."

See also Lévy-Bruhl, *L'Ame primitive*[2] (Paris, 1927), pp. 263, 412 ff.—A. Hilka, *Beiträge zur Kenntnis der indischen Namengebung: Die altindischen Personennamen* (Breslau, 1910), pp. 5 ff.—A number of facts are collected in J. Gonda, *Notes on Names* . . . (see above, n. 2).

14. P. Hacker, "Eigentümlichkeiten der Lehre und Terminologie Śaṅkaras: Avidyā, Nāmarūpa, Māyā, Īśvara," *ZDMG.* 100 (1950), pp. 259, 264-266. "In Ś. most often in the dual *nāmarūpe*, less often in the collective *nāmarūpam*," *ibid.*, p. 258, n. 1. We may note that the dual *upādhibhyām* is used apropos *nāman* and *rūpa*, in *Taittirīyopaniṣad-bhāṣya*, II, 6 (p. 74):

ato nāmarūpe sarvāvasthe brahmaṇaivātmavatī, na brahma tadātmakam. te tatpratyākhyāne na sta eveti tadātmake ucyete. tābhyāṃ copādhibhyāṃ jñātṛjñeyajñānaśabdārthādisarvasaṃvyavahārabhāg brahma. (Cf. *supra*, p. 44, n. 31 end.)

15. *nāmarūpād vimuktaḥ*, *Muṇḍ.Up.* III, 2, 8; *nāmakāyā vimutto*, *Sn.* 1074. Cf. *supra*, p. 166 and n. 117; Oldenberg, "Buddhistische Studien," *ZDMG.* LII (1898), p. 689.—With the Upaniṣad one may

further compare, *Cullavagga*, IX, 1, 4 (*Vin.* II, p. 239 = *Ud.* V, 4, p. 55; cf. *A.* IV, p. 202). The meaning of this latter passage is, however, different. The expression used is, moreover, *nāmagotta*, and not *nāmarūpa* or *°kāya*: *seyyathā pi, bhikkhave, yā kāci mahānadiyo seyyathīdaṃ: Gaṅgā Yamunā Aciravatī Sarabhū Mahī, tā mahāsamuddaṃ pattā (pa)jahanti purimāni nāmagottāni, mahāsamuddo tv eva saṃkhaṃ gacchanti (gatāni), evam eva kho, bhikkhave, cattāro ('me) vaṇṇā: khattiyā brāhmaṇā vessā suddā, te Tathāgatappavedite dhammavinaye agārasmā anagāriyaṃ pabbajitvā jahanti purimāni nāmagottāni, samaṇā sakyaputtiyā tv eva saṃkhaṃ gacchanti.* Cf. also *D.* III, p. 84 (*supra*, pp. 123-124); E. J. Thomas, *The History of Buddhist Thought*[2] (London, 1951 [reprint: 1953]), p. 97, n. 1. We may recall that the *brahman* is called *anāmagotra* (*Subāla-Up.* III: Radhakrishnan, *Up.*, p. 865). Cf. also Kshiti Mohan Sen, *Hinduism* ("Penguin Books," 1961), p. 105: "There are many classes of men amongst the *Bāuls*, but they are all just *Bāuls*; they have no other achievement or history. All the streams that fall into the Ganges become the Ganges."

According to Oldenberg (*Buddha*[1], p. 450; cf. Oldenberg-Foucher[4], p. 255, n. 1), the *Mahānidāna-Sutta* (*D.* II, p. 62) would also be using the word *nāma*, in *nāmarūpa*, in the sense of "name." It does not however seem to us that this interpretation can be right. Cf. Buddhaghosa, *Sumaṅgalavilāsinī*, II, p. 501.

16. Cf. Oldenberg, *Buddha*[1], p. 451; cf. Oldenberg-Foucher[4], p. 255, n. 1.—"It is obvious that the theory of 'name-and-form' and that of the 5 skandhas are borrowed from different sources and that no amount of sophistry will succeed in identifying them," H. Kern, *Histoire du Bouddhisme dans l'Inde*, I (= *Annales du Musée Guimet, Bibliothèque d'études*, t. X, Paris, 1901), p. 340 (361), n. 2.—After a different fashion, F. O. Schrader, cited by C. Strauss, *Indische Philosophie* (München, 1925), Anm. 74: "According to the view of F. O. Schrader (in a verbal communication) the theory of *khandha* arose from a wish to represent *nāman* as a composite of four parts, analogous with *rūpa* which consists of four elements—i.e. as something equally transitory."—See also E. Frauwallner, *Geschichte der indischen Philosophie*, I (Salzburg, 1953), p. 207.

17. On scholastic speculations on the subject of *nāma*, see Buddhaghosa, *Atthasālinī*, §§ 147, 804-805; *Visuddhimagga*, XVII, 51; XVIII, 3-4 (ed. Warren-Kosambi, *HOS.* 41).—*Abhidharmakośabhāṣya*, III, 30, p. 142 (*AK.* III, pp. 94-95).

18. *Supra*, p. 21.

APPENDIX V

On the "Suicide" of the Delivered[1] *and on the idea of Personal Deliverance*

The ancient Upaniṣads do not mention suicide. It is only in later Upaniṣads, such as the *Jābāla*,[2] that suicide is expressly permitted the Delivered.

We have the feeling that Buddhism had undergone a similar evolution. Suicide, which, according to some texts of the Pāli Canon,[3] may be committed by the Delivered, that is, by one who has transcended his phenomenal existence,[4] seems to us to be incompatible with the spirit of ancient Buddhism, which has as its aim, we have seen, not the personal salvation of man, but universal salvation.[5]

This doctrine entailed, however, a very serious moral danger. From the instant that the Delivered was authorized to put an end to his life, false candidates for suicide were bound to multiply: Deliverance is something not easy to determine from outside, especially when the accent is put upon its personal nature. As we have suggested above,[6] it is, it would seem, to slow down the rush towards suicide that the distinction was introduced between "Deliverance acquired in this life" (*jīvanmukti = sa-upādisesa-nibbāna/sopadhiśeṣa-nirvāṇa*) and "Deliverance acquired through death" (*videha-mukti = anupādisesa-nibbāna/ anupadhiśeṣa-nirvāṇa*). This distinction is foreign, as much to the ancient Upaniṣads as to ancient Buddhism.

Classical Vedānta, we have seen, strove to justify this distinction.[7] The explanation that it gives is, however, hardly convincing. The *Vivekacūḍāmaṇi* itself recognizes that the distinction between the two Deliverances is nothing but a concession to popular opinion.[8]

It is certain, in any case, that the Delivered no longer had the right to quit life prematurely. According to an identical verse, found in both Hindu and Buddhist texts, aspiring neither to life nor to death, the Delivered must await the ultimate moment "as the servant waits for his salary."[9] "The Arahants do not put an end to what is not yet ripe; the sages await the maturing."[10]

The position of the Mahāyāna, which is, we believe, more faithful to the spirit of Buddhism, is different. The problem of "suicide" does not arise for the Bodhisattva. Renouncing his personal salvation,[11] he gives himself *fully* to others, identifying himself with them.[12] Having gone beyond the idea of the small I, he has recourse to that of the Great I (*mahātma-dṛṣṭiṃ śrayate mahārthām*); and without expectation of reward, he works *spontaneously* for the good of all, as if he were acting for his own good (*sarvārthakartā na ca kārakāṅkṣī yathātmanaḥ svātmahitāni kṛtvā*), for the other and the self are identical in his eyes (*sattvātmasamānabhāvāt*).[13] Now, no gift is so great, so complete, as that of one's own person. The bodhisattva does not hesitate, therefore, to accomplish it when it is necessary. Moreover, he accomplishes it without having any consciousness of accomplishing it; he has no consciousness of his individual existence.

On the idea of personal Deliverance.—It may be wondered how such an idea could come into being in the Vedānta and in Buddhism. If transcending my phenomenal existence means: realizing the *ātman,* the Being which I am in the depths of my being, by virtue of this realization itself, I am one with the rest of existence. I am, therefore, not delivered as long as the rest of existence is not. Before Deliverance, it was simply a question of *my* Deliverance; now, it is a question of the Deliverance of *all.* My Deliverance is, therefore—paradoxical as it may seem—my "deepest and most extensive bond."[14]

Such an idea of Transcendence, however, was bound to be incomprehensible to the majority of people. How may one remain in the world, if he has genuinely transcended the world?[15] Hence, a new conception of Transcendence, more ordinary and thus more accessible to understanding: it is no longer a question of transcending the world within the world and of transfiguring it,[16] but of evading the world; and this evasion can only be personal. The things of the world, instead of *revealing* Being, lose all their value. In order for his perfection to be accomplished, the sage must die; and, by the same token, death, which was nothing but the effacing of an evanescent appearance,[17] takes on a fundamental importance.

This, then, is a tendency, foreign, it would seem to us, to the Upaniṣads and to original Buddhism, but to which bear clear witness, first of all, the valorization of suicide and, secondly to the doctrine of the two Deliverances. It could not but provoke another consequence: passive detachment from the world, against which the Mahāyāna was in revolt.[18]

Notes to Appendix V

1. Cf. *supra*, p. 72, n. 77; p. 175, n. 174.
2. *Jābāla Upaniṣad*, 5, in F. O. Schrader, *The Minor Upaniṣads*, I (*Saṃnyāsa-Upaniṣads*), Madras, Adyar Library, 1912.
3. Cf. *supra*, p. 72, n. 77.
4. Strictly speaking, the question is therefore no longer one of "a suicide."
5. *Supra*, p. 17 and n. 113. It is interesting to note that *D.* II, p. 332, and *Mil.*, pp. 195-196, still evoke the "good of the greatest number" to justify the interdiction against suicide of which we are shortly going to speak.
6. P. 175, n. 174.
7. *Supra*, p. 144.
8. *Supra*, p. 175, n. 174. Cf. below.
9. *Supra*, p. 175, n. 174.
10. *na ca arahanto apakkaṃ pātenti, paripākaṃ āgamenti paṇḍitā*, *Mil.*, p. 44.—*na kho, rājañña, samaṇabrāhmaṇā sīlavanto kalyāṇadhammā apakkaṃ paripācenti, api ca paripākaṃ āgamenti paṇḍitā*, *D.* II, p. 332.
11. *Supra*, p. 16.

12. Cf. *supra*, p. 217.
13. *Supra*, pp. 14-15 (*MSA*. XIV, 37-38; 41).
14. *Supra*, p. 14 (*MSA*. XIV, 39).
15. Cf. *Vivekacūḍāmaṇi*, 462, cited above, p. 175, n. 174.
16. See *supra*, pp. 12 ff.
17. *Supra*, p. 46, n. 38a (p. 49); cf. p. 144.
18. *Supra*, p. 17. Cf. also Barth's remarks on the subject of pessimism (*supra*, p. 46, n. 37).

Appendix VI

nibbānaṃ paññatti anattā sabbe dhammā anattā

aniccā sabbe saṃkhārā dukkhānattā ca saṃkhatā |
nibbānañ c' eva paññatti anattā iti nicchayā ||
(*Vin.* V, p. 86 [*Parivāra,* III, 1]).

Miss Horner translates this stanza as follows:

Impermanent are all constructs, painful, not self, and constructed,
And certainly nibbāna is a description meaning not-self.[1]

Our critics may perhaps say that all our efforts have been in vain: Nirvāṇa, which appeared to us to be identical with *brahman* and, in consequence, with the Upaniṣadic *ātman,* is here called *anattā.* The *saṃkhārā* are *anattā,* but Nirvāṇa also is *anattā*; there is, therefore, no *ātman*![2]

Let us, nevertheless, see if another interpretation of this stanza is possible. The conditioned (*saṃkhata*) elements of the empirical world are not the *ātman,* or, if preferred, they are "lacking in own-nature" (*anattā*: nominative plural masculine of the adjective *anatta*[*n*][3]). But, since these elements are thus, their destruction or rejection[4] which is Nirvāṇa, must also be non-Ātman (or "lacking in own-nature": *anattā* = nominative singular feminine of the adjective *anatta,* qualifying *paññatti*[5]). What, in fact, are *saṃsāra* and *nirvāṇa,* if not simply "designations" (*paññatti* = Sanskrit *prajñapti*)? In the transcendent sense, there is neither *saṃsāra* nor *nirvāṇa,* neither *bandha* nor *mokṣa.* The conditioned (*saṃskṛta/saṃkhata*) is simply the "veiled form"[6] of the Unconditioned (*asaṃskṛta/*

asaṃkhata); it has, as its "essential nature" (*svarūpa, svabhāva* = *ātman*) the Unconditioned. That which we commonly call "bond" (*bandha*) is nothing but an error, one which confuses the true and the false, appearance and that which appears.[7] "Deliverance" (*mokṣa*) consists, simply, in the destruction of that error,[8] and *nirvāṇa/nibbāna* is nothing but a "designation" of that destruction of the error, in other words, of the *unveiling of the Being.*

Therefore, *saṃsāra* and *nirvāṇa* are, fundamentally, nothing but Being, seen from two different points of view, in other words, two "appearances" of the same Being. The stanza from the *Parivāra* asserts, to our mind, this identity of *saṃsāra* and *nirvāṇa,* an identity upon which the Mahāyāna, especially, will insist.[9]

It still remains for us to speak of the well-known formula: *sabbe dhammā anattā.* On this subject, the teaching of the Nikāyas is clear:[10] by *dhamma* in this formula, must be understood the "conditioned" *dhammas*:

> *rūpaṃ aniccaṃ, vedanā aniccā, saññā aniccā, saṃkhārā aniccā, viññāṇaṃ aniccam. rūpaṃ anattā, vedanā anattā, saññā anattā, saṃkhārā anattā, viññāṇaṃ anattā. sabbe saṃkhārā aniccā, sabbe dhammā anattā, M.* I, pp. 228, 230; *S.* III, pp. 132-134.
>
> *dhammā aniccā . . . dhammā dukkhā . . . dhammā anattā, S.* IV, pp. 3 ff.
>
> *sabbasaṃkhāresu dukkhānupassī viharati . . . sabbesu dhammesu anattānupassī viharati . . . nibbāne sukhānupassī viharati, A.* IV, p. 14.
>
> Cf. *Dhammapadaṭṭhakathā*, III, p. 407 (on *Dhp.* 279: *sabbe dhammā anattā*): *tattha sabbe dhammā ti pañcakkhandhā va adhippetā.*

The itinerant monk, Vacchagotta,[11] came to ask the Buddha whether there was an *ātman* or not. The Buddha did not reply. Later, explaining the reason for his silence to Ānanda, he said: "To reply that there is an *ātman,* would have been to adopt the eternalist point of view (*sassatavāda*)[12] and to contradict the truth according to which no *dhamma* is the *ātman* (or: has self nature)[13] [*sabbe dhammā anattā*]; and, if I had answered that there is no *ātman*, I would have been adopting the nihilistic point of view (*ucchedavāda*), and, moreover, I would have been adding to the folly of Vacchagotta. . . ."

The *ātman* which Vacchagotta was seeking, the so-called individual *ātman*, is impossible to find: no *dharma* can be the *ātman*, which is the foundation of all *dharmas*. Even so, the Buddha could not deny it: being in becoming, it has an intermediate reality between being and non-being, it is not nothing.[14] He could deny it only by referring to the universal and absolute *ātman*. But the spiritual state in which Vacchagotta was, did not permit him to conceive of such a reality; if there was an *ātman*, it could only be for him, an individual substance. If the Buddha had replied that that *ātman* of his imagination did not exist, he would simply have thought: "I had an *ātman*, and that *ātman* no longer exists!"[15] In the circumstances, the Buddha preferred to keep silent.

From the Mahāyānic point of view: all *dharmas*, *saṃskṛta* and *asaṃskṛta*, are *anātman*, in two ways: 1. The objectively existing *dharmas* are not *pudgalas* "individuals," and neither are there any *pudgalas* beyond them (*pudgalanairātmya*);—2. In "expressible things," there is no *dharma* the essential nature of which could be made to consist in all these expressions (*dharmanairātmya*). *punaḥ sarvadharmāṇāṃ bodhisattvaḥ saṃskṛtāsaṃskṛtānāṃ dvividhaṃ nairātmyaṃ yathābhūtaṃ prajānāti: pudgalanairātmyaṃ dharmanairātmyaṃ ca. tatredaṃ pudgalanairātmyaṃ yan naiva te vidyamānā dharmāḥ pudgalāḥ, nāpi vidyamānadharmavinirmukto 'nyaḥ pudgalo vidyate. tatredaṃ dharmanairātmyaṃ yat sarveṣv abhilāpyeṣu vastuṣu sarvābhilāpasvabhāvo dharmo na saṃvidyate. evaṃ hi bodhisattvaḥ sarvadharmā anātmāna iti yathābhūtaṃ prajānāti, Bodhisattvabhūmi*, pp. 280-281 (ed. Wogihara, Tokyo, 1930-1936; passage translated by Walpola Rāhula, "Asaṅga," *Encyclopaedia of Buddhism*, II, 1, 1966, p. 12 [offprint]).—All expressible (that is to say, objectively grasped) *dharmas*, whether conditioned *dharmas* or the Nirvāṇa, are, in fact, void of self-nature; they are "simply designations" (*prajñapti*): *yeyaṃ svalakṣaṇaprajñaptir dharmāṇāṃ yad uta rūpam iti vā vedaneti vā pūrvavad antato yāvan nirvāṇam iti vā, prajñaptimātram eva tad veditavyam, na svabhāvo nāpi ca tadvinirmuktas tadanyo vāg-gocaro vāg-viṣayaḥ. evaṃ sati na svabhāvo dharmāṇāṃ tathā vidyate yathābhilapyate, ibid.*, pp. 43-44.—Cf. *supra*, p. 109, n. 243.

Notes to Appendix VI

1. I. B. Horner, *The Book of the Discipline*, VI (= *Sacred Books of the Buddhists*, XXV, London, 1966), p. 123.

2. Cf. H. von Glasenapp, *Vedānta und Buddhismus* (= *Abhandlungen der Akademie der Wissenschaften und der Literatur in Mainz: Geistes- und Sozialwissenschaftlichen Klasse*, 1950, NR. 11), pp. 13-14 (1023-1024). The author also mentions *Ud.* VIII, 2: *duddassaṃ anattaṃ nāma na hi saccaṃ sudassanaṃ.* On the reading *anattaṃ*, however, cf. F. L. Woodward, *The Minor Anthologies of the Pāli Canon*, part II (= *Sacred Books of the Buddhists*, VIII, London, 1935 [reprint: 1948]), p. 98, n. 1.

3. H. von Glasenapp (*op. cit.*, p. 11 [1021]) has shown that the Pāli Canon uses, indiscriminately, the substantive *anattan* (nominative singular *anattā*) and the adjective *anatta.* Thus *S.* III, p. 56 (ed. Nālandā: vol. II, p. 286): *anattaṃ rūpaṃ anattā rūpan ti yathābhūtaṃ na pajānāti, anattaṃ vedanaṃ anattā vedanā ti yathābhūtaṃ na pajānāti, anattaṃ saññaṃ anattā saññā ti yathābhūtaṃ na pajānāti, anatte saṃkhāre anattā saṃkhārā ti yathābhūtaṃ na pajānāti, anattaṃ viññāṇaṃ anattā viññāṇan ti yathābhūtaṃ na pajānāti.—Ibid.*, p. 114 (ed. Nālandā: II, p. 335): *anattaṃ rūpaṃ anattaṃ* (variant: *anattā*) *rūpan ti yathābhūtaṃ na pajānāti* . . .

The *ātman* is the "self-nature" (*svarūpa, svabhāva*; cf. *supra*, p. 114, n. 249) of all things. It is not, however, identical to anything in particular, for, if it were identical to a thing, it would be the *ātman, svarūpa* or *svabhāva* of that thing; it would thus cease to be the *ātman*, universal *svarūpa* or *svabhāva* (cf. *supra*, p. 43, n. 31). Consequently, no thing has an *ātman* (= *svarūpa* = *svabhāva*) peculiar to it.

It is in this sense, therefore, that the equivalence of the substantive *anattā* and the adjective *anatta* is to be understood.

4. Cf. *supra*, p. 140.

5. See *Some Thoughts*, p. 19, n. 51.

6. *Supra*, p. 137.

7. *Supra*, p. 54, n. 60; cf. p. 46, n. 38 (last paragraph).

8. *bhramamātrasaṃkṣaya, avidyāpratibandhamātra, ajñānahṛdaya-granthināśa, kalpanākṣaya* (*supra*, p. 54, n. 60; p. 10).

9. See also *supra*, p. 46, n. 38 (last paragraph); p. 54, n. 60; p. 157, n. 60; pp. 137 ff.

10. See also M. and W. Geiger, *Pāli Dhamma*, pp. 86-87. Cf. *Some Thoughts*, p. 19, n. 51.

11. *S.* XLIV, 10 (vol. IV, pp. 400-401). Cf. *supra*, p. 86, n. 119; p. 25.

12. Cf. *supra*, p. 51, n. 53; p. 18 and n. 119.

13. Cf. *supra*, p. 238 and n. 3; "Some Thoughts on Ātman-Brahman in Early Buddhism," *Dr. B. M. Barua Birth Centenary Commemoration Volume* (Calcutta, Bauddha Dharmankur Sabha [Bengal Buddhist Association], 1989), p. 73, n. 12.

14. *Supra*, p. 18 and n. 119.

15. *ahu vā me nūna pubbe attā, so etarahi n' atthi.*—Cf. *supra*, p. 25.

Abbreviations and Bibliographic Indications

Except where the contrary is indicated, we have used the PTS. editions for the Pāli texts, wherever they existed. We also made use, however, of the more recent editions of Nālandā (*Nālandā Devanāgarī Pāli Series*), which are, in some ways, clearly superior to those of the PTS.

For the Upaniṣads, with commentary by Śaṅkara, we have used the Poona editions (*Ānandāśrama Sanskrit Series*; second edition, with the exception of the *Śvetāśvatara*, of which we know but one edition, that of 1889. As is well known, the attribution of the commentary of that Upaniṣad to Śaṅkara is extremely uncertain).

A. = *Aṅguttara-Nikāya.*

AAĀ. = Haribhadra, *Abhisamayālaṃkārāloka.* See below, *ASP.*

Abhidharmakośabhāṣya: Abhidharm-Koshabhāṣya of Vasubandhu, edited by P. Pradhan, Patna, K. P. Jayaswal Research Institute, 1967 (*Tibetan Sanskrit Works Series*, Vol. VIII).

Ait. Ār. = *Aitareya-Āraṇyaka: Ānandāśrama Sanskrit Series*, 38, Poona, 1898 (with the commentary by Sāyaṇa).

Ait. Up. = *Aitareya-Upaniṣad.*

AK. = *Vasubandhu, Abhidharmakośa: L'Abhidharmakośa de Vasubandhu*, translated and annotated by Louis de la Vallée Poussin, Paris-Louvain, 1923-1931.

ASP. = *Aṣṭasāhasrikā Prajñāpāramitā: Aṣṭasāhasrikā Prajñāpāramitā*, with Haribhadra's Commentary, called *Āloka*, edited by P. L. Vaidya, Darbhanga, 1960 (*Buddhist Sanskrit Texts*, No. 4, published by the Mithila Institute of Post-Graduate Studies and Research in Sanskrit Learning).

Aṣṭāvakra-Gītā: Die Aṣṭāvakra-Gītā, edited and translated by Richard Hauschild, Berlin, 1967 (*Abhandlungen der Sächsischen Akademie der Wissenschaften zu Leipzig: Philologisch-historische Klasse*, Band 58, Heft 2).

Ātmabodha: Ātmabodhaprakaraṇa of Śaṅkarācārya with a commentary ascribed to Madhusūdana Sarasvatī, edited with an introduction and notes by Dinesh Chandra Bhattacharya, Calcutta, 1961 (*Calcutta Sanskrit College Research Series*, No. XVII).

Barth, *Œuvres* = *Œuvres de Auguste Barth*, Paris, 1914-1927.

BĀU. = *Bṛhadāraṇyaka-Upaniṣad.*

BCA. = Śāntideva, *Bodhicaryāvatāra: Bodhicaryāvatāra of Śāntideva, with the Commentary Pañjikā of Prajñākaramati*, edited by P. L. Vaidya, Darbhanga, 1960 (*Buddhist Sanskrit Texts*, No. 12).

BCAP. = Prajñākaramati, *Bodhicaryāvatāra-pañjikā*: cf. above, *BCA.*

BEFEO. = *Bulletin de l'École française d'Extrême-Orient.*

Belvalkar-Ranade = S. K. Belvalkar and R. D. Ranade, *History of Indian Philosophy*, II (The Creative Period), Poona, 1927.

Bhāgavata-Purāṇa, Nirṇaya-Sāgara Press, Bombay, 1894.

BhG. = *Bhagavadgītā*, Gujarati Printing Press, Bombay, 1912, 1938 (in two volumes, with nineteen commentaries). French translations: E. Senart (second edition, Paris, 1944); S. Lévi and J.-T. Stickney (Paris, 1938).

ChU. = *Chāndogya-Upaniṣad.*

D. = *Dīgha-Nikāya.*

Deussen: *AGPh.* = P. Deussen, *Allgemeine Geschichte der Philosophie*: I, 1 (*Allgemeine Einleitung und Philosophie des Veda bis auf die Upanishad's*), Leipzig, 1906 (second edition);—I, 2 (*Die Philosophie der Upanishad's*), Leipzig, 1920 (fourth edition).

———. *Up.* = *Sechzig Upanishad's des Veda*, Leipzig, 1897.

Dhp. = *Dhammapada.* Editions of S. Sumaṅgala Thera and of H. C. Norman (with the commentary), PTS. Cf. also edition-translation of P. S. Dhammārāma, *BEFEO.* LI, 2 (1963), pp. 239 ff.

Edgerton, *Grammar, Dictionary* = F. Edgerton, *Buddhist Hybrid Sanskrit Grammar and Dictionary*, New Haven, Yale University Press, 1953.

ERE. = *Encyclopaedia of Religion and Ethics*, edited by James Hastings, Edinburgh-New York, 1908-1926.

Festschrift Nobel = *Jñānamuktāvalī: Commemoration Volume in Honour of Johannes Nobel, on the Occasion of his 70th Birthday*, edited by Claus Vogel, New Delhi, International Academy of Indian Culture, 1959 (*Sarasvatī-Vihāra Series*, 38).

M. and W. Geiger, *Pāli Dhamma* = *Abhandlungen der Bayerischen Akademie der Wissenschaften: Philosophisch-philologische und historische Klasse*, XXXI. Band, 1. Abhandlung (München, 1920).

W. Geiger, *Dhamma und Brahman* = *Untersuchungen zur Geschichte des Buddhismus*, II (München-Neubiberg, 1921).

W. Geiger, *Pāli Literature and Language* = *Pāli Literatur und Sprache*, authorized English translation by B. Ghosh, University of Calcutta, second edition, 1956.

HJAS. = *Harvard Journal of Asiatic Studies.*

HOS. = *Harvard Oriental Series.*

IHQ. = *Indian Historical Quarterly* (Calcutta).

IIJ. = *Indo-Iranian Journal* (Leiden).

It. = *Itivuttaka.*

JA. = *Journal asiatique.*

JAOS. = *Journal of the American Oriental Society.*

Jāt. = *Jātaka* (ed. Fausböll, London, 1877-1896; reprint: 1962-1964).

Jayatilleke = K. N. Jayatilleke, *Early Buddhist Theory of Knowledge*, London, 1963.

JPTS. = *Journal of the Pāli Text Society.*

JRAS. = *Journal of the Royal Asiatic Society of Great Britain and Ireland.*

JUB. = *Jaiminīya-Upaniṣad-Brāhmaṇa*, ed. V. P. Limaye-R. R. Vadekar, in *Eighteen Principal Upaniṣads*, I, Poona, Vaidika-saṃśodhana-maṇḍala, 1958.

Kauṣ.Up. = *Kauṣītaki-Upaniṣad: The Kaushītaki-Brāhmaṇa-Upaniṣad with the Commentary of Śaṅkarānanda*, edited with an English translation by E. B. Cowell, Calcutta, 1861 (*Bibliotheca Indica*).

Keith, *RPhVU.* = A. B. Keith, *The Religion and Philosophy of the Veda and Upanishads*, Cambridge (Mass.), 1925 (*HOS.* 31-32).

Lamotte: *Histoire* = E. Lamotte, *Histoire du Bouddhisme indien*, I, Louvain, 1958 (*Bibliothèque du Muséon*, 43).

———. *Somme* = E. Lamotte, *La Somme du Grand Véhicule d'Asaṅga* (*Mahāyānasaṃgraha*), II (Translation and Commentary), Louvain, 1938-1939 (*Bibliothèque du Muséon*, 7).

———. *Traité* = E. Lamotte, *Le Traité de la Grande Vertu de Sagesse de Nāgārjuna* (*Mahāprajñāpāramitāśāstra*), Louvain, 1944, 1949 (*Bibliothèque du Muséon*, 18).*

* The third and fourth volumes of this important translation appeared in 1970 and 1976 (*Publications de l'Institut Orientaliste de Louvain*, 2 and 12).

Lamotte: *Vimalakīrti* = *L'Enseignement de Vimalakīrti* (*Vimalakīrti-nirdeśa*), translated and annotated by Étienne Lamotte, Louvain, 1962 (*Bibliothèque du Muséon*, 51).

Laṅk. = *Laṅkāvatāra-Sūtra*, ed. B. Nanjio, Kyoto, 1923.—Cf. ed. P. L. Vaidya, Darbhanga, 1963 (*Buddhist Sanskrit Texts*, No. 3).

La Vallée Poussin, *Siddhi* = *Vijñaptimātratāsiddhi: La Siddhi de Hiuan-tsang*, translated and annotated by Louis de la Vallée Poussin, Paris, 1928-1929.

M. = *Majjhima-Nikāya.*

MaiU. = *Maitri-Upaniṣad*, in *Thirty-two Upaniṣads, Ānandāśrama Sanskrit Series*, 29, Poona, 1895 (with the commentary of Rāmatīrtha).

Māṇḍ.Kār. = Gauḍapāda, *Māṇḍūkya-Kārikā: Ānandāśrama Sanskrit Series*, 10, second edition, Poona, 1900 (with the commentary of Śaṅkara).—Cf. Vidhuśekhara Bhaṭṭācārya, *Gauḍapādīyam Āgama-śāstram* (in Sanskrit), University of Calcutta, 1950.

Māṇḍ.Up. = *Māṇḍūkya-Upaniṣad.*

Manu = *Manusmṛti: The Manusmṛti, with the Commentary Manvartha-muktāvalī of Kullūka*, edited with critical and explanatory notes, etc., by Nārāyaṇ Rām Āchārya, Bombay, Nirṇayasāgara Press, tenth edition, 1946.

May = J. May, *Candrakīrti: Prasannapadā Madhyamakavṛtti* (Twelve chapters translated from the Sanskrit and from the Tibetan . . .), Paris, 1959.

Mbh. = *Mahābhārata.* Editions used: Calcutta Edition; Bombay Edition, with the commentary of Nīlakaṇṭha; Poona critical edition.—If we have not been able to draw all our references from one single edition, this is because none of these three editions were permanently available to us.

Mélanges Louis Renou = *Mélanges d'indianisme à la mémoire de Louis Renou*, Paris, 1968 (*Publications de l'Institut de Civilisation indienne*, fascicule 28).

Mil. = *Milindapañhā* (ed. Trenckner, London, 1880; reprint: 1962). [For the title, cf. Geiger, *Pāli Literature and Language*, p. 26, n. 7.]

MK. = Nāgārjuna (*Mūla-*) *Madhyamaka-Kārikā*, ed. L. de la Vallée Poussin, Saint-Petersburg, 1903-1913 (*Bibliotheca Buddhica*, IV).

MKV. = Candrakīrti, *Prasannapadā*: Commentary on *MK.* (above).

MSA. = *Mahāyāna-Sūtrālaṃkāra*, edited and translated according to a manuscript brought from Nepal, by Sylvain Lévi, Paris, 1907 and 1911 (*Bibliothèque de l'École des Hautes Études, Sciences historiques et philologiques*, fascs. 159 and 190).—Cf. G. M. Nagao, *Index to the Mahāyāna-Sūtrālaṃkāra*, I, Tokyo, 1958.

Muṇḍ.Up. = *Muṇḍaka-Upaniṣad.*

Murti = T. R. V. Murti, *The Central Philosophy of Buddhism: A Study of the Mādhyamika System*, London, 1955.

Netti = *Nettippakaraṇa.*

NIA. = *New Indian Antiquary.*

Oldenberg: *Buddha* = H. Oldenberg, *Buddha: sein Leben, seine Lehre, seine Gemeinde.*—The most often used edition, with the translation by Foucher (Oldenberg-Foucher[4], Paris, 1934), is that of 1961 ("Goldmanns Gelbe Taschenbücher," Band 708/709, München: edited by Helmuth von Glasenapp). We have also used the "Excurse" of the first edition (Berlin, 1881).

———. *LUAB.* = *Die Lehre der Upanishaden und die Anfänge des Buddhismus*, second edition, Göttingen, 1923.

———. *WBT.* = *Die Weltanschauung der Brāhmaṇa-Texte*, Göttingen, 1919.

PTS. = Pāli Text Society (London).

PTS. Dictionary = *The Pāli Text Society's Pāli-English Dictionary*, edited by T. W. Rhys Davids and William Stede, London, 1959 (reprint).

Radhakrishnan, *Up.* = *The Principal Upaniṣads*, edited with Introduction, Text, Translation and Notes by S. Radhakrishnan, London, 1953.

Ratnagotravibhāga = *Ratnagotravibhāga-Mahāyānottaratantraśāstra*, ed. E. H. Johnston-T. Chowdhury, Patna, Bihar Research Society, 1950.*

RV. = *Ṛg-Veda-Saṃhitā* (ed. Max Müller, second edition, London, 1890-1892).

S. = *Saṃyutta-Nikāya.*

Śaṅkara: *Brahmasūtra-bhāṣya*, ed. Mahāmahopādhyāya Anantakṛṣṇa Śāstrī, Bombay, Nirṇayasāgara Press, second edition, 1938.

* Cf. now, in addition to the work of J. Takasaki, mentioned above, p. 41, n. 20, D. Seyfort Ruegg, *La théorie du Tathāgatagarbha et du Gotra: Études sur la Sotériologie et la Gnoséologie du Bouddhisme*, Paris, 1969 (*Publications de l'École française d'Extrême-Orient*, LXX).

Śaṅkara: *Upadeśasāhasrī*, in *Minor Works of Śrī Śaṅkarācārya*, edited by H. R. Bhagavat, second edition, 1952 (*Poona Oriental Series* No. 8).—Commentary of Rāmatīrtha in *The Pandit*, III-V (Benares, 1868-1870).

(For the commentaries of the Upaniṣads, cf. above, p. 243, and for the commentary of the *Bhagavadgītā*, above, *BhG.*)

ŚB. = *Śatapatha-Brāhmaṇa: The Çatapatha-Brāhmaṇa in the Mādhyandina-Çākhā with extracts from the commentaries of Sāyaṇa, Harisvāmin and Dvivedagaṅga*, edited by Albrecht Weber, Berlin-London, 1855.

Sn. = *Suttanipāta* (ed. D. Anderson-H. Smith, PTS.; cf. also ed. P. V. Bapat, Poona, 1924).

Some Thoughts = K. Bhattacharya, *Some Thoughts on Early Buddhism with special reference to its relation to the Upaniṣads*, Pune, Bhandarkar Oriental Research Institute, 1998 (Post-graduate and Research Department Series No. 41, "Acharya Dharmananda Kosambi Memorial Lectures," [Third Series]).

Śvet.Up. = *Śvetāśvatara-Upaniṣad.*

TB. = *Taittirīya-Brāhmaṇa* (*Ānandāśrama Sanskrit Series*, 37, Poona, 1898).

Triṃśikā: see below, *Viṃśatikā.*

TS. = Śāntarakṣita, *Tattvasaṃgraha*, ed. Embar Krishnamacharya, Baroda, 1926 (*Gaekwad's Oriental Series*, XXX-XXXI; with the *Pañjikā* of Kamalaśīla).

TSP. = Kamalaśīla, *Tattvasaṃgraha-pañjikā*: cf. above, *TS.*

TU. = *Taittirīya-Upaniṣad.*

Ud. = *Udāna.*

Venkata Ramanam = K. Venkata Ramanan, *Nāgārjuna's Philosophy as presented in the Mahā-Prajñāpāramitā-Śāstra*, Rutland-Tokyo, 1966 (Harvard-Yenching Institute Publication).

Vimalakīrtinirdeśa: Study Group on Buddhist Sanskrit Literature, The Institute for Comprehensive Studies of Buddhism, Taisho University, *Vimalakīrtinirdeśa: A Sanskrit Edition Based upon the Manuscript Newly Found at the Potala Palace*, Tokyo, Taisho University Press, 2006.

Viṃśatikā: *Vijñaptimātratāsiddhi, deux Traités de Vasubandhu: Viṃśatikā (La Vingtaine), accompagnée d'une explication en prose, et Triṃśikā (La Trentaine) avec le commentaire de Sthiramati*, Sanskrit original published for the first time based on manuscripts from

Nepal by Sylvain Lévi, Paris, 1925. (*Bibliothèque de l'École des Hautes Études, Sciences historiques et philologiques,* fasc. 245).—Cf. S. Lévi, *Matériaux pour l'étude du Système Vijñaptimātra,* Paris, 1932 (*Bibliothèque de l'École des Hautes Études,* fasc. 260).

Vin. = *Vinaya-Piṭaka* (ed. Oldenberg, London, 1879-1883).

Vivekacūḍāmaṇi: Edition-translation of Swāmī Mādhavānanda, second edition, Mayavati, Advaita Ashrama, 1926.

WZKM. = *Wiener Zeitschrift für die Kunde des Morgenlandes.*

WZKS[O]. = *Wiener Zeitschrift für die Kunde Süd- und Ostasiens* [then *Südasiens*] *(und Archiv für indische Philosophie).*

ZDMG. = *Zeitschrift der Deutschen Morgenländischen Gesellschaft.*

www.ingramcontent.com/pod-product-compliance
Lightning Source LLC
Chambersburg PA
CBHW062206270326
41930CB00009B/1659
* 9 7 8 0 8 8 1 8 1 0 0 6 6 *